Population Economics

Springer
Berlin
Heidelberg
New York
Barcelona
Hong Kong
London
Milan
Paris
Tokyo

Titel in the Series

Holger Bonin

Generational Accounting

Theory and Application

With 32 Figures
and 33 Tables

 Springer

Dr. Holger Bonin
Forschungsinstitut zur Zukunft der Arbeit (IZA)
Schaumburg-Lippe-Straße 7–9
53113 Bonn
Germany

Printed with the support of the Deutsche Forschungsgemeinschaft D 25/10

ISBN 3-540-42266-8 Springer-Verlag Berlin Heidelberg New York

Library of Congress Cataloging-in-Publication Data applied for
Die Deutsche Bibliothek – CIP-Einheitsaufnahme
Bonin, Holger: Generational Accounting: Theory and Application / Holger Bonin. – Berlin;
Heidelberg; New York; Barcelona; Hong Kong; London; Milan; Paris; Tokyo: Springer, 2001
   (Population Economics)
   ISBN 3-540-42266-8

Springer-Verlag Berlin Heidelberg New York
a member of BertelsmannSpringer Science+Business Media GmbH

http://www.springer.de

© Springer-Verlag Berlin · Heidelberg 2001
Printed in Germany

Hardcover-Design: Erich Kirchner, Heidelberg

SPIN 10843044   42/2202-5 4 3 2 1 0 – Printed on non-aging paper and on acid-free paper

Preface

> We see which way the stream of time doth run
> And are enforced from our most quite sphere
> By the rough torrent of occation.
>
> *William Shakespeare*

During the next decades, as a consequence of fertility decline combined with ever-decreasing mortality, progressive population aging hits most developed societies. The demographic transition ahead will put severe pressure on government budgets, as the sizeable demands on public transfers made by the elderly who collect public pensions and a major share of health and nursery care spending, are largely unfunded by the current systems of social security. Growing awareness that present fiscal policy assumes commitments impacting on public budgets only in the longer-term, has stimulated research on fiscal indicators that incorporate the intertemporal effects of today's government policies.

Among the new methods to evaluate the long-term implications of current fiscal policy measures, certainly the concept of generational accounting, put forward in a series of papers by Alan Auerbach, Jagadeesh Gokhale and Laurence Kotlikoff, has become the most prominent. Generational accounting is based on the fundamental notion of neoclassical dynamic analysis that fiscal policy is restricted by the requirement to balance the intertemporal budget of the public sector. This means that in the long term, the present value of taxes paid by present and future generations must be sufficient to finance the present value of projected government spending, including interest due on the net liabilities of the public sector.

Defining the present value of taxes net of transfers paid by a representative member of an age cohort over the remaining life cycle as a generational account, the reference to the intertemporal financing constraint of the government can provide a number of closely related insights. Firstly, by linking the cohort set of generational accounts to a long-term demographic projection, one can analyze whether a set of tax and spending parameters selected by the government is sustainable in the long term, i.e. consistent with an intertemporally balanced public budget. Sustainable fiscal policy is generationally balanced in the sense that it would allow to impose identical lifetime net tax burdens on just-born and future generations. If continuation of current fiscal policy violates against the intertemporal public budget constraint, consumption opportunities are redistributed between generations, because envisaged tax and transfer levels cannot stay unchanged unless government non-transfer spending is reduced. Generational accounting illustrates the value of the government's unfunded spending commitments by the dimension of the required policy revision.

Secondly, generational accounting indicates how fiscal burdens are spread across generations. The method judges fiscal policy changes by the corresponding age-specific changes in lifetime net tax payments, which contributes to the understanding of possible fiscal policy effects on cohort welfare, as well as on capital formation and growth. Finally, generational accounting may help in identifying policies that are intertemporally sustainable, or would move public finances that are not toward a generationally more balanced outcome.

In the decade since its invention, generational accounting has had considerable success among analysts, as is illustrated by the large number of international country studies currently before the public. While the basic ideas of the generational accounting concept have not changed, practical experience has lead to methodological and empirical sophistication. The principal aim of this book is to survey the current theory and practice of generational accounting. It combines an in-depth and up-to-date introduction to the method with a comprehensive empirical application.

The theoretical first part of the study, which runs from chapters 1 to 4, addresses the various methodological issues involved in the construction of generational accounts, so far scattered over the literature, from a unified perspective. Special attention is paid to the shortcomings of the original residual concept to construct the generational accounts of future generations, which prompted the invention of the sustainability approach that has started to replace the residual concept recently. It is shown how the sustainability approach yields demographically unbiased estimates for the future generational accounts. Furthermore the properties of the different indicators of intertemporal fiscal imbalance provided by what seems to become the new methodological standard of generational accounting are discussed.

The empirical part of the book uses the example of German public finances for an application of the generational accounting method. The comprehensive country study of chapters 5 to 7 allows to discuss in detail the practical problems faced by analysts implementing generational accounting. It is demonstrated how generational accounting can be used to assess the long-term solvency of overall government and of isolated social insurance finances, and to analyze both intertemporal and inter vivos redistribution of resources between generations induced by reforms of fiscal policy.

In detail, the book is organized as follows. For an introduction, Chapter 1 gives a theoretical motivation of generational accounting. It is shown that contemporaneous deficits provide ill-defined indicators in an intertemporal context, provided agents are rational life cycle planners. The fiscal balance rule is derived, which provides the fundamental reference of generationally balanced policy used by generational accountants.

Generational accountants typically make a clear distinction between the net tax burdens of current and future generations. While the accounts of living generations are treated as given by current fiscal policy, the net tax burdens faced by future generations are derived endogenously respecting the requirement to balance the intertemporal public budget. The layout of chapters 2 to 4 follows this distinction. Chapter 2 presents the construction of generational accounts under the conditions of current fiscal policy, and discusses the implications of the underlying status quo perspective. Chapter 3 introduces the intertemporal budget constraint of the government and explains how it is interpreted by generational accountants in order to draw a link between the net tax burdens of present and future generations.

Chapter 4 explains how generational accountants illustrate fiscal imbalance by computing the changes in current fiscal policy required to balance the intertemporal public budget. First the original residual approach to derive the tax burden of future generations and the corresponding conventional indicator of generational redistribution – the relative change in lifetime tax rates between just-born and future generations – are described. It is also demonstrated that the concept of generational balance is independent from aggregate redistribution between current and future generations. The analytical shortcomings of the original approach to measure fiscal imbalance are discussed in section 4.5. As an alternative, Section 4.6 presents the sustain ability approach, which indicates the long-term solvency effects of current fiscal policy by adding the correspondent present value of future primary deficits to the initial net liabilities of the government. It is shown that the resulting *sustainability gap* can provide a range of indicators translating the crude intertemporal liabilities of the government into more illustrative measures of generational redistribution.

In Chapter 5, the sustainability approach is applied to an analysis of the intertemporal state of government finances in Germany. Besides implementing the new methodological concept, the material presented in this book is distinguished from previous German generational accounting studies by using a new, extended set of profiles allocating tax payments and government spending between age groups. Furthermore the calculations make an effort to incorporate cohort effects, by designing maturation of statutory Social Security benefits and the long-term development of civil servant pensions.

The results of the generational accounting analysis indicate that status quo of fiscal policy in Germany is unsustainable. Moreover, the degree of generational redistribution due to current debt, demographic aging and the unfunded costs of German unification, is possibly large. Chapters 6 and 7 deal with possible policy measures to improve the sustainability of public finances. In Chapter 6, the extent to which demographic rejuvenation through immigration can alleviate intertemporal generational redistribution is analyzed. It is shown that immigrants' contribution to the intertemporal public budget is on average positive so that immigration is financially beneficial for the incumbent population. However, although the fiscal gains from immigration can be increased by active migration policy aiming at higher immigrant quality, immigration even well above historic levels is unlikely sufficient to restore sustainable public finances in Germany.

Chapter 7 analyzes the generational consequences of different strategies to reform statutory pension insurance whose unfunded spending commitments are a major source of fiscal imbalance in Germany, as construction of separated generational accounts for the pension system reveals. The approach taken to evaluate the impact of policy reform distinguishes between aspects of intertemporal generational redistribution (between current and future generations), measured by changes in the sustainability gap, and aspects of inter vivos redistribution (between current generations), indicated by the deviation of cohort reform burdens relative to an age-neutral reform that would tax all individuals with a uniform fraction of their pre-reform wealth.

The results indicate that plausible reforms keeping to the institution of pay-as-you-go financing, like a cut in pension replacement rates and a turn to a broader revenue base using indirect taxation, are hardly sufficient to assure long-term viability of the German pension system. In contrast, implementation of a partially funded pension system, though suitable to reduce intertemporal fiscal pressure, requires careful design to avoid sizeable redistribution between current generations. The book concludes in Chapter 8 with a brief outline of possible topics for future research on generational accounting.

The present volume came into life as a doctoral thesis at the University of Freiburg. This is the occasion to thank all colleagues and friends whose help and encouragement was essential to accomplish my thesis. In particular, I owe a lot to my supervisor Bernd Raffelhüschen who introduced me to the world of generational accounting, and to Laurence Kotlikoff and Jan Walliser who made it possible for me to learn its practice at Boston University. My special thanks go to Karen Feist and Erik Lüth for many hours of discussions, not only about generational accounting. The former is also the co-author of the paper on which much of Chapter 7 is based. Finally, I would like to thank Daniel Besendorfer and Christoph Borgmann who rendered me far more than technical support.

Bonn, April 2001   *Holger Bonin*

Contents

1. The Rationale for Generational Accounting

The extent to which fiscal policy, and government debt in particular, leads to redistribution across generations is a long-debated topic in economics. Government policy is defined to redistribute intergenerationally if it expands the consumption opportunities of one generation at the expense of some other generation. The view that public debt causes intergenerational redistribution as it slows down capital formation, and burdens future generations who have to service public liabilities through increased levels of taxation, has become generally accepted among analysts since the seminal work of Buchanan (1958) and Modigliani (1961).[1]

The interpretation of public debt as a device of intergenerational redistribution leaves conventional deficit accounting as an inappropriate instrument to measure the stance of fiscal policy.[2] Based on the neoclassical paradigm that rational agents face a life-cycle optimization problem with regard to consumption and savings, Summers (1981), Chamley (1981) and Kotlikoff (1979), among others, showed that in a dynamic macroeconomic context, the issue of intergenerational redistribution through fiscal policy is disconnected from the reported sequence of budget deficits. In fact, from a neoclassical perspective, policies that generate different time paths of deficits can be identical in terms of generational redistribution. Stated differently, policies that generate an identical sequence of reported deficits may differ substantially in terms of intergenerational redistribution.

This observation prompted Kotlikoff (1986, 1988a,b) to a radical critique of conventional deficit budgeting, which he dismissed as arbitrary. *Yearly* deficit concepts fail to include the long-term revenue and expenditure implications of present fiscal policy, obviously relevant if agents make their economic decisions with a life-cycle perspective. The attempt to measure and evaluate fiscal policy in terms of agents' lifetime budget constraint inspired

---

[1] Cf. Vaughn and Wagner (1992) and Gandenberger (1981) for critical reviews.

[2] Traditional deficit indicators are surveyed by Blejer and Cheasty (1991). An early critique of short-term budgeting focused on the omission of unfunded Social Security liabilities was put forward by Feldstein (1974). Chouraqui et al. (1990), Blanchard (1993) and Gramlich (1990) have suggested various indicators for a long-term oriented analysis of fiscal policy.

the invention of generational accounting, which rationalizes on the *intertemporal* deficit associated with current fiscal policy.

This chapter serves as an introduction to the paradigmatic background of the generational accounting procedure. First, some simple bookkeeping exercises show that the perspective on annual budget deficits does not allow to investigate issues of generational redistribution. In a second part, the intertemporal financing problem of the government is analyzed in the context of an overlapping generations model, in order to derive the *fiscal balance rule* proposed by Kotlikoff (1993) to judge intergenerational redistribution due to fiscal policy. This rule provides the benchmark for generationally balanced policy generational accountants refer to.[3]

1.1 Deficit Accounting and Generational Redistribution

The proposition that annual budget deficits have no definite relationship to generational redistribution due to fiscal policy can be illustrated in a simple accounting framework. Consider a model of two overlapping generations, a young generation and an old generation, living in each period i. Consecutive generations grow at a rate n. If $P_{i,k}$ denotes the size of a generation born in period k during period i, this implies $P_{i,i} = (1+n)P_{i-1,i-1}$. Excluding premature death, one may also write $P_{i,i} = (1+n)P_{i,i-1}$, because $P_{i,i-1}$ equals $P_{i-1,i-1}$. In this model, one can show that two policies that (depending on how fiscal policy is labeled) result in a balanced budget and rising budget deficits respectively, are equivalent in economic terms, as they have the same distributional impact on all generations.

For a first scenario, the government introduces, in period i, a policy that redistributes resources from the young generation to the old generation. In each period, the members of the young generation are taxed with a constant lump sum of z. Aggregate tax revenue is distributed evenly, in the same period, to the members of the old generation. The periodical budget impacts of this policy, which might be interpreted as a pay-as-you-go Social Security system, are displayed by Table 1.1. As transfers to the old generation are defined by the yield of the lump-sum tax on the young generation, government spending equals government revenue in each period. Therefore, reported government deficits are zero. As the young generation is larger than the old generation living at the same time by n percent, the lump-sum transfer to the old exceeds the per capita tax levied on the young by n percent, too.

In order to evaluate generational redistribution due to the specified tax and transfer scheme, one has to aggregate the present value of taxes paid and transfers received by each cohort over the life cycle. Let r denote the rate of

---

[3] There are several useful introductions to the methodological background of generational accounting, including Raffelhüschen (1999a) and Auerbach et al. (1994). The following ows in particular to Kitterer (1996).

Table 1.1. Generational Redistribution with Periodically Balanced Budget

Revenue	Expenditure
Period i	
Tax Payment of Young Generation	Transfer to Old Generation
$zP_{i,i}$	$zP_{i,i} = z(1+n)P_{i,i-1}$
Period i+1	
Tax Payment of Young Generation	Transfer to Old Generation
$zP_{i+1,i+1}$	$zP_{i+1,i+1} = z(1+n)P_{i+1,i}$

discount that takes future payments back to the present, supposed constant for convenience. Then, for the generation being young when the policy is introduced, the present value of lifetime tax payments net of transfer receipts is given by

$$zP_{i,i} - \frac{z(1+n)P_{i+1,i}}{1+r} = \frac{r-n}{1+r}zP_{i,i}, \tag{1.1}$$

considering that $P_{i+1,i} = P_{i,i}$ by assumption. According to equation (1.1), if the interest rate exceeds the rate of population growth, as it is the case in a dynamically efficient economy [Blanchard and Fischer (1989, p. 103)], a policy transferring resources from the young to the old generation, imposes a net lifetime burden on the generation born in period i. Provided that the interest rate is constant, the policy also imposes a burden on each subsequent future generation. This burden, in per capita terms, is equal to the burden on the generation young in the introductory period.[4] The aggregate burden on the present young and future generations serves to finance the introductory gain of the generation $P_{t-1,t-1}$, whose lifetime resources are extended by an amount $zP_{i,i}$. The fact that the policy under investigation redistributes resources to the disadvantage of future generations, however, is not indicated by conventional public deficit measures, as the government budget stays always in balance.

In an alternative scenario, a deficit occurs. In period i, the government takes up a loan of z units per capita from the young generation, in order to pay a lump-sum transfer of $(1+n)z$ to each member of the then old generation, as before. Table 1.2 shows the budget impacts of this policy. In terms of deposit and disbursement flows, the public budget remains balanced in period i. In economic terms, however, as the government loan from private individuals does not constitute a revenue, financial assets of the public sector

---

[4] The burden is explained by the fact that pay-as-you-go financing, in a model without productivity growth, yields only a biological rate of return [Samuelson (1958)].

Table 1.2. Generational Redistribution with Budget Deficits

(a) Cash-Flows

Deposit	Disbursement
Period i	
Loan from Young Generation	Transfer to Old Generation
$zP_{i,i}$	$zP_{i,i} = z(1+n)P_{i,i-1}$
Period i+1	
Loan from Young Generation	Transfer to Old Generation
$zP_{i+1,i+1}$	$zP_{i+1,i+1} = z(1+n)P_{i+1,i}$
Tax Payment of Old Generation	Redemption of Loan
$(1+r)zP_{i+1,i}$	$zP_{i,i}$
	Interest on Loan
	$rzP_{i,i}$

(b) Revenue and Expenditure

Revenue	Expenditure
Period i	
Deficit	Transfer to Old Generation
$zP_{i,i}$	$zP_{i,i} = z(1+n)P_{i,i-1}$
Period i+1	
Tax Payment of Old Generation	Transfer to Old Generation
$(1+r)zP_{i+1,i}$	$zP_{i+1,i+1} = z(1+n)P_{i+1,i}$
Deficit	Interest on Loan
$nzP_{i,i}$	$rzP_{i,i}$

are reduced. Put differently, a deficit occurs, which amounts to the transfer payment given to the old generation.

As for period $i + 1$, consider the following policy. First, the government maintains the transfer strategy of the previous period. Each member of the old generation receives a lump-sum transfer financed by a per capita loan z taken up from the young generation. In addition, the government redeems the loan taken up from the young (now old) generation in the previous period. Credit redemption and interest due are financed via a uniform tax payment levied on the old generation. Since the payment requirement adds up to $(1+r)zP_{i,i}$ and all previously young survive through period $i + 1$ by assumption, the per capita tax on the old equals $(1+r)z$.

Parallel to the situation in period i, deposit and disbursement flows are balanced with this policy. The loan from the young equals the transfer to the old, while the simultaneous tax payments of the old generation balance government spending to service debt. However, from the perspective of government revenue and expenditure which excludes credit transactions, the public budget stays in imbalance. Government tax revenue from the old generation is smaller than expenditure on transfer benefits and interest by an amount of $nzP_{i,i}$. It is easy to check that the deficit will grow at a rate of n percent is subsequent periods, if the specified tax and transfer policy is maintained.

Although the time path of reported deficits is fundamentally different, the described policy is equivalent to the above pay-as-you-go strategy. Consumption possibilities of present and future generations are affected in the same way. The generation old in the introductory period of the policy again faces a windfall profit of $zP_{i,i}$. All other generations, made responsible for the service of government debt, lose. Aggregation of the present value of life cycle flows between the generation born in period i and the government sector, displayed in Table 1.2(a), yields

$$zP_{i,i} + \frac{(1+r)zP_{i+1,i}}{1+r} - \frac{zP_{i,i} + rzP_{i,i} + z(1+n)P_{i+1,i}}{1+r} = \frac{r-n}{1+r}zP_{i,i} \quad (1.2)$$

Comparing equations (1.1) and (1.2), we find that the lifetime net transfer of resources from generation i (representative for all subsequent generations) to the public sector is the same, irrespective of the fact that transactions between the private and government sector are labeled differently by the two specified policies.

One could construct different policies leading to the same generational redistribution to the disadvantage of future generations as that measured by equations (1.1) and (1.2), but are associated with a reported budget surplus. Yet the messages from the above exercise seem clear enough. First, the government may influence the size of reported deficits by a simple re-organization of intergenerational tax and transfer programs. More importantly, the size of the annual deficit is no measure of intertemporal generational redistribution due to fiscal policy. It does not reveal how continuation of present fiscal policy would affect agents' consumption opportunities over their life cycle. Therefore, if individuals are indeed long-term planners and free from fiscal illusion, the time path of government deficits is unrelated to individual economic decision making.

1.2 Generational Redistribution and the Economy

1.2.1 An Overlapping Generations Model

In the previous section, it was taken for granted that intertemporal generational redistribution due to fiscal policy matters, without specifying the intertemporal optimization problem of the household exactly. Moreover, possible macroeconomic feedbacks of the policies, which could affect generational redistribution by changing factor returns, were neglected. To address the impacts of generational redistribution through fiscal policy more precisely, a simple two generations life cycle model is convenient. Consider a representative member of the generation born in period i, who lives for two periods. In the first period, when young, the individual works and receives a wage income w_i, which is either consumed or saved. Let c_i^1 and s_i^1 denote consumption and savings of a representative young agent during period i respectively. Then, supposed no taxes or transfers, it holds that $w_i = c_i^1 + s_i^1$. When old, the individual does not work, but dissolves savings (which create a return $r_{t+1}s_i^1$) to finance consumption. Thus, abstracting from bequests and government activity, private consumption is given by $c_{i+1}^2 = (1 + r_{t+1})s_i^1$.

The agent chooses the consumption profile (c_i^1, c_{i+1}^2) by maximizing the intertemporal utility function $U_i = U(c_i^1, c_{i+1}^2)$ subject to the periodical budget constraints when young and old. The optimal consumption plan determines optimal savings during youth. The solution to the optimization problem is given by the demand functions

$$
\begin{aligned}
c_i^1 &= c_i^1(w_i, r_{i+1}), \\
c_{i+1}^2 &= c_{i+1}^2(w_i, r_{i+1}), \\
s_i^1 &= s_i^1(w_i, r_{i+1}).
\end{aligned}
\tag{1.3}
$$

Without government activity, the distribution of consumption over the life cycle, as well as private savings, depend on the wage income w_i and the interest rate faced when old r_{t+1}. In addition, individual time preference, as a parameter of the intertemporal utility function, determines the sequence of consumption over time and therefore the level of savings during youth.

Now add a non-distortionary public tax and transfer system to the model. Suppose government levies taxes and pays benefits in each period of the life cycle, and let m_i^1 represent the net tax payments, i.e. the tax payments net of transfers received, during youth and m_{i+1}^2 net tax payments during retirement of an individual born in period i. Accounting for fiscal policy, the periodical budget constraint when young changes to $w_i = c_i^1 + m_i^1 + s_i^1$, and the budget constraint when old to $c_{i+1}^2 + m_{i+1}^2 = (1 + r_{i+1})s_i^1$. Solving the second constraint for s_i^1, and substituting the result into the periodical budget constraint during youth leads to the intertemporal budget constraint faced by a representative agent born in period i:

$$
c_i^1 + \frac{c_{i+1}^2}{1 + r_{i+1}} = w_i - \left[m_i^1 + \frac{m_{i+1}^2}{1 + r_{i+1}} \right].
\tag{1.4}
$$

Equation (1.4) states that the present value of life cycle consumption is determined by the present value of life cycle net income, i.e. gross income net of life cycle net tax payments.

For notational convenience, define $m_i := m_i^1 + m_{i+1}^2/(1 + r_{i+1})$. This simplification allows to summarize the distribution of net tax payments between generations that characterizes a specific fiscal policy, with help of a parameter $0 \leq a \leq 1$, defined by

$$a = \frac{m_i^1}{m_i}. \tag{1.5}$$

According to equation (1.5), the parameter a represents the share of net tax payments during youth in the present value of aggregate net tax payments over the life cycle. If $a = 1$, net taxes are paid only by the young generation, whereas if $a = 0$, life cycle net taxes are concentrated in retirement.

We are now prepared to analyze the impacts of fiscal policy on the optimal consumption and savings decisions of the representative agent. With taxation, individuals choose the consumption profile maximizing the intertemporal utility function subject to the modified intertemporal budget constraint (1.4). The optimal consumption plan is described by

$$\begin{aligned} c_i^1 &= c_i^1(w_i, r_{i+1}, m_i), \\ c_{i+1}^2 &= c_{i+1}^2(w_i, r_{i+1}, m_i). \end{aligned} \tag{1.6}$$

If $m_i \neq 0$, the government interferes with the lifetime consumption opportunities. Agents adapt their decisions to the present value aggregate of lifetime net tax burdens. Supposed gross wage income and the rate of return on savings remain constant, the specific sequence in time of the net tax payment m_i does not change individuals' life cycle consumption plan, as was claimed in the previous section. Consequently, periodical cash flow indicators, reflecting only present tax and transfer policy, are of little relevance in a microeconomic context.

From a macroeconomic perspective, however, the timing of net tax burdens over the life cycle matters, because it affects capital formation. If the life cycle sequence of payments associated with a given net tax burden m_i varies, agents can only maintain their consumption profile by adaptating personal savings. To see this, insert Marshallian consumption demand according to equation (1.6) into the agents' periodical budget constraint when young and rearrange to yield

$$s_i^1 = s_i^1(w_i, r_{i+1}, m_i; a) = w_i - c_i^1(w_i, r_{i+1}, m_i) - am_i. \tag{1.7}$$

Equation (1.7) reveals that, for a given lifetime net tax burden m_i, optimal savings vary inversely with the relative tax burden during youth, as described by the parameter a. Ceteris paribus, concentration of net tax payments in old-age raises savings. Agents wishing to maintain their original life cycle consumption plan save more to finance net tax payments during retirement.

Due to this effect, the overall impact on capital formation of a tax and transfer policy reducing lifetime net income by an amount m_i is uncertain. For an illustration of this proposition, suppose first that net tax payments are levied only on the young generation so that $a = 1$. Provided that consumption during youth and old-age are superior goods, the reduction in optimal consumption in period i due to the net tax burden m_i is smaller than the reduction in net income due to taxation. Agents distribute the aggregate tax burden over the life cycle by cutting down both present and future consumption. In response to reduced consumption in retirement, savings during youth decline. Now consider a policy that levies the amount m_i exclusively on the old generation ($a = 0$). As optimal consumption during youth, compared to the first policy, does not change, savings increase according to equation (1.7). Although agents, as before, reduce both present and future consumption due to their reduced net income, they must increase savings, in order to finance net tax payments when old.

The microeconomic reaction of savings to public tax and transfer policy is essential in a macroeconomic context, since it determines aggregate capital formation and therefore the long-term capitalization of the economy, which in turn affects factor returns.[5] As a consequence, the initial generational distribution of after-tax income could change. For example, if a policy redistributing resources to the disadvantage to the old generation raises private savings, it is possible (given that there are no other compensating changes in pre-tax income) that burdens in the event slide from future to present generations.[6]

Inspection of a life cycle model of consumption shows that life cycle net tax burdens, rather than annual government budget parameters, enter the optimization of rational, non-myopic individuals. Adding a macroeconomic perspective to this, which stresses the impacts of private savings decisions on aggregate capital formation, the specific sequence of net taxes over the life cycle becomes important. Therefore, it is useful to analyze also the relative generational distribution of lifetime net tax payments, which again is disconnected from the short-term budget parameters.

1.2.2 The Fiscal Balance Rule

So far, we have illustrated that reported cash-flow deficits do not provide an indicator for generational redistribution due to fiscal policy, from a microeconomic as well as from a macroeconomic perspective. This section discusses what might be a more meaningful benchmark to assess generational redistribution through fiscal policy. This benchmark is provided by the *fiscal balance rule*, suggested by Kotlikoff (1993), which aims at defining a non-

---

[5] This follows from combining the individual savings decision with a neoclassical growth model, i.e. the classic Diamond (1965) model.

[6] Cf. Lindbeck and Weibull (1986) for an analysis of generational redistribution through different tax and transfer policies in a growth framework with overlapping generations.

distortionary rule for setting fiscal policy in an intertemporal context.[7] The fiscal balance rule is based on the government budget constraint in general equilibrium. To derive the equilibrium budget, start from the periodical budget constraint of the government. Assume that in each period i, government spends an amount G_i. Assume further that the government is indebted with an amount of B_i in period i, which requires payments totalling $r_i B_i$ to serve interest. In each period, the government finances its spending from net tax payments of the young generation (M_i^1) and the old generation (M_i^2), and from issuing new bonds. Under these conditions, the periodical budget constraint of the government reads as

$$M_i^1 + M_i^2 + (B_{i+1} - B_i) = G_i + r_i B_i. \tag{1.8}$$

In a steady-state, all budget items are constant in per capita terms. Supposed population grows at a constant rate n, division of equation (1.8) by the cohort size of the young generation gives us the steady-state condition

$$m^1 + \frac{m^2}{1+n} = g + (r - n)b, \tag{1.9}$$

where b represents government debt per capita of the young generation, and m^1 and m^2 denote the net tax payment per capita of the young and the old generation, respectively. Equation (1.9) states the well-known result that in a dynamically efficient economy, credit financing raises per capita taxes in the long term, because interest payments grow at a faster rate than the population.

After some simple manipulation of equation (1.9), one can state the financing constraint implied by a steady-state budget in terms of generations' life cycle net tax burden[8]

$$m = g + \frac{r-n}{1+n}\left[(1+n)b - \frac{m^2}{1+r}\right]. \tag{1.10}$$

Abstracting from macroeconomic feedbacks, one might interpret the relation between the fiscal policy parameters of the government described by equation (1.10) as a fiscal balance rule. Generational redistribution occurs whenever the government varies one of its fiscal parameters (the lifetime net tax burden and the net tax payment extracted from the elderly, government consumption and government debt) without counterbalancing the long-term budget impacts of this policy by adaptation of at least one other parameter. Put differently, fiscal policy that were in a steady-state is restricted in its

---

[7] Besides the original paper by Kotlikoff (1993), our presentation of the fiscal balance rule makes use of Boll (1994, pp. 32n) and, in particular, the reinterpretation of the fiscal balance rule by Kitterer (1996).

[8] Deriving equation (1.10), it helps to note that $\frac{m^2}{1+n} = \frac{m^2}{1+r} + \frac{(r-n)m^2}{(1+r)(1+n)}$.

options by equation (1.10) if it wants to stay there and prevent generational redistribution.

This concept of generationally balanced fiscal policy has nothing in common with the conventional notion of periodical budgetary balance. Using equation (1.10) it is easy to show that the existence of government deficits does not contradict generational fiscal balance. Consider a steady-state without debt ($b = 0$), where only the young generation pays taxes to finance government spending so that $m^1 = m = g$. Now, a temporary change in fiscal policy introduces government debt. Supposed constant government consumption, the steady-state condition (1.10) for a balanced budget condenses to $m = g + (r - n)b$, which leads to the conventional result that in a dynamically efficient economy, government debt burdens future generations.

However, this distributional outcome is by no means certain. Suppose that apart from issuing bonds the government also introduces a tax in old-age equaling debt per capita of the old. Then, $\frac{m^2}{1+r} = (1 + n)b$, so that equation (1.10) changes to $m = g$. In this case, the introduction of government debt does not change the lifetime tax payment in the steady-state and is therefore consistent with generational balance. This implies that the tax burden during youth m^1 needs to be reduced, since $m^2 > 0$ under the specified policy. Stated differently, generational redistribution due to government debt (from the young to the old) is counterbalanced by redistribution through the tax and transfer system (from the old to the young).

Similarly, it can be shown that generational redistribution could occur with non-deficit policies. Consider a pay-as-you-go system where in each period tax payments of the young equal transfer payments to the old. In per capita terms of the young generation, this restraint can be written as $(1 + n)m^1 = -m^2$. Supposed no government consumption and no debt, inserting the pay-as-you-go constraint into the status-quo budget condition leads to $m = \frac{(r-n)m^2}{(1+r)(1+n)} > 0$. This confirms the previous result, expressed in equation (1.1), that introduction of a pay-as-you-go system transferring resources from the young to the old, though not associated with periodical deficits, is a generationally imbalanced policy. It requires to raise tax levels, in order to return to a (new) budget steady-state.

The fiscal balance rule described by equation (1.10) is valid for a partial equilibrium. It abstracts from the macroeconomic repercussions of fiscal policy. In order to derive a fiscal balance rule in general equilibrium, the steady-state budget condition of the government sector needs to be combined with the steady-state condition of the private sector. In a neoclassical growth model, the steady-state of the economy is determined on the capital market. Private savings must balance the capital demand of investors and the government. [9] In a model with two overlapping generations where the

---

[9] For an introduction into the neoclassical growth model, consult Barro and Sala-i-Martin (1995).

old dissave capital accumulated when young the savings of the young generation determine the capitalization of the economy in the subsequent period. Let k denote capital per capita of the young generation. Then, in per capita terms of the young generation, capital market equilibrium in a steady-state is represented by

$$s^1 = (1+n)(k+b). \tag{1.11}$$

Equation (1.11) states that, in order to keep the capitalization of the economy constant in per capita terms, savings by the young generation must exceed private and government capital demand $(k+b)$ by an amount of n percent. The young must take over the existing capital stock as well as government bonds from the old generation, and finance the extra demand for capital due to population growth.

Substitution of the capital market equilibrium condition (1.11) into the periodical budget constraint of a representative agent during retirement yields

$$m^2 = (1+r)(1+n)(k+b) - c^2(w,r,m). \tag{1.12}$$

Equation (1.11) describes the level of taxation in old-age consistent with dynamic general equilibrium. Finally, substitution of equation (1.12) into the steady-state budget condition (1.10) gives us, after some manipulations,

$$m = g + \frac{r-n}{1+r}\left[\frac{c^2(w,r,m)}{1+n} - (1+r)k\right]. \tag{1.13}$$

Equation (1.13) represents the fiscal balance rule in general equilibrium, as derived by Kotlikoff (1993, p. 34).[10] The fiscal balance rule has a range of interpretations. First, it explains the life cycle tax burden observed in general equilibrium. For a given level of government consumption, life cycle net tax payments differ from government consumption in a steady-state, if consumption during old-age differs from the amount of capital accumulated during youth, including returns on savings, which is represented by $(1+r)k$.[11] If, for example, consumption during retirement exceeds the personal funds acquired through savings when young because of a public transfer given to the old generation, life cycle tax burdens must exceed government spending in the long term. Accordingly, the introduction of a tax and transfer policy that

---

[10] Differences between equation (1.13) and the original representation of the fiscal balance rule are due to the inclusion of population growth in our model.

[11] Note that the bracketed term on the RHS of equation (1.13) is expressed in per capita terms of the young. In a steady-state equilibrium without government activity, it is always true that $(1+r)k = c^2/(1+n)$. Agents finance their consumption in old-age by selling the capital stock accumulated during youth to the present young generation. In addition, they can consume the return on their investment.

extends the consumption opportunities of the old leads to intergenerational redistribution. It raises the equilibrium life cycle tax burden.

According to this interpretation, the fiscal balance rule appears as a tool to analyze generational redistribution due to a specific fiscal policy through the corresponding changes in equilibrium life cycle taxes m. One could interpret the fiscal balance condition also in a more rigid sense – 'extract enough from each successive generation such that if you were in the stationary state you would stay there and not impose a larger or smaller burden .. on subsequent generations.' [Kotlikoff (1993, p. 34] This statement understands the fiscal balance rule as an instruction for setting non-distortionary fiscal policy. Given that the economy is in equilibrium and supposed no discrete shocks, the economy will not deviate from its equilibrium growth path, if policy guarantees a constant life cycle tax payment. If the government changes the time path on one of its fiscal choice parameters, the time path of other fiscal parameters has to be adapted as well, in order to counterbalance generational redistribution caused by the initial policy change, and to keep the economy on the equilibrium growth path.

Finally, if the economy is in disequilibrium, for example as a consequence of a discrete change in fiscal policy, the fiscal balance rule describes how to return to a new equilibrium, by selecting a life cycle tax payment m that is maintained over time. In disequilibrium, the fiscal balance rule determines neither the amount of the lifetime tax payment m nor the exact transition to generationally balanced policy. As a consequence, the long-term equilibrium and the generational welfare impacts effected by adhering to the fiscal balance rule are indefinite.[12] Nevertheless, the fiscal balance rule provides a theoretical justification for the normative claim of equal net tax burdens for present and future generations, prerequisite to achieve an equilibrium.

The fiscal balance rule sets the theoretical benchmark of generational accounting, which is an empirical exercise to test if the sequence in time of government revenue and spending associated with a specific fiscal policy is consistent with intertemporal budget balance, thus permitting to impose identical life cycle net taxes on current and future generations. Furthermore, if fiscal policy deviates from the fiscal balance rule, generational accounting serves to assess the exent of the policy change required to lead government finances back onto a generationally balanced path.

---

[12] This is shown by simulations of different policies to implement the fiscal balance rule in a disequilibium, investigated by Kotlikoff (1993, pp. 35n).

2. Net Taxes of Living Generations

The previous chapter illustrated the relevance of present value life cycle net taxes, henceforth referred to as *generational accounts*, on individual consumption and savings decisions, which in turn affect the equilibrium growth path of the economy and the generational distribution of consumption opportunities. Furthermore, it was shown that fiscally balanced policy avoiding generational redistribution by the government sector, would require to set fiscal choice parameters so as to meet the steady-state budget constraint of the public sector, and to maintain life cycle taxes across generations.

Generational accounting aims at an empirical indication of the life cycle net taxes set by fiscal policy empirically. In order to test for generational fiscal balance, the method analyzes whether the time path of fiscal parameters selected by the government is consistent with the intertemporal budget constraint of the public sector. If the constraint is violated, fiscal policy breaks the fiscal balance rule. The government redistributes consumption opportunities intergenerationally, as it is forced to adjust net tax levels over time. Inspired by the fiscal balance rule, sustainability of fiscal parameters is the central criterion used by generational accountants to judge government tax and spending schemes. If fiscal policy is sustainable, life cycle net taxes are identical for present and future generations. Accordingly, if the economy were in equilibrium, welfare of all cohorts would be the same. There would be no incentives to revise economic decisions so that the equilibrium state of the economy could be preserved. If the economy were in disequilibrium, sustainable public finances would lead the economy back to an equilibrium state.

Measuring lifetime net tax payments, generational accountants in general make a clear distinction between cohorts alive and generations not yet born. This chapter deals with the construction of generational accounts for agents already living. Chapter 3 provides a discussion of the restraints on tax and transfer policy, imposed by the requirement to balance the intertemporal government budget, which serve as the link between the fiscal burdens of present and future generations. Chapter 4 deals with the construction of generational accounts for future generations and discusses the implications of different measures to indicate the degree of fiscal imbalance.

2.1 Generational Accounts Defined

To give a comprehensive account of the generational distribution of fiscal burdens, it would be desirable to follow the net tax payments made by living generations over their entire lifespan. This would be a highly data consuming task. Generational accountants usually are less ambitious. They compute generational accounts in a strictly forward-looking manner that incorporates only net tax payments occurring after a specified base period.[1] In its simplest version, generational accounting indicates, for each age cohort alive, the net tax burden faced by a representative member over the remaining life cycle.

For all agents born in or prior to the base year, the present value of net tax payments upon death is constructed by subjecting the discounted average net taxes imposed on different age groups to the age-specific survival probabilities of a given cohort. In technical terms, the generational account of a representative individual born in period k who is resident in the base year period t, denoted by $GA_{t,k}$, is defined as

$$GA_{t,k} = \sum_{i=t}^{k+D} t_{i,k} S_{i,t,k} (1+r)^{t-i} \qquad (2.1)$$

for cohorts $t - D \leq k \leq t$. In equation (2.1), $S_{i,t,k}$ represents the fraction of a generation born in period k and resident in period t who survives until period $i \geq t$ and $t_{i,k}$ stands for the per capita net taxes paid in period i by a representative agent born in period k. Furthermore, D defines the maximum age and r represents the pre-tax interest rate applied to take future payments back to the base period, supposed constant.

Since $S_{i,t,k}$ represents a survival probability, it must satisfy $0 \leq S_{i,t,k} \leq 1$. In particular, it is true that $S_{t,t,k} = 1$, and $S_{k+D+1,t,k} = 0$. Given a population forecast, where $P_{i,k}$ represents the number of agents born in period k who are resident in a period i, it seems straightforward to compute the cohort-specific survival rates entering equation (2.1) as

$$S_{i,t,k} = \frac{P_{i,k}}{P_{t,k}} \qquad (2.2)$$

for all $t \leq i \leq k + D$ and $t - D \leq k \leq t$. Substitution of equation (2.2) into equation (2.1) leads to an alternative definition of the generational accounts for living generations, more common in the generational accounting literature:

---

[1] A notable exception is a study for the United States by Auerbach, Gokhale and Kotlikoff (1995) who make a courageous attempt to account for the past net tax payments of cohorts born since 1900. However, as historic fiscal data tend to be seriously inadequate, the calculations involve some heroic assumptions. Ablett and Tseggai-Bocureziou (2000) and Van Kempen (1996) report somewhat less ambitious backward-looking generational accounts for Australia and the Netherlands, respectively, which also must be approached with caution.

$$GA_{t,k} = \frac{\sum_{i=t}^{k+D} t_{i,k} P_{i,k} (1+r)^{t-i}}{P_{t,k}}. \tag{2.3}$$

However, as pointed out by Ablett (1997), this conventional definition of generational accounts is only correct without migration. Immigration adds members to the cohort of k-born agents alive in the base period, whereas emigration reduces cohort size other than by death. Therefore, in the presence of migration, future cohort size $P_{i,k}$ does not only reflect the survival probabilities faced by the start cohort $P_{t,k}$, but also the extent to which it will be affected by migration in the future. Due to this distortion, the cohort-specific survival ratios of base year residents are measured incorrectly by equation (2.2). In fact, if prospective net immigration is sufficiently large, it is possible that cohort survival even exceed unity for certain age groups.

As a consequence, as soon as immigration is a relevant demographic factor, the conventional definition of generational accounts according to equation (2.3) yields biased estimates of residents' fiscal burdens. In the case of net immigration, for example, the net tax payments of future migrants who are born in period k prior to the base year are wrongly assigned to base year residents born in the same period. Considered the typically favorable age composition of immigrants, which is likely to go along with positive rest-of-life net tax payments, the conventional procedure of generational accounting tends to overstate the actual fiscal burden on resident cohorts.

The distortion of generational accounts via immigration effects can be avoided, if the underlying survival ratios are derived explicitly from the individual annual survival ratios of the different resident cohorts. Let $\zeta_{j,j-k}$ denote the probability that a representative agent who is of age $j - k$ at the beginning of period j survives until the beginning of period $j + 1$, reaching age $j + 1 - k$. Then, the likelihood that a k-born agent resident in period t is still alive in period i is given by

$$S_{i,t,k} = \prod_{j=t}^{i-1} \zeta_{j,j-k} \tag{2.4}$$

for all $t < i \leq k + D$. Throughout this study, the conventional – implicit – evaluation of cohort survival ratios is replaced by equation (2.4). Explicit construction of cohort survival ratios requires forecasting survival probabilities by age and generation, i.e. predicting the future development of the death table. Although very long-term projections of the death table are in general not readily available from official sources, they can be obtained recurring to standard models of demography.

The projection of mortality trends adds an element of arbitrariness to the calculation of generational accounts. It is necessary to specify the development of life expectancy conditional on age, and to make assumptions about how a variation in life expectancy will translate into changes of age-specific survival rates. Demographic uncertainties can be avoided only if the initial death table is maintained indefinitely. Such a procedure improves the indicator quality of the accounts, and would be consistent with the method's status quo approach to fiscal policy (discussed below). Nevertheless, generational accountants usually make an effort to design changes in life expectancy, since gains in longevity are likely to be an important source of intertemporal fiscal imbalance.

Given that the choice of mortality parameters is fundamental for the generational accounts, most of the generational accounting literature pays curiously little attention to analyze the possible fiscal impacts of changing mortality. The selected mortality scenarios typically remain rather cautious with regard to expected changes in life expectancy, typically designing a moderate gain in longevity that comes to an end soon. Considered the very long-term time horizon of the concept, the use of short-sighted mortality assumptions does not seem fully convincing in the generational accounting context. This approach, likely to design long-term mortality conditions quite inadequately, seems to evade a decision whether generational accounts are designed to provide a fiscal indicator that reflects present fiscal and demographic conditions, or a realistic estimate of cohorts' lifetime fiscal burdens.

From a methodological viewpoint, as the prognostic quality of long-term demographic projections might be poor,[2] a satisfactory solution to deal with demographic uncertainties is to define a benchmark set of generational accounts based on the base year death table. Alternative mortality scenarios processing additional information on mortality trends can then be judged against this *status quo* perspective. This standardized demographic approach could also ease cross-country comparisons of generational accounts, which are often difficult due to diverging approaches to the design of future mortality.[3]

2.2 The Meaning of Net Taxes

In addition to the specification of future mortality rates, calculation of generational accounts according to equation (2.1) requires a projection of the age-specific net tax payments by cohort, $t_{i,k}$. In order to generate this projection of personal fiscal parameters, generational accountangs first break net tax payments down into a set of per capita tax and transfer payments satisfying

---

[2] Cf. Feichtinger (1979) and Grohmann (1980) for a debate of the prognostic quality of conditional demographic forecasts.

[3] Fiscal policy in Denmark, for example, according to the generational accounts seems rather well-balanced, compared to other European countries [Jensen and Raffelhüschen (1999a,b)].) However, this positive outcome is partially attributable to absence of aging from the top distinguishing the Danish generational accounts [Bonin and Raffelhüschen (1999)].

$$t_{i,k} = \sum_l t_{i,k}^l. \tag{2.5}$$

In equation (2.5), $t_{i,k}^l$ indicates the average taxes or transfers of type l paid or received by a representative k-born agent in period $i \geq t$, hence of age $i - k$. By convention, $t^l > 0$ defines a tax payment from the personal to the public sector. Correspondingly, $t^l < 0$ indicates a transfer payment from the public to the personal sector.

Standard generational accounts, in order to capture generational distribution of fiscal burdens through public sector budgets, seek to incorporate the taxes paid to and transfers received from all federal levels of government, including off-budget authorities. In particular, the accounts take into account all contributions net of transfer receipts paid to social insurances. Still, the exact concept of net taxes differs widely between generational accounting studies. Typically the accounts include all monetary tax and transfer flows between the public and personal sector that immediately affect private consumption opportunities. The treatment of government expenditure not registering in the balances of the private households, however, is far from uniform. This concerns government consumption in terms of the National Accounts, i.e. public sector expenditure on goods and services, but also government investment and public subsidies to private companies.

Constructing generational accounts, the benefit character of certain types of public non-transfer expenditure is acknowledged in the generational accounting literature more often than not. Since the work of Franco et al. (1992), it is frequent practice to consider government spending that is plausibly assignable by age as a transfer reducing the individual net tax burden. This procedure has been justified with the argument that government spending provides public goods otherwise bought (presumably at identical cost) by agents themselves, thus reducing their consumable income. This is an opportunity cost argument that assigns the role of an intermediator to the government whose only function is the provision of public goods making the private sector better off. In generational accounting practice, this view on government expenditure is usually limited to public spending on education. Only occasionally, it is extended to public institutions providing for old-age care [Jensen and Raffelhüschen (1999a)].

Recently, some analysts have reconsidered the established generational accounting approach to net tax burdens. Extending the conventional concept of in-kind transfers, Raffelhüschen (1999a) and ter Rele (1997) also distribute non-age specific government spending as a transfer to individuals. Public spending, they claim, yields identical per capita benefits for all age groups. This extension of the transfer concept alters the interpretation of the generational accounts. As long as material consumption of the public sector is not considered to reduce net tax burdens, generational accounts indicate changes in disposable rest-of-life income due to fiscal policy. From the perspective of the life cycle theory of consumption, changes in pre-tax income induced by fiscal policy are obviously most relevant under allocative aspects. This is true provided that agents do not draw a link between their net tax payment and the level of public sector benefits not redistributed via monetary transfers. The exclusion of in-kind transfers from the definition of net taxes accentuates that government spending other than on in-cash transfers is an exogenous parameter in the objective function of private individuals.

This interpretation of the generational accounts, which places stronger emphasize on who pays for government expenditure rather than on who benefits from it, has been criticized as one-sided [Havemann (1994), Buiter (1997)]. It actually might distract from the fact that net tax payments of the private sector could create public goods in return that enhance individual welfare. If, for example, the government were to cut its spending on defense completely, the generational accounts of the living would not change at all. Still, it does not seem reasonable to conclude that personal welfare would remain unaffected by this policy. Put differently, if generational accounts are supposed to reflect changes in individual well-being induced by government budgets, they should include all types of public expenditure translating into private benefits.

In the light of this argument, the established generational accounting practice to recognize government spending as a transfer only if it falls on clearly identifiable age groups appears unconvincing. It stops halfway between the two different interpretations of the net tax burden. In fact, many immaterial public goods provided by the public sector are age-neutral by their very nature. One may think of public goods like political freedom, social peace or judicial security, all of which are associated with the – costly – existence of government.

The interpretation of benefits derived from public goods as a transfer requires specification of how public spending translates into private benefits. For a rough approximate, one might assume that personal welfare from public goods is identical, on average, to their input value, or more precisely to the per capita money spent by the government. However, this approach could be misleading for several reasons. First, the social value of a public good might differ from its market value, if it generates externalities. Secondly, if benefits from public spending are assigned according to their input cost to agents, efficiency gains in the government sector that allow to provide an identical set of public goods less costly, would lead to an increase in the net fiscal burden. A welfare loss is indicated, although private well-being does not change [McCarthy and Bonin (1999)].

Finally, an even distribution of benefits among all age cohorts is likely to misrepresent the incidence of government spending on public goods. This is straightforward for government spending on education or old-age care, but age-neutral distribution of benefits could also be inappropriate for other types of public investment or subsidies that do not fall on clearly identifiable age cohorts. At the margin, the cost of the public investment must be equal to the (possibly infinite) sequence of benefits generated by the investment. If it were not, the investment would not be profitable for the government. Consequently, to indicate the distributive impact of the public investment correctly, the sequence of welfare gains needs to be allocated across cohorts alive when the benefits occur, rather than across cohorts alive when the investment is made.

One could argue that public investment is typically more beneficial for cohorts comparatively young, since they have the chance to benefit from the returns on the investment over a longer remaining lifespan. Provided that this line of argument is empirically relevant,[4] it would be preferable to suppose a downward-slope for the age-specific benefits originating from public investment. However, construction of the exact personal benefit profiles seems empirically difficult. It requires detailed information on the structure of government investment and the corresponding time structure of returns.[5] In addition, the introduction of a specific benefit profile would draw a wedge between the time structure of public revenue and spending on the one hand, and the personal burdens and benefits on the other. As a consequence, the intertemporal budget constraint of the public sector, which determines the intertemporal changes in net tax burdens, would be constructed according to a different principle than the generational accounts.

To summarize, if one wishes to assign government spending as an in-kind transfer, one usually has to be satisfied with a lump-sum distribution of the potential benefits (approximated by input costs). Interpreting the resulting generational accounts as welfare indicators, however, one should be aware that this procedure, as was criticized by Havemann (1994, p. 101) tends to exaggerate the actual future net fiscal burden of future generations. It concentrates the entire benefits of public goods in the year when they are purchased.

Despite the difficulties to assign benefits from government expenditure properly, omission of in-kind transfers from the concept of a net tax burden does not completely satisfy as an alternative. First, it encourages the misleading interpretation that someone burdened with a positive generational account would be better off, if the government did not exist at all. More importantly, the generational accounts measure intergenerational redistribution through public sector budgets incompletely, if the analysis does not account for benefits derived from public consumption and investment. These argu-

---

[4] Empirical evidence suggests that the impact of public investment on private sector output or growth is weak. This is true, whether public infrastructure is financed through credit [Kellermann and Schlag (1998), Kitterer (1994)], or taxes [Holtz-Eakin (1994), Barro (1990)].

[5] The age-related spending profiles for government subsidies and investment employed by Cardarelli and Sefton (1999) in a generational accounting study for the United Kingdom do not reflect differences in benefits by age, but variations in costs.

ments notwithstanding, a conservative definition of net taxes, in principle limited to in-cash transfers between the public and private sector, will be favored in the empirical part of this volume. In any case, the two concepts lead to identical results, if generational accounting is used to analyze the cohort-specific impact of changes in fiscal policy that only affect taxes or transfers.

To conclude this discussion of alternative net tax concepts, it is worth mentioning that neither perspective on net fiscal burdens implies that aggregate net taxes collected from private agents equal overall public revenue net of total expenditure. First, transactions between the public and private sector generating an exchange in return do not constitute a burden or benefit. For example, fees paid for usage of public services do not add to the tax burden, while interest payments on outstanding government debt are a return on private investment, rather than a transfer. Secondly, government revenue from foreign transfers does not impose a fiscal burden on the internal personal sector, unless one would be willing to argue that being dependent on foreign money creates a welfare loss for the individual citizen. This aspect is especially relevant when preparing generational accounts for developing countries,[6] but also for some European countries relying on support by the European Union.[7]

2.3 The Projection of Taxes and Transfers

It is now time to return to the problem of how to acquire the long run estimates for future age specific tax and transfer payments, $t_{i,k}^l$, prerequisite for the calculation of representative rest-of-life net tax burdens according to equation (2.5). As a starting point, generational accountants observe that age-specific per capita tax payments and transfer receipts, $t_{t,k}^l$, are subject to a fundamental restriction – in the base year, the sum of age-specific individual payments, weighted with cohort size, must equal the corresponding macroeconomic tax or transfer aggregate, denoted by T_t^l. Thus,

$$T_t^l = \sum_{k=t-D}^{t} t_{t,k}^l \, P_{t,k}. \qquad (2.6)$$

In general, micro data on fiscal transactions between single individuals and the state are difficult to gather and where available, tend to be afflicted with inaccuracies. On the other hand, the corresponding macroeconomic data, typically taken from National Accounting statistics, are utmost exact. Therefore,

---

[6] Cf. Kakwani and Krongaew (1999) and Altamiranda (1999) for examples.

[7] Ireland is a prominent example. The EU transfers received by the Irish government amount to almost two percent of GDP. While foreign transfers are not part of the generational accounts, they need to be considered projecting aggregate public revenue [McCarthy and Bonin (1999)].

while the identity (2.6) must hold in theory, no existing statistics on individual tax and transfer flows between the private and public sector would ever guarantee that this relation holds empirically.

To cope with deficiencies in the micro data, generational accountants proceed in two steps. First, age-specific information regarding average tax payments or transfer receipts per agent is collected. The goal at this stage is to capture the relative fiscal position of different age groups as accurately as possible. Therefore, the relative tax and transfer profiles by age not necessarily have to relate to the base period, if this allows a gain in accuracy. Satisfactory statistics on fiscal parameters by age are not readily available from official sources quite often. The construction of generational accounts typically relies on estimates for individual tax and transfer payments by age retrieved from large-sample survey data, like national consumption and expenditure surveys or panel studies.

Even where using panel data, generational accountants so far have not made serious efforts to distinguish between age and cohort effects. For many tax and transfer types, the available data would not allow to draw this distinction anyway. Hence, the vector of relative per capita tax payments and transfer receipts by age, $(\tau^l_{t,t-D}, ..., \tau^l_{t,k}, ..., \tau^l_{t,t})$, where $\tau^l_{t,k}$ denotes the relative fiscal position in period t of a representative agent born in period k with respect to the tax or transfer l, in most empirical applications contains purely cross-sectional information.

In a second step, the estimated relative age distribution of different tax and transfer payments is tallied with the corresponding macroeconomic aggregates T^l_t by application of a proportional, non-age-specific benchmarking factor, denoted by θ^l in the following. Re-evaluation of the relative distribution of individual tax and transfer payments by age according to

$$t^l_{t,k} = \theta^l \ \tau^l_{t,k} \tag{2.7}$$

for all living generations $t - D \leq k \leq t$, where θ^l is defined by

$$\theta^l = \frac{T^l_t}{\sum^t_{k=t-D} \tau^l_{t,k} P_{t,k}}, \tag{2.8}$$

assures that equation (2.6) is satisfied. For the easy proof, substitute equation (2.8) into (2.7) and rearrange.[8]

In general, the base year cross section of absolute tax or transfer payments per capita $(t^l_{t,t-D}, ..., t^l_{t,k}, ..., t^l_{t,t})$ derived from equation (2.7) is the starting

---

[8] Following Auerbach et al. (1991), it has become common practice to relate the basic relative age profiles to a *numéraire* before re-evaluation. In technical terms, this means to employ a vector $(\tau^l_{t,t-D}/\tau^l_{t,k}, ..., 1, ..., \tau^l_{t,t}/\tau^l_{t,k})$ instead of $(\tau^l_{t,t-D}, ..., \tau^l_{t,k}, ..., \tau^l_{t,t})$ in equations (2.7) and (2.8). It is easy to see that this intermediate step is unnecessary. The procedure merely inflates the the scaling factor by the payment assigned to the *numéraire* generation, $\tau^l_{t,k}$.

point for the projection of future taxes and transfers by age required to construct generational accounts. However, tax and transfer profiles could change significantly after the initial period. Setting aside economic growth for the moment, it is evident from equation (2.8) that two factors would affect the development of absolute per capita tax and transfer profiles. First, changes in fiscal policy could alter the level of future of tax and transfer aggregates $(T_i^l \neq T_t^l)$, while leaving the relative fiscal position of individual cohorts unchanged. For example, variations in proportional payroll contribution rates, might be assumed to work in this way. In order to design a development of this kind, one has to substitute the projected time path of T_i^l into the nominator of equation (2.8), which shifts the original absolute age profile of tax or transfer payments uniformly by a factor T_i^l / T_t^l.[9]

Secondly, the vector $(\tau_{t,t-D}^l, ..., \tau_{t,k}^l, ..., \tau_{t,t}^l)$, indicating the relative position of individual age cohorts in the base year, may not stay constant. If the initial vector is replaced by an estimate of future age-specific payments $(\tau_{i,i-D}^l, ..., \tau_{i,k}^l, ..., \tau_{i,i}^l)$, the scaling factor θ^l defined by equation (2.8) varies accordingly. The resulting change in the tax or transfer aggregate is determined by first substituting the corrected scaling parameter into equation (2.7), and in turn equation (2.7) into (2.6).[10] Variations in the relative fiscal position of age groups might be a response to fiscal policy reforms that are directed at specific age cohorts only. A typical example is an increase in standard retirement age, which demands to adjust average labor tax payments and pension receipts close to retirement. Apart from fiscal policy, changes in demographics could affect future average taxes and transfers by age.[11]

Even without changes in fiscal policy, the relative fiscal position by age of the base year living may indicate the prospective age distribution of individual tax and transfer payments inadequately. Cohort effects are likely to change the cross-sectional relative fiscal profiles over time. The design of cohort effects requires specifying a matrix containing projected per capita tax and transfer payments $\tau_{i,k}^l$ for all generations k and all periods i. Generational accountants usually do not adopt this approach, but maintain the initial cross-sectional relative position of each age group indefinitely, except for the design of fiscal policy impacts. The loss in predictive quality using cross-sectional data in empirical microeconomics is known from econometric

---

[9] If future tax or transfer aggregates vary due to demographic changes, this does not affect the per capita position regarding taxes and transfers determining the generational accounts. Demographic factors always cancel out in equation (2.8), as they change the nominator and the denominator in the same proportion.

[10] For sake of argument, we assume that the base year population does not change. Considering demographic changes, two adjustment processes would overlap.

[11] For example, the relation between mortality parameters and health transfers might be important [Lee and Skinner (1999)].

analysis of consumer behavior.[12] It also needs to be considered commenting on the generational accounts. In particular, the life cycle net tax burdens reported for younger base year generations tend to be biased due to the neglect of cohort effects.

These arguments show that a realistic specification of the future age-specific tax and transfer payments underlying the construction of generational accounts is a difficult task. Taking equations (2.7) and (2.8) as the starting point, detailed assumptions regarding future fiscal policies and their influence on both the absolute and relative fiscal position by age, as well as an assessment of potential cohort effects, are required. Acknowledging that long-term conditional projections are inevitably marked by prognostic errors and growing statistical variance, generational accountants normally do not attempt to design in detail what they consider as most likely economic developments. Instead, base case projections of age-specific tax and transfer payments generally postulate that the observed relative levels of taxes and transfers will stay unchanged in the future.

The assumption that in the future government policy will alter neither the absolute nor the relative fiscal position of individual age groups, has been rejected as unrealistic. Governments, some analysts argue, are reactive and adjust net taxes if keeping to present fiscal policy turns out unsustainable. Furthermore, as agents adapt to the resulting change in tax and transfer levels, also relative age profiles are unlikely to stay constant. For these reasons, generational accounts have been dismissed as being of little empirical interest [Diamond (1996), Havemann (1994)]. However, this criticism misses the character of the generational accounting exercise. It is actually the postulate of unchanged fiscal parameters, which transforms generational accounts from simplistic estimates of lifetime net tax burdens into meaningful indicators for the current state of public finances. Rather than predicting net tax burdens by generation, the method of generational accounting condenses multidimensional information regarding the complex interplay between current fiscal policy, cohort behavior and demographic parameters into a compact set of indicators.

It is worth noting that the strategy to translate multidimensional cross-sectional data into summarizing life cycle indicators is well known from demographics. For example, life expectancy at birth does not project the average lifespan of a birth cohort, but states the average number of years survived given that current mortality rates do not change over the life cycle. Similarly, the net reproduction rate of females summarizes the base year conditions regarding fertility and mortality by assuming that both stay constant during the lifetime of a representative woman. Although these demographic mea-

---

[12] Cf. Ronning (1991) and Bartenwerfer (1990). The validity of a cross-sectional approach for constructing generational accounts is questioned by Banks et al. (2000). Fullerton and Rogers (1993) have shown how to estimate lifetime income tax burdens incorporating cohort effects.

sures lose information transforming a cross-sectional status quo into a fictive life cycle concept – cohort indicators would be superior of course – one could not argue that they are empirically void. The loss in predictive quality is exchanged for a gain in interpretative clarity. The same can be said with respect to generational accounts that reflect the status quo of fiscal policy.

For the sake of a well-defined indicator concept, the assumption that fiscal policy will maintain base year tax and transfer levels should serve as the guiding principle behind a basic set of generational accounts. In practice, generational accountants have to moderate this rule occasionally, if present fiscal policies exhibit their revenue and expenditure impacts only in the future. In order to design the stance of base year policy properly, generational accountants typically consider also those legal amendments, enacted in or prior to the base year, as *present* fiscal policy, whose future budgetary impacts can be predicted reasonably well. Frequently, the status quo perspective is loosened further to incorporate official short- and medium-term budget forecasts.[13] The latter approach should be adopted with some caution. In many instances, government projections of the medium-term budget are embellished by optimistic assumptions about the immediate future.

In any case, projections regarding future budget developments aiming at a more accurate design of what is considered as current government policy, add uncertainties to the analysis. After all, even the short-run development of aggregate budget variables is difficult to predict, not the least because of business cycle effects. Therefore, conservative strategies interfering little with the original absolute and relative fiscal profiles, seem preferable, as they enhance the indicator quality of the generational accounts. A rigid status quo approach does not limit the analytical scope of generational accounting. On the contrary, the impacts of more sophisticated, arguably more realistic specifications of future budget developments on the generational accounts can be judged persuasively only against a neutral reference.

Uncertainties entering through the design of policy scenarios command thorough sensitivity tests. Still, due to the long-term character of the calculations, which inflates parameterization errors, generational accounts beyond a pure indicator concept always need careful interpretation. By no means, they represent statistical forecasts. Nevertheless, contrasting the accounts under projected alternative time paths of fiscal policy with lifetime net tax burdens under *status quo* conditions, is a powerful means to evaluate policy options in terms of their generational incidence.

To conclude this section, it is worth pointing out that the status quo approach might contradict to institutional arrangements. In particular, the continuation of current tax and transfer levels implies that payroll contribu-

---

[13] For example, the official generational accounting results for the US published in OMB (1994, pp. 21n) consider official 10-year budget forecasts. Bovenberg and ter Rele (1999b) employ official budget projections to update their 1995 base year budget table until the year 1999.

tion and social insurance replacement rates are preserved, even if this leads to a violation of the annual budget constraint of pay-as-you-go financed social insurance schemes when the composition of the population changes. This approach avoids to decide how future fiscal policy will react to imbalances in social insurance budgets. After all, policymakers could select any combination of defined benefit and defined contribution strategies, or accommodate imbalances with (temporary) borrowing or lending. The counterfactual approach to the projection of pay-as-you-go net contributions makes clear once again that predictive quality is not the core analytical interest of generational accountants.

2.4 Accounting for Economic Growth

The argument of the previous section abstracted from real economic growth.[14] Of course, productivity gains will affect both the absolute and relative level of future age-specific tax payments and transfer receipts. However, as with fiscal policy and cohort behavior, generational accountants generally do not attempt at forecasting productivity effects on individual tax and transfer payments, or merely productivity growth rates. Rather, they deal with the uncertainties regarding the fiscal impacts of productivity growth by assuming that economic growth, ceteris paribus, does not affect life cycle net tax rates on human capital (or labor income).

Accordingly, age specific tax payments or transfer receipts per capita are usually projected by subjecting fiscal profiles of the base period to a constant and time invariant productivity growth rate. If g denotes the annual rate of labor productivity growth, and if the design of current fiscal policy does not require modification of relative and absolute tax or transfer payments, this rule can be transcribed as

$$t^l_{t+j,k} = (1+g)^j \, t^l_{t,k-j} \tag{2.9}$$

for generations $t - D < k \leq t$, where $1 \leq j \leq k + D - t$.[15] Equation (2.9) postulates that each agent who reaches age $t + j - k$ in the future will experience the same tax or transfer payment as the representative $t + j - k$-year-old in the base year, uprated for annual economic growth. For example, the vector of life cycle net tax payments for a representative member of the cohort born in the base year, $(t_{t,t}, ..., t_{t+j,t}, ..., t_{t+D,t})$, is supposed to equal

---

[14] Generational accounts are defined in real terms. Nominal effects due to price inflation cancel out if all net tax payments are expressed in base year prices. This does not mean that inflation is supposed absent. Seignorage, or the implicit tax burden due to inflation, is a topic in Section 5.2.2.

[15] Since agents born in year $t - D$ do not survive the base year, a projection is not required for this cohort. The remaining lifetime net taxes paid by a representative cohort member are equal to $t_{t,t-D}$.

$(t_{t,t}, ..., (1+g)^{j}t_{t,t-j}, ..., (1+g)^{D}t_{t,t-D})$. Thus, the projected cohort net tax burden incorporates the cross-sectional absolute net tax profile observed in the base period.

As future taxes and transfers are uprated on the microeconomic level, generational accounting considers economic growth in terms of output per worker, rather than in terms of gross domestic product (GDP). Therefore, with competitive labor markets, per capita wage income also grows at the rate g for each cohort. Then, application of equation (2.9) is sufficient to guarantee that life cycle cohort net tax rates on labor income do not change due to productivity growth, if fiscal policy stays unchanged.

The uprating rule defined by equation (2.9) implies that without demographic, behavioral and fiscal policy changes, tax and transfer aggregates grow at a constant annual rate of g. Since the calculations perpetuate the base year state of the business cycle in the consequence, one would ideally choose a period with average capacity utilization (representing the long-run trend in economic growth) as the starting point. Notwithstanding, generational accountants frequently base their analysis on the most recent year for which the required set of data can be assembled.

Interpreting the generational accounts, one has to stay aware of business cycle effects. Status quo net tax payments typically develop pro-cyclically. In a boom, government tax revenue tends to increase while spending falls, whereas the opposite is true in a depression. Thus, net tax levels tend to appear more or less sustainable, depending on the initial macroeconomic economic conditions.[16] Occasionally, it is necessary to take a likely economic downturn or recovery into account, in order to assess the state of public finances adequately.[17]

Mechanical forecasting rules as given by equation (2.9) are typically justified by noting that per capita tax and transfer payments cannot grow at a different rate than productivity and hence labor income in the long term [CBO (1995, p. 13)]. If they did, the share of the corresponding aggregate in national income would converge either to zero (for growth rates smaller than g) or infinity (for growth rates higher than g). Nevertheless, even if business cycle effects are negligible, equation (2.9) could poorly design the short-term response of tax and transfer profiles to future economic growth. Constant growth uprating implies that the tax (transfer) system is not progressive (regressive) with regard to economic growth.

This assumption imposes a rather strong restriction on fiscal legislation. Government is supposed to redesign tax and transfer regulations per-

---

[16] The fact that generational accounts ary considerably over the business cycle is evident from a sequence of studies for Norway. The severe generational imbalance indicated by the accounts for the year 1992 [Auerbach et al. (1993)] has vanished by the year 1996 due increased petroleum revenue and improved unemployment figures [Steigum and Gjersem (1999)].

[17] A generational accounting study starting in a deep recession and therefore designing economic recovery to medium productivity growth is Feist et al. (1999).

manently, adjusting for example, tax tariffs and transfer benefit schemes annually in accordance with real income growth. Administrative practice frequently does not meet this rigid requirement. In fact, tax and transfer regulations are often adapted to economic progress with considerable time lags. If current legal settings provide automatic annual adjustments of tax or transfer regulations, these are typically linked to price inflation, rather than to economic growth.

The uprating rule described by equation (2.9) claims that if appropriate adjustments to productivity gains are not carried out annually, temporary gains in public revenue or losses in private transfers are fully compensated by periodical legal amendments at some later point of time. This status quo perspective postulates that base year transfer replacement and tax rates are guaranteed in the long term, which may contradict to the intentions of policymakers who would use delayed productivity adjustments as a deliberate means to increase tax levels or to reduce transfer levels.[18] If this is indeed the case, one may prefer to temporarily suspend the standard uprating rule of equation (2.9), in order to design the actual stance of current fiscal policy. Nonetheless, at some tax and transfer level (which should be subject of a sensitivity test), government must return to productivity indexation.

Equation (2.9) implies that economic growth reproduces the initial relative fiscal position by age for all cohorts alive, if at a different level. This assumption rules out that productivity gains favor specific age groups at the expense of others. In fact, productivity effects are likely to be cohort specific, being stronger for younger generations if they depend on agents' capacity to innovation. More generally, the application of a uniform growth factor to the age profiles of taxes and transfers implies that productivity gains do not entail changes in the structure of the economy.

Put differently, while fiscal policy is assumed to maintain the average payments of taxpayers or transfer recipients in terms of life cycle income, productivity gains are assumed to leave the likelihood to pay taxes or to receive transfers unaffected.[19] This implies, for example, that labor market conditions are not changed by gains in productivity, with unemployment rates staying constant at their base year level. Furthermore, behavioral changes due to rising wage income are ruled out, although at least labor force participation is likely to be responsive. As with fiscal policy effects, generational accountants are ready to sacrifice more realistic estimates for cohort specific productivity impacts on lifetime net taxes for a gain in indicator quality.

---

[18] For example, price indexation of minimum pensions in the United Kingdom has been interpreted as a policy to reduce the share of these pensions in transfers [Cardarelli and Sefton (1999)].

[19] The age-specific net tax payment per capita $t_{t,k}$ can be factorized into the likelihood of being a net tax payer, given by the fraction of net tax payers in the entire cohort, and the average net tax payment per net tax payer.

Although generational accountants in general do not question the growth uprating rule defined by equation (2.9), it seems worth noting that it represents only a sufficient condition to assure that tax and transfer aggregates grow at the same rate as GDP in the long term, not a necessary one. A less restrictive postulate is that individual *lifetime* tax payments and transfer receipts grow at the same rate as labor productivity for consecutive cohorts. Assuming uniform survival rates for all birth cohorts, this more general requirement can be stated as

$$\sum_{i=k+j}^{k+j+D} t^l_{i,k+j} = (1+g)^j \sum_{i=k}^{k+D} t^l_{i,k}. \qquad (2.10)$$

It is easy to show that projecting absolute age-specific tax payments according to equation (2.9) is consistent with this less restrictive condition quite generally. However, as was noted by Levy and Doré (1999) and , in some instances a different uprating scheme could design the impacts of fiscal policy more accurately. Referring to their example, the primary insurance amount offered by public pensions, i.e. the pension payment provided by a statutory pension insurance at entry to retirement, is often closely related to lifetime labor income (or any fraction of it). In retirement, however, adjustments of pension benefits frequently insure against the inflation risk only. Given this arrangement, the primary insurance amount for consecutive cohorts of retirees increases at a rate g in line with lifetime labor income, whereas cohort specific pension benefits in retirement remain constant upon death in real terms. Therefore, it would be preferable to design age-specific transfer receipts over the life cycle of subsequent cohorts according to

$$t^l_{k+j,k} = (1+g)\, t^l_{k-1+j,k-1} \qquad (2.11)$$

for generations $t - D < k \leq t$, where $0 \leq j \leq D$. The productivity growth rule defined by equation (2.11) is consistent with the sufficient long-term growth condition (2.10), but processes longitudinal data. Although the growth uprating schemes defined by equations (2.9) and (2.11) are equivalent under very specific conditions,[20] economic and institutional fluctuations of the past showing in the base year cross-section could make the latter routine superior.

---

[20] For the sketch of the proof, consider the vector of life cycle payments for a base year-born individual, $(t^l_{t,t}, ..., t^l_{t+k,t}, ..., t^l_{t+D,t})$. According to equation (2.11), $t^l_{t+1,t}$ equals $(1+g)t^l_{t,t-1}$. Furthermore, $t^l_{t+2,t}$ is defined as $(1+g)t^l_{t+1,t-1}$. Given equation (2.11) is valid for the cohorts born in years $t-1$ and $t-2$, $t^l_{t+1,t-1}$ can be written as $(1+g)t^l_{t,t-2}$. Substitution of the latter term into the definition of $t^l_{t+2,t}$ yields $t^l_{t+2,t} = (1+g)^2 T^l_{t,t-2}$. By a similar line of reasoning, one can rewrite all future $t^l_{t+i,t}$ as $(1+g)^i t^l_{t,t-i}$, for $1 \leq i \leq D$. Thus, the vector of future age-specific payments of the generation born in t is transformed into an expression in terms of the base year cross-section, which reads $(t^l_{t,t}, ..., (1+g)^j t^l_{t,t-j}, ..., (1+g)^D t^l_{t,t-D})$ and is identical to the life cycle profile of payments projected by equation (2.9).

Evidence suggests that growth uprating by equation (2.11) rather than by equation (2.9) leads to less pronounced pension expenditure growth, and increases net taxes paid by the base year living [Levy and Doré (1999), Cardarelli and Sefton (1999)]. Still, cohort growth uprating in line with equation (2.11) cannot replace standard cross-sectional uprating. It requires estimation of a longitudinal payment profile $(t^l_{k,k}, ..., t^l_{k+i,k}, ...t^l_{k+D,k})$ to start from, which adds uncertainties, to be balanced against the potential analytical gain, to the analysis. Ideally, as soon as generational accounts are based on cohort uprating in line with equation (2.11), one would test the sensitivity of the findings against the conventional productivity adjustment.

All arguments considered, there seem to be good reasons to believe that the tax and transfer profiles observed in the base year will not follow the growth path defined by equation (2.9), in particular in the short term. The resulting bias in the generational accounts is generally more prominent for older base year cohorts, whose net tax payments in the first years of the projection, which are less likely to be dominated by long-run productivity trend, are important due to a short remaining lifetime. As a consequence, the generational accounts computed for the elderly should be approached with particular caution. Fortunately, considered the small population share of the oldest-old, measurement errors affecting the accounts of the elderly are of little relevance on a macroeconomic level.

As for younger generations, the assumption that tax and transfer payments will develop in line with long-run productivity growth over their life cycle, at least on average, appears more likely. Nevertheless, in face of uncertainty about the appropriate specification of a long-term productivity growth rate, also their generational accounts require sensitivity tests.

2.5 General Equilibrium Considerations

The application of time invariant growth and interest factors to construct the generational accounts and, more generally, the assumption that generational accounts provide satisfactory indicators of generational redistribution of welfare ignores possible interrelations between individuals' present value life cycle net tax payments and pre-tax factor income in the economy. Strictly, this would be appropriate only if the economy were in equilibrium in the base year, and if fiscal policy were consistent with the fiscal balance rule. In practice, ignoring the possibility of macroeconomic disequilibrium and changing

---

This argument requires the assumption that growth uprating according to equation (2.11) properly describes the relation between the life cycle payments of all presently living cohorts (the oldest born a century ago) and hence the economic (and legislative) conditions of the past. Only under this condition, the cross-sectional base year fiscal profile would incorporate the growth effects, which equation (2.11) postulates to be effective only in the future.

pre-tax factor incomes may limit the empirical validity of the generational account measures. The static perspective passes over two aspects in particular, which could be essential to judge fiscal burdens accurately – the impacts of demographic changes on the macroeconomic environment, and the generational distribution of the deadweight loss associated with a specific setting of tax and transfer parameters.

Changes in the composition of the population, especially marked demographic aging and corresponding population decline, are likely to affect productivity growth and before-tax labor income per capita.[21] The direction of the response to demographic transitions is far from unambiguous though, both theoretically and empirically. On the macroeconomic level, ceteris paribus, relative shortage of labor supply or, put differently, higher capitalization per worker, tends to improve labor productivity and therefore gross wages. From the microeconomic perspective, if labor supply is responsive, improved labor market conditions may raise labor supply, compensating for a declining population at working age. Furthermore, demographic aging may change the rate of (labor augmenting) technical progress.[22]

If continuation of present fiscal parameters or realization of fiscal reform alter the incentives to consume and to invest, the resulting transition toward a new macroeconomic equilibrium could render the present value of generations' life cycle net tax payments a poor indicator for actual changes in utilities. In addition to the immediate net tax burden measured by the generational accounts, dynamic incidence analysis would have to incorporate the generational welfare impacts of changes in gross-of-tax factor incomes and of tax avoidance activities, including income as well as substitution effects. If dynamic incidence effects were to dominate changes in utility, the generational accounting approach to measure generational redistribution by first-order distribution of net tax payments would be inadequate. If they do, is essentially an empirical question.

Integrating generational accounting into a general equilibrium framework with two overlapping generations, Raffelhüschen and Risa (1997) have analyzed the transition to a funded Social Security system as a reaction to a demographic aging shock. They show that life cycle net tax burdens may actually provide bad approximations for changes in cohort utility, as changes in pre-tax income due to the demographic transition prevail over the direct tax effects. This finding is qualified, however, by simulation experiments conducted by Fehr and Kotlikoff (1997) who used the 55-overlapping-generations

---

[21] The growth rate of per capita labor income can deviate from the growth rate of labor productivity as a result of changes in average lifetime labor force participation.

[22] Disney (1996, chapter 6) summarizes theoretical and empirical evidence on the relation of demographic variables and both productivity growth and labor supply decisions. For Germany, the impacts of population decline on economic growth have been analyzed by Färber (1988) and Felderer (1983).

dynamic simulation model designed by Auerbach and Kotlikoff (1987) to compare changes in generational accounts with changes in generations' utility for a large number of stylized fiscal policies. The results suggest that the welfare change due to changes in lifetime net tax payments approximates the overall change in generations' utility quite well in general, provided that capital adjustment costs are negligible.[23] Still, conventional generational accounts may indicate generational distribution of fiscal burdens inadequately for some fiscal policy strategies. This seems to hold in particular investigating policies that affect the progressivity of the tax and transfer system, and analyzing small open economies characterized by more immediate variations in factor returns.

In general, measurement errors associated with ignorance of the behavioral reactions to fiscal policy and demographic changes accumulate over time, as the corresponding macroeconomic adjustments come to the fore only gradually. As a consequence, first-order redistribution induced by present value net tax payments, as indicated by the generational accounts, is the more likely to differ from the actual changes in individual welfare the younger cohort age. In fact, the generational accounts typically provide the least accurate approximation of total welfare changes due to fiscal policy for generations not yet alive in the base period. Therefore, analyzing policies that distribute net taxes to the advantage of young and future generations, the generational accounts are likely to indicate only the lower bound of the actual welfare improvement faced by these cohorts. In the opposite case, if policies redistribute to the advantage of older base year cohorts, generational accounts, neglecting welfare impacts of probably adverse repercussions on capital formation, tend to understate the fiscal burden of young and future cohorts [CBO (1995, p. 44)].

This bias, the direction and strength of which are difficult to predict generally, is the price to pay for the empirical and methodological simplicity achieved when restricting generational accounting to a fundamentally static perspective. Interpreting the resulting indicators of generational redistribution, one should stay aware that the construction of generational accounts (not unlike the calculation of budget deficits or surpluses in this respect) stays basically an accounting exercise, despite the apparent sophistication of the concept. The look ahead into the long-term future underlying the generational accounts must not be mistaken for a dynamic analysis, for it has no place for ongoing behavioral adjustments to fiscal policy or to demographic changes. Thus, generational accounts primarily make a statement about the present, rather than painting a sophisticated picture of the uncertain economic future.

---

[23] With capital adjustment costs, the overall return to capital is likely to be dominated by stock market revaluations which would influence generations' utility even in the short-run. However, the empirical evidence for the existence of considerable capital adjustment costs is weak [Cutler (1988)].

2.6 Breaking Down Generational Accounts

Provided that the available micro data are sufficiently detailed, one may break the generational account of a representative cohort member down to measure the rest-of-life tax payments faced by members of distinct subpopulations. Disaggregation of the generational accounts is a welcome extension, as it allows to evaluate the generational impacts of current fiscal policy and the incidence of policy reforms on different groups within the population.

If generational accounts are separated, the rest-of-life tax burden indicated for a representative member of each age cohort is a weighted average of the generational accounts for representative members of the distinct population groups. It is shown in the Appendix A.1 that the age-specific weights are given by the share of the subpopulations in the initial population. Hence,

$$GA_{t,k} = \sum_m \frac{P_{t,k}^m}{P_{t,k}} GA_{t,k}^m. \qquad (2.12)$$

Here and in the following, the superscript m to a variable indicates that it refers to a particular population subgroup $m = 1, ..., n$. Furthermore, it must hold that set of subpopulations adds up to the base year population, i.e. that $\sum_m P_{t,k}^m = P_{t,k}$. In equation (2.12), the subgroup generational accounts are derived parallel to the standard definition of rest-of-life tax burdens given by equation (2.1) in connection with equation (2.4). Therefore, the construction of generational accounts for different population groups requires group-specific survival probabilities and per capita tax payments, as well as the base year age structure of the subpopulation.

After distinguishing tax and transfer age profiles between subpopulations, the individual tax or transfer payments must still aggregate to the corresponding budget variable. This restriction serves to re-evaluate the subgroup-specific relative fiscal position by age to the macroeconomic data. Extending equation (2.6) while respecting (2.8) yields the uniform benchmarking parameter θ^l, by solving

$$T_t^l = \sum_m \sum_{k=t-D}^t t_{t,k}^{l,m} P_{t,k}^m = \theta^l \sum_m \sum_{k=t-D}^t \tau_{t,k}^{l,m} P_{t,k}^m. \qquad (2.13)$$

Equation (2.13) implies that the original relative position of the subgroup observations within each age group, $(\tau_{t,t-k}^1, ..., \tau_{t,t-k}^m, ..., \tau_{t,t-k}^n)$, stays unchanged by the benchmarking procedure. Projecting future subgroup tax and transfer payments, generational accountants for a base case typically use uniform forecasting rules in line with the principles discussed in the previous sections. This procedure preserves the initial relative fiscal position of the distinct population groups for the future.[24]

---

[24] This approach implies that there are no transitions between fiscally distinct population groups that would change average net taxes.

Although application of uniform uprating rules for all subpopulations is consistent with the status quo character of generational accounting, it might be seriously misleading on some occasions. Economic recovery of the East German states unleashed by German unification is one example in this regard. A design of the convergence process requires specification of region-specific growth rates to design the lifetime fiscal position of East and West German residents adequately. To give a more universal example, continuing emancipation of the female labor force may imply that average net tax payments of women for some period of time will grow at a faster rate than that of men. As always, conservative parameterizations are preferable when designing differential tax and transfer projections for population subgroups. If such need to be incorporated into the status quo set of generational accounts, careful sensitivity tests are in order.

As the generational accounts are strictly forward-looking and neglect net tax payments prior to the base year, one must not compare the remaining lifetime net tax payments faced by representative members of different age cohorts. Variations in rest-of-life net tax burdens not only indicate cohort differences in net tax levels but also differences in remaining lifetime. However, one may compare the generational accounts of agents who are members of the same birth cohort, but belong to distinct population groups. If life expectancy conditional on age varies across subpopulations, the resulting net tax differentials are an integral part of agents' average remaining lifetime tax burden and relevant for assessing redistribution between population groups due to fiscal policy. Allowing for differential mortality does not question the validity of comparing generational accounts across subpopulations, but adds the dimension of personal welfare to the analysis.

2.7 Ambiguities of Generational Accounts

The set of generational accounts for living cohorts is not only useful to assess differential impacts of fiscal policy on distinct population groups. An even more powerful application is to evaluate representative remaining lifetime net tax payments by age (and possibly by population group) under different time paths of fiscal policy. The counterfactual scenario of constant tax and transfer parameters over the lifetime of base year cohorts provides a benchmark by which to judge generational redistribution due to specific fiscal policy measures, supposed that deviations from the status quo are not anticipated. If they were, differential incentive effects among living cohorts, at work in or even prior to the base year, would render changes in generational accounts, which measure future net income effects of fiscal policy only, an insufficient indicator for generational redistribution among the living.

Selecting from a range of possibilities to design future fiscal policy and the development of the economy, generational accountants are exposed to the usual problems of conditional projections, which cannot be resolved by scientific reasoning. The degree of freedom in parameter choice when designing more realistic alternatives to the indicator concept of constant fiscal and demographic parameters opens space for bad specification and even intentional manipulation. Facing uncertainty about the future, it is a matter of scientific integrity that any particular assumption entering the projections different from the status quo is based on empirical or theoretical evidence and clearly documented for the public.

While uncertainties involved with the specification of realistic future scenarios for the economy could render generational accounting prone to manipulation, the status quo indicator perspective seems less susceptible to wilful procedures. Nevertheless, as was criticized, among others, by Havemann (1994, p. 107), the statement of some advocates of generational accounting that the method, in contrast to cash-flow budgeting, would be immune against manipulation [Auerbach et al. (1991, 1994)]) seems overly optimistic even with regard to benchmark generational accounts derived under the condition of constant base year parameters – recall that this chapter showed a number of reasons not to follow this rigid procedure.

First, as the notion of net taxes is not unambiguous, reported fiscal burdens can be manipulated by eliminating particular taxes or transfers from the generational accounts. Less obvious would be an omission of parts of the overall government budget. After all, as generational accounting starts from a periodical cash-flow budget, manipulations of the reported deficit are not automatically fixed by transition to an intertemporal cohort perspective. Finally, there are no definite solutions how to derive the profiles of tax and transfer incidence by age underlying the measurement of generational net tax burdens. Manipulations at this preliminary stage of the generational accounting procedure hardly can be traced.

The generational accounting studies currently before the public actually indeed show great diversity regarding fiscal incidence assumptions and the assignment of micro tax and transfer variables to specific age cohorts. This observation remains true despite recent efforts to provide large scale cross-country studies based on a uniform methodological framework.[25] Drawing comparisons of generational accounts across countries, even if keeping to the respective status quo benchmark, one should stay aware of the possible generational impacts of different approaches to construct relative tax and transfer profiles by age.

---

[25] The twelve country studies collected by the European Commission (1999), though superior to a similar collection by Auerbach et al. (1999) in using a single computational algorithm, show diverging approaches to construction of relative tax and transfer profiles. For example, while inheritance taxes are generally assigned to heirs, Cardarelli and Sefton (1999) allocate the tax burden to testators. Bovenberg and ter Rele (1999b) relate indirect tax payments to annual income, whereas life cycle distribution of consumption purchases is the base for the indirect tax profiles used in the remaining country studies.

Non-standardized treatment of relative tax and transfer profiles remains a major weakness of current generational accounting practice. Methodological ambiguities are frequently due to deficiencies in the available empirical sources. Not everything theoretically sound can be realized working on a usually highly limited micro data base. Nevertheless, in order to reduce conceptual arbitrariness, development of consistent conventions guiding the construction of relative tax and transfer profiles seems indispensable for the future, in particular if generational accounting were to complement traditional deficit accounting as an official statistical statement. An agreement on a well-defined standard is also prerequisite to harmonize the collection of age-related data with the requirements of generational accounting.

Thus, there seems to remain scope to advance the fiscal indicator quality of the generational accounts, which are not free from methodological and empirical ambiguities yet. In the meantime, application of the rigid status quo benchmark outlined in this chapter offers a second-best solution to derive a set of generational accounts for living cohorts providing a well-defined indication of government interference with individual consumption opportunities, which could be meaningfully pursued over time and compared across countries.

3. The Intertemporal Public Budget

Continuation of current fiscal policy does not only redistribute consumption opportunities among living generations. Tax burdens are also shifted intertemporally, onto cohorts not yet born. In order to assess the possible extent of intertemporal generational redistribution associated with a specific tax and transfer policy, generational accountants construct stylized generational accounts for future generations. In the terminology of generational accounting, fiscal strategies that require different fiscal treatment of current and future generations considered their entire life cycle are defined as intergenerationally imbalanced. Alternatively, policies that require correction of the initial tax and transfer parameters, thus affecting the fiscal burden of present and/or future cohorts, are called unsustainable.

To calculate the – hypothetical – net life cycle tax burden representative for future generations, generational accounting starts from the observation that the net tax payments faced by present and future generations are linked by a fundamental macroeconomic constraint. Over an indefinite time horizon, the choices of fiscal policy are restricted by the requirement to balance the intertemporal budget constraint of the public sector. This chapter gives an introduction to the revenue and expenditure components of this intertemporal fiscal policy constraint, and discusses its economic implications.

3.1 The Intertemporal Budget Constraint

Generational accounting is based on the neoclassical formulation of the intertemporal public budget constraint. In a dynamically efficient economy, where the interest rate is smaller than the rate of population growth (adjusted for technical progress), deficits of public sector budgets cannot be financed by issuing new bonds indefinitely. As a consequence, the present value of prospective net tax payments to the public sector, imposed on either living or future born agents, plus the aggregate return from government net assets must be sufficient to finance the present value of projected government purchases. In present value terms of the base year, this intertemporal constraint to public sector finances can be expressed as

$$\sum_{k=t-D}^{t} N_{t,k} + \sum_{k=t+1}^{\infty} N_{t,k} + W_t = \sum_{y=t}^{\infty} G_{t,y}. \qquad (3.1)$$

Equation (3.1), or some variant with identical meaning, is shared by all generational accounting studies. In equation (3.1), $G_{t,y}$ stands for projected net government purchases made in period y, in present value terms of period t, and W_t represents the value of government net assets in the base period. Finally, $N_{t,k}$ denotes the present value as of period t of future net taxes paid until death by the members of the generation born in the year k. Consequently, the first term on the LHS of equation (3.1) aggregates the rest-of-life net taxes paid by agents alive in the base period, whereas the second term cumulates the life cycle payments of cohorts not yet born. Since net tax payments of future born generations enter the intertemporal public budget constraint in present value terms, their aggregate converges below infinity, provided that the rate of discount exceeds the growth rate of generations' aggregate net taxes, at least in the long term.[1] This condition is always satisfied, as the economy cannot remain in a dynamically inefficient state.

The cohort-specific net tax aggregates $N_{t,k}$ encompass all taxes and transfers included in the construction of the generational accounts on the individual level. Correspondingly, on the RHS of equation (3.1), $G_{t,y}$ comprises all government purchases not allocated as a transfer to the personal sector, net of public revenue that does not impose a tax burden on the individual agent. As an exception, $G_{t,y}$ typically excludes net returns from government holdings of net assets, the reasons for which will be explained below. As the intertemporal budget constraint is defined in present value terms, the predicted amount of net government purchases in each year y is discounted to the base year by application of a uniform discount factor. Again, if the economy is dynamically efficient, the present value of aggregate government purchases remains finite.

In the generational accounting literature, the variable $G_{t,y}$ has been addressed as *government consumption* frequently, and more recently as *non-age-specific government expenditure*.[2] Neither term is really satisfying. Obviously, the former label is running a risk of being mistaken for government consumption in the literal sense of the National Account statistics, where it measures the value of all government services provided free of charge. Generational accountants' view on net government purchases is clearly different. In fact, government consumption in terms of National Account terminology is not

---

[1] This follows from a basic rule for infinite summation. Assumed that the growth of net tax payments by cohort converges to the rate g' in the long-run, the present value of net taxes develops with $x = (1 + g')/(1 + r)$. The cumulated weights of future net tax payments, $\sum_{k=0}^{\infty} x^j = (1 - x)^{-1} < \infty$, converge only if $|x| < 1$.

[2] The latter appears in country studies conducted for the European Commission (1999).

included in $G_{t,y}$, if one adopts a transfer concept that assigns government services as a personal transfer.

Although in generational accounting public spending excluded from the generational accounts is frequently distributed evenly across generations, the term *non-age-specific government expenditure* is not a satisfactory label for $G_{t,y}$ either. It obscures the fact that age-dependency is not a relevant criterion for the definition of government net purchases. First, lump-sum tax and transfer payments would register in the generational accounts. More importantly, government spending on consumption, subsidies or investment, which typically accounts for the major share of government net purchases, are not necessarily independent of age. Although the correlation is often difficult to establish in practice, several generational accounting studies incorporate empirical evidence indicating that some government purchases vary with age.[3]

To summarize, while the expenditure and revenue items abridged to the variable $G_{t,y}$ are very clearly defined in the framework of generational accounting, it is difficult to provide a satisfying, economically meaningful label for them. In this book, $G_{t,y}$ is continually referred to as *government (net) purchases*, as opposed to government net tax revenue aggregated on the LHS of the intertemporal budget constraint of the public sector. It seems worth noting that terminology issues raised above become irrelevant, if the selected definition of personal transfers is sufficiently broad. Provided that the generational accounting analysis regards all government activity (or more precisely the related government expenditure) as an implicit transfer, net government purchases vanish and the RHS of the intertemporal budget constraint reduces to zero [Raffelhüschen (1999a)].

The third term on the LHS of the intertemporal public budget constraint, the base year stock of net government wealth, W_t, represents the sum of real government surpluses (or deficits) in the past, mirroring the spending and revenue history of the public sector. Government assets constitute an additional source of revenue to the public coffers, which can be used to finance prospective net government purchases. Of course, net government wealth is not necessarily positive. If the government sector faces net liabilities, as its financial and tangible assets are smaller than financial debt, it would be more appropriate to include W_t on the RHS of the intertemporal budget constraint, for it adds to the government's debit that eventually needs financing from net tax revenue.[4]

---

[3] For example, Feist et al. (1999) and Cardarelli and Sefton (1999) consider that government subsidies are not spread evenly among cohorts.

[4] In the literature, one meets this variant of the intertemporal budget constraint occasionally. Cf. Auerbach et al. (1992a, 1997) for examples.

3.2 Determinants of Government Wealth

The measurement of public net assets raises difficult conceptual and valuation issues. With government net wealth, a stock variable enters the intertemporal budget constraint of the public sector, which contains payment flows besides. In theory, given perfect capital markets, the value of government assets equals the present value of aggregate prospective future returns exactly. To illustrate this proposition, let d_y denote the annual return to nominal government net assets in year, regarded constant for convenience, so that $d_y = d$. Discounting at a uniform annual interest rate, denoted by r, perfect capital markets evaluate assets by the aggregate present value of the interest stream accruing to them. Thus,

$$W_t = \sum_{y=t+1}^{\infty} \frac{d_y}{(1+r)^{y-t}} = \frac{d}{r}. \tag{3.2}$$

Equation (3.2), which exploits the rules of infinite summation, shows that if the annual interest yield on nominal assets deviates from the market rate a priori ($d \neq rW_t$), the value of the asset on the capital market, W_t, varies accordingly to restore the equality. On perfect capital markets, arbitrage would guarantee that government net assets, evaluated at their market price, always bear the average market rate of return. In accordance with this proposition, generational accountants typically use the stock of public net wealth as an equivalent to the discounted stream of revenue from government asset holdings.

As equation (3.2) reveals, in order to represent prospective government net interest revenue correctly, it is precisely the *market* value of base year net wealth that has to be included in the intertemporal budget constraint. In practice, assessing the market value of government assets is a difficult task, in particular with regard to the tangible assets of the government, which frequently by their very nature are not tradable on markets,[5] but also with respect to financial assets (or liabilities), which are reported in *nominal* terms in the financial statistics. If the nominal value of government assets differs from the market value, as they do not bear the market rate of return, the former would perhaps significantly misrepresent the actual present value of aggregate future interest revenue.[6]

Nevertheless, it is established practice in the generational accounting literature to approximate the market value of government net wealth by the reported nominal value.[7] This approach imposes quite strong assumptions. It

---

[5] Tangible assets are typically evaluated by replacement cost.

[6] If r' denotes the rate of return to government assets, it is easy to show using equation (3.2) that the market value differs from the nominal value by a factor r'/r.

[7] Cf. Oreopoulos (1999) and Bonin et al. (1999) for examples.

postulates that financial and tangible assets of the government bear precisely the average market rate of return, supposed equal to the discount rate.[8] Also the interest rate on public borrowing must average the capital market interest rate. If these conditions are satisfied, it is guaranteed that the present value of aggregate interest payments, measured by W_t, is independent of the capital market interest rate. This eases sensitivity analyses with regard to the discount factor. As follows from equation (3.2), W_t responds to variations in interest rates, if the rate of return to government capital differs from the market rate of return.

Instead of using the reported nominal amount of government net assets, some analysts prefer estimating the base year market price of assets explicitly, capitalizing a discounted stream of projected net asset revenue, in line with equation (3.2). Ideally, one would specify the entire sequence of prospective returns on government net wealth, $(d_1, ..., d_\infty)$. However, doing so requires precise data concerning both the actual composition of government net wealth and the specific return on different public assets, which are difficult to gather. For a second best solution, one may assume that base year net revenue from public assets, d_t, excluding income from asset sales which represents a non-recurring gain, remains constant over time so that $d_t = d$. Then, dividing the observed net return to government wealth by the constant *nominal* interest rate yields the corresponding market value of public sector wealth.[9] Since the generational accounts are constructed in real terms, the base year return to capital, which reflects nominal interest, needs correction for the projected rate of long-term price inflation.

In several recent applications of generational accounting, the elementary constant returns to capital approach has been replaced by an alternative rule to predict returns to government tangible assets.[10] It is assumed that the sequence of prospective capital revenue develops according to

$$d_y = \frac{d_t \, (1+g)^{y-t} \, \sum_{k=y-D}^{y} P_{y,k}}{\sum_{k=t-D}^{t} P_{t,k}} \tag{3.3}$$

for all periods $y > t$. Equation (3.3) postulates that the future annual return to tangible assets equals the return observed in the base year, corrected for changes in labor productivity and population size.

This is a strong normative statement requiring that gains in labor productivity cause higher absolute returns to government assets. To justify this assumption, one could argue that productivity gains allow to exploit govern-

---

[8] In general, these two rates deviate. The problem of the adequate discount rate for generational accounting will be discussed in Section 5.2.4.

[9] This approach was used in the pioneering study by Auerbach et al. (1991).

[10] Cf., for example, the country reports collected by the European Commission (1999). The procedure is rather obscured in these studies, as revenue from tangible assets is balanced against aggregate purchases of the government.

ment tangible assets more effectively, thus leading to a permanent gain in public revenue from the initial stock of assets. The connection between total population size and absolute returns to public tangible wealth established by equation (3.3) appears somewhat less plausible. Unless one wishes to argue with uncertain economies of scale, this approach suggests that returns to government assets resemble a user charge on citizens for the utilization of state-owned assets. Taking this perspective, it seems meaningful to assign a constant yield to a representative agent.

This seems to be a very restrictive interpretation of the returns to tangible assets. In fact, there are good reasons to believe that changes in population size are going to affect per capita capital revenue. For example, per capita revenue is likely to increase in case of rapid population decline, as the stock of government assets does not simply deteriorate due to reduced population size. In this scenario, government finances would develop more favorably than is indicated by the user charge approach. Nevertheless, the user charge perspective is in line with the status quo character of generational accounting analysis. Per capita uprating of capital income avoids uncertain statements about the behavior of public asset revenue during periods of demographic transition. It is also a sufficient condition to guarantee that this source of government revenue does not grow at a faster rate than GDP and converges to a stable share in the long term.

The approach to approximate unobservable net government wealth on the base of observed returns to capital by means of clear-cut rules of thumb has clear advantages. It is easy to implement and avoids conceptual arbitrariness, which becomes part of the analysis as soon as the sequence of future returns to capital is projected explicitly. Of course, for specific applications, empirical evidence might suggest that the stylized capital return approach is inadequate. If this is the case, it seems advised to deviate from the standard procedures, at least to provide for a sensitivity test. For example, projecting aggregate revenue from government tangible assets, Bovenberg and ter Rele (1999b) take into account that returns from public housing ownership in the Netherlands lag systematically behind the uniform interest rate used elsewhere to compute the generational accounts. They show that, compared to a scenario determining government assets in the conventional manner, explicit design of prospective capital revenue changes the generational accounting outcome markedly.

In a similar spirit, it would be useful to consider the base year interest structure of government liabilities explicitly. The initial average interest rate on government bonds does not necessarily reflect the constant long-term interest rate on which the generational accounts are based. For instance, if the base year stock of financial liabilities was mainly emitted during a period of high interest, the government may initially face a higher interest rate than the market rate, as it can exchange outstanding bonds for lower priced securities only gradually. The resulting expenditure effects have drawn curiously little attention in the generational accounting literature so far. A hint at the distortions that could result from unqualified application of the discount rate to government bonds was found by ter Rele (1997) using generational accounting to conduct long-term budget forecasts. In this application, to arrive at a meaningful sequence of budget deficits, it turns out necessary to design convergence of the base year average interest rate to the supposed long-term interest rate explicitly.

Finally, modeling the revenue stream from government net wealth as infinite is misleading with respect to public ownership of natural resources like minerals. Revenue from state-owned or publicly controlled natural resources contributes significantly to public budgets in several countries. Since natural resources are depletable, it is necessary to design the corresponding revenue flow as finite. Moreover, as prices on markets for minerals tend to be volatile, the standard assumption that base year public revenue from natural resources stays constant in the future is often too strong in this context. Although computation of the actual present value of public sector revenue from depletable natural resources is empirically difficult,[11] Auerbach et al. (1993) and Steigum and Gjersem (1999) have provided estimates in generational accounting studies for Norway, to adequately capture the impacts of petroleum wealth on the fiscal position of future generations. Similarly, Bovenberg and ter Rele (1999b) have taken the present value of Dutch gas resources into account, which are expected to dry up within the next decades.

To summarize, adequate specification of government net wealth, which is an essential determinant of intertemporal generational redistribution, is an highly intricate matter. It adds a serious ambiguity to the analysis, which cannot be solved in an economically well-defined or even unique way.[12] With no ideal measure of government net wealth available, a sensitivity test comparing the effect of different approaches to measure net government wealth, is definitely in order, if generational account analysis addresses the intertemporal stance of current fiscal policy. The difficulty to determine government wealth is less serious when generational accounting is applied to compare alternative fiscal policy options. The differential impact of policy changes effective in the future is not affected by government asset holdings, which reflect fiscal policy of the past.

---

[11] Among other things, it requires specification of the prospective time path of world market prices for the resource, of the speed of resource depletion, and of investment costs.

[12] As argued by Ablett (1996, p. 98), generational accountants, through the intertemporal public budget constraint, may replace the ill-defined government deficit concept with an ill-defined notion of net government wealth.

3.3 The No-Ponzi Game Condition

The incorporation of revenue from depletable natural resources in the intertemporal budget constraint of the public sector constitutes a special case. Natural wealth cannot yield revenue for the government other than by being sold on the market and being exhausted in the consequence.[13] In general, however, the intertemporal constraint to public sector revenue and expenditure is less restrictive.[14] It does not claim that the government, in order to fulfill the financing demands of government spending, is required to sell off its assets completely. Correspondingly, if the government is in debt ($W_t < 0$), the budget constraint does not say that taxes need to be raised in the future, in order to redeem the base year stock of government bonds. This is already obvious from the argument made in the previous section, which showed that the base year stock of government wealth considered in equation (3.1) represents the present value of interest flows accruing to government net assets. Of course, the government sector may sell part of its initial wealth, or retire part of its initial debt in the future. However, given perfect capital markets, the resulting net profits do not bring fiscal relief. In present value terms, they entail a loss in revenue from government net assets of equal size. Selling government net wealth and receiving an infinite interest stream are equivalent.

Rather than assuming that asset holdings of the government decrease to zero upon infinity, the intertemporal budget constraint of the public sector states that prospective revenue from public wealth cannot be invested to accumulate additional wealth over infinite periods of time. If it were, interest revenue derived from government's assets would grow at a faster pace than economic output in a dynamically efficient economy and government wealth per capita would grow to infinity in the consequence. In this case the measurement of lifetime tax burdens is obviously irrelevant. Thus, the intertemporal budget constraint of the public sector implies that prospective government revenue from base year wealth is employed to lower tax burdens of either present of future generations.

The argument behind the above line of reasoning is more familiar in the context of government debt, i.e. negative public wealth, where it is frequently referred to as the *no-Ponzi game condition*.[15] The Ponzi condition demands that outstanding debt does not grow asymptotically at a faster rate than interest payments. Otherwise the public sector would enter into a vicious

---

[13] Of course, the government may delay exploitation, in order to profit from higher market prices when resources become scarce. However, in a deterministic model, there is no reason for the government to preserve its natural resources over an infinite time horizon.

[14] The restrictions on government wealth imposed by the intertemporal public budget constraint are discussed extensively by the CBO (1995, Appendix A).

[15] Cf., for example, Blanchard and Fischer (1989, pp. 49n) who also give a formal definition of the no-Ponzi game condition.

circle of ever increasing per capita debt. In a dynamically efficient economy, a sufficient condition to fulfil the Ponzi condition is that interest payments on outstanding public sector bonds are not financed by issuing new bonds, thereby increasing the initial stock of debt. Put differently, base year public debt invariably induces an increase in net tax payments (or alternatively a reduction in net government purchases) at some point of time in the future.[16]

By incorporating the no-Ponzi game condition in the intertemporal budget constraint of the public sector, generational accounting precludes that an infinitely living government could pay the bill on base year debt at the Greek calends. In fact, the opposite position that the state would have the opportunity to hand over an ever increasing debt burden from generation to generation without being forced to raise taxes to pay interest, gets only weak theoretical support. In a dynamically efficient economy, it requires to assume that issuing public debt opens a chance for risk pooling in incomplete financial markets, which do not offer the low-risk equities private agents demand.[17] Even if part of the observed interest differential between equities and government bonds could be explained with risk-pooling on incomplete financial markets [Mehra and Prescott (1985)], the empirical evidence seems hardly sufficient to base long-term fiscal policy decisions exclusively on this hypothesis.[18]

In any case, acting as if infinite debt rollover were impossible provides a kind of intergenerational insurance. It prevents that some future generation is left alone with an enormous fiscal bill, if handing over debt upon infinity turns out not successful eventually [Ball et al. (1998)]. From this perspective, the intertemporal budget constraint of the government states that less distant (present) generations have to tolerate a risk premium and therefore must contribute to retire the initial public debt (or to serve the correspondent interest payments) by paying higher net taxes.

Although the no-Ponzi game condition restricts the extent to which the public sector can become indebted, it is consistent with the existence of primary budget deficits in the long term. The intertemporal budget constraint only demands that the resulting increase in government debt is counterbalanced by an equal increase in the present value of aggregate net tax payments, or by a respective cut in net government purchases, in order to pay for the corresponding aggregate interest payments. There is no other option for the government, considered that debt financing of interest payments is not feasible. By the same line of argument, the intertemporal budget constraint of the public sector is consistent with long-term primary budget surpluses, as

---

[16] For a proof within a general equilibrium framework, cf. Atkinson and Stiglitz (1980, pp. 249n). Note that this was also the result of our elementary partial equilibrium model in Chapter 2.

[17] This argument against the no-Ponzi game condition goes back to Blanchard and Weil (1992).

[18] The CBO (1995, p. 55) discusses this issue in more detail.

long as interest return on the accumulation of government wealth is employed
to lower the tax burden of at least one generation, or to increase future net
government spending.

3.4 The Mechanics of the Intertemporal Budget

Inspecting the intertemporal budget constraint of the government, the zero-
sum character of fiscal policy is in evidence. The present value of future
government purchases finally must be in balance with government revenue,
taxed from either living or future generations if revenue accruing to initial
government wealth is not sufficient. As long the aggregate present value is
equal, the sequences in time of government spending and revenue are independent and unrestricted by short-term budget considerations. Respecting
the intertemporal budget constraint in particular does not require an annually balanced public budget.

As the state outlives its citizens upon infinity, the government has the
opportunity to discriminate intergenerationally with its fiscal policy, and to
redistribute net tax burdens between present and future generations.[19] The
intertemporal budget constraint of the public sector suggests a simple ceteris
paribus interpretation, which can reveal the link between the aggregate lifetime net tax payments of present generations and those of cohorts not yet
born. Consider for example, a policy that raises the present value tax burden upon death of the current living. Then, provided that the tax increase
does not serve to accommodate additional government purchases, according
to equation (3.1), the aggregate net tax burden of future generations must
fall by the same amount. If the tax increase for the living is used to augment government net assets, i.e. to retire part of the initial public debt or
to accumulate assets, future generations benefit from the additional interest
yield. Which cohort would actually benefit from the possible tax reduction,
is indefinite though.

Fiscal policy may redistribute consumption opportunities also in the opposite direction. Reducing the net tax payments of the present living, ceteris
paribus, increases periodical budget deficits. Future generations face higher
lifetime net tax burdens in the consequence, as they are required to finance
interest due on the additional government debt. An increase in government

---

[19] In theory, as is well-known from the seminal work of Barro (1974), the time
horizon of mortal private individuals approaches infinity, if they behave perfectly altruistic. If this is the case, the government loses its power to spread
effective net tax burdens over different cohorts, as individuals counteract with
their decisions to bequeath. However, empirical evidence on bequest behavior
does not support the hypothesis of intergenerational altruism in general. Cf.
Boskin and Kotlikoff (1985), Altonji et al. (1992, 1997) and Wilhelm (1996),
among others. Laitner and Juster (1996) were able to show the existence of weak
altruism.

purchases not accommodated by a tax raise for the living would work in the same direction, but leave the generational accounts of present generations unchanged. Finally, fiscal policy may redistribute between present and future generations, by not allocating interest payments accruing to public assets in a generationally equitable way. If, for example, the public sector is in debt, net taxes levied on the living might not be sufficient to let them share in retiring outstanding liabilities, or more precisely, in paying interest.

The distinction between the aggregate net tax payments of living and future cohorts established by this mechanical interpretation of the intertemporal public budget constraint is convenient for analytical purposes. However, from the perspective of practical fiscal policy, the confrontation of current and future generations may appear as an artificial and even ill-defined concept. The life spans of generations born prior to the base period and of future birth cohorts overlap and it seems unlikely that policymakers could implement strategies discriminating against simultaneously living cohorts by year of birth. Although fiscal policy has some instruments to differentiate by cohort, it is not realistic to assume that the government would be able to levy significantly different net taxes on consecutive birth cohorts (like the base year birth cohort and its immediate successor).

In practice, fiscal policy will add more specific constraints on the relation between the aggregate tax net tax burdens of present and future generations than a mechanical interpretation of the intertemporal public budget constraint focusing on aggregate present value terms suggests. Quite generally, policies that favor the present living should be expected to favor some subsequent future generations, too. This holds in particular for policy measures directed at the current young, whereas fiscal policy parameters set for older living generations are much less a pre-commitment for future fiscal policy. These arguments notwithstanding, generational accountants construct the tax burden of future generations on the base of the simple mechanics explained above, precluding possible pre-commitments of present fiscal policy with regard to future birth cohorts. Put more generally, generational accounting avoids to add structure to the intertemporal budget constraint, which would limit the free interplay of its four aggregate components.

This approach does not mean that generational accountants do claim that a differential treatment of present and all future generations could actually work. The intention of the ceteris paribus approach is to eschew ambiguous statements regarding possible intergenerational constraints on fiscal policy. Considered this methodological simplification, it is obvious that also the generational accounts of future generations do not provide realistic estimates for the lifetime net tax burdens to be expected in the future. While the generational accounts of the present living are based on the unlikely scenario of an unchanged status quo, the accounts for future generations do not take into consideration intergenerational fiscal policy constraints that in practice restrict fiscal policy over considerable periods of time.

4. Assessing Fiscal Imbalance

While the basic idea of generational accounting has remained unchallenged, current practice shows a growing diversity of approaches. Methodological differentiation, which reflects the novelty of the general concept, concerns the construction of the generational accounts for future generations and the measurement of intergenerational imbalance.

In the first three sections of this chapter, we give an introduction to the traditional residual method to derive the net tax burden for prospective newborn residents, still dominating the literature, and debate the resulting indicator of fiscal sustainability. Conventionally, in line with the original concept advocated by Auerbach et al. (1991), the relative change between the life cycle net tax rates observed for the base year newborn and a representative future born agent is used as the principal indicator of intergenerational fiscal imbalance.

Section 4.4 analyses generational accounting's conception of fiscal sustainability and how it is related to aggregate redistribution between living and future generations in more detail. Next, Section 4.5 illustrates the analytical shortcomings of the residual approach and the traditional measurement of intergenerational imbalance. As will be explained in Section 4.6, possible ambiguities of the residual approach have lead to the alternative sustainability approach to construct future generational accounts, offering a more sophisticated set of long-term fiscal indicators.

4.1 The Residual Approach

Written as in equation (3.1), the budget constraint of the public sector states an intertemporal macroeconomic identity. In order to provide the indicator for individual future net tax burdens generational accounting is searching for, it requires further disaggregation. The second aggregate term on the LHS of the intertemporal budget constraint incorporates the generational accounts and the respective cohort size of future generations. However, there is no unique procedure how to determine this aggregate and how to translate it into the lifetime tax burdens of representative future agents.

Conventionally, generational accountants have relied on the basic mechanics discussed in the previous chapter, regarding the individual components of the intertemporal budget constraint as non-interdependent. From this *ceteris paribus* perspective, the aggregate net tax burden imposed on future generations is determined as a residual. In technical terms, this is a simple rearrangement of the intertemporal public budget constraint:

$$\sum_{k=t+1}^{\infty} N_{t,k} = \sum_{y=t}^{\infty} G_{t,y} - \sum_{k=t-D}^{t} N_{t,k} - W_t. \tag{4.1}$$

As the generational accounting purpose is to evaluate the impacts of present fiscal policy on the fiscal burden of future generations, the three components entering the RHS of the equation (4.1) are treated as determined by current tax and spending levels. Then, aggregate net tax payments of future born cohorts are endogenous, since they have to guarantee the equality.

The postulate that some components of the intertemporal budget constraint are pre-determined limits the choice variables of the government. If present fiscal policy violates the intertemporal budget constraint, the government has other options than to adjust the aggregate tax burden of future generations. It may adapt net purchases or the net taxes levied on the present living. Recognizing that it is impossible to anticipate the policy selected, generational accountants opt for a solution that tends to exaggerate the differential between the eventual net tax burdens of present and future cohorts. Consider a situation where the intertemporal budget constraint of the government is in deficit. From the perspective of equation (4.1), the adjustment burden spreads among future generations, raising generational accounts. If the government burdens living cohorts as well, the change in lifetime tax burdens for future generations is smaller, reducing fiscal imbalance.

Implementation of the residual approach requires to compute the three components constituting the residual aggregate financing burden levied on future taxpayers. Section 3.2 dealt with the problem how to determine the present value of interest yield from public wealth, W_t. Therefore, we can limit the discussion to the aggregate net tax payments of the living and the present value of government purchases.

As the residual left to future generations is calculated under the assumption of constant fiscal policy for the present living, aggregate net tax payments by living generations can be inferred from their generational accounts, derived under the same assumption. Noting that $N_{t,k}$ represents the present value of lifetime net tax payments by *all* members of a generation born in period k, it apparently suffices to combine cohort size of the living, born between periods $t - D$ and t, with the present value of *individual* lifetime net tax payments, as given by the generational accounts:

$$\sum_{k=t-D}^{t} N_{t,k} = \sum_{k=t-D}^{t} P_{t,k} GA_{t,k}. \tag{4.2}$$

However, equation (4.2) is incomplete, as only the net tax payments of base year residents are considered. The contribution of future immigrants who are born in or prior to the base period and take residency during the lifetime of the base year residents, inflating initial cohort size, are omitted.[1]

To account for immigration, equation (4.2) must be extended to include aggregate net tax payments made by prospective migrants after arrival. Let $M_{y,k}$ denote the number of immigrants born in period k who enter the country in period $y \geq t$, aged $y - k$ years when taking residence. Then, the aggregate net tax payments of living generations are given by

$$\sum_{k=t-D}^{t} N_{t,k} = \sum_{k=t-D}^{t} P_{t,k} GA_{t,k} + \sum_{y=t}^{t+D} \sum_{k=y-D}^{t} M_{y,k} \frac{GA_{y,k}^{M}}{(1+r)^{y-t}}. \qquad (4.3)$$

Equation (4.3) considers future migrants with their remaining lifetime net tax payments after taking residency, expressed in terms of migrant-specific generational accounts. $GA_{y,k}^{M}$ denotes the rest-of-life net taxes paid by a representative immigrant born in period k who enters the host country in period y as a present value of the same year. The migrant generational account is taken back to the base year by application of a discount factor. The inner part of the double summation in equation (4.3) limits aggregation of migrant net tax payments to immigrant cohorts alive in the base year, while the outer summation determines the year in which an immigrant takes residency.

Supposed fiscal parameters and survival rates do not change, migrant net tax payments depend on age when taking residency, but not on the year of immigration. The rest-of-life tax payment of a representative immigrants of age $y - k$ equals the growth-uprated generational account faced by a base year resident of the same age: $GA_{y,k}^{M} = (1+g)^{y-t} GA_{t,t-(y-k)}$. However, if fiscal or mortality parameters vary over time, migrants' rest-of-life net taxes payments require explicit construction, as they vary with the year of entry to the host country. Migrant generational accounts are defined similar to those of residents, but aggregation of age-specific personal net taxes subject to mortality only starts when the migrant enters the country in period y. Thus,

$$GA_{y,k}^{M} = \sum_{i=y}^{k+D} t_{i,k} S_{i,y,k} (1+r)^{y-i}. \qquad (4.4)$$

In equation (4.4), $S_{i,y,k}$ stands for the fraction of a (migrant) cohort born in period k and resident in period y who survives until period i, which is determined by age- and cohort-specific survival rates.

In order to project future government purchases, generational accountants basically follow the principles set for net tax payments. However, as

---

[1] If not indicated otherwise, *immigration* in this text refers to *net* immigration, i.e. the balance of gross immigration and emigration. Furthermore, it is taken for granted that immigration is positive. We do not refer to (net) emigration explicitly, as it is empirically irrelevant in most OECD countries. With emigration, all statements considering immigration need to be reversed.

government purchases are not assigned to specific cohorts by definition, payments are projected by period, rather than by cohort. For a forecast, the age profile of government purchases per capita in the base period is uprated for productivity growth and linked to the demographic projection. Let $t_{t,k}^g$ denote the amount of government purchases, assigned to a representative agent born in period k, in period t.[2] If one assumes that age-specific government purchases stay constant except for productivity gains, aggregate government net expenditure in period $y \geq t$, in present value terms of period t, is given by

$$G_{t,y} = \sum_{k=y-D}^{y} t_{t,t-(y-k)}^g P_{y,k} \left(\frac{1+g}{1+r} \right)^{y-t}. \tag{4.5}$$

for all periods $y > t$. Equation (4.5) assigns the amount of government purchases made for a representative individual of age $y - k$ in the base period to each individual who will reach the same age in the future, uprated for productivity growth.

Projection of government purchases according to equation (4.5) is consistent with generational accounting's general conception of status quo fiscal policy. As with tax and transfer payments, predicted government purchases do not allow for possible scale effects due to demographic changes and neglect macroeconomic repercussions. Mechanical growth uprating also precludes that government services could turn less costly in per capita terms, if labor gets more efficient. These assumptions serve to assure that the share of government purchases in domestic product stays constant in the long term.

In generational accounting practice, government purchases are frequently treated lump-sum. If this is the case, the projection follows

$$G_{t,y} = \frac{T_t^g \sum_{k=y-D}^{t} P_{y,k} \left(\frac{1+g}{1+r} \right)^{y-t}}{\sum_{k=t-D}^{y} P_{t,k}}, \tag{4.6}$$

for all periods $y > t$, where T_t^g denotes aggregate government purchases in period t, supposed to spread evenly among all living generations who are aggregated by the denominator. According to equation (4.6), projected aggregate government purchases vary parallel to changes in absolute population size, in addition to productivity growth.

Substitution of equations (3.2), (4.2) and (4.5), or of the respective alternatives, into the RHS of the rearranged intertemporal budget constraint (4.1) determines the residual aggregate net tax payment, to be financed by generations born after the base period. Aggregate revenue demand to balance the intertemporal public budget constraint imposes a restriction on net

---

[2] To derive $t_{t,k}^g$, generational accountants proceed parallel to equations (2.6) to (2.8), benchmarking a relative age-specific profile of government purchases against net government purchases in the base year.

taxes extracted from future agents. How the revenue need of the government translates into a per capita burden depends on future cohort size. Parallel to equation (4.2), combining the size of future birth cohorts with the respective present value life cycle net tax payments of a representative cohort member yields the aggregate net tax payments of future generations. In present value terms of the base period, it holds that

$$\sum_{k=t+1}^{\infty} N_{t,k} = \sum_{k=t+1}^{\infty} P_{k,k} \frac{GA_{k,k}}{(1+r)^{k-t}}, \tag{4.7}$$

Equation (4.7) states an identity. Containing an infinite number of unknowns, it cannot be solved for the sequence of generational accounts faced by future generations, $(GA_{t+1,t+1}, ..., GA_{\infty,\infty})$. The analytical scope of generational accounting is less ambitious. In order to test for sustainability, the method asks whether present fiscal parameters are consistent with the fiscal balance rule, i.e. would allow to maintain life cycle tax rates constant. Therefore, generational accountants only ask whether *some* future generation must experience a change in its lifetime net tax burden, as compared to other generations who can be traced over their entire life cycle.

To avoid speculation which cohorts would be affected by generationally imbalanced fiscal policy, generational accounting claims that government follows the fiscal balance rule for all generations born after the base year. The generational accounts for all future generations are derived under the proposition that government distributes the aggregate financing need, as computed from equation (4.1), evenly across future generations, holding life cycle tax rates constant. This approach must not be mistaken for a normative statement. Generational accountants neither claim that the government would have the ability to conduct fiscal policy in an equitable way, nor that politicians should have the ultimate ambition to do so. The normative task to formulate objectives for how to distribute possible future tax burdens (or tax reliefs) that emanate from continuation of base year fiscal policy remains with the political decision makers.

However, in order to judge the fiscal sustainability of selected fiscal policy parameters, the exact sequence of of future generational accounts implemented is of little importance. In fact, any distribution rule would be feasible for this analysis. In the static framework of generational accounting, gambling against time, or more precisely between distinct birth cohorts, is always a zero-sum-game. Hence, the observation of non-sustainability prevails, irrespective how fiscal burdens are distributed among future generations. To see this, consider a fiscal policy that is fiscally imbalanced to the disadvantage of future generations. If the fiscal burden is distributed evenly among all future birth cohorts, a representative future agent faces a higher life cycle tax burden compared to a current newborn. If instead, the government decides to exempt some future generations from the necessary revision of fiscal policy or to implement the necessary adaptation gradually, the additional fiscal burden to be imposed on the remaining future cohorts are even higher. Thus, the convention to distribute intertemporal fiscal burdens evenly among prospective taxpayers indicates only the minimum possible increase in life cycle income tax rates hitting some future generation.[3]

Among the possibilities to distribute the intertemporal budget residual, application of the fiscal balance rule to future generations is the most convenient. The assumption that generational accounts stay identical except for life cycle income growth restricts the choice parameters of fiscal policy. This allows to express all generational accounts of future birth cohorts in terms of the account assigned to a representative agent born immediately after the base period. As lifetime wages of two consecutive cohorts grow at the annual rate of labor productivity,[4] implementation of the fiscal balance for future generations implies that

$$GA_{t+j,t+j} = (1+g)^{j-1} GA_{t+1,t+1} \qquad (4.8)$$

for $1 < j < \infty$. Equation (4.8) provides a set of additional constraints that allow solution of equation (4.7). Substitution of the constraints into equation (4.7) and some simple rearrangements yield the lifetime net tax burden for a representative agent born in period $t+1$, imposed through the intertemporal budget constraint of the government, as

$$GA_{t+1,t+1} = \frac{(1+r) \sum_{k=t+1}^{\infty} N_{t,k}}{\sum_{k=t+1}^{\infty} P_{k,k} \left(\frac{1+g}{1+r}\right)^{k-(t+1)}}. \qquad (4.9)$$

The generational account for a member of the birth cohort $t+1$ given by equation (4.9) stands representative for the fiscal burden of future generations. The remaining set of future life cycle tax burdens does not contain additional information, as it differs by the exogenous growth factor only, according to the fiscal balance constraint (4.8). Henceforth, referring indifferently to *the* future generational account, we precisely address the life cycle net tax burden of the $t + 1$-born generation, representative for all subsequent cohorts under the residual approach.

4.2 The Conventional Sustainability Index

On the base of the representative future generational account, it is straightforward to judge the intertemporal sustainability of currently selected tax

---

[3] In the opposite case, if maintaining base year fiscal policy allows to unburden future generations, equal treatment of all prospective newborns yields a lower bound of the tax cut.

[4] The working life span of two successive generations overlaps completely except for one year. Assuming that age-specific labor supply and the employment profile do not vary, life cycle wage income of the later born cohort exceeds income of the preceding cohort by exactly the productivity gain in this single year.

and spending parameters by comparing the future life cycle tax burden to the fiscal burden faced by a representative newborn of the base period. Unlike members of other living cohorts, whose generational accounts are biased by a shorter remaining lifespan, present newborns are traced over the same number of years as future born agents.[5] By definition, fiscal policies raising the future life cycle taxes compared to those of base year newborns, are unsustainable. Fiscal parameters valid for living generations cannot be maintained, as they offend against the intertemporal financing constraint of the government.

As noted in Chapter 2, a policy that requires to vary life cycle tax burdens across generations, is distortionary. If the economy were in equilibrium in the base year, deviation from the fiscal balance rule gives impetus to leave the equilibrium growth path determined by present fiscal parameters. The extent to which future lifetime tax payments deviate from those experienced under present conditions gives an indication for the degree of government intervention into the long-term course of the economy. On the contrary, if the economy is not in equilibrium (or sufficiently close to it), observation of fiscal balance between present and future generations does not allow easy conclusions. A change in life cycle tax burdens found necessary to balance the intertemporal public budget could be explained by an ongoing move toward a new steady-state, following a past fiscal shock. If this is indeed the case, the difference in present and future life cycle net tax burdens actually may not interfere with the fiscal balance rule to maintain equal fiscal burdens, in order to keep the economy on its track to equilibrium.

Although real economies are hardly ever to be found in equilibrium, generational accountants rely on the fiscal balance rule as an analytical benchmark. In the light of the argument made above, this approach must not be mistaken for a normative statement. Whether policy should strive for balance of life cycle tax payments between present and future newborns, cannot be decided within the generational accounting framework. Reference to fiscal balance provides a theoretically neutral benchmark, by which the possible intertemporal consequences of present fiscal conditions can be evaluated. It does not relieve of judging fiscal imbalance indicated by the generational accounts against the current and prospective state of the economy, as well as against past fiscal policy. Certainly, evaluation of the sustainability measures provided by generational accounting, not unlike the exegesis of annual budget deficits in this respect, is prone to interpretative contentions.

Reservations of this kind notwithstanding, the fiscal balance criterion seems to provide a meaningful analytical tool to assess the extent to which present fiscal policy redistributes consumption opportunities over time. Pro-

---

[5] The average lifespan of present and future generations could differ by a small degree, if the projections account for declining mortality. However, changes in generational accounts due to mortality changes between subsequent generations are generally negligible.

vided that bequests and transfers *inter vivos* are insignificant, policies that require to raise future lifetime fiscal burdens, ceteris paribus, reduce individual welfare of future birth cohorts.[6] In the long term, unsustainable fiscal strategies redirect a higher share of private income into unproductive use, to finance government consumption or redistribution through the tax and transfer system (yielding less than the market rate of return), thereby crowding out the private capital stock and stunting economic growth. The opposite is true, if fiscal policy redistributes private tax burdens from future to present generations.

The change between present and future generational accounts required to balance the public budget intertemporally can be reported in different ways. Ideally, one would measure the extent of intergenerational redistribution by the variation of lifetime labor tax rates due to continuation of present fiscal parameters. Supposed no bequests, the present value of gross labor income provides a reference by which to judge agents' fiscal burden, as it defines individual consumption opportunities before government intervention. From a present value perspective, capital income does not extend life cycle consumption opportunities. On perfect capital markets, the present value of returns just equals the amount originally saved from human capital income.

To stay within the general accounting framework, the present value of life cycle labor income is preferably computed parallel to the generational accounts, subjecting estimates on age-specific average wage earnings per capita (re-evaluated to fit total labor income) to cohort mortality. Although the additional data requirements set up hardly an obstacle to this procedure, generational accountants do not regularly report explicit lifetime tax rates. Instead, the degree of intergenerational redistribution is generally indicated by the relative change in life cycle tax rates between present and future newborns. This practice avoids calculation of lifetime wages, as the ratio of future and base year life cycle tax rates, conventionally denoted as π, can be shortened by the present value of life cycle labor income. Supposed constant productivity adjustment of wages, gross lifetime income of the cohort born in period $t + 1$ exceeds that of the base year born generation exactly by the productivity growth factor. Thus, the relative change in life cycle net tax rates is given by

$$\pi = \frac{GA_{t+1,t+1}}{(1+g)GA_{t,t}}. \tag{4.10}$$

Indicating fiscal imbalance by equation (4.10) loses information, for it lacks a benchmark by which to assess the reported magnitude of the relative change in fiscal burdens. Therefore, as an indicator of generational redistribution, π is certainly inferior to a measurement of absolute variations in life cycle income tax rates associated with unsustainable public finances. Nevertheless,

---

[6] This argument abstracts from macroeconomic repercussions of course, which could work in the opposite direction.

the generational account ratio provides a meaningful and accessible index to judge fiscal sustainability. If the index π equals unity, the parameters of present tax and transfer policy are sustainable, as maintaining base year lifetime tax rates is consistent with the intertemporal budget constraint of the government.

Otherwise, base year policy shifts fiscal burdens between present and future cohorts. For π greater than unity, fiscal policy reallocates consumption opportunities of future generations to the base year living. Some future cohort (though not necessarily the $t+1$-born) will experience a higher taxation of life cycle labor income, in order to maintain net income, i.e. gross income net of generational accounts, and consumption prospects of living agents. Intergenerational redistribution works in the opposite direction, if π is smaller than unity. Government policy taxes consumption opportunities of living generations to expand consumption of future generations, who are faced with a lower net tax rate on labor income.

The fact that the standard sustainability index π sets into relation payment streams that are expressed in present value of two different periods has generated confusion. In fact, the nominator of equation (4.10) is frequently taken back to the base year, adopting a procedure that goes back to the original launch of generational accounting by Auerbach et al. (1991). This approach has been recognized as wrong only recently.[7]

Understanding that π represents the relative change of lifetime net tax rates between base year and future generations, rather than the ratio of their absolute life cycle net tax burdens, it is quite easy to show that discounting of future net taxes $GA_{t+1,t+1}$ to the base period is misleading. The tax rate of future generations is invariant to the discounting procedure, as it affects nominator (lifetime net taxes) and denominator (lifetime gross income) alike. Put differently, if one discounts the future generational account in equation (4.10) back to the base year, one would have to discount life cycle income of future generations (canceled out), too. Doing so leads back to the above definition of π, as it reintroduces the interest factor.

To formalize this argument, let $GA_{t,k}^{w}$ denote the lifetime gross wage income attributed to a k-born individual in present value of year t. Then the following relation is true:

$$\pi = \frac{\frac{GA_{t+1,t+1}}{GA_{t+1,t+1}^{w}}}{\frac{GA_{t,t}}{GA_{t,t}^{w}}} = \frac{\frac{GA_{t,1+1}}{GA_{t,1+1}^{w}}}{\frac{GA_{t,t}}{GA_{t,t}^{w}}} = \frac{\frac{(1+r)GA_{t,1+1}}{(1+g)GA_{t,t}^{w}}}{\frac{GA_{t,t}}{GA_{t,t}^{w}}} = \frac{GA_{t+1,t+1}}{(1+g)GA_{t,t}}. \qquad (4.11)$$

The nominator of equation (4.10) can be justified also with an economic argument. Discounting the representative future generational account $GA_{t+1,t+1}$

---

[7] The original formula, which replaces the nominator of equation (4.10) by $GA_{t,t+1}$, unfortunately, reached textbook level, like in Raffelhüschen and Walliser (1996). Even some fairly recent contributions to the literature, for example Jagob and Scholz (1998), keep to this error.

back to period t implies that future generations could reduce their absolute net tax burden by paying it prematurely in the base year. However, agents are not free to shift tax burdens beyond the limited horizon of their own lifetime. Tax payments are bound to the physical existence of the tax subject. Therefore, they cannot predate the birth of a generation. As a consequence, from the point of view of the individual agent, the expected lifetime tax burden cannot be discounted back to any period that lies prior to her birth.[8]

To look at this argument from the opposite angle, assume that $GA_{t,t+1}$ is substituted for the nominator of equation (4.10). Assume further that fiscal policy is consistent with equalization of present and future generational accounts in terms of base year present value. Finally, for sake of simplicity, suppose zero productivity growth. Under the given assumptions, although π indicates sustainability, fiscal policy is generationally imbalanced. Even if perfect capital markets give credit to agents not yet born, who fulfil their tax obligation to the public sector $(GA_{t,t})$ already in the base year, life cycle consumption opportunities of future generations are reduced by more than the generational account of the base year newborns. When born in period $t + 1$, agents have to redeem the loan and to pay interest. Therefore, their life cycle income is actually burdened with an amount $(1 + r)GA_{t,t}$. The reduction in disposable lifetime income equals the present value of the net tax burden as of its birth period, so that $GA_{t+t,t+1} > GA_{t,t}$. To indicate correctly that fiscal policy is imbalanced in this stylized scenario, one must return to the original version of equation (4.10).

4.3 Subgroup Accounts and Fiscal Sustainability

If the generational accounts for the living distinguish between subpopulations, the lifetime tax burden of a representative future agent can be broken down accordingly. As for generations alive, the future generational account defined by equation (4.9) is a weighted average of the accounts assigned to members of different subpopulations. Thus, equation (2.12) holds for any future generation, too. In particular, it is true that

$$GA_{t+1,t+1} = \sum_m \frac{P^m_{t+1,t+1}}{P_{t+1,t+1}} GA^m_{t+1,t+1}. \tag{4.12}$$

Similar to equation (4.7), a unique solution of equation (4.12) for the m group-specific accounts $GA^m_{t+1,t+1}$ requires introduction of additional constraints. Risking to neglect more definite information, the residual approach relies on

---

[8] If discounting were possible, the economic 'lifetime' of base year and future generations would differ by one year. One would have to abandon the discounting of future payments for that year, in order to arrive at a meaningful base of comparison, tracing base year and future newborns over an identical number of years.

the assumption that required changes in fiscal parameters do no affect the relative fiscal position of different population groups observed maintaining present fiscal policy. The ratio of the generational accounts for members of any two population groups, indexed by m and n, valid for present newborns is supposed to stay constant in the future, which means

$$\frac{GA_{t,t}^m}{GA_{t,t}^n} \overset{!}{=} \frac{GA_{t+1,t+1}^m}{GA_{t+1,t+1}^n}. \tag{4.13}$$

In order to derive a set of future generational accounts for different subpopulations on the base of equation (4.13), the lifetime tax burden of an arbitrary n-th cohort serves for a numéraire. Rearrangement of equation (4.13) for $GA_{t+1,t+1}^n$ and substitution of the resulting expression into equation (4.12) leaves

$$GA_{t+1,t+1} = GA_{t+1,t+1}^n \sum_m \frac{P_{t+1,t+1}^m}{P_{t+1,t+1}} \frac{GA_{t,t}^m}{GA_{t,t}^n}, \tag{4.14}$$

which is easily solved for the numéraire generational account of cohort n. Finally, re-substitution of $GA_{t+1,t+1}^n$ into equation (4.13) yields the future accounts for the remaining population groups $m \neq n$.

Though useful for illustrative purposes, breaking down future generational accounts in general does not add relevant information regarding fiscal sustainability. It is obvious inspecting equation (4.14) that subgroup-specific generational accounts, under the given assumptions, represent linear transformations of the lifetime tax burden faced by a representative individual. As a consequence, the magnitude of the relative change in lifetime tax burdens required to balance the intertemporal public budget is identical in the population subgroups, provided that their population share does not change in the future.[9]

This result reduces the data requirements for an analysis of fiscal imbalance considerably. In order to derive valid sustainability indicators, per capita tax and transfer profiles of a representative agent can be employed without loss of generality. In particular, it is not necessary to distinguish between genders (unless the intention is to evaluate fiscal redistribution inter vivos), as the gender ratio at birth can surely be regarded as a natural constant.[10] The assumption that population shares of fiscally distinct population classes stay unchanged is not a severe restriction quite generally and fits the status quo character of the generational accounting analysis. However, it might be

---

[9] The easy proof is given in the Appendix A.2.

[10] This is worth mentioning, as introductions to generational accounting often seem to suggest that distinction between men and women is fundamental to the method. The sustainability results of generational accounting studies that do not consider gender differentials due to data deficiencies [Feist et al. (1999), Bovenberg and ter Rele (1999b)] are fully comparable to studies that do.

too rigid for some analytical purposes, for example, when one distinguishes between native and migrant residents. As soon as population shares of fiscally distinct subpopulations are expected to change, an additional restriction affecting generational fiscal imbalance enters the analysis. If, for example, a population group who currently pays high taxes (or receives small transfers) gains a higher weight in future cohorts, the relative increase in fiscally potent agents will reduce the relative tax increment for a representative cohort member.

To determine intergenerational redistribution when cohort composition is assumed to change, the development of the fiscally distinct population groups needs to be traced explicitly. Respecting that equation (4.12) holds for the accounts of all future birth cohorts and singling out the accounts of the reference cohort n, equation (4.7) can be broken down into

$$\sum_{k=t+1}^{\infty} N_{t,k} = \sum_{k=t+1}^{\infty} \frac{P_{k,k}^n GA_{k,k}^n + \sum_{m \neq n} P_{k,k}^m GA_{k,k}^m}{(1+r)^{k-t}}. \tag{4.15}$$

Supposed that the development of future generational accounts is restricted parallel to equation (4.8) for all population groups, all subgroup accounts in equation (4.15) can be expressed in terms of the net tax payments of $t+1$-born members. Imposing the additional constraint that the relative fiscal position of the different population classes does not change, compared to that observed in the base year birth cohort, allows to express all generational accounts in terms of the life cycle net tax burden faced by a member of the reference group n. Then, some simple manipulations of equation (4.15) lead to a modified version of equation (4.9), which serves to determine the numéraire future generational account:

$$GA_{t+1,t+1}^n = \frac{(1+r)\sum_{k=t+1}^{\infty} N_{t,k}}{\sum_{k=t+1}^{\infty} \left(P_{k,k}^n + \sum_{m \neq n} \frac{GA_{t,t}^m}{GA_{t,t}^n} P_{k,k}^m\right)\left(\frac{1+g}{1+r}\right)^{k-(t+1)}}. \tag{4.16}$$

The denominator of equation (4.16) transforms, in fiscal terms, future individuals who belong to group m into members of the reference cohort n. The size of the different population groups is weighed in accordance with their fiscal potential relative to members of group n, indicated by the generational account ratio measured within the base year birth cohort.[11]

The numéraire generational account $GA_{t+1,t+1}^n$ is sufficient to judge generational fiscal imbalance. The net tax burdens assigned to all other population

---

[11] If, for example, base year newborns of group m bear twice the net lifetime tax burden of a member of group n, each future m-type individual counts for two members of the reference cohort. Obviously, if the ratio of subgroup-specific accounts equals unity, equation (4.16) simplifies to equation (4.9). Disaggregation into separate population groups is trivial, unless they exhibit distinct fiscal characteristics when considering the entire life cycle.

groups are derived as simple linear transformations of the reference generational account, using the constraints set up by equation (4.13), and change by the same relative magnitude. As a consequence, it is also redundant to calculate the average generational account $GA_{t+1,t+1}$. As a weighted average of the subgroup-specific accounts, it exhibits the same relative change as any of its components.

4.4 Sustainability and Generational Redistribution

Generational accounting's conception of fiscal sustainability emphasizes the distributional conflict between living and future generations. Ignoring that government is a reactive institution, the latter are made responsible to meet any imbalance in the intertemporal budget constraint of the public sector, accumulated by maintaining present fiscal policy parameters over the remaining lifetime of all agents alive. The approach to assign the budget residual accumulated by the base year living exclusively to future generations has been misconceived occasionally. In fact, one may think that the tax burden of future agents is *a priori* biased. Calculated from the intertemporal budget residual, the generational accounts of future generations, in contrast to the accounts of the present living, seem loaded with government wealth and non-transfer purchases by the government.[12]

However, this perspective confuses the relation between the size of the intertemporal budget residual and the sustainability outcome. Unsustainable fiscal policy does not occur due to a residual financing requirement left to future generations. As a matter of fact, fiscal sustainability is compatible with any shift of aggregate fiscal burdens between present and future generations, as measured by the intertemporal public budget residual. The extent to which generationally balanced policy requires future newborns to share intertemporal fiscal burdens is determined exclusively by the life cycle net tax burden assigned to present newborns. Their generational account sets the exogenous reference for the sustainability analysis.

The intertemporal budget residual coinciding with a fiscally sustainable situation is a function of the generational account faced by a base year newborn, $GA_{t,t}^S$.[13] Setting π equal to unity and substituting the generational account ratio expressed by equation (4.10) into the definition of the future generational account (4.9) yields, after some manipulations, the constraint

---

[12] This impression seems to guide Havemann (1994), where he criticizes the assumption of generational accountants that 'the set of future generations ... must ... pay off the existing national debt ...' (p. 97), suggesting that the present living ought share part of this burden.

[13] Here and in the following, the superscript S is used to indicate a sustainable life cycle tax burden.

on the aggregate net tax payments of living generations necessary to achieve fiscal balance. This condition reads as

$$\left[\sum_{y=t}^{\infty} G_{t,y} - W_t\right] - \sum_{k=t-D}^{t} N_{t,k} \overset{!}{=} GA_{t,t}^{S} \sum_{k=t+1}^{\infty} P_{k,k} \left(\frac{1+g}{1+r}\right)^{k-t}. \quad (4.17)$$

The RHS of equation (4.17) aggregates the tax payments made by all future generations, which supposed fiscal balance, are determined by the generational account of a base year newborn. The LHS of equation (4.17) represents the residual of the intertemporal public sector budget constraint that does not offend against fiscal balance. The sustainable intertemporal budget residual is positively correlated to the life cycle net tax payments to be maintained ($GA_{t,t}^{S}$).

The higher (lower) the lifetime net tax payments of a present newborn and therefore the net taxes of her descendants maintained by generationally balanced fiscal policy, the larger (smaller) the public sector liabilities that the remaining base year living generations are allowed to accumulate. If keeping to present fiscal parameters yields large (small) tax revenue from future generations, the present living, apart from the base year newborn, must contribute less (more) to finance that part of net government purchases in excess of revenue from government wealth, as indicated by the bracketed term on the LHS of equation (4.17). Note that the special case of a zero residual in the intertemporal budget constraint is consistent with fiscal sustainability only if the generational account of the base year newborn approaches zero, too.

To reverse the above interpretation of the sustainability condition, a unique relation between the absolute amount of the budget residual and the sustainability outcome does not exist. If the residual approach is used, policies redistributing resources among the present living could affect the degree of intergenerational sustainability without changing the intertemporal budget residual. Therefore, accumulated wealth or debt 'inherited' by the base year living to their descendants does not constitute an appropriate indicator to measure fiscal imbalance. For a meaningful indicator of aggregate generational redistribution, one would have to correct the residual of the intertemporal public budget constraint for the amount of intertemporal liabilities compatible with fiscal sustainability, as indicated by the LHS of equation (4.17). Interpretation of the conventional intertemporal budget residual as the overall public sector liabilities, which indicate the explicit and implicit pre-commitments of the government is useful for illustrative purposes, but seems to obscure the origin of intergenerational imbalance. Generational accountants' reference to fiscal balance does not predetermine the level of generational redistribution between present and future generations.

Furthermore, the necessary condition for intergenerational balanced policy (4.17) reveals that the benchmark of fiscal balance does not establish a rule how financing of government purchases that are not paid by interest accruing to government wealth, should be distributed between the living and future cohorts. The concept of fiscal sustainability only requires that living generations take over that part of excess government purchases not shared between present and future newborns.

The unresolved distributional conflict among generations is highlighted by two polar scenarios. First, suppose that fiscal policy sets the life cycle net taxes of all newborn agents so that to equal a growth-adjusted share in government purchases (net of government wealth). Then, the fiscally balanced generational account of present and future newborn generations is given by

$$
GA_{t,t}^{S} = \frac{\sum_{y=t}^{\infty} G_{t,y} - W_t}{\sum_{k=t}^{\infty} P_{k,k} \left(\frac{1+g}{1+r} \right)^{k-t}},
\tag{4.18}
$$

and all other living generations could go out free. Substituting equation (4.18) into the sustainability condition (4.17), it is easy to see that the bracketed term on the LHS cancels out. Under the given conditions, fiscal sustainability only requires that the aggregate tax payments of the base year living (apart from newborns) are sufficient to meet their own aggregate transfer receipts.

In the opposite extreme, if life cycle tax payments balance life cycle transfer receipts of the present newborn, i.e. if $GA_{t,t}^{S}$ equals zero, fiscal policy does not ask them and future generations to participate in financing non-transfer spending in excess of government wealth. Nevertheless, this policy can be sustainable, provided that aggregate net taxes imposed on other living generations are sufficient to balance unfunded government spending. Inspection of these distributional extremes illustrates that fiscal policy could set any life cycle tax burden as a benchmark for generationally balanced policy without coming into conflict with the sustainability goal, provided that the generational distribution of net tax payments raises sufficient tax revenue from the remaining living cohorts. From this perspective, the fiscal balance criterion sets a restriction on the set of generational accounts for living generations other than the newborn cohort.

For a better understanding of the interplay between generational accounts, the intertemporal public sector budget residual and the concept of fiscal sustainability, it might be useful to illustrate the above reasoning with a numeric generational accounting example. Table 4.1 calculates the generational accounts and the corresponding intertemporal budget residual for a stylized economy. To keep the presentation simple, aggregate government purchases are set to zero. The initial population is separated into only three age groups, which one may identify as the young respectively 'newborn' (age 1), the working aged (age 2) and the retirees (age 3). Furthermore, the population is assumed to be in a stable stationary state so that the initial age composition reported in the second column of Table 4.1 is also valid in the future. Then, supposed no immigration, age- and cohort-specific survival rates can be inferred from the base year composition of the population. In detail, the likelihood for a base year young to reach working age amounts to 50 per-

Table 4.1. Sustainability of fiscal policies with identical intemporal budget residual

(a) Unsustainable fiscal policy

Age	$P_{t,k}$	$t_{t,k}$	$GA_{t,k}$	$N_{t,k}$	W_t	$\sum G_{t,y}$			
1	1,000	10	21	21,000					
2	500	20	22	11,000					
3	200	5	5	1,000					
Residual				33,000	+	-33,000	−	0	= 0

(b) Sustainable fiscal policy

Age	$P_{t,k}$	$t_{t,k}$	$GA_{t,k}$	$N_{t,k}$	W_t	$\sum G_{t,y}$			
1	1,000	-32	0	0					
2	500	62	64	32,000					
3	200	5	5	1,000					
Residual				33,000	+	-33,000	−	0	= 0

cent. The chance to reach retirement equals 20 percent. Finally the likelihood that a working aged reaches retirement is 40 percent.

Linking the survival ratios to the age-specific per capita net tax payments $t_{t,k}$, specified in the third column of Table 4.1, allows us to calculate the generational accounts $GA_{t,k}$ for the base year living generations on the base of definition (2.1). For simplicity of calculation, we do not submit individual tax payments to productivity growth, and set the discount factor applied to post-base year payment streams to unity. The resulting rest-of-life tax payments for a representative member of each living generation are reported in the fourth column of the table.[14]

First consider an age-specific distribution of net tax payments as specified for scenario (a). Under the given assumptions, the corresponding generational accounts are positive for all age groups. As rest-of-life tax payments to the government exceed transfers received from the public sector for the different age groups, all base year living contribute to redeem base year government debt, supposed to equal 33,000 currency units. In particular, a representative base year newborn reduces public debt rolled over to future generations by 21 currency units. Turning from the tax burden of individual agents to the macro economic level, aggregation of net tax payments made by present generations ($N_{t,k}$) reveals that their contribution to the government budget

---

[14] To give an example, in the unsustainable fiscal policy scenario, the generational account for the youngest generation is calculated as $GA_{t,t} = 10+0, 5*20+0, 2*5$.

(33,000 currency units) is sufficient to pay off explicit liabilities of the public sector. As a consequence, the residual of the intertemporal public budget constraint to be financed by future generations equals zero provided that initial fiscal parameters are maintained over the lifetime of the base year living. Distributing the budget residual uniformly among the prospective newborns according to equation (4.9), the generational account assigned to a representative future agent equals zero, too.

A comparison of the generational account of a representative future newborn (0 currency units) to the account of a base year newborn (21 currency units) indicates that fiscal policy in the specified scenario cannot be maintained, although there do not exist public liabilities that are shifted from present to future generations. Non-existence of an intertemporal public budget residual is not sufficient to achieve generational fiscal balance. In scenario (a), fiscal policy is imbalanced between base year and future newborns. While the former are asked to redeem part of outstanding public debt, future generations are not and hence are endowed with larger consumption opportunities. Redistribution of resources from present newborns to future generations is made possible by the funds raised from the working aged and pensioner cohorts alive in the base period.

There is no unique policy to restore fiscal sustainability. In the present scenario, as the generational account of the base year newborn is too high in comparison to the tax burden of future birth cohorts, one strategy is to create liabilities rolled over to future generations, by lowering per capita net taxes for at least one of the three distinct age groups. For example, fiscal policy could reduce the net tax burden during youth ($t_{t,t}$) without changing age-specific net tax payments at other stages of the life cycle. The marginal reduction in the generational account for a representative member of the base year birth cohort resulting from this measure leaves parts of the outstanding government wealth to be financed by future generations. As a consequence, the life cycle tax payment to be levied on future generations increases by a small margin. Following this strategy, one can find the extra tax payment during youth that assures the corresponding generational account $GA_{t,t}^S > 0$ to become sustainable.

The above strategy achieves fiscal sustainability by accumulation of an intertemporal public budget deficit, which leaves both present and future newborns with a positive tax burden, to let either share in financing public liabilities. However, attaining sustainability does not necessarily require changing the aggregate tax burden on the present living. As the policy specified in Table 4.1(b) demonstrates, also the original zero intertemporal residual can be consistent with fiscal sustainability. Since the zero intertemporal budget residual leads to a zero generational account of future generations, fiscal balance requires that the lifetime net tax payment for a base year newborn equals zero. To achieve fiscal sustainability with a zero generational account for newborn generations, fiscal policy needs to adjust per capita net tax payments by age, while preserving aggregate revenue of 33,000 currency units from the living.

This calibration problem has no unique solution. It is solved in scenario (b) by preserving per capita tax payments of the old. Respecting this condition, restoration of sustainability demands redistribution of resources from the working-age generation to the young. When young, base year newborns receive a net transfer of 32 currency units, while the working aged face a net tax burden of 62 units per capita. Accounting for mortality, distribution of net taxes as displayed in Table 4.1(b) implies zero life cycle payments to the state from the base year newborn. In the specified scenario, mainly the working aged are left with repayment of base year government debt, as present and future newborns are relieved completely from this obligation.

A comparison of the sustainable scenario (b) with the non-sustainable scenario (a) illustrates once more that the relative change in tax burdens between present and future newborns is not correlated unequivocally to the size of the intertemporal public budget residual. When assessing the degree of fiscal sustainability indicated by the generational accounts, one should stay aware that the sustainability criterion does not predetermine *aggregate* redistribution between living and future cohorts, measured by the imbalance of intertemporal public finances left to future generations. Any generational account assigned to the base year born can be sustainable, as long as other living generations are willing, or can be forced, to accommodate the intended net tax level.

The fact that the absolute tax level of newborns remains indefinite adds a degree of freedom to the sustainability analysis that might be regarded as a methodological shortcoming. In fact, generational accounting fails to provide a benchmark to rank distinct fiscal sets of fiscal parameters identified as sustainable. Selecting among sustainable fiscal strategies, one may give preference to policies that accomplish sustainability at the lowest lifetime income tax rate, in order to minimize economic distortions effected by the tax and transfer system in the long term. However, as alternative sustainable fiscal policies distribute tax burden among present generations differently, this criterion could turn out inadequate.

Consider for example, fiscal policy in scenario (b) and a reform of scenario (a), which exclusively lowers the tax burden during youth, as discussed above. While either tax and transfer scheme is fiscally balanced, one cannot decide within the generational accounting framework which policy is preferable. Policy (b) could appear superior, as it guarantees a smaller generational account for future birth cohorts, but it comes at the cost of a more significant intervention into the remaining consumption opportunities of the working aged. To arrive at a well-measured conclusion, the economic repercussions generated by the generational distribution of net tax burdens in the two scenarios requires consideration. At this stage, pure accounting of age-specific payment flows hits its limits. A more definite evaluation of fiscally balanced strategies can be achieved only by rigid dynamic macroeconomic welfare analysis.

The message of this section is not limited to the special case of sustainable fiscal policy. Also if fiscal parameters are unsustainable, it is true that a specific relative change of life cycle tax burdens between newborn cohorts can be associated with any amount of aggregate redistribution between present and future generations. Hence, the sustainability criterion fails to incorporate a parameter to assess the distributional impacts of fiscal policy across present and future generations. This conceptual ambiguity renders a comparison of alternative fiscal policies and of fiscal imbalance across countries difficult. Meaningful comparisons cannot be based exclusively on the sustainability index provided by the relative change in lifetime tax burdens. Interpreting fiscal imbalance, one has to take into account also the generational distribution of net tax burdens among the living and the level of generational accounts faced by present and future birth cohorts.[15]

Generational accountants have not invented yet clear-cut concepts to supplement sustainability analysis with these aspects. In Chapter 7.2, we will try to add one element, developing a framework that allows to condense the distributional consequences of fiscal policy on the base year living into a single index figure. Still, invention of a coherent concept incorporating both sustainability aspects of fiscal policy and aggregate redistribution between present and future generations, seems to remain a task that is open to future research.

4.5 Analytical Shortcomings of the Residual Approach

Until recently, the residual approach to construct the stylized life cycle net tax payment of a representative future agent and the sustainability index π dominated the generational accounting literature. However, with a growing number of empirical applications, some serious shortcomings of the residual method and the traditional indicator concept have come to light. These are the topic of the present section, which first discusses the failure of the residual approach to design the fiscal potential of future born resident cohorts adequately, before addressing the problematic algebraic properties of the traditional measure for generational fiscal imbalance. The methodological refinements invented to overcome the imperfections of the original generational accounting approach are left to section 4.6.

---

[15] For example, according to the sustainability indicator π, intertemporal redistribution through fiscal policy in Argentina and Norway appears very similar [Kotlikoff and Leibfritz (1999, Table 4.2)]. However, the fiscal imbalance of about 60 percent observed in the two countries is reached at considerably different tax burdens (22,700 versus 106,300 US-dollar for the base year newborn) and in a markedly distinct demographic environment. It would be careless to conclude that the long-term economic impacts of fiscal policy in the two countries are comparable, despite similar relative generational imbalance.

4.5.1 Ambiguous Policy Implications

A too simplistic distribution of the intertemporal public budget residual across future generations has proved as the major drawback of the residual approach. The procedure to distribute the intertemporal financing demand of the government evenly among future newborns, in accordance with equation (4.9), does not design the tax and transfer parameters faced by future generations explicitly. As a consequence, it does not allow to design variations in the demographic and economic structure that could affect the fiscal potential of future generations and therefore the average tax burden levied on a representative future agent.

In particular, as was pointed out by Bonin et al. (2000), the traditional assignment of the intertemporal budget residual omits the fiscal contribution of future migrants who are born after the base period.[16] Migrants who enter or leave the country at non-zero age are not represented in equation (4.9), as it focuses on cohort size at birth. Therefore, conventional future generational accounts are biased in the presence of migration. Provided that immigration raises population size, the residual approach overstates the net payments imposed on a member of future resident birth cohorts, as it distributes the intertemporal budget residual among a too small number of prospective tax-payers. In the opposite case, if emigration reduces population, the method understates the tax burden on future resident newborns. Thus, given that migration is a relevant demographic parameter, it is misleading to compare the net tax burden of present newborns, reflecting the net tax burden of resident cohorts, with the generational accounts of future newborn generations, which take over tax burdens borne by immigrants.

A similar point can be made, if the long-term projections underlying the intertemporal budget residual account for socio-economic trends changing the fiscal potential of a representative tax payer. For example, the assumption of rising female labor force participation could render future taxpayers, on average, more potent fiscally than today [Berenguer et al. (1999)]. In principle, long term trends of this kind can be incorporated into the standard residual approach by assigning changing fiscal weights to future newborns [Raffelhüschen and Walliser(1999)]. However, as the residual perspective does not provide an explicit model of future tax and transfer policy, these weights remain invariably *ad hoc*.

Returning to the case of immigration, in order to correct the biased generational account of future resident cohorts, one would have to define how a revision of fiscal policy due to the intertemporal financing constraint of the government will affect net tax payments of immigrants after taking residency. Staying within the boundaries of the residual approach, parallel to the standard assumption applied for different fiscal groups within the newborn

---

[16] Net tax payment of immigrants born *prior* to the base period enter the budget residual via equation (4.3).

cohort, one may claim that migrants will face the same relative change in net tax payments as newborn residents. This assumption allows to transform the possible fiscal contribution of migrants into units of net taxes paid by newborn residents. However, as was noted by Auerbach and Oreopoulos (2000) this is hardly a likely outcome of realistic fiscal policy. In fact, if prospective policy adjustments had to guarantee an equal proportional change of lifetime net tax burdens for all age groups, this would require highly discriminating interventions in the existing tax and transfer system. A proper design to evaluate the fiscal contribution of future immigrants requires specification of the government response to unsustainable finances. This approach would allow to assess net tax burdens over the life cycle of future generations, which could then be assigned to future migrants dependent on age when taking residency.

Implausible policy implications also hurt the residual approach to distinguish between the future tax burdens of fiscally distinct population groups although, other than in the case of immigration, the measurement of generational imbalance is not distorted. The constraint that revisions of fiscal parameters to balance the intertemporal public budget change the life cycle tax payments of all future newborns by the same proportion, as is postulated by equation (4.13), fails to acknowledge the restrictions plausible fiscal policy has to respect. To address the most prominent example, it seems unconvincing to assume that a revision of fiscal policy to balance the intertemporal budget changes the life cycle net tax payments of male and female agents in the same proportion. Considered that the composition of net tax payments over the life cycle is gender-specific, realistic fiscal policy is likely to affect men and women differently.

As a consequence, the conventional practice to distribute the intertemporal budget residual without reference to the fiscal parameters that distinguish population groups within the living cohorts could poorly indicate the future impacts of policy revisions on different subpopulations. Moving beyond a basic sustainability test of present fiscal parameters, it is advised to employ additional economic structure, if one intends to derive a set of future generational accounts for different population groups. Doing so would allow to work out the spectrum of fiscal imbalance, which could vary across different population groups, in particular with regard to fiscal burdens by gender.

This empirical improvement comes at a cost. Acknowledging that relative changes in lifetime tax burdens may vary within future birth cohorts, the degree of intergenerational fiscal imbalance turns more difficult to assess. Considering distinct population groups, variation in lifetime tax payments depends on the specific policy selected to balance the intertemporal budget. To preserve a clear-cut indicator of fiscal imbalance nonetheless, one has to base the sustainability analysis on the relative change in generational accounts of a representative agent. Since her absolute generational represents a weighted average of the subgroup accounts, it stays invariant with respect to the specific distribution of the intertemporal public budget residual among future newborns.[17] Hence, the conventional sustainability indicator π stays unique, as long as it is based on the life cycle tax burden of representative members of present and future newborn cohorts.

4.5.2 Sensitivity to the Concept of Net Taxes

Besides the difficulties to design the fiscal potential of future birth cohorts in an adequate way, the algebraic properties of the traditional concept to indicate fiscal imbalance have raised concern.[18] First, the special case $GA_{t,t} = 0$ is not in the domain of the π, as this would involve division by zero. In practice, the asymptotic properties of the indicator if the generational account for a present newborn approaches zero, are more problematic. In order to evaluate the limit of sustainability index, it is useful to write π as a function of $GA_{t,t}$,

$$\pi(GA_{t,t}) = \frac{GA_{t+1,t+1}(GA_{t,t})}{(1+g)GA_{t,t}}, \tag{4.19}$$

where the sign of the partial derivative is given by $\frac{\partial GA_{t+1,t+1}}{\partial GA_{t,t}} < 0$. The inverse relation of present and future newborns' generational accounts is explained by the intertemporal zero-sum character of government policy due to the static conception of the intertemporal public budget constraint, although the exact functional relation of the accounts would be difficult to specify. In general, a variation in the life cycle net tax payments of the present newborn leads to a change in the generational accounts of other living cohorts as well, which makes it difficult to assess the overall public revenue effect of a marginal change in the life-cycle tax payment of present newborns.

Noting that the change in the future generational account induced by a marginal change in the generational account of a base year newborn is finite,[19] we observe that $\lim_{GA_t \to 0} \pi$ equals infinity in absolute terms, except for the special case $GA_{t+1,t+1}(0) = 0$.[20] The sign of the left-side limit and the right-side limit of the sustainability indicator differ and are determined by the sign of the nominator of equation (4.19), evaluated at $GA_{t,t} = 0$. In particular, if a zero generational account for the base year newborn imposes a positive tax burden on future generations, it holds that

---

[17] Recall equation (4.12), p. 58. While this relation is true for the absolute change of future generational accounts, it does not hold for the relative variation of tax burdens.

[18] The argument in this section is strongly influenced by Raffelhüschen (1996).

[19] To see this, substitute equations (4.1) and (4.2) into (4.9), and differentiate the resulting expression for $GA_{t+1,t+1}$ with respect to $GA_{t,t}$.

[20] In this unlikely but conceivable case (compare scenario (b) in Table 4.1), application of l'Hôpital's rule yields $\lim_{GA_t \to 0} \pi = \frac{\partial GA_{t+1,t+1}/\partial GA_{t,t}}{1+g}$, which is finite.

$$\lim_{GA_t \to 0^+} \pi(GA_{t,t}) = \infty \quad ; \quad \lim_{GA_t \to 0^-} \pi(GA_{t,t}) = -\infty. \qquad (4.20)$$

If $GA_{t+1,t+1}(0)$ is negative, the signs in equation (4.20) are reversed. Due to this asymptotic behavior, the standard sustainability indicator turns highly sensitive in absolute terms, if the generational account measured for a representative member of the base year birth cohort is close to zero. If this is the case, a high numeric value of π dominantly reflects a low life cycle tax burden for a present newborn and does not hint at intertemporal fiscal imbalance between generations. Put differently, the conventional relative measure of fiscal sustainability turns arbitrary, as soon as government intervention into the life cycle consumption opportunities of base year newborns is insignificant.

Several generational accounting studies report a low life cycle net tax burden for a representative base year newborn. In particular, the denominator of π tends to move close to zero, if inter-gender redistribution is sizeable, as demonstrated by Jensen and Raffelhüschen (1997) for the Danish case. In many classical welfare states, generous public benefit programs bring women into the position of lifetime net transfer recipients, which, on a weighted average, might counterbalance the positive lifetime net tax burden observed for male members of the base year born cohort. However, the outcome that the generational account for the present newborn is close to zero is not restricted to the case of significant redistribution between genders. It could also reflect modest redistribution across age groups, as it is the case in New Zealand, where fiscal policy balances taxes paid with transfers received over the entire life cycle of present newborns, though gender redistribution is not prominent [Auerbach et al. (1997)].

Finally, the procedure to allocate government non-transfer expenditure (partially) as a personal benefit could lead to arbitrary reactions of the standard sustainability measure. As the intertemporal public budget residual aggregates net government expenditure for present and future generations, while considering public transfers only for the base year living, approaching government purchases as an in-kind transfer invariably lowers the intertemporal budget residual. The corresponding reduction in the generational account of future generations moderates indicated fiscal imbalance. However, at the same time, the broader transfer concept reduces the life cycle net tax payment assigned to current newborn agents, raising the index of fiscal sustainability. Which of the two opposing effects dominates, depends crucially on the extent to which the change in the transfer concept moves the generational account of the base year generation closer to zero, rendering the sustainability indicator π more sensitive.

Thus, using the residual approach, the classification of government purchases and personal transfers matters. A well-defined indicator would be invariant to changes in the categorization of overall government spending. In order to evaluate if tax and government spending parameters can stay unchanged in the future, it is irrelevant whether government expenditure creates a private benefit for the individual agent or not, but only whether government revenue is sufficient to finance envisaged total spending. Considered that the distinction between the categories of transfer spending and government purchases is ambiguous both theoretically and empirically, the fact that the sustainability indicator reacts to changes in the notion of transfers renders the residual approach susceptible to manipulation. By renaming parts of net government consumption as a personal transfer, or a personal transfer as net government consumption, one may maneuver reported generational fiscal imbalance in a specific direction.

Quite obviously, the standard concept to evaluate fiscal imbalance by the relative change in generational accounts is ill-defined also, if the generational accounts of present and future generations are of opposite sign. This is empirically relevant in particular where a wide transfer concept is employed to define net taxes. Incorporating government purchases as a transfer in the generational accounts, the net tax burden of current present newborns is typically negative.[21]

4.5.3 Fiscal Policy Indicators

To derive a measure of fiscal imbalance that is well-defined over the entire domain of $GA_{t,t}$, Jensen and Raffelhüschen (1997) and Auerbach and Kotlikoff (1999) propose to use sustainable policy as a benchmark to evaluate fiscal imbalance due to current fiscal policy. The basic idea is to report the required change in present tax and/or transfer parameters that would allow to maintain the corresponding generational account of the present newborn generation indefinitely. As the government has an infinite choice of policies to achieve fiscal sustainability, measurement of fiscal imbalance turns dependent on the selected balancing policy.

Reference to standardized policy experiments helps to avoid conceptual arbitrariness. For example, one could compute the proportional immediate and permanent change in all tax payment consistent with fiscal balance, given that all other present parameters of fiscal policy stay unchanged. Let $GA_{t,k}^{+} > 0$ denote the remaining lifetime tax payment of a representative agent born in period k in present value terms of period t, given present tax parameters, and $GA_{t,k}^{-} < 0$ the analogous life cycle transfer received, so that $GA_{t,t} = GA_{t,t}^{+} + GA_{t,t}^{-}$. Then, the proportional scaling factor α, equalizing the generational account of present and future newborns, is obtained by solving

$$\alpha = \frac{\sum_{y=t}^{\infty} G_{t,y} - W_t - \sum_{k=t-D}^{t} P_{t,k} GA_{t,k}^{-} - \sum_{k=t+1}^{\infty} P_{k,k} GA_{t,t}^{-} \frac{(1+g)^{k-t}}{(1+r)^{k-(t+1)}}}{\sum_{k=t-D}^{t} P_{t,k} GA_{t,k}^{+} + \sum_{k=t+1}^{\infty} P_{k,k} GA_{t,t}^{+} \frac{(1+g)^{k-t}}{(1+r)^{k-(t+1)}}}$$

$$(4.21)$$

---

[21] Provided that government purchases are regarded as personal transfers, present newborn agents are life cycle net transfer recipients in all member states of the European Union except Italy [Raffelhüschen (1999c, Table 5)]

Interpretation of equation (4.21) is straightforward. The nominator aggregates the present value of aggregate public expenditure not financed from revenue from government wealth, under the condition that present transfer parameters stay unchanged for all generations (uprating for productivity growth). Similarly, the denominator of equation (4.21) aggregates taxes paid by living and future generations, supposed present tax parameters stay constant. It is easy to check that if the latter are increased by a uniform proportion α, the aggregate tax yield just equals projected government spending. The corresponding sustainable generational account for newborn cohorts is given by $GA_{t,t}^S = \alpha GA_{t,t}^+ + GA_{t,t}^- := \beta GA_{t,t}$.[22]

Though not a realistic policy option, this standardized policy experiment offers a clear-cut indication of fiscal imbalance. By definition, present fiscal parameters are sustainable, if α equals unity. If maintaining present transfer parameter requires a tax raise ($\alpha > 1$), fiscal policy is unsustainable. Both present and future generations face a tax increase, required to balance unfunded intertemporal spending commitments. Note that the assumption that each generation contributes to finance the revenue gap avoids the possibly misleading confrontation of present and future generations marking the conventional indicator of fiscal imbalance π. For $\alpha < 1$, the public sector runs an intertemporal revenue surplus, which allows to reduce the net tax burden of some present or future generation. The more distant the adjustment parameter α from unity, the more significant (ceteris paribus) generational redistribution occurring under present fiscal parameters.

However, the value of the fiscal policy indicator α not only reflects the extent of fiscal imbalance, but also the initial composition of the public sector budget. For a given intertemporal revenue need expressed by the nominator of equation (4.21), low (high) aggregate tax revenue in the base period predisposes a low (high) numeric value of the sustainability indicator. Variations in the policy parameter α due to differences in the structure of net taxes between policy scenarios (or across countries) can be corrected, if one relates the necessary policy adjustment to a neutral reference. For example, the policy change required for a fiscally balanced outcome could be related to economic output, which means reporting the corresponding variation in the base year tax quota.

Of course, one could specify other policy experiments to assess fiscal imbalance than a uniform tax increase. Proportional tax adjustment could be restricted to specific public revenue categories, like indirect taxes or social insurance contributions. Alternatively, one could calculate the proportional change in public transfer spending or government purchases assuring that $\pi = 1$.[23] If keeping to present tax parameters requires a reduction in govern-

---

[22] Note that $\beta = \alpha + (1 - \alpha)(GA_{t,t}^-/GA_{t,t})$. Obviously, $\beta > 1$ for $\alpha > 1$, and $\beta < 1$ for $\alpha < 1$, provided that $GA_{t,t} > 0$.

[23] The respective policy parameters are constructed parallel to equation (4.21). Supposed all transfers are adjusted, the sustainable generational account is given

ment spending for a sustainable outcome, fiscal policy tends to redistribute from present to future generations. In the opposite case, fiscal policy is disposed to favor living cohorts.

The idea to employ hypothetical policy scenarios to overcome the shortcomings of the sustainability measure π seems immediately appealing. In fact, it is used in most recent contributions to the generational accounting literature, as a complement to the traditional generational account ratio. However, if computation of future generational accounts rests on the standard residual method, the behavior of fiscal policy indicators is sensitive to the prospective demographic environment. As a consequence, fiscal policy measures could disorder the sustainability ranking generated by the conventional sustainability measure π. Therefore, cross-country comparisons that rely on the policy indicator concept must be approached with some caution.[24] Depending on future cohort size, fiscal imbalance might be indicated incorrectly, provided that the future net tax payment is derived on the base of the residual approach.

To illustrate this proposition, it is convenient to analyze the impacts of a fertility increase raising prospective cohort size, on the alternative measures of fiscal imbalance.[25] First consider the conventional sustainability indicator π. Since the fertility increase does not affect the fiscal parameters faced by living generations, the generational account ratio is affected only by the change in the net tax burden of future generations due to the fertility change. In theory, the response of the future generational account to variations in prospective cohort size is indefinite. Empirically, as sensitivity tests reported in the generational accounting literature suggest, future cohort size and the net tax payment per future agent required to balance the intertemporal public budget vary inversely.

In fact, the necessary condition for this *normal* reaction of the future net tax payment to occur is rather weak. The generational account decreases with rising population size, if the marginal gain in public revenue from an additional newborn, $GA_{t+t,t+1}$, exceeds the marginal increase in net government expenditure caused by the new population member.[26] The fraction of his or her net tax payment that does not serve to finance additional govern-

---

by $GA_{t,t}^S = GA_{t,t}^+ + \alpha GA_{t,t}^- = \beta GA_{t,t}$, where $\beta = 1 + (\alpha - 1)(GA_{t,t}^-/GA_{t,t})$. Note that the sustainable net tax payment differs from that with adaptation of taxes. Adjusting government purchases, the sustainable generational account equals that under current tax and transfer parameters: $GA_{t,t}^S = GA_{t,t}^+ + GA_{t,t}^-$.

[24] Cf. Kotlikoff and Raffelhüschen (1999) in particular. The international survey by Kotlikoff and Leibfritz (1999) focuses less on this approach.

[25] The analytical results supporting the following argument are derived in the Appendix A.3.

[26] Note the analogy to the membership problem of a public club [Cornes and Sandler (1996, p. 359)]. However, as generational accounting rules out externalities of absolute population size on both public revenue and expenditure, an optimal future cohort size does not exist.

ment purchases spills over to all other future born, lowering the per capita net tax burden. Therefore, assessing the sustainability of a given fiscal status quo for two demographic developments, $P_{k,k}^0$ and $P_{k,k}^1$, where $P_{k,k}^1 \geq P_{k,k}^0$, with inequality holding for at least one period $k > t$, it is typically true that $\pi(P_{k,k}^1) < \pi(P_{k,k}^0)$.

To analyze the corresponding reaction of the fiscal policy indicator, suppose that present fiscal policy is imbalanced to the disadvantage of future generations. Then, a fiscally balanced situation can be achieved by a uniform tax increase or a uniform cut in public spending. Unless one analyzes a cut in government purchases, hypothetical policy adjustment equalizes the generational accounts of present and future newborns from two directions. First, it increases the net tax payments of the base year living, including those of the newborn generation. Secondly, the net tax burden of future agents falls due to the corresponding reduction of the intertemporal public budget residual.

The response of present newborns' generational account to changes in fiscal policy parameters raising life cycle net taxes by a proportion β, is independent of the future demographic environment. Since $GA_{t,t}(\beta; P_{k,k}^0) = GA_{t,t}(\beta; P_{k,k}^1)$, demographic sensitivity of the fiscal policy indicator is due to the fact that the response of the future generational account to the fiscal policy experiment depends on prospective cohort size. If the residual method is used, a specific tax increase or transfer cut always generates a constant amount of additional revenue, not influenced by prospective fertility, since the intertemporal public budget residual takes into account aggregate net tax payments of the base year living only. However, computing the future net tax burden, the extra public revenue due to the policy change is distributed among a changing number of future residents, depending on the fertility development. The larger future cohort size, the smaller is the relief each individual future agent derives from a net tax increase imposed on the living. Therefore, the future generational account reacts more sensitively to a revenue generating policy measure, if future cohort size is small.

The consequences for the policy indicator concept are illustrated in Fig. 4.1, which draws the growth-adjusted future generational account as a function of the policy adjustment parameter β. Future cohort size is a shift parameter of this functional relation which, as explained above, turns less elastic with a growing number of tax bearers. The generational account of the base year newborn generation, $GA_{t,t} > 0$, is characterized by $\beta = 1$. As Fig. 4.1 is drawn, fiscal policy is imbalanced to the disadvantage of future generations in either demographic scenario, $P_{k,k}^0$ and $P_{k,k}^1$, distinguished as before. Furthermore, a normal reaction of fiscal imbalance to rising future cohort size is assumed. This is easily checked noting that the generational account ratio π is represented by the tangent of a ray from the origin, which hits the growth-adjusted future generational account evaluated at $\beta = 1$. In either demographic scenario, the ray from the origin is steeper than the 45°-line, which is the locus of equal life cycle net tax rates for present and

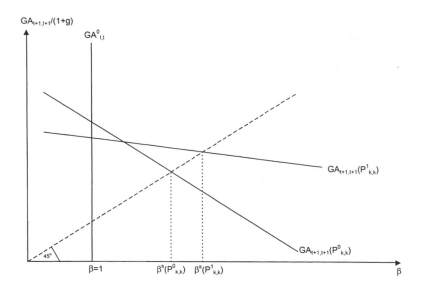

Fig. 4.1. Demographic Sensitivity of Future Generational Accounts

future newborn agents. In addition, the ray is flatter for the high fertility scenario $P^1_{k,k}$, reflecting the postulated normal reaction of the future net tax burden.

In the present example, as fiscal policy is imbalanced to the disadvantage of future generations, the generational accounts for the living need to be increased for a generationally balanced result. In Fig. 4.1, the sustainability generating adjustment of the generational account faced by base year newborns is found where the corresponding future generational account, corrected for income growth, intersects with the 45°-line. In the depicted scenario, $\beta^s_0(P^1_{k,k}) > \beta^s_0(P^0_{k,k})$. Equalization of present and future generational accounts requires a more significant policy change, if the demographic course turns more favorable. Thus, the policy adjustment indicator suggests a generationally more imbalanced situation, while fiscal policy actually moves closer to sustainability due to the fertility gain. This misleading outcome is not merely a theoretical possibility, as demographic sensitivity tests of Spanish generational accounts performed by Berenguer et al. (1998) demonstrate. Using fiscal policy indicators, they find that fiscal policy turns more imbalanced as fertility increases, although the necessary conditions for a normal reaction of the future tax burden are met.

The paradoxical behavior of the policy indicator is not a necessary outcome either. Technically, it requires that the two functions of future generational accounts cross at a point above the 45°-line.[27] Whether they do depends on a set of factors, in particular the value of the initial intertemporal budget residual and the relative size of present and future cohorts. Still, even if the policy indicator does not distort the sustainability order of alternative population developments *within* a country, the demographic bias of the concept is problematic, as it limits the comparability of sustainability measures *across* countries. The policy indicator tends to favor countries with comparatively small prospective cohort size. Therefore, one must be careful to infer a sustainability ranking from the reported order of the necessary changes in fiscal policy.

The demographic bias of the stylized tax and transfer experiments is due to the asymmetric treatment of present and future cohorts by the residual approach. Since net tax payments of future birth cohorts are not designed explicitly, a change in fiscal parameters increasing the net tax payments of the living does not lead to a gain in public revenue from future generations that would vary positively with future cohort size. For an unbiased alternative, one could base the fiscal policy indicator on an unmitigated proportional cut in government purchases which, in contrast to net taxes, are allocated to all generations in the same manner. Therefore, the revenue gain from a uniform cut in government purchases and the fiscal relief for future generations invariably increase with future cohort size. Unfortunately, basing the fiscal policy indicator on government purchases is not always possible, in particular if the analysis relies on a broad transfer concept. Supposed that fiscal policy is imbalanced to the disadvantage of future generations and that the aggregate present value of government purchases is small, even cutting government purchases to zero could not be sufficient to achieve generational fiscal balance.

4.6 The Sustainability Approach

The flaws of the residual approach are mainly due to its failure to provide an explicit model of the tax and transfer design generating the sequence of future generational accounts balancing the intertemporal public budget. The non-structural proceeding tolerates a loss in information. First, the matrix of the future population is reduced to the vector of future newborns. Demographic trends affecting cohort size at a later stage of the life cycle are not respected. Secondly, the fiscal policy determining the prospective net tax burden remains obscure. Hence, economic trends other than productivity

---

[27] In the special case where $GA_{t+1,t+1}(\beta, P_{k,k}^{0})$ and $GA_{t+1,t+1}(\beta, P_{k,k}^{1})$ meet on the 45°-line, the policy indicator indicates that the demographic change has no impact on fiscal sustainability at all.

growth affecting the fiscal potential of a representative future agent cannot be integrated in a straightforward manner. Structural restrictions on future net taxes, for example due to long-term oriented reforms, are not modelled either.

Finally, the residual approach to future generational accounts seems incoherent from a methodological point of view. The sustainability outcome depends on the theoretically and empirically ambiguous distinction between public transfers and net government expenditure, as the method treats the two types of public spending differently. While public transfers are determined from the intertemporal budget residual only implicitly, prospective government purchases are calculated explicitly on the base of age-specific spending and the future population matrix. The resulting indefiniteness of the generational account ratio π is not overcome using stylized fiscal policy indicators due to a demographic bias, again caused by the non-structural computation of the future net tax burden.

4.6.1 The Sustainability Gap

An obvious response to the shortcomings of the residual approach is to consider the prospective fiscal and demographic structure explicitly deriving future generational accounts. This alternative approach was formalized first by Boll (1996) and Auerbach (1997), and has been advanced by Raffelhüschen (1999a) recently. For a starting point, the method treats net tax payments allocated to future born generations in the same manner as government purchases under the residual approach. It is assumed that present tax and transfer parameters stay unchanged indefinitely, disregarding that fiscal policy is actually restricted by the intertemporal budget constraint of the public sector. This assumption allows to determine the aggregate public revenue demand built up keeping to present fiscal parameters. The value of the unfunded expenditure commitments provides a basic measure to judge the fiscal policy adjustments necessary to balance the intertemporal public budget.

As this alternative concept to analyze the intertemporal fiscal imbalance of public finances proceeds in a first step as if generational accounts were sustainable for present and future generations, it might be called the *sustainability approach*, in contrast to the residual approach, which regards net tax payments of future agents as endogenous from the start. Accordingly, we henceforth use the term *sustainability gap* to identify the deficit in the intertemporal government budget arising from continuation of current fiscal policy.[28] The sustainability gap measures the present value of public revenue

---

[28] As the sustainability approach has turned popular only recently, unanimous terminology is not reached yet. In the literature, the sustainability gap is also addressed as the *generation balance gap* [Cardarelli et al. (2000)] and as *intertemporal public liabilities* [Raffelhüschen (1999a)].

that is lacking to render the present set of fiscal policy parameters sustainable. By definition, if continuation of present fiscal policy does not violate the intertemporal budget constraint, the sustainability gap amounts to zero.

If the sustainability gap is positive, the present value of implicit spending commitments made by the government exceeds the present value of prospective public revenue, if present fiscal policy conditions continue. At some point of time, net taxes need to be increased in order to meet the intertemporal financing demand. In case the sustainability gap is negative, present fiscal policy generates an intertemporal budget surplus. Net tax payments can be reduced for some present or future generation. In either scenario, the timing of this policy revision is uncertain. It requires additional restrictions on fiscal policy to infer the generational distribution of adjustment burdens from the sustainability gap.

In technical terms, the sustainability gap is defined by the familiar components of the intertemporal public sector budget. However, net tax payments of future generations are treated as determined by present tax and transfer parameters. The resulting long-term imbalance in the intertemporal public budget defines the sustainability gap in present value terms of the base year t, denoted by SG_t, as

$$SG_t = \sum_{y=t}^{\infty} G_{t,y} - \sum_{k=t-D}^{t} N_{t,k} - \sum_{k=t+1}^{\infty} \bar{N}_{t,k} - W_t. \qquad (4.22)$$

Here and in the following, we add a bar to a variable where necessary to clarify notation, indicating that a variable is evaluated under the condition of constant present policy. Comparing equation (4.22) to the definition of the intertemporal public budget residual given by equation (4.1), it is evident that the sustainability gap differs from the residual concept by exactly the aggregate present value of net tax payments projected for future cohorts. As a consequence, the sustainability gap reveals even less about aggregate redistribution between living and future generations than does the traditional intertemporal budget residual.

This is no serious drawback to the analysis. As we noted in section 4.4, aggregate redistribution between living and future cohorts is not directly related to the concept of fiscal sustainability. In fact, a zero sustainability gap can be consistent with any amount of liabilities transferred from present to future generations, provided that the generational account of a representative present newborn, and therefore the net tax payments of future generations, are sufficiently large. In the opposite extreme, all newborn generations can receive a life cycle net transfer, if this policy is made feasible by an aggregate surplus drawn from living cohorts.

What the sustainability gap actually reveals is the amount of government spending pre-commitments that, from the base year perspective, remain unfunded by expected public revenue. Some of these spending obligations are assumed explicitly by the government and protected by personal property rights. This applies to interest payments on government bonds, but is also true, for example, for entitlement to transfer benefits living generations acquire with their contributions to statutory social insurance. As reported public debt does not mirror the latter spending commitment, the sustainability gap provides a more comprehensive measure of the long-term state of public finances. The remaining government liabilities entering the sustainability gap are less explicit in nature. They derive from the postulate not to discriminate fiscally between birth cohorts, i.e. to follow the fiscal balance rule.

Incorporation of this theoretical concept distinguishes the sustainability gap from the long-established measurement of hidden long-term liabilities that accrue from explicit spending promises made by the government.[29] When interpreting the sustainability gap, one should stay aware that it represents a theory laden statistical indicator, whose scope is far more ambitious than to lay bare public payment obligations definite in the base year, omitted by the inadequate cash-flow accounting of public deficit statistics.

In order to determine the base year present value of future generations' net tax payments, added to the conventional intertemporal budget residual by the sustainability approach, one can proceed parallel to the computation of aggregate net tax payments made by the base year living. Taking into account net taxes paid by future born immigrants, aggregate net revenue from future generations, supposed present tax and transfer policy persists, is given by

$$
\sum_{k=t+1}^{\infty} \bar{N}_{t,k} = \sum_{k=t+1}^{\infty} P_{k,k} \overline{GA}_{k,k} (1+r)^{t-k} + \sum_{y=t+1}^{\infty} \sum_{k=k'}^{y} M_{y,k} \overline{GA}_{y,k}^{M} (1+r)^{t-y},
$$

(4.23)

where $k' = \max\{t+1, y-D\}$. The first term on the RHS of equation (4.23) aggregates the discounted generational accounts of agents born after the base period who stay resident during their entire life cycle. The set of generational accounts for future residents entering equation (4.23) is derived parallel to the definition of generational accounts for living generations, as given by equation (2.1), under the assumption that present net tax parameters persist. However, summation of age-specific net tax payments starts from period k and payments are discounted back to the birth year of the respective generation.

The double summation on the RHS of equation (4.23) aggregates net tax payments by future born migrants. As noted above, the residual approach omits government revenue from this source, which biases the net tax burden of future resident cohorts, if migration is a relevant demographic factor.

---

[29] The literature on this topic, which deals with long-term net liabilities of public pension schemes in particular, is extensive. Cf. Van den Noord and Herd (1993) for an example with a European perspective. Franco (1995) provides a critical assessment of this approach, which stands somewhere between annual deficit accounting and the sustainability approach to generational accounting.

While the outer summation determines the year in which an immigrant cohort takes residency, the inner summation limits aggregation to payment of migrants who are born after the base year. The set of migrant-specific generational accounts is defined parallel to equation (4.4), serving to determine the accounts of immigrants alive in the base year.

Calculation of the generational accounts for future resident and migrant generations requires to extend the projection of age-specific net taxes per agent, used to evaluate net tax burdens of the living, upon infinity. Hence, the entire matrix of projected relative net tax burdens by age is included in the sustainability gap. Incorporation of additional economic structure is the fundamental advantage of the sustainability approach. It allows to design long-term fiscal trends that change the fiscal position of future birth cohorts, and to judge the adjustment burden to balance the intertemporal public budget more accurately.

Furthermore, the sustainability gap is invariant against the ambiguous distinction between personal transfers and net government expenditure, as it incorporates an explicit projection of transfer benefit spending. If government purchases are assigned as a personal transfer by the generational accounts, the corresponding reduction in the aggregate present value of government purchases balances the higher aggregate net tax payments assigned to present and future generations.[30] It is obvious from equation (4.22) that the sustainability gap does not change in this case. The residual approach, in contrast, omits the higher personal transfers received by future born agents, which reduces the intertemporal public budget residual.

4.6.2 A Set of Sustainability Indicators

If the only intention of generational accounting analysis were to ascertain the sustainability or non-sustainability of a specific fiscal policy, the sustainability gap defined by equation (4.23) provides a sufficient indicator. Fiscal policies that create a positive (negative) sustainability gap, tend to distribute personal consumption opportunities intertemporally to the disadvantage (advantage) of future generations. Accordingly, any reform of public finances reducing an existent sustainability gap is regarded favorably, from an intertemporal generational point of view. However, the sustainability gap lacks a yardstick, by which to judge the extent of intertemporal redistribution and the corresponding economic burden. The sustainability approach offers several concepts to translate the sustainability gap into more substantial measures of fiscal imbalance, whose merits are discussed in the following.

---

[30] We pass over the proof, which requires some lengthy but easy manipulations of the different components of the sustainability gap, noting that age-specific per capita government purchases and transfer benefits vary by the same amount in absolute terms if one changes the definition of net taxes.

Macro Indicators

As the sustainability gap evaluates unfunded spending commitments of the government on a macroeconomic level, it is useful to set it into relation with an aggregate measure of economic activity. In fact, in order to judge the degree of fiscal imbalance, some analysts have reported the sustainability gap in terms of present GDP.[31] This measurement approach has the advantage that it is compatible to the familiar debt-to-GDP quota. A comparison of the two rates reveals the extent to which present fiscal policy (which is still under control of the government) imposes restraints on future budgets in addition to those deriving from fiscal policy decisions of the past (which are *datum* for future fiscal policy).

Stating the sustainability gap as a fraction of base year GDP apparently eases comparison of intertemporal public liabilities across countries, as it corrects for differences in the level of economic activity. However, relating the sustainability gap to a short-term measure of economic activity does not capture a country's capability to cope with aggregate fiscal imbalance, which also depends on future GDP. Comparing the sustainability gap in countries, whose economic or demographic prospect is disparate, it is inadequate to use a benchmark that ignores the future growth prospect.[32] Moreover, the approach is not suited to perform meaningful sensitivity tests analyzing the sustainability gap under different demographic and economic parameters, which would also affect the future time path of the GDP.

To overcome these problems, Boll (1996) suggests to report the sustainability gap in terms of the base year present value of aggregate future national product. Let $GDP_{t,y}$ denote gross domestic product projected for period y in present value terms of period t. Then, this indicator, denoted by κ, can be stated as

$$\kappa = \frac{SG_t}{\sum_{y=t+1}^{\infty} GDP_{t,y}}. \tag{4.24}$$

Inspecting equation (4.24), one finds that κ has a straightforward interpretation. The indicator measures the constant share in gross domestic product fiscal policy has to direct into the public coffers (in addition to net tax revenue under present fiscal parameters) in each future year,[33] if it wants to meet the intertemporal public budget constraint. For each year that the indicated extra public revenue is not collected, κ rises even further.

---

[31] For example, the European cross-country comparison of the intertemporal state of public finances by Bonin and Raffelhüschen (1999) is exclusively based on this concept.

[32] One may put forward the same argument against the debt-to-GDP indicator. However, it seems more relevant within the intertemporal context of generational accounting.

[33] Alternatively, the policy revision could start from year t.

This interpretation of κ precludes that adaptation of fiscal policy to meet the intertemporal financing constraint could affect the future development of GDP. Under this condition, the elementary growth model used to construct the generational accounts is satisfactory to conduct the projection of future GDP required to implement the indicator concept described by equation (4.24). To project aggregate output, one may link output per worker in the base period, uprated for constant labor productivity growth, to a forecast of the work force combining age-specific labor force participation rates (supposed constant) with a demographic projection. This procedure is unlikely to provide a good prognosis of future growth trends. However, it is consistent with the concept of persisting economic parameters underlying the construction of the sustainability gap.

Micro Indicators

The macroeconomic indicator suggested above reports unfunded intertemporal liabilities of the public sector, as a fraction of cumulated national income, burdened with the corresponding adjustment of fiscal policy. A parallel concept can be realized on the microeconomic level, transforming the aggregate sustainability gap into changes in individual net tax payments set into relation to life cycle income. This idea leads to a set of sustainability indicators resembling the measures of fiscal imbalance provided by the residual approach. Despite the aggregate character of the sustainability gap, the microeconomic viewpoint to assess fiscal imbalances seems more adequate, as it highlights the extent to which fiscal policy redistributes consumption opportunities between generations, which is the core interest of generational accounting.

To convert the sustainability gap into a set of personal tax burdens, one might presume that all living generations are exempt from necessary changes in fiscal policy. This assumption resumes the original proceeding of the residual approach with its clear distinction of living and future cohorts. Deriving possible sequences of future generational accounts, the sustainability method starts form the set of individual rest-of-life net tax payments that establishes the sustainability gap. Policies to balance the intertemporal government budget redesign the matrices of age- and cohort-specific tax and transfer parameters $\bar{t}^{l}_{i,k}$ generating the initial set of generational accounts. To avoid conceptual ambiguities, it is recommended to base the construction of future generational accounts on hypothetical policy concepts. For example, on could opt for a uniform proportional adjustment of tax or transfer parameters across all age groups.[34] Hence, despite explicit specification of prospective fiscal policy

---

[34] This stylized procedure does not conflict with the central idea of the sustainability approach to model long-term trends in fiscal and demographic trends, in order to capture fiscal capability of future generations. Generation-specific differences in fiscal potential are not ironed out by a proportional adjustment of per capita taxes or transfers.

(lacking from the residual approach) the sustainability method does not yield a realistic prognosis of future tax burdens either.

For a specific policy experiment, the corresponding set of future generational accounts is derived in two steps. First, the proportional adjustment factor is determined which, if applied to the addressed matrix of per capita taxes or transfers, raises additional net revenue to the extent of the sustainability gap. In a second step, the corresponding rest-of-life net tax payments are added to the set of generational accounts under present fiscal conditions. For an example, suppose the sustainability gap is closed by a uniform variation in all tax payments of future born agents. Let $\overline{GA}^+_{k,k} > 0$ represent the the present value life cycle tax payment of a representative agent born in period $k > t$, assumed that present tax parameters persist, and $\overline{GA}^{M+}_{y,k} > 0$ the tax payment upon death of a k-born immigrant after taking residency in period y. Then, the proportional variation μ in tax levels balancing the sustainability gap is obtained solving

$$\mu = \frac{SG_t}{\sum_{k=t+1}^{\infty} P_{k,k} \frac{\overline{GA}^+_{k,k}}{(1+r)^{k-t}} + \sum_{y=t+1}^{\infty} \sum_{k=k'}^{y} M_{y,k} \frac{\overline{GA}^{M+}_{y,k}}{(1+r)^{y-t}}} \tag{4.25}$$

with $k' = \max\{t+1, y-D\}$. The denominator of equation (4.25) duplicates equation (4.23), but is restricted to the tax components of the generational accounts. It represents the aggregate tax revenue received from future born agents provided that present tax parameters are maintained. As personal tax payments by age and generation are adjusted uniformly, all accounts of remaining lifetime tax payments exhibit the same proportional change.

As the denominator of equation (4.25) is positive, the direction of the required tax reform is established by the sign of the sustainability gap. If maintaining present fiscal accumulates an intertemporal deficit ($SG_t > 0$), tax revenue from future generations must increase and hence $\mu > 0$. In the opposite case, if an intertemporal budget surplus occurs ($SG_t < 0$), the original tax load on future generations can be reduced so that $\mu < 0$. Provided that the sustainability gap equals zero, application of equation (4.25) assures that $\mu = 0$. Since fiscal policy is sustainable, the initial tax levels can be kept for all future born.

In case of non-sustainable fiscal policy, correcting the initial net tax payments for the necessary change in life cycle taxes yields a sequence of future generational accounts not offending against the intertemporal budget constraint of the public sector. One obtains $GA_{k,k} = (1 + \mu)\overline{GA}^+_{k,k} + \overline{GA}^-_{k,k} = \nu_k \overline{GA}_{k,k}$ for resident cohorts born in year $k > t$, where $\overline{GA}^-_{k,k} < 0$ denotes the life cycle transfer receipt of a representative resident born in period k, which analyzing balancing tax policy is determined by present transfer parameters. Note that ν_k is indexed to future generations' period of birth. The proportional variation in net tax burdens is a function of the share of life cycle tax payments in the total generational accounts, which can differ between birth cohorts.[35] As a consequence, if future generations are fiscally distinct, it can be misleading to assess intertemporal fiscal imbalance by the relative change in life cycle tax burdens between base year newborn residents and their immediate successors, as it is done by the residual approach. Although variations in future generational accounts are likely to be modest in most empirical applications, this problem gains relevance, if the projection of fiscal parameters designs very long-term policy developments. In some instances, this could be even necessary to design a satisfactory status quo benchmark.[36] Incorporation of long-term trends in life expectancy, affecting life cycle net taxes through changes in survival patterns, could add to differentiation of future generational accounts between cohorts.

Even if growth-adjusted generational accounts do not vary at all across future generations, the relative change in the lifetime net tax burdens of present and future newborns yields an ambiguous indicator of intertemporal fiscal imbalance. In general, using the sustainability method, the set of future generational accounts is dependent on the selected policy experiment. If, for example, the sustainability gap is closed through a uniform proportional cut in public transfers,[37] life cycle net taxes of future born residents change compared to the tax policy experiment, provided that division of the aggregate adjustment burden between residents and migrants changes. In fact, the set of future generational accounts is invariant to the policy selected to balance the sustainability gap only if migration does not occur and if net tax burdens before adjustment are identical for future generations.[38]

---

[35] The tax-adjusted generational accounts of migrants can be written as $GA^M_{y,k} = \nu_{y,k}\overline{GA}^M_{y,k}$ for all $y > t$ and $y \geq k \geq \max\{t+1, y-D\}$. Even if the share of tax payments in the generational account does not differ between future resident birth cohorts, it certainly changes with migrant age when taking residency. Hence, one does not observe a uniform proportional variation of migrants' generational accounts. A similar argument can be made, if the analysis distinguishes between resident subpopulations.

[36] Maturation of the recently introduced pay-as-you-go pension scheme in the United Kingdom and the transition to a resettled pension system in Italy provide examples for long-term status quo developments, unfolding over half a century, that have been analyzed in a generational accounting framework. Cf. Cardarelli et al. (2000) and Franco and Sartor(1999), respectively.

[37] This requires to replace the set of tax accounts in equation (4.25) with an analogous set of transfer accounts.

[38] For a sketch of the proof, suppose government wealth and net government purchases are zero to limit notation. Furthermore, suppose no migration. Then, if fiscal policy balances the intertemporal public budget constraint by adaptation of fiscal parameters for future generations, it must hold that $\sum_{k=t+1}^{\infty} P_{k,k}GA_{t,k} = \sum_{k=t-D}^{t} P_{t,k}GA_{t,k}$. Supposed net tax burdens do not vary across future cohorts, it is also true that $\sum_{k=t+1}^{\infty} P_{k,k}GA_{t,k} = GA_{t,t+1}\sum_{k=t+1}^{\infty} P_{k,k}(1+g)^{k-(t+1)}$. Inserting this condition into the intertemporal public budget constraint and rearrangement yields $GA_{t,t+1} = \sum_{k=t-D}^{t} P_{t,k}GA_{t,k} / \sum_{k=t+1}^{\infty} P_{k,k}(1+g)^{k-(t+1)}$.

In the light of these arguments, reference to the generational account ratio π seems useful mainly for illustrative purposes, if the sustainability method is employed to derive future tax burdens. As the asymptotic properties of the generational account ratio discussed in section 4.5.2 are not overcome by switching to just a different method to construct the set of future generational accounts, π might be ill-defined anyhow. For an alternative, one could report the absolute variation in growth adjusted personal lifetime tax burdens of agents born in the base year and one year after.[39] However, considered that the generational account of the $t+1$ born agent could be neither representative nor unique, this does not seem a fully satisfactory solution to the indicator problem and perhaps adds an ambiguity to cross-country comparisons.

Besides, the focus on the absolute net tax differential between current and future newborns misses the implicit statement on life cycle consumption opportunities made by the relative indicator π. Neglecting this reference, sensitivity tests of generational imbalance can become seriously misleading. Alternative parameters for productivity growth and the discount factor affect the present value of expected life cycle income at time of birth. This income change must be taken into account, judging the impact of the observed absolute variation in net tax payments on personal welfare. Furthermore, analysis of absolute tax differentials fails to control for differences in mortality between countries. All other things equal, the fiscal burden corresponding to a specific absolute variation in life cycle generational accounts is likely to be the higher, the shorter the expected lifespan at time of birth.[40] Adequate evluation of generational fiscal burdens requires to consider net tax payments in terms of life cycle consumption opportunities.

Fiscal Policy Indicators

As a unique set of future generational accounts in general does not exist under the residual approach, the corresponding net tax rate differential is not unique either. Therefore, one might be satisfied to characterize the sustainability of public finances by the policy revision necessary to balance the

---

Thus, under the given conditions, the representative future generational account is unique, as the terms on the RHS are determined by initial fiscal policy parameters and exogenous demographics. As a corollary, the sustainability and the residual method yield identical future accounts.

[39] This is the approach taken by the generational accounting studies collected by the European Commission (1999) where π is inapplicable due to application of a broad concept of personal transfers.

[40] This aspect gains particular relevance comparing fiscal sustainability between developing and more advanced countries. But even within Western Europe, the current variation of life expectancy reaches almost four years, comparing Ireland [McCarthy and Bonin (1999)] and Sweden [Lundvik et al. (1999)].

intertemporal public budget constraint. In the above example, the value of the proportional adjustment factor μ applied to all taxes is actually sufficient to identify the intertemporal burden imposed by present fiscal policy parameters. Transformation into a cohort-specific parameter ν_k does not add relevant information with regard to fiscal sustainability, although it provides an illustration of the corresponding individual burdens.

Selecting a policy indicator to judge fiscal sustainability, it is essential to understand the (algebraic) properties of this measure. For sake of argument, suppose for the moment that a deficit in the intertemporal public budget occurs ant that it is balanced by a once-and-for all uniform tax raise for future generations. Then, for a given revenue demand indicated by the sustainability gap, the value of the tax adjustment parameter depends on demographic and fiscal factors. With respect to demographics, it is easy to see from equation (4.25) that the balancing increment in the net tax payments of future generations varies inversely with the size of future born resident and migrant cohorts, $P_{k,k}$ and $M_{y,k}$. Therefore, as one would claim, a more favorable demographic development invariably reduces the policy indicator of fiscal sustainability. The paradoxical behavior, which could invalidate the fiscal policy indicator under the residual approach, does not occur basing the same approach on the sustainability gap concept.

This observation does not imply that the policy adjustment parameter would always exhibit a *normal* reaction. As the value of the sustainability gap is affected by changes in fertility and migration patterns, fiscal sustainability is not necessarily improved with rising future cohort size. A necessary condition for a normal reaction of the policy adjustment indicator is that the additional tax revenue gained from a new population member (serving to finance the sustainability gap) exceeds the marginal expansion of the sustainability gap occurring provided that the increase in net government expenditure attributed to the extra population member exceeds her rest-of-life net tax payments under present fiscal conditions.[41]

The second influence on the tax adjustment parameter comes from economic variables. The necessary revision of the initial tax parameters the more significant, ceteris paribus, the smaller the base year present value of

---

[41] This requirement actually comprises a set of necessary conditions, as one has to distinguish between resident and migrant cohorts. This set of conditions represents a generalization of the condition for a normal reaction under the residual approach. It can be derived parallel to Appendix A.3, writing the policy adjustment factor μ first as a function of residents' and migrants' cohort size: $\mu(P_{k,k}, M_{y,k}) = SG_t(P_{k,k}, M_{y,k})/f(P_{k,k}, M_{y,k})$, where $f(\cdot)$ represents the denominator of equation (4.25). Differentiating $\mu(\cdot)$ with respect to $P_{k,k}$ for all $k > t$, and furthermore with respect to $M_{y,k}$ for all $y > t$ and $y \geq k \geq \max(t+1, y-D)$ yields the set of necessary conditions. Even if fiscal policy does not discriminate between future birth cohorts, one is left with a set of D necessary conditions, $D-1$ of which apply to immigrants, depending on their age when taking residency.

tax accounts entering the denominator of equation (4.25). The present value aggregate depends on three elements – the tax rates effective in the economy, the assumptions on productivity growth and the interest factor, and the distribution of tax payments during lifetime. The last determinant might be less obvious. If taxation is deferred, on average, to a later stage of the life cycle, the revenue base for the tax experiment declines (and therefore μ increases), since tax payments at older age are more heavily discounted.

It would be useful to control for these influences, in particular when attempting at cross-country analysis. Similar to the policy indicator concept under the residual approach, variations in effective tax rates between countries or different policy scenarios can be monitored reporting the required policy adjustment in terms of the corresponding change in macroeconomic tax quotas. However, supposed that the adjustment burden is levied on future generations, this change in tax rates is not instantly observable. The policy adjustment experiment unfolds its full effect only when the last agent exempted from the adjustment will have died (after a period of D years). Ideally, one would project pre- and post-adjustment tax rates over this time span. For a much simpler measure, which neglects the impact of prospective demographic changes but avoids a projection of aggregate production, one might apply the adjustment factor μ to the tax payments of present residents and set the resulting aggregate into relation with GDP in the base period.

As far as cross-country analysis is concerned, the sensitivity of the policy indicator concept to variations in growth and interest factors is no serious obstacle, provided that comparative results are derived under an identical long-term economic environment.[42] However, sensitivity tests of fiscal sustainability within a country turn ambiguous. The policy indicator shows a downward bias for increasing growth and decreasing interest rates, as the aggregate value of generational accounts under present fiscal policy falls in present value terms. Like other absolute measures of fiscal sustainability (the sustainability gap, the difference of generational accounts between current and future newborn) the policy index misses a benchmark relating the departure from initial tax parameters to future economic conditions. Again, evaluation of long-term macroeconomic tax rates could introduce a meaningful reference.

The impacts of cross-country or policy-related differences in tax incidence by age on the policy adjustment factor seem more difficult to eliminate in a satisfactory way. If one does not wish to argue that these effects are quite negligible in practice, one could select specific taxes for the adjustment ex-

---

[42] It is not always meaningful to define the baseline of cross-country analysis around a uniform growth and interest rate. For example, in order to design the specific economic conditions of what is still a developing country in many ways, the special baseline for Argentina [Villela Malvar (1999)] deviates significantly from the standards set for the world-wide generational accounting studies collected by Auerbach et al. (1999).

periment, whose microeconomic age profiles stay unchanged under different policy scenarios or show little variation across countries. Of course, lump-sum taxes, if existent, would provide the perfect reference to achieve age-neutrality of the adjustment experiment. The lump-sum indicator of fiscal imbalance suggested below will take up this aspect.

Reviewing the properties of a policy indicator concept under the sustainability approach, we assumed that this indicator would be based on a uniform tax adjustment borne by future generations. Our above argument is just as valid for other counterfactual policies. For example, one could ask for the uniform proportional transfer reduction balancing the sustainability gap, or combine tax increments with a spending cut. However, tax experiments circumvent the ambiguous distinction between personal transfers and net government expenditure. The value of transfer benefit indicators can be manipulated by changing the transfer concept, as long as there is no established standard to base this type of policy experiment on the broadest possible definition of government spending.

Rather than distributing the entire adjustment burden among future born cohorts, the sustainability gap can be allocated to current and future generations alike.[43] This strategy seems preferable in some ways, as it does not rely on the artificial and possibly confusing confrontation of the two parties implying that policy pursues two distinct fiscal regimes at the same time. Reporting fiscal imbalance in terms of the unmitigated once-and-for-all policy revision balancing the sustainability gap closely resembles the idea of fiscal policy measures under the residual approach. Nevertheless, in general the two concepts are not equivalent.[44] The residual approach alleges intertemporal fiscal balance between current and all future newborn residents (which is likely to offend against government's intertemporal budget constraint, depending on immigration). The sustainability approach, in contrast, assures a zero sustainability gap by policy adjustment (which is likely to tolerate variations in the generational accounts of present and future birth cohorts).

Lump-Sum Indicators

Policy indicators of fiscal sustainability illustrate intertemporal redistribution against the background of the specific organization of the tax and transfer system under investigation and its prospective development. As noted above, structural influences on the resulting indicators could render adequate comparisons of fiscal sustainability across countries or fiscal policy strategies difficult. Given that the premise of a uniform variation of personal tax and/or

---

[43] To conduct, for example, a tax experiment, one has to add equation (4.3), restricted to the tax accounts of living generations, to the nominator of equation (4.25).

[44] They are, under the very special conditions that render the sustainability and the residual approach interchangeable.

transfer rates represents by no means a likely policy option, one might overcome this difficulty by selecting an even more stylized policy rule. Assuming that the sustainability gap is closed by means of a uniform tax payment or transfer receipt per capita, allocated lump sum to future birth cohorts or, alternatively, to both present and future generations, clears the sustainability measure from fiscal peculiarities. By definition, neither differentials in tax and transfer structure nor in the distribution of net taxes by age make a difference in this fictive lump-sum scenario.

Age-neutral taxes or transfers are rarely observed in reality. Therefore, adopting a lump-sum strategy, one could not report intertemporal fiscal imbalance in terms of a required change of initial policy, as do the conventional policy indicators of sustainability. Instead, one has to rely on a microeconomic viewpoint, reporting the adjustment burden in terms of a newly introduced personal lump-sum tax or transfer receipt. At first sight, this proceeding seems to exchange certain deficits of the policy approach for the more serious shortcomings of an absolute measure of generational imbalance, debated above. However, exploiting the lump-sum perspective, these shortcomings are alleviated considerably, for the assumption that intertemporal fiscal liabilities are levied evenly on all population members irrespective of age allows to translate the sustainability gap into an annual per capita payment that is constant in growth-adjusted present value.

If only future birth cohorts are made responsible for the imbalance in the intertemporal public budget, the amount of the yearly lump-sum payment balancing the sustainability gap, LS_t, in terms of base year present value, is determined by

$$LS_t = \frac{SG_t}{\sum_{y=t+1}^{\infty} \sum_{k=k'}^{y} P_{y,k} \left(\frac{1+g}{1+r}\right)^{y-t}} \tag{4.26}$$

where $k' = \max\{t+1, y-D\}$. Equation (4.26) distributes the sustainability gap evenly among all future born agents. The denominator aggregates, for each period $y > t$, cohort size by age, $P_{y,k}$, of generations born after the base period (including migrant cohorts). The periodical population is subjected to productivity growth to incorporate changes in income.[45]

Analyzing fiscal imbalance on the base of a yearly burden in lieu of an absolute life cycle payment has some advantages. First, it facilitates to control for variations in life expectancy, especially relevant in a cross-country context. A given absolute life cycle adjustment ceteris paribus translates into a higher yearly lump-sum payment, pointing at a higher welfare loss. More importantly, the proposed annual indicator is less seriously affected on the whole by growth and interest rate variations than the conventional lifetime measurement of absolute fiscal burdens.

---

[45] If the lump sum amount is assigned to living and future generations, an analogous formula applies, where the outer summation begins in year t, while the inner summation always starts from the birth year of the oldest agent, $y - D$.

Adopting a life cycle perspective, the present value of absolute net tax differentials is subject to a downward bias when interest rates go up, as life cycle burdens are more heavily discounted. However, one must not interpret this trend as an improvement of fiscal balance, considered that the present value of pre-tax consumption opportunities is reduced at the same time. Using the annual lump-sum payment as an alternative avoids the possibly misleading discounting bias. All other things equal, a given life cycle tax burden translates into a higher yearly tax burden if the underlying interest factor is increased.[46] In a similar way, the indicator controls for the increase in the absolute difference of generational accounts due to more favorable assumptions on prospective productivity growth, which inflate absolute payments. Still, personal welfare does not necessarily move in the same direction as the lump-sum indicator. Variations in aggregate life cycle income before taxation could outweigh changes in the lifetime yearly payment. As stressed repeatedly in this section, pre-tax income changes require explicit consideration, if one wishes to judge the impacts of fiscal imbalance on individual agents adequately.

To summarize, there is a range of different approaches to illustrate the sustainability gap associated with continuation of a specific set of fiscal policy parameters. The discussion in this section showed that none of the indicators suggested by generational accountants copes with all aspects of intertemporal generational redistribution perfectly. Therefore, instead of favoring a single sustainability measure, one would typically use a variety of sustainability indicators for a generational accounting analysis. The in-depth case study occupying the second part of this study chooses deliberately from the toolbox of sustainability indicators suggested above. Doing so will allow us to offer a comprehensive description of the generationally imbalanced state of present fiscal policy in Germany and the severe generational conflicts, which might be the consequence.

---

[46] This is evident from equation (4.26), as $\frac{\partial LS_t}{\partial r}\big|_{dSG_t=0} < 0$. The overall impact of an interest rate increase is indefinite, as the sustainability gap is also a negative function of the interest factor.

5. The Intertemporal State of German Public Finances

5.1 Introduction

Empirical applications of the generational accounting concept have spread around the globe. To the knowledge of the author generational accounts, mainly computed according to the flawed residual method, have been used to examine the intertemporal sustainability of public finances in 22 countries, which are surveyed by Table 5.1.[1] In the remainder of this study, the generational accounting framework is applied to analyze the sustainability of German public finances. For several reasons, Germany seems suited for a stimulating case study. First, the institutional design of public sector finances is somehow representative for a number of OECD countries. In particular, the provision of Social Security through a comparatively mature, pay-as-you go type of statutory pension insurance is archetypal for the Bismarckian social insurance systems frequent in western and southern Europe.

Secondly, Germany's population, in the aftermath of the baby bust, will age severely 'from the bottom' over the next decades. This threat to public finances is aggravated further by an ongoing trend of declining mortality. Although double aging is typical for the majority of OECD countries [Hagemann and Nicoletti (1989)], it is especially pronounced in Germany. This allows to highlight the impact of demographic processes on the intertemporal sustainability of public sector budgets. Thirdly, the German case study provides an example for the computation of region-specific generational accounts. With East Germany still struggling for recovery from the economic shock of unification, Germany remains divided into two economically distinct areas. The resulting regional differences in individual net tax burdens must be taken into consideration when evaluating the intertemporal sustainability of German fiscal policy. This extension of the standard analysis could be applicable to other countries suffering from strong regional disparities.

Furthermore, Germany has developed into a major destination for immigration over the past decades. Since migrant-specific age profiles of net tax

---

[1] Many of the country studies are collected in volumes edited by the European Commission (1999) and by Auerbach et al. (1999). Summaries of the main findings are given by Kotlikoff and Raffelhüschen (1999) and Kotlikoff and Leibfritz (1999). Studies for Iceland and Switzerland are forthcoming.

Table 5.1. Generational Accounting Country Studies

Country	Source	Approach
Argentina	Altamiranda (1999)	Residual
Australia	Ablett (1996, 1997, 1999)	Residual
Austria	Keuschnigg et al. (1999, 2000)	Sustainability
Belgium	Lüth and Dellis (1999)	Sustainability
	Stijns (1999)	Residual
Brazil	Villela Malvar (1999)	Residual
Canada	Oreopoulos (1999)	Residual
Denmark	Jensen and Raffelhüschen (1999a)	Sustainability
	Jensen et al. (1996)	Residual
	Jensen and Raffelhüschen (1997, 1999b)	Residual
Finland	Feist et al. (1999)	Sustainability
France	Crettez et al. (1999)	Sustainability
	Levy and Doré (1999)	Residual
Germany	Bonin et al. (1999)	Sustainability
	Raffelhüschen and Walliser (1997)	Residual
	Besendorfer et al. (1998)	Residual
	Gokhale et al. (1995)	Residual
	Boll et al. (1994)	Residual[a]
	Boll (1994, 1996)	Residual
Ireland	McCarthy and Bonin (1999)	Sustainability
	McCarthy (1995)	Residual
Italy	Franco and Sartor(1999)	Sustainability
	Sartor (1999)	Residual
	Franco et al. (1992)	Residual

[a] Isolated Social Security system.

payments can be identified from the available micro data, the generational accounting framework may be used to assess the fiscal position of migrants relative to German natives, and to assess the intertemporal fiscal effect of demographic rejuvenation through immigration. Since political decision-makers do not consider Germany as an immigration country and are reluctant to take steps toward active immigration policy, the results of this analysis should be exemplary for countries which do not make an effort to screen immigrants.

Finally, the microeconomic database in Germany is vastly superior compared to most other countries. More comprehensive sets of micro profiles,

Table 5.1. (continued) Generational Accounting Country Studies

Country	Source	Approach
Japan	Takayama et al. (1999)	Residual
Netherlands	Bovenberg and ter Rele (1999b)	Sustainability
	Bovenberg and ter Rele (1999a)	Residual
New Zealand	Baker (1999)	Residual
	Auerbach et al. (1997)	Residual
Norway	Steigum and Gjersem (1999)	Residual
	Auerbach et al. (1993)	Residual
Portugal	Auerbach et al. (1999)	Residual
Spain	Berenguer et al. (1999)	Sustainability
	Bonin et al. (2001)	Sustainability[a]
	Berenguer et al. (1998)	Residual
Sweden	Lundvik et al. (1999)	Sustainability
	Hagemann and John (1997, 1999)	Residual
Thailand	Kakwani and Krongaew (1999)	Residual
	Kotlikoff and Walliser (1995)	Residual
United Kingdom	Cardarelli and Sefton (1999)	Sustainability
	Cardarelli et al. (2000)	Residual
United States	Auerbach and Oreopoulos (1999)	Sustainability
	Auerbach et al. (1991, 1992b, 1994)	Residual
	Gokhale et al. (1999)	Residual

[a] Isolated Social Security system.

to our knowledge, have been gathered only for Denmark and the United Kingdom. Comparatively detailed information on personal tax and transfer incidence allows us to design a variety of policy options, exemplary for the debate on long-term oriented fiscal reform, and to compute their impact on fiscal burdens across generations.[2]

---

[2] This is not always possible. For example, generational accounting for Argentina relies on micro data taken from foreign countries to compensate data deficiencies. Therefore, it is difficult to investigate fiscal policies affecting the age distribution of net taxes [Altamiranda (1999, p. 117)]. Even in countries whose statistics is more advanced, sufficiently detailed micro data is not always available. In the Netherlands, for example, it was necessary to assign indirect taxes on the base

This is by no means the first study using generational accounts to assess the intertemporal sustainability of public finances in Germany.[3] Since an initiatory study by Boll et al. (1994) who applied generational accounting to assess generational redistribution through pay-as-you-go social insurance as well as different pension reform strategies, generational accounts have been compiled repeatedly, getting increasingly refined. The first fully developed generational accounting studies for Germany, based on the post-unification public sector budget of year 1992, were presented by Gokhale et al. (1994, 1995).[4] Distinguishing between the net tax payments of East and West Germans, Gokhale et al. constructed region-specific generational accounts in order to identify the cohort distribution of unification related tax and debt burdens. Since this pioneering study, differentiation between region-specific accounts is standard practice in generational accounting studies for Germany.

The standard-setting generational accounts presented by Gokhale et al. have been updated several times. Based on a revised set of personal tax and transfer profiles, the German *Bundesbank* (Federal Bank) assessed the intertemporal generational imbalance of fiscal policy in consecutive years: Boll (1996) is based on the 1994 overall public sector budget, while the rather basic sustainability analysis published by the Deutsche Bundesbank (1997) starts from the budget of year 1996.

Raffelhüschen and Walliser (1997, 1999) maintain the original set of East and West German tax and transfer profiles used by Gokhale et al. (1995), but update the corresponding aggregate data to the 1995 budget. In addition, they introduce a less restrictive concept of personal transfers that include public education spending not representing public investment as a personal transfer. As Raffelhüschen and Walliser employ the residual approach to indicate fiscal sustainability, this incidence assumption affects the sustainability outcome.

Bonin et al. (1999), also starting from the public sector budget of 1995, use an even wider concept of personal transfers. Government purchases not assignable by age are distributed as a personal transfer evenly among all generations. In order to obtain meaningful indicators of intergenerational fiscal imbalance despite base year born agents being net transfer recipients, Bonin et al. change to the sustainability approach.

---

of age-specific income, although this incidence assumption contradicts the life cycle hypothesis of consumption [Bovenberg and ter Rele (1999, p. 332)].

[3] Greiner and Semmler (1999) approach the issue of the fiscal sustainability from a very different angle. Based on time-series data, they use econometric tests to show that German fiscal policy did not meet the no-Ponzi game condition in the past, thus offending against the intertemporal budget constraint of the public sector.

[4] At the same time, Boll (1994) provided an elementary sustainability analysis for overall government sector finances, but the study, unfortunately, was yet limited to the pre-unification state of the (West) German budget.

More recently, Besendorfer et al. (1998) and Raffelhüschen (2001a) have constructed generational accounts for Germany which start from the government budgets of 1996 and 1997, respectively. Both studies investigate the generational impacts of different strategies for long-term pension reform.[5] The former, in direct tradition of Raffelhüschen and Walliser (1997, 1999), derive the generational accounts on the base of the residual approach and incorporate the entire public sector. Education expenditure is partially allocated as a personal transfer. In contrast, Raffelhüschen (2001a) employs the sustainability approach and isolates generations' net contributions to pay-as-you-go financed social insurance schemes.

The following in-depth generational accounting analysis of German public sector and social insurance finances is based on the sustainability approach. The case study continues previous work by Bonin et al. (1999), but extends it in a number of directions. First, the analysis is based on a completely revised set of personal tax and transfer profiles by age. The revision of the micro data set improves the fiscal differentiation between East and West Germans, and models the present age distribution of transfer benefits more faithfully. In particular, the cohort distribution of pension benefits is specified more exactly. Secondly, the present study updates the available 1995 generational accounts for the budget years 1996 and 1997. Application of a uniform generational accounting framework to three consecutive budgets allows to assess the sensitivity of the generational accounting outcomes with respect to base year choice.

Thirdly, a conservative definition of net taxes is employed, omitting in-kind transfers – including education – from the generational accounts. Restricting the net tax concept to cash payments, the generational accounts are defined to measure changes in cohort wealth. This approach ensures plausible lifetime income tax rates. Finally, constructing the overall public sector budget, the substantial corrections for inter-governmental and inter-administrative payments, typical for German generational accounting studies, are withdrawn as far as possible. While this extension of the public sector budget neither changes the overall generational accounts nor the sustainability outcome since taxes and transfers are affected alike, it is prerequisite to effectively isolate the cohort-specific net tax payments to the different branches of the German social insurance system.

The subsequent examination of German public sector finances proceeds as follows. The remainder of this chapter exposes the basic data sets and assumptions underlying the calculations, and presents a comprehensive sustainability analysis of public sector finances in Germany. Demographic aging is identi-

---

[5] The generational accounts presented by Jagob and Scholz (1998), which use 1996 for a base year and only take into account net contributions to Social Security, are invalidated by serious data deficiencies. Apparently lacking a long-term population projection, Jagob and Scholz perpetuate the population structure of the year 2040 indefinitely, which seriously misrepresents the demographic transition.

fied as the major source of severe intertemporal fiscal imbalance. Chapter 6 evaluates to what extent immigration, and systematic immigration policy in particular, could contribute to mitigate generational redistribution caused by an aging society. It is shown that even sizable and screened migration inflows are unlikely to restore the sustainability of German public finances. Consequently, Chapter 7 investigates the generational impacts of different pension reform policies on the political agenda in Germany. The reforms are judged by their effects on intertemporal generational imbalance, which are contrasted with the redistributive outcome among living generations.

5.2 The Demographic and Fiscal Scenarios

Almost a decade after unification, Germany remains divided into two economically and demographically distinct areas. As the economic and social disparities in united Germany and the ongoing process of regional convergence influence the future development of public sector budgets, it is necessary to identify region-specific generational accounts for the East and West German states. Therefore, our long-term projections of demographic parameters, personal tax payments and transfer receipts underlying the construction of generational accounts have been conducted separately for the two different regions. If not indicated otherwise, all projections start from 1996. However, to test the sensitivity of the generational accounts with regard to base year choice, also projections starting from the years 1995 and 1997, respectively, were conducted. These projections are designed according to the same principles as the central forecast starting from the year 1996 is discussed in the following.

5.2.1 Demographic Scenarios

Construction of generational accounts for living and future generations requires a projection of survival ratios by age, as well as the prospective size and composition of the population. Forecasting the population development basically calls for a specification of three fundamental demographic parameters: mortality, fertility and immigration. In accordance with the methodological guidelines developed in Chapter 2, three different demographic scenarios will be used – a status quo projection extrapolating the demographic parameters of the base year 1996, which provides the analytical benchmark, and two more realistic forecast variants, modeled after the recent 'ninth' coordinated population projection conducted by the Federal Statistical Office (*Statistisches Bundesamt*). All projections extend to the year 2200, when the predicted population structure will have reached a stable state. The key assumptions of the demographic scenarios are summarized in Table 5.2. The more specific assumptions are discussed in Appendix B, which gives a detailed account of

Table 5.2. Key Assumptions of the Demographic Scenarios

	Year	Status Quo	Low Mortality	High Fertility
Total Fertility Rate[a]	1996	1.30/0.95/1.51	1.30/0.95/1.51	1.30/0.95/1.51
	2005	1.30/1.30/1.51	1.30/1.30/1.51	1.60/1.60/1.60
Life Expectancy[b]				
at Birth	1996	73.6/79.9	73.6/79.9	73.6/79.9
	2025	73.6/79.9	76.4/82.7	76.4/82.7
	2050	73.6/79.9	78.6/84.9	78.6/84.9
at Age 65	1996	14.9/18.7	14.9/18.7	14.9/18.7
	2025	14.9/18.7	16.7/20.8	16.7/20.8
	2050	14.9/18.7	18.3/22.5	18.3/22.5
Net Immigration	1996	353.500	353.500	353.500
	2000	242.500	242.500	242.500
	2010	200.000	200.000	200.000

[a] West/East/Non-naturalized residents of foreign origin and immigrants.
[b] Males/Females.

the computable cohort population model used for the demographic projections.

In the status quo scenario, the total fertility rate of West German natives is maintained indefinitely at the current value of 1.30, which is well below replacement level.[6] This rigid status quo assumption is not feasible for East Germans. Fertility in the East German states dropped dramatically during the turmoil of unification, and has not fully recovered yet. In 1996, the East German total fertility rate was as low as 0.95. However, there is strong evidence that the fall in East German fertility rates is a temporary phenomenon caused by an increasing proliferation age. In fact, young East German women seem to have adapted to the fertility behavior of West German women of the same age [Lechner (1998)]. To design the ongoing assimilation process, the

---

[6] The total fertility rate indicates, for a given year, the average number of children born per woman of reproductive age. Without immigration, the total fertility rate must range about 2.1 in order to guarantee reproduction of the parent cohort. Application of the cross-sectional total fertility rate concept to predict cohort fertility resembles the fundamental generational accounting procedure to forecast cohort net taxes on the base of cross-sectional net tax profiles. Demographic data were taken from various issues of the Statistical Yearbook [Statistisches Bundesamt (1996, 1997a, 1998)], or were provided on request by the Federal Statistical Office.

status quo projection linearly raises the East German total fertility rate to the current Western level until the year 2005.

The fertility pattern of alien residents, whose fertility rate exceeds that of German natives, is kept constant at the initial level of 1.51. The same fertility rate is also assigned to future immigrants. Although immigrants are likely to show a different fertility behavior after arrival than the current migrant population who took residence on average more than a decade ago, data shortcomings prevent us from reproducing the gradual adaptation of immigrant fertility more precisely. The demographic assimilation of second-generation foreigners[7] is modeled by strictly adopting the principle of *ius soli*. After the base year, children born to alien residents are treated as German natives. This assumption, which does not correspond to the rather strict application of the *ius sanguinis* principle in Germany, is likely to overstate the speed of the assimilation process [Kane (1986)]. Again, shortage of data on immigrant assimilation forestalls the desirable distinction between first-generation and second-generation immigrants.

With respect to mortality, the demographic projections do not differentiate between the three population groups so that variations in the generational accounts within a cohort only reflect differences in individual net tax burdens. This procedure neglects existing differences in mortality. Life expectancy at birth in the East German states currently lags by about two years behind that in West Germany [Sommer (1994)], whereas life expectancy of migrant residents, according to the available statistical data, exceeds that of German natives by almost seven years [Birg (2000)].[8] However, considered that the assimilation process of the different population groups would be difficult to predict, it seems preferable to work with average mortality data. In the status quo scenario, life expectancy at birth is held fixed at the base year level of 73.6 years for males and 79.9 years for females. Correspondingly, life expectancy conditional on the standard retirement age of 65 stays constant at 14.9 and 18.7 years for men and women respectively.[9]

Whereas the status quo scenario serves as a useful analytical reference, it ignores the secular trend in mortality. In the past, life expectancy at birth increased by about 1.5 years per decade in Germany. Gains in longevity may continue at a similar rate in the future, given the evidence on the develop-

---

[7] Cf. Höhn et al. (1990) for an in-depth analysis.

[8] The latter is only partially attributable to favorable self selection among foreigners [Mammey (1990)]. To significant extent, the high life expectancy measured for foreigners reflects underreporting of immigrant mortality, as migrants frequently return abroad unnoticed shortly before their death [Bretz (1986)].

[9] Conditional life expectancy at birth derives from the abridged life table of 1996. To construct the corresponding set of age-specific mortality rates, the mortality model introduced in the Appendix B was applied to the most recent complete life table for West Germany, as published by the Statistisches Bundesamt (1991).

ment of cohort mortality rates.[10] The latest population forecast conducted by the Federal Statistical Office, in contrast to earlier projections, designs the expected long-term fall in mortality in a more realistic manner. Life expectancy at birth is supposed to rise continually by five years until 2050.[11] The second demographic scenario, termed *low mortality scenario*, differs from the status quo scenario by incorporation of this officially predicted mortality trend. From 1997 on, age-specific mortality rates are gradually reduced so that life expectancy at birth reaches 78.6 years for men and 84.9 years for women by the year 2050, and remains constant thereafter. The specified reduction in mortality is assumed to be beneficial for all age groups, but for the elderly in particular. Although some analysts predict that mortality decline continues over the entire twenty-first century [Birg (1998)], the official mortality projection is not extended beyond 2050. With a further increase in life expectancy, the generational accounting assumption that the age profiles of net taxes are stable over time would be hardly plausible.

The third demographic scenario, termed the *high fertility scenario*, also adopts the mortality development predicted by the Federal Statistical Office. In addition, a more optimistic assumption on future fertility is used, which serves to assess the impact of fertility developments on the generational account measures. In the high fertility projection, total fertility of all population groups increases linearly to 1.6 children per woman by the year 2005, and remains constant thereafter. A more significant recovery of fertility rates seems unlikely from today's perspective, considered that in Germany, like in most OECD countries, reproduction rates persist well below replacement level for more than two decades, due to a fundamental change in the social position of women.[12]

The three demographic scenarios share the assumption on the prospective development of net immigration which, given the high volatility of migrant figures in the past,[13] is difficult to predict. The assumptions used reflect the recent decline from the extraordinarily high number of immigrants observed in the early nineties. While 398,000 and 354,000 net immigrants took residency in 1995 and 1996 respectively, net immigration had declined to a number of 239,000 in 1997. In line with the central migration variants of other recent population projections,[14] the projections account for 200,000 net immigrants of foreign origin per year from 2000 on. In addition, immigration of

---

[10] Cf. Dinkel et al. (1996) and in particular Bomsdorf (1993).

[11] In the previous (eighth) population projection, life expectancy was held constant from year 2000 on [Sommer (1994)]. Therefore, the medium variant of this projection closely resembles our status quo scenario.

[12] Cf. Bretz (1986). Even in the GDR where strong incentives promoted fertility the total fertility rate did not exceed 1.7 after the early seventies.

[13] Cf., among others, Schmidt and Zimmermann (1992).

[14] Cf. Prognos (1998), BMI (1996) and in particular Birg et al. (1998).

ethnic Germans from Eastern Europe, predicted to total 600,000 migrants, is taken into account. Net immigration of migrants with German ethnicity gradually declines from 50,000 in year 1997, and ceases by the year 2010. In order to assign aggregate net immigration by age and gender, the composition of net immigrants observed in 1996 is assumed to stay constant over the entire projection period. The structure of net immigration has been considerably more stable in recent years than the aggregate number of net immigrants. Therefore, it might be justified to take the immigrant structure of the base year as representative for the future.[15]

The consequences of the demographic assumptions are displayed in Table 5.3, which summarizes the projected age composition of the German population until the year 2070. At that period, the demographic transition induced by the baby boost will have come to its end.[16] In the status quo scenario, the population declines, after a temporary increase, from 2004 on when net immigration turns insufficient to compensate the excess of deaths over births in the resident population. Population decline accelerates over time. While the population decreases at a rate of 0.50 percent per annum in the decade between 2020 and 2030, the annual rate of population decline reaches 0.74 percent in the decade between 2060 and 2070, and stabilizes at this level thereafter.[17]

Population decline is accompanied by considerable changes in the age composition of the population. As fertility persists below replacement level, the population share of children and teen-agers (younger than 18) falls permanently below the base year level of 19.4 percent. It reaches a minimum of 14.7 percent between 2030 and 2040. In the long term, the population share of the young stabilizes at a rate of about 15 percent. Also the fraction of the population of employable age (18 to 65), almost constant until the year 2020, falls markedly in the long term, from 65.0 percent in the base year to a minimum 58.5 percent in 2037 when the last strong cohorts born in the early 1960's will have retired. The population share of the working aged converges to a long-term level of about 59 percent thereafter.

At the same time, the proportion of the population aged 65 and above steadily increases. Whereas only 15.6 percent of the population had reached

---

[15] A sensitivity test, varying both the aggregate number and the composition of the immigrants, is deferred to Chapter 6.

[16] From 2050 on, the demographic projections turn increasingly unrealistic, as the majority of the population is born after the base year. However, the very long-term demographic development has little impact on the generational accounts, since it is heavily discounted.

[17] Continuation of this process leads to an implausibly small aggregate population in the final years of the projection. We refrain from designing a demographic process, which would stabilize population size in the very long term. Exclusion of (unpredictable) endogenous demographic reactions is consistent with the static projections of net tax payments. Level effects likely associated with population decline [Färber (1988)] are neglected.

Table 5.3. Projected Age Composition of the German Population

Year	1996	2000	2010	2020	2030	2040	2050	2060	2070
				Status Quo Scenario					
Total Population (millions)	81.8	82.6	82.0	79.6	75.7	70.9	65.3	60.1	55.8
Population Share (percent)									
< 18	19.4	19.0	16.6	15.5	15.1	14.7	14.7	14.9	15.1
18 – 64	65.0	64.9	64.0	64.2	60.8	58.8	59.7	59.1	59.3
> 64	15.6	16.1	19.3	20.3	24.1	26.5	25.7	25.9	25.6
> 80	3.6	3.0	3.8	4.6	4.7	5.6	7.3	6.2	6.5
Median Age	38	39	43	46	46	48	48	47	47
				Low Mortality Scenario					
Total Population (millions)	81.8	82.6	82.6	81.1	78.3	74.6	70.1	65.2	60.7
Population Share (percent)									
< 18	19.4	19.0	16.5	15.3	14.7	14.1	13.8	13.9	14.0
18 – 64	65.0	64.9	63.7	63.4	59.3	56.5	56.4	55.4	55.6
> 64	15.6	16.1	19.8	21.4	26.0	29.4	29.9	30.7	30.5
> 80	3.6	3.1	4.1	5.4	6.0	7.7	10.8	10.1	10.3
Median Age	38	39	43	46	47	49	50	50	50
				High Fertility Scenario					
Total Population (millions)	81.8	82.8	83.9	83.6	82.2	80.3	77.7	74.8	72.3
Population Share (percent)									
< 18	19.4	19.2	17.8	17.4	16.9	16.8	16.8	16.9	17.1
18 – 64	65.0	64.7	62.7	61.8	58.3	55.9	56.3	56.4	56.6
> 64	15.6	16.1	19.5	20.8	24.8	27.3	26.9	26.8	26.3
> 80	3.6	3.1	4.0	5.2	5.7	7.1	9.7	8.8	8.6
Median Age	38	39	43	45	46	46	46	46	46

retirement age in the base year, this figure grows by more than ten percentage points to 26.5 percent in 2040, and is still close to 26 percent in 2070. Even more significant is the development predicted for the population share of the oldest-old. By 2050, compared to the base period, the fraction of the population aged 80 and above (7.3 percent) is more than doubled. As a consequence of the shifting age composition, the median age of the population increases by a decade. In 1996, a fraction of 50 percent of the population was younger than 38. Five decades later, between 2040 and 2050, the median age reaches 48. It never falls below age 46 in the remaining projection period.

Of course, the demographic aging process is even more pronounced assuming a more realistic mortality trend. In the low mortality scenario, the population share of the retirees almost doubles to a value of 30.7 percent close to the year 2060, compared to 25.6 percent in the status quo scenario. The fraction of the oldest-old permanently exceeds ten percent after 2050. Accordingly, the population shares of the young and in particular of the working-aged fall in comparison to the status quo scenario. The mortality decline adds three years to the long-term median age, which stays constant at age 50 from 2040 on. The significant impact of increasing life expectancy on the projected aging process in Germany is typical for a demographic environment marked by low fertility and mortality [United Nations (1988, p. 56)]. The gain in longevity also retards the population decline. By the year 2070, the total population in the constant fertility scenario exceeds that under status quo conditions by almost 5 millions. However, as the size of future birth cohorts is hardly affected by the reduction in mortality, the eventual (negative) rate of population growth is not significantly different in the two scenarios.

In contrast, the fertility increase underlying the high fertility scenario enlarges future cohort sizes. Population decline slows down, approaching a rate of 0.34 percent per annum by the year 2070. The total population falls only by 9.5 millions until then. Corresponding demographic rejuvenation from the bottom gradually alleviates the aging process, if mainly in the long term. Compared to the low mortality scenario, the population share of the elderly is 0.6 percentage points smaller by the year 2020. The difference increases to 2.1 percentage points in 2040, when the fraction of elderly reaches a minimum, and to more than four percentage points after 2070. Nevertheless, the population share of retirees exceeds that under status quo conditions, even in the very long term. Moreover, the fraction of working-aged is not significantly larger than in the low mortality scenario, as the weight of youth cohorts increases (which also lowers the median age). These findings confirm that realistic variations in fertility behavior are very unlikely to counterbalance the adverse structural effect of increasing life expectancy, let alone the demographic transition caused by the baby boost.

Figure 5.1 displays how the changing age composition in the three demographic scenarios translates into old-age dependency ratios. The old-age dependency ratio, here defined as the number of persons aged 65 and older per hundred of persons of working age 18 to 64, provides a basic indicator for the fiscal burdens induced by population aging. Its construction reflects the fundamental implicit contract between generations, which lets active labor force participants support the elderly in retirement through income transfers.[18] In all three demographic scenarios, old-age dependency increases sharply over the next decades. Whereas a hundred persons of working age had to support

---

[18] One may construct more refined old-age dependency measures, like the pensioner-to-workers ratio. However, unless labor force participation rates or pensioner quotas are subjected to a change, these measures show the same variation as the basic old-age dependency ratio.

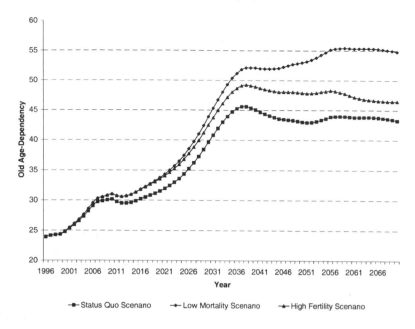

Fig. 5.1. Development of old-age dependency ratio for alternative demographic scenarios. Old-age dependency ratio defined as numer of persons of age 65 and older per hundred persons of age 18 to 64.

about 24 persons in retirement in the base year, this number almost doubles to 46 in the years around 2035 even under status quo conditions. The boost in old-age dependency takes place in two different stages. A first phase of moderate aging occurs in the first decade of the new century when the dependency ratio rises by about six percentage points. After a short period of recovery, the aging process accelerates. In the decade between 2020 and 2030, old-age dependency increases by eight percentage points. After the year 2035, the ratio of the elderly to the working-aged declines, because the first cohorts affected by the fertility decline of the 1960's enter retirement. However, even then the dependency ratio remains as high as 43.

In the low mortality scenario, the change in life expectancy raises old-age dependency, as it prolongs the average lifespan in retirement. By the year 2035, two persons of working age will have to support one person older than 65. Furthermore, as the mortality decline continues until 2050, a third phase of population aging occurs, shifting the period of most serious old-age pressure forward by more than two decades. Between the years 2035 and 2060, the dependency ratio increases by another five percentage points, finally stabilizing at 55 percent.

A moderate fertility increase would be sufficient to counterbalance this third wave of population aging. In the high fertility scenario, similar to the status quo projection, old-age dependency starts declining shortly after 2035. Although the change in fertility behavior enlarges (younger) working-age cohorts, it can offset only partially the effects of rising life expectancy on generations in retirement. Compared to the status quo scenario, 100 members of active cohorts have to support three additional retirees in 2035.

In any case, a comparison of the three demographic scenarios reveals that effects of realistic variations in future demographic parameters on old-age dependency are quite negligible, compared to the long-term impact of the fundamental changes in demographic parameters, which took place in the past.

5.2.2 Relative Tax and Government Spending Profiles

Apart from demographic projections, computation of generational accounts demands specification of age-specific personal tax and transfer payments characterizing current fiscal policy. In addition, for a projection of net government expenditure, one has to take into account that some non-transfer spending by the government may depend on the age composition of the population. As outlined in Chapter 2.3, allocation of government revenue and spending to specific age groups proceeds in two steps. First, the relative fiscal position of different age groups is identified on the base of personal or household micro data. At the second stage, to overcome data deficiencies on the micro level, the relative age profiles are benchmarked against the overall public budget.

General Principles

The comprehensive set of tax and government spending age profiles used to construct the generational accounts presented in this study is mainly based on cross sectional survey data taken from the German Consumer Expenditure Survey (*Einkommens- und Verbrauchstichprobe*), henceforth referred to as the CES, conducted by the Federal Statistical Office in 1993. The CES provides a large sample of about 40,000 households with more than 100,000 members. It consists of two sub-samples of East and West German households, which can be blown up separately to represent the socio-economic household structure in the East and West German states.[19] This allows to identify region-specific differences in the age distribution of fiscal burdens.[20]

---

[19] The CES omits households with a monthly income exceeding DM 35,000 and persons who live in institutions. This may cause a bias of certain tax or transfers profiles, as capital income earners and old transfer recipients are underrepresented in the sample. For a critique of the CES, cf. Kitterer (1986).

[20] In previous generational accounting studies for Germany, relative age profiles derived from the CES were retrieved from the 1988 sample, which, of course, only contained West German households. As a consequence, region-specific differences

The CES data are classified either by household or by the individual household members. As a general rule, we have assigned tax and transfer data on the personal level directly to the individual household member, when the tax or transfer payment is observed. This incidence assumption is debatable, in particular with respect to transfer receipts. First, redistribution within households, which to some extent could be displaced by public transfers, is neglected. Suppose, for example, that provision of public pensions would reduce private intra-family transfers, or increase accidental bequests made by the old generation.[21] In either case, personal welfare of the pension beneficiary is not affected by the public transfer. The transfer incidence slides on household members of younger age. If this is the case, generational accounts based on the assignment of pension benefits to the transfer recipient are misleading as a welfare indicator. In the light of this argument, incorporation of a more rigid study of age-specific incidence seems in order when constructing the relative tax and transfer profiles underlying the accounts. Unfortunately, this would be an empirically difficult and highly data consuming task, preferably to be combined with a micro simulation study.

Secondly, assignment of tax and transfer payments on the personal level ignores that the reported amount of taxes and transfers may be a function of the number of dependents supported by the taxpayer or transfer recipient. In Germany, for example, the replacement level of unemployment benefits depends on the existence of children in the family. Income taxation discriminates against the number of children, as well as the marital status of the taxpayer. Still, for lack of more adequate data, it seems tolerable to assign the entire payment amount to the transfer recipient or taxpayer, since it is his or her social and economic status that causes the tax or transfer to occur. This proceeding is indeed fairly unproblematic, provided that the socio-economic composition of households will not change over time, for example, as a consequence of changes in demographic parameters. If fertility decline reduces the average number of children per household, income taxes paid by a representative adult increase on average, as tax credits for children are reduced. However, one could not identify the exact variation of the income tax profile, as long as payments attributable to dependents are not isolated in the initial profile.

Fiscal data that are only classified by household in the CES are allocated by assuming that the total amount reported is distributed evenly among the relevant household members. Again, this assignment is likely to misrepresent the actual incidence of tax and transfer payments within the household. In particular, as data limitations require equal treatment of household members

---

in personal fiscal parameters had to be designed on the base of region-specific aggregate household data, neglecting actual variations in the age and gender distribution of payments.

[21] This example is drawn from CBO (1995, pp. 10n). Lampmann and Smeeding (1983), for example, have analyzed the intra-family incidence of transfer benefits.

irrespective of sex, net tax differentials by gender are measured inadequately. Nevertheless, an effort is made to disaggregate the relative micro profiles used for construction of the generational accounts by gender whenever possible.[22] Analyzing the resulting gender-specific generational accounts, one should be aware that the underlying incidence assumptions by gender are perhaps rather inaccurate.

In order to capture the generational impact of public sector budgets more precisely, the set of age, gender and regional profiles built from the CES is complemented with age related data provided by the Federal Statistical Office, social insurance statistics and other government institutions. If possible, the construction of the additional age profiles follows the same principles as that of the CES based profiles.

In a final step, the age profiles were corrected for outliers and smoothed through application of a three-year moving average where necessary. For most profiles, the variance in the data is especially large for the oldest age cohorts due to small sample sizes. Therefore, we aggregate all available observations for persons above age 90, and distribute them uniformly among the oldest old. Still, the age profiles derived for the very old should be approached with caution.[23] After these general remarks, we now turn to explain the data sources and the specific assumptions employed to construct the individual tax and government spending profiles underlying the generational accounts.

Taxes and Contributions

Labor income taxes are assigned to age cohorts using CES data. Unfortunately, the CES classifies wage and assessed personal income taxes *(veranlagte Einkommensteuer)* only by household.[24] Therefore, in order to assign labor income tax payments to individuals, it is necessary to proceed in two stages. In a first step, gross labor income, classified by individuals in the CES, is subjected to the income tax tariff valid in 1993 when the survey was made. The resulting fictive tax liabilities, which neglect the socio-economic characteristics of the household but design the progressivity of the German income tax system, are assigned to individuals by age. In a second step, aggregate

---

[22] Even in the case of household data, gender-specific differentials in relative tax and transfer profiles are observed. These reflect differentials in household composition by age. The number of single households increases particularly in old age, which renders gender differences more prominent for the elderly. In general, gender differences identified from household data, where observable, remain moderate.

[23] In face of the small population share of this age group in the base year, this does not seem to be a serious problem. However, considered the predicted increase in the number of oldest old, the exact distribution of net taxes among this population group will become more important.

[24] This is not the place for describing the German fiscal system in detail. Readers unfamiliar with the German tax and transfer system are referred to the useful surveys presented by Börsch-Supan (1994a) and Leibfritz et al. (1998).

wage and assessed income tax payments of the household, which reflect the tax relevant socio-economic status, are allocated to the individual household members according to their share in the fictive income tax liabilities of the entire household, derived in the first step.[25]

Flat-rate payroll contributions to the different branches of state-organized, pay-as-you-go financed social insurance – the public pension scheme, statutory health insurance and unemployment insurance - are allocated by age using a similar two-staged approach. First, fictive contributions on individual gross labor income are determined, taking into account the indirect regressivity of the contribution payments caused by contribution thresholds and the possibility to opt out for high income earners. Next, household payroll contributions as reported by the CES are assigned to household members employed with mandatory insurance, according to their fictive contribution share. Payroll contributions are assigned fully to workers. By assuming that incidence does not slide, at least partially, to employers, payroll taxes are regarded as an integral part of gross wages.

Payroll contributions to statutory accident insurance and nursing care insurance, not surveyed by the CES,[26] are allocated parallel to the payroll contributions to health insurance, in view of the fact that they are determined under analogous legal conditions. Contributions of pensioners to the statutory health and nursing care schemes, which are strictly proportional to pension income, are assigned by age with the relative age distribution of pension benefits (discussed below).

Incidence of capital income taxes, defined as the taxes on private capital income, the corporate tax *(Körperschaftsteuer)* and the trade tax on income *(Gewerbeertragsteuer)*, is supposed to fall on private individuals according to their annual revenue from private wealth, as reported by the CES, which consists of revenue from interest and dividends, as well as rental and leasing income. To construct the capital income profile, the surveyed household data on wealth income are distributed evenly among the adult members of each household not classified as dependent children. As capital income tax burdens are measured indirectly, no attempt is made to design the progressivity of capital taxation in Germany through the income tax system.[27]

The incidence assumption regarding capital income taxation is debatable for several reasons. First, in small open economies, international mobility of capital could shift the fiscal burden induced by capital income taxa-

---

[25] The use of the income tax payment to construct the *labor* income tax profile could lead to distortions, as the income tax includes taxes on capital. However the bias, mainly occurring in older age groups, is likely to be small.

[26] The nursing care insurance was not introduced before 1995.

[27] As Germany uses the full imputation system, corporate and personal income taxation are fully integrated. Therefore, the tax rate on distributed corporate profits (dividends) equals the marginal rate on personal income [Fehr (1999, p. 21)].

tion from owners of capital to suppliers of labor, at least partially. In fact, this argument has been used in some generational accounting studies, like Auerbach et al. (1997), to justify the allocation of capital income taxes according to wage income over the life cycle. However, in face of evidence on the considerable wage rigidities prevailing on the German labor market, it might be justified to assume that corporate income taxes are ultimately borne by the capital owners [Turner et al. (1993)].

Secondly, as argued by Auerbach et al. (1991), investment incentives could lead to redistribution between the owners of different assets. For example, if accelerated depreciation is allowed, the returns on new investment increase. The relative tax advantage of new capital capitalizes on perfect capital markets. As a consequence, the market value of new capital tends to increase,[28] while owners of existing capital experience a loss which constitutes a fiscal burden [Auerbach and Kotlikoff (1987, chapter 9)]. Put differently, in the presence of investment incentives, the effective marginal tax rate on (new) capital differs from the observed average tax rate on (old) capital. Devaluation of old relative to new capital causes intergenerational redistribution. A one-time tax is imposed on older living cohorts who own the existing capital stock. On the other hand, younger and future generations who are going to invest, or can buy the existing capital stock from the old at reduced cost, are better off.

Nevertheless, we do not make an effort to assign the potential fiscal burden from capital devaluation due to tax incentives to living generations. Empirical evidence (which is scarce) suggests that investment incentives do not affect the market value of the existing capital stock in Germany too seriously.[29] In fact, although investment incentives have been greatly increased in the course of German unification, in order to promote economic growth in the East German states, it seems unlikely that the West German capital stock has depreciated [Deutsche Bundesbank (1995)]. More importantly, a change in the market value of capital, despite being induced by fiscal policy, can be interpreted as an income transfer within the private sector. As generational accounting is a static concept, it seems inconsistent to incorporate macroeconomic repercussions only in this specific context. In any case, devaluation of the private capital stock does not generate a payment stream between the personal and private sector that would enter the intertemporal budget constraint of the public sector.

As more specific data is lacking, the relative age profile of capital income is also used to assign some minor taxes levied on the ownership or acquisition

---

[28] This is known as the taxation paradox [Sinn (1987, p. 145)]. Accelerated depreciation can increase the market value of (new) capital, because it shifts tax burdens into the − more heavily discounted − future.

[29] The generational accounts for Germany computed by Gokhale et al. (1995) assign devaluation of old capital as a one-time tax to living generations. They make use of estimates on effective capital tax rates taken from Leibfritz (1993), which imply that devaluation equals 18 percent of western German physical capital.

of capital, like the private wealth tax or the property tax.[30] Furthermore, the profile is applied to allocate seignorage, i.e. the private fiscal burden associated with the creation of money by the central bank. The expansion of the monetary base increases the opportunity costs of holding money balances (the nominal rate of return on other assets). Therefore, it reduces the value of real balances for agents who have to acquire the additional money [Wagner (1992)]. This inflation 'tax' on private real balances extends the expenditure opportunities of the government, since the printed value of the extra money exceeds its real value. Accordingly, although generational accounts are expressed in real terms, the corresponding fiscal burden must be distributed among age groups. By assigning seigniorage according to capital income, it is supposed that private holdings of money balances are closely related to age-specific private wealth.

Indirect tax payments are not surveyed in the CES, but can be inferred from the comprehensive data set on household consumption. The turnover tax *(Umsatzsteuer)*, also referred to as value-added tax, is assigned to all adult household members (aged 18 or above), with an equal share of taxable aggregate household consumption. This procedure differs from previous retrievals of turnover tax profiles for Germany, which distributed a fraction of the indirect tax burden among infant household members, by assigning speculative consumption weights to dependent children.[31] In accord with our standard incidence assumption, we prefer to assume that indirect taxes are borne by those paying the taxes, which excludes that the indirect tax burden would slide from parents to their offspring (who pay the tax by means of an intra-familiar transfer). Using the terminology of population economics, this approach treats children as a consumption good whose quality, which is related to their commodity consumption, enters the parents' utility function, but is a substitute for parents' own consumption of commodities [Razin and Sadka (1995, p. 14)]. Adopting this perspective, both the level and the relative age distribution of consumption do not necessarily vary in line with fertility. Therefore, it is also justified to assume that the initial value-added tax profile stays unchanged when the average number of children per household falls in the course of the demographic transition.

To assign turnover tax payments, two separate age profiles are used, distinguishing between the acquisition of goods that are subject to the general tax rate (16 percent in 1996), and the consumption of commodities taxed at the reduced rate of seven percent. The reduced tax rate is mainly levied on goods satisfying daily needs, whose share in total purchases varies with

---

[30] This supposes that the age distribution of taxed asset holdings is identical to the age distribution of capital revenue. This incidence assumption might be problematic regarding taxation on conveyance of assets, like inheritance taxation.

[31] The relative age profiles for value-added taxes used in most German generational accounting studies to date weigh the consumption of agents younger than 18 with a factor 0.7.

age. Therefore, the average tax rate levied on consumption depends on age as well, which necessitates disaggregation of aggregate consumption spending according to the differential tax treatment. In fact, the tax-rate specific relative age patterns of value-added tax burdens retrieved from the CES are clearly distinct.

The assignment of other indirect taxes to specific age cohorts follows the principles developed for the turnover tax payments. Tax burdens are treated as proportional to the amount of aggregate household transactions subject to the respective tax, and distributed evenly among all adult household members. In this way, we have derived specific age profiles for excise duties on stimulants (mainly on alcohol and tobacco), the duty on gasoline and mineral oil, the insurance tax and the vehicle tax. Several petty taxes, whose relative age distribution cannot be satisfactorily estimated from the CES data, are assigned as a lump sum among all age cohorts.[32]

Transfer Receipts and Government Spending

Constructing relative age profiles for pension benefits, the profound age related statistics provided by the Social Security institutions are convenient [VDR (1996)]. The data set reports the absolute number of pension cases by age as well as the average tax payments per pension case. To derive the missing average pension payment per agent, it is sufficient to relate the cohort-specific total of pension cases to the corresponding cohort size. Combining the resulting pension frequency in a given age cohort with the average pension amount yields the required age-specific per capita benefit. Pension profiles are derived separately for old-age pensions, survivors pensions and orphan pensions.

The accuracy of the pension data allows to design maturation effects, which are likely to change the relative age distribution of pension receipts for future pensioner cohorts. Inspecting the initial cross-section, it seems unlikely that it could actually represent a life cycle profile of pension receipts: both average pension receipts and the fraction of pension cases vary substantially across present pensioner cohorts, reflecting past differences in working careers. In particular, the average pension receipts of the oldest-old are substantially lower than those of younger retirees. Therefore, assuming that the original cross sectional age pattern of pensions stays constant in the future, as would be the standard procedure, implies that pension receipts decline in the course of the pension career.

In order to avoid this implausible outcome, it is necessary to specify the matrix of future relative pension profiles explicitly.[33] This requires differ-

---

[32] Since aggregate revenue from these taxes amounts to less than one percent of total tax revenue, the possible error is negligible.

[33] A similar treatment of maturation effects within a generational accounting framework is proposed by Bonin et al. (2001).

entiating between old-age pensions and survivors pensions. With respect to old-age pensions, we assume that average pension receipts in the initial cross section, for each cohort older than standard retirement age 65 in the base year, remain constant over the remaining life cycle (apart from productivity growth). For younger base year cohorts and all future generations, the original cross-sectional relative age profile upon legal retirement age is applied. From age 65 on, at which *per capita* old-age pensions irrespective of gender is at or close to the maximum at present, the pension amount is held fixed unchanged until death.[34]

As far as survivors pensions are concerned, the relative age distribution of benefits in the cross section is maintained upon reaching the maximum close to age 80. Until this age, the age-related increase in the population share of beneficiaries clearly dominates the variations in the average benefit per widow or widower. For all cohorts aged 80 or younger in the base year, the survivors pension is assumed to stay constant from age 80 on. The initial cross-sectional pension receipt is maintained over the remaining life cycle of all older base year cohorts.

How maturation of the pension system, according to our projections, affects the relative age profile of pension benefits, is illustrated by Fig. 5.2. It compares, for women resident in the West German states, the 1996 cross section of old-age and survivors pensions to the age profile assigned to the 1996 birth cohort, which equals the long-term cross section.[35] As is evident from Fig. 5.2, mechanistic uprating of the original cross section would underestimate the pensions actually received by younger women. In the base year cross section, decline in average old-age pensions begins to offset the rising frequency of widows pensions from age 75 on and even leads to a relative decline in average pensions for the oldest-old cohorts. In contrast, the mature pension profile continues to rise until age 80, before stabilizing about 20 percent above the pension level in the cross section. The implicit increment in average pensions due to maturation effects is by no means negligible, considered the future increase in the absolute of oldest-old.

In addition to maturation effects, a realistic projection of pension benefits in Germany needs to take into account the impact of the 1992 Pension Reform Act on cohorts not yet retired. The reform will progressively reduce incentives for early retirement over the period from 2000 to 2005 [Schmähl (1992)]. Designing what might be the impact of the reform on pension spending, we follow Boll et al. (1994) who assume that retirement participation rates grad-

---

[34] The *average* old-age pension amount (per pension case) is markedly higher for base year cohorts in early retirement, which seems to suggest that the pension level could increase even further. However, this phenomenon is mainly attributable to self-selection among early retirees.

[35] The example refers to women, since maturation effects are less marked for men. As the maturation process in the East German states is overshadowed by regional convergence, Fig. 5.2 reports West German data only.

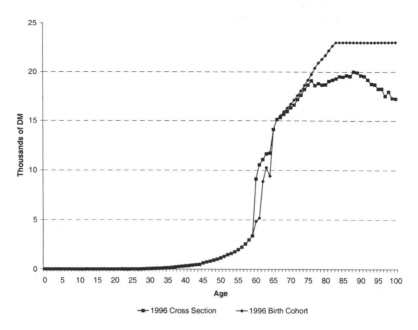

Fig. 5.2. Projection of Maturation Effects in the German Pension System. Average Old-Age and Widow's Pension of West German Females. Payments of 1996 birth cohort, corrected for economic growth.

ually fall in the age bracket from 60 to 65 when the reform comes into effect.[36] The corresponding reduction in average pensions explains why the long-term pension profile displayed in Fig. 5.2 ranges below the original cross section before age 65. We furthermore assume that the projected increase in average labor force participation of older working-age cohorts does not affect the per capita pension receipts after reaching standard retirement age. This requires that the additional pension loss of early retirees due to the 1992 pension reform compensates the rising fraction of retirees with additional service years.

Similar to pension benefits provided by statutory pension insurance, the future development of the pension claims by civil servants, financed from general tax revenue, requires explicit design.[37] Retrieving both the age-specific pension per civil servant and the cohort share of civil servants from the CES

---

[36] To be specific, we assume that early retirement decreases by 28, 30 and 12 percent for men aged 60, 61 and 62 to 64, respectively, and by 47, 51, 20, 12 and 20 percent, respectively, for women aged 60 to 64. Payroll contributions in these age groups rise accordingly. The adjustment parameters are based on estimates on the labor supply distortions caused by the current incentives for early retirement, which are reported by Börsch-Supan (1991).

[37] Since generational accounts refer to representative agents, the pensions of civil servants need to be included. On average, each agent has a certain chance to become a civil servant, and thereby to be a recipient of state pensions.

data, one can observe that the latter varies significantly, not only among current retirees, but also throughout the working-age population. The changing age pattern of this status variable is going to affect the prospective relative age distribution of transfer receipts. To give an example, the fraction of civil servants among older women (and hence the average state pension per capita) is extremely low at present. However, the amount of state pensions per woman is going to rise considerably, as soon as younger female generations, in which the share of civil servants is higher, start entering retirement. The upswing of state pensions per capita will be even more significant in the East German states: shortly after unification, hardly any civil servant had reached retirement in the base year. Moreover, the civil service machinery was still in the process of formation.[38]

Projecting the development of state pension receipts, we discriminate among base year cohorts according to age. First, parallel to pay-as-you-go pensions, the initial per capita state pension is maintained upon the death of all cohorts already in retirement, only accounting for the growing amount of survivors pensions. Secondly, for generations younger than standard retirement age but older than 45, the initial cross- sectional state pensions is adjusted for prospective variations in the cohort share of civil servants, set constant over the remaining working career.[39] Again, the per capita pension reached at standard pension age is held unchanged during retirement. Finally, in accordance with status quo practice of generational accounting, it is assumed that government policy regarding civil servants will not change for all cohorts younger than 45. Accordingly, they face the same civil servant career as the present 45 year-old. With respect to the East German states, we suppose that the civil service is gradually built up from the bottom and eventually converges on the West German structure.

As for the remaining relative age profiles employed to assign government spending, the standard status quo rule is applied, which maintains the original cross-sectional age pattern indefinitely. The allocation of statutory health care benefits by age relies on highly dependable health insurance administration data, which are used for compensating risk differentials caused by age structure variations between competing health insurers.[40] Although health insurance benefits in Germany are mainly received in kind by individuals,

---

[38] According to the CES data, the cohort share of civil servants in the East German states exhibits a characteristic downward slope throughout all working- age cohorts, irrespective of gender.

[39] This *ad hoc* assumption reflects certain age ceilings for entering the civil service set by legislation. Our approach claims that changes in the population share of civil servants among agents older than 45 are only due to cohort effects, reflecting past policy changes. In the 1970's the number of civil servants expanded rapidly, while measures to reduce state personnel were taken later on.

[40] These data are published in BMA (1996a). Our profile builds on the relative age pattern of health benefits and excludes disability pensions administered by statutory health insurance. This profile is employed also to project health support

they should be included equivalent to a (monetary) transfer in the generational accounts. In the present static context, the fact that insurers clear the balances for medical treatment on behalf of the insurant is largely an administrative formality of little economic relevance.[41]

Data regarding the age pattern of transfers received from the newly introduced statutory nursing care insurance, which had not come into full effect until 1997, is extremely scarce yet. For lack of more reliable data, we assume that nursery care spending is proportional to the population share of transfer recipients.[42] Since the introduction of statutory nursery care insurance is directed at partially substituting certain social welfare benefits providing for long-term care, we suppose that the distribution of nursery spending by age is valid also for this type of social welfare transfers.

As for the construction of the remaining age profiles of personal transfer receipts, we rely on CES data. Relative profiles assigning unemployment insurance benefits, accident insurance benefits, permanent social welfare assistance *(Sozialhilfe zum Lebensunterhalt)*, maternity benefits (only received by females) and education support *(BAföG)* to age cohorts are designed on the base of the respective average transfer receipts, classified by individuals in the CES.

Additional age profiles regarding public housing support *(Wohngeld)*, welfare benefits cushioning temporary burdens in life *(Sozialhilfe in besonderen Lebenslagen)*, and family allowances were constructed on the base of household data. Housing support benefits received by the household are distributed evenly among all adult household members. For the two other transfer categories, we suspend our general assumption that the transfer recipient is also the beneficiary. Whereas temporary social welfare payments are assigned with an equal share to all household members, family allowances are allocated to those household members who are classified as dependent children. This design is in order, as in either case the presence of children in the household is the main determinant of the payment.[43] The assumption that the initial relative age pattern of transfers, which reflects the past evolution of fertility, stays

---

payments to civil servants, taking into account the predicted change in the age composition of the civil service.

[41] Of course, the procedure changes the principle-agent relationship on the insurance market. However, the assessment of the resulting welfare changes would go beyond the analytical scope of generational accounting.

[42] This figure is derived from the absolute number of beneficiaries, published by the BMA (1996b). While preliminary, the age profile is consistent with projections of the age distribution of nursing care benefits predating the introduction of the insurance scheme published by BMA (1991).

[43] This is obvious for family allowances, but holds also for temporary welfare support. As inspection of the relative age profile reveals, benefits are concentrated in infant age. Since the number of households receiving temporary social welfare payments is small, we cannot distinguish region-specific relative profiles.

constant in the course the demographic transition would be questionable, if these mainly child-related transfers were assigned to the formal recipient.

Projecting net government expenditure, it is taken into account that public youth services and education, though not included in the generational accounts representing in-kind benefits, are dependent on age. Expenditure on education is forecasted by assuming that spending is proportional to the fraction of an age cohort enrolled in the educational system. Making use of school enrolment statistics from the Ministry of Education [BBF (1998)], it is possible to distinguish relative age profiles for primary education and lower-secondary schools, secondary schools, vocational schools and universities. Spending on pre-school education is distributed according to kindergarten attendance, as surveyed in the microcensus.

Finally, youth services are projected in accordance with participation rates in youth service programs, derived from age-related data on the absolute number of beneficiaries.[44] Remaining net government purchases are projected by allocating base year aggregate spending lump sum to all age cohorts.

5.2.3 Aggregate Budget and Absolute Net Tax Payments

To translate the cohort structure of government revenue and spending into meaningful values of average payments by age, the relative micro data profiles discussed above need to be re-evaluated in order to assure that aggregated per capita tax and transfer payments by age are consistent with the corresponding budget aggregates. As the aim of generational accounting is to measure generational redistribution through public sector budgets comprehensively, the budget used to re-evaluate the relative fiscal profiles considers all federal levels of government activity, including social insurance schemes and off-budget authorities. In particular, the budgets of several debt funds created in the course of German unification are taken into account, as well as those of publicly owned companies.

The overall budget of the public sector underlying the generational accounts, displayed in Table 5.4, rests on National Accounts tables, supplemented with data from annual financial reports by government authorities. In principle, one could benchmark the distinct relative fiscal profiles for the East and West German states against the united public sector budget on display in Table 5.4, using equation (2.13). However, with the East German economy being in a process of rapid transformation, the tax and transfer level of East Germans relative to Westerners is likely to have changed considerably even in the short period since the CES was made in year 1992. Moreover,

---

[44] The data employed are reported by the Statistisches Bundesamt (1997a), tables 19.16 (kindergarten) and 19.15.1 (youth services). Like data on education enrolment, they are not region-specific. Considered that assimilation of East Germans is likely to affect younger cohorts first, it seems tolerable to work with uniform education and youth support profiles.

Table 5.4. The Structure of the German Public Sector Budget 1996

Revenue	Billions of DM	Percent of Total	Expenditure	Billions of DM	Percent of Total
Taxes			Social Insurance		
Labor Income	315.6	19.3	Social Security[a]	446.0	27.3
Capital Income	108.6	6.6	Statutory Health[a]	247.0	15.1
Seignorage	7.0	0.4	Nursery Care	20.4	1.2
Turnover[b]	243.8	14.9	Unemployment	105.4	6.4
Excise	33.6	2.1	Accident	17.9	1.1
Gasoline	68.3	4.2	Maternity Assistance	7.0	0.4
Insurance	14.3	0.9	Child Allowances	37.3	2.3
Vehicle	13.7	0.8	Social Welfare	50.0	3.1
Other	2.0	0.1	Housing Support	6.6	0.4
Contributions			Education Support	3.1	0.2
Social Security	299.3	18.3	Youth Services	25.8	1.6
Statutory Health	234.6	14.3	Education[c]	118.9	7.3
Nursery Care	22.6	1.4	Government Purchases[d]	419.7	25.7
Unemployment	88.7	5.4			
Accident	19.8	1.2			
Deficit[e]	163.5	10.0	Interest Payments	130.5	8.0
Total	1635.5	100.0	Total	1635.5	100.0

[a] Includes transfers to civil servants.
[b] Includes duty.
[c] Net of investment.
[d] Non age-specific spending.
[e] Includes provision for pension of civil servants.
Source: Author's calculations based on BMA (1997), BMF (1997), Statistisches Bundesamt (1997a,b) and BLK (1997)

some of the relative profiles, for example regarding health spending, merely cover the relative frequency of services, rather than the respective spending levels in East and West Germany. Therefore, it is necessary to adjust the region-specific relative payment profiles separately, wherever identification of separate East and West German budget aggregates is still possible.[45]

Some of the figures reported in Table 5.4 are not immediately comparable with the fiscal statistics from which they were originally drawn. In order to meet the requirements of generational accounting, certain budget variables

---

[45] The separate budgets compiled for East and West Germany are documented in the Appendix C.

are balanced or consolidated. Boll (1994, chapter 4) describes the procedure of how to arrive at the revenue and spending aggregates behind the generational accounts for Germany in detail. Therefore, we can contain ourselves to highlight some peculiarities that seem of interest for the less specialized reader.

On the revenue side of the budget, differentiation between taxation on labor and capital income is ambiguous, since assessment of direct taxes in Germany is based on the amount of personal income and not on the sources of income [Deutsche Bundesbank (1996, p. 40)]. In order to estimate the level of revenue from the assessed income tax and the trade tax on income that actually represents a tax on labor, we claim that the share of labor income in the tax base is equal to the share of aggregate labor income (including imputed entrepreneurial wages) in national income, which amounted to 83.8 percent in 1996. Although this approximation adds an uncertainty to the analysis, it seems superior to the procedure of Boll (1996) who restricts the aggregate tax burden on labor income to the wage tax. Note that corporate taxes levied on retained earnings are regarded as taxes on capital.

Regarding payroll contributions to statutory social insurance schemes, this study does not follow the established practice in German generational accounting to correct social insurance balances for inter-administrative payments. While inclusion of payment flows between different institutions of government does not affect the overall generational accounts, it is prerequisite to state the fiscal burdens or benefits from individual taxes or transfers correctly. For an example, consider pensioners' contributions to statutory health insurance, which are conventionally eliminated from the budget used for generational accounting. As a consequence, the fiscal burden imposed by the public health system is underreported. Since transfer benefits from the public pension scheme are underreported by the same amount, the net tax payment to the public sector is measured correctly by the generational accounts. However, the net tax payment to the public pension scheme alone is exaggerated.

For sake of interpretative clarity, it appears preferable to avoid clearing the social insurance budgets from inter-governmental payments that do not influence intergenerational redistribution. This approach inflates the public sector budget, because various payments between the highly interrelated social insurance institutions appear twice – as an expenditure of one social insurance, and as a revenue of another. Referring to our example, pensioners' contributions to statutory health insurance increase both the level of aggregate pension spending and the contribution revenue accounted for in the public health budget.

As for Social Security and health care spending, expenditure aggregates reported in Table 5.4 include transfer payments to civil servants. These payments are assigned lump sum as part of government purchases in previous generational accounting studies for Germany. This approach seems inadequate for two reasons. First, as mentioned above, it neglects the transfer character of old-age income and health care support payments to civil servants, which do not involve a service in return.[46] More importantly, even if one would be ready to assume that income support payments to civil servants actually represent personnel spending of the public sector (and thereby government consumption), it is unsatisfactory to design them as independent of age. Doing so would actually miss a major pressure on future public budgets in Germany.[47]

Government purchases as reported in Table 5.4 include public spending that a) supposedly does not constitute a transfer to private households and b) cannot be assigned reliably to specific age groups. In particular, in addition to what is literally government consumption of goods and services (including administrative costs of the social insurance schemes), government purchases cover public subsidies[48] and public net investment. Characterization of government investment as a government purchase that intertemporally requires financing from net tax revenue, is controversial. This approach denies that accumulation of tangible assets can create a return, which may pay off the initial investment. In the extreme, the present value of aggregate returns would just equal the cost of investment. Our construction of government purchases opts for the opposite extreme, assuming that public investment in infrastructure does not generate a *monetary* return that could be used to redeem intertemporal liabilities of the public sector. In fact, infrastructure is mainly provided free of charge in Germany.[49] Some sensitivity test will be performed in the course of our analysis, which attempts to bracket what would be the actual return on public investment.

As displayed in Table 5.4, government purchases are balanced against public revenue from tangible assets, which for a baseline, in accordance with our theoretical considerations regarding the estimation of government wealth, are predicted to develop in proportion to aggregate population size. To arrive at the base year amount of net government purchases in the sense of generational accounting, one has to add government spending on youth services and various education institutions (net of investment), which are age-specific, but not accounted for as a personal transfer due to the rigid in-cash definition of net taxes favored in this study.

While returns on government assets are considered as government revenue in the calculations (reducing the net worth of government purchases), financial liabilities of the government are approximated by their base year

---

[46] This is the basic criterion defining public transfers. Cf. Andel (1998, p. 26).

[47] Cf. Deutsche Bundesbank (1998b) and Färber (1997).

[48] Public subsidies represent a government transfer to the business sector, which does not slide to private agents by assumption.

[49] This argument is borrowed from Auerbach et al (1994) who also allocate public investment as a government purchase.

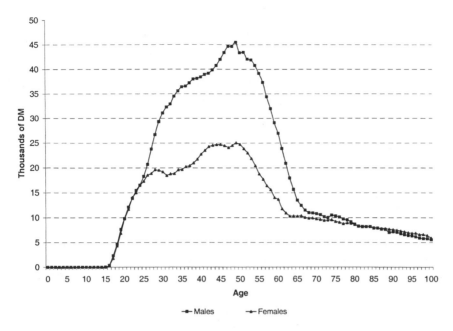

Fig. 5.3. Age-specific tax payments. Cross section of year 1996

nominal value, which amounted to DM 1,993 billion at the beginning of the base year, or 56.6 percent of the 1996 GDP (DM 3,524 billion).[50] Therefore, the corresponding flow of interest payments does not enter the long-term fiscal constraint to the government as an expenditure. The alternative approach to deduct the market value of financial assets by indefinite aggregation of base year interest payments, will be tested in the sensitivity analysis.

Benchmarking the relative tax and transfer profiles against the base year budget and aggregating all individual taxes respectively transfers, reveals the absolute fiscal burdens or benefits of representative agents as a function of age. The corresponding age pattern of absolute net tax burdens is fundamental for the sensitivity of public sector budgets to demographic influences. Figure 5.3 displays the absolute age profile of tax payments according to the base year cross section. Irrespective of gender, taxes are concentrated in working age. Agents do not start paying taxes before age 17, as indirect taxes are assigned to their parents. Since labor income taxes and payroll contributions, in Germany, are the main of source of revenue for the public sector (they ac-

---

[50] Cf. Deutsche Bundesbank (1999b, p. 55*). One has to be careful not to confuse the periodicity of the data. Revenue and expenditure flows reported in Table 5.4 occurred in the course of 1996. They added to the stock of financial liabilities at the beginning of the year. It is wrong to start from the liabilities measured at the end of the base year, as several analysts, for example Bonin et al. (1999), have done.

counted for 59.9 percent of total revenue in 1996) the aggregate tax profile is dominated by the life cycle distribution of average wage income. Accordingly, average tax payments of men rise continuously after entering the labor force, reflecting gains in productivity. After reaching a peak around age 50, male per capita tax payments decline sharply upon standard retirement age, as a consequence of rising unemployment and progressive exit from the labor force to enter early retirement.

Average tax payments of women start lagging behind those of men at age 25 in the consequence of family formation. Both average labor force participation rates and average income of women stay smaller than men's for the remainder of the working career, resulting in about 50 percent lower average tax payments. Figure 5.3 also shows that, in the base year cross section, women retire earlier than men, because of the lower standard retirement age. Women's absolute tax payments turn to the pattern of moderate tax burdens characteristic for pensioner cohorts about five years earlier than men's. In retirement, the absolute tax burden is governed by indirect tax payments, whose share in government revenue is considerably lower (22.1 percent) than that of taxes on labor. In the course of retirement, absolute tax payments moderately decline with age, as the propensity to consume decreases. Unlike in working age, the absolute tax burdens in retirement do not differ greatly by sex, since consumption is spread more evenly among genders than income.

The 1996 cross section of age-specific absolute transfer receipts, displayed in Fig. 5.4, is dominated by pension and statutory health care benefits. In the base year, the share of these two transfer payments in the entire transfer expenditure amounted to 47.7 and 26.4 percent, respectively. Until age 55, the absolute transfer pattern mainly reflects the relative age distribution of health care benefits. Therefore, transfers to the youngest age groups and to women of child-bearing age are relatively high. Besides, gender-specific differences in transfer receipts are negligible. From age 55 on, pension benefits become the most important determinant of average transfer receipts. For both sexes, the increment in transfer benefits is especially marked at age 60. This suggests that the transfer estimates are fairly consistent with the ongoing trend toward early retirement in Germany, which had lowered the mean retirement age to 59,7 years in 1992 [Börsch-Supan (1998a)].

During retirement, the average transfer receipts of males and females differ substantially. Government transfers to women rise continuously upon age 90. The increase in overall benefits is more pronounced than the increment in old-age pensions caused by survivors pensions, due to rising health and nursery care benefits. For the oldest old, average transfer receipts decline, as rising costs of morbidity do not compensate the reduction in average pensions in the initial cross section. Since statutory pension insurance in Germany is characterized by strong tax-benefit linkage, (pension) transfers received by men exceed those of women, mirroring differentials in labor force participation. For men, the increment in average transfer benefits after reach-

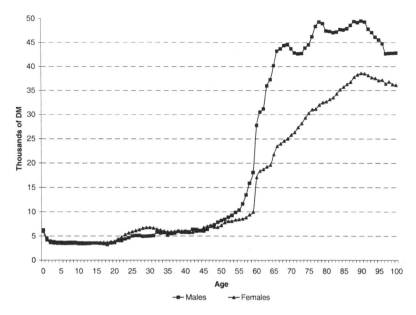

Fig. 5.4. Age-specific transfer receipts. Cross section of year 1996

ing standard retirement age 65 is less significant than for women. It largely reflects variations in average health and nursery care benefits, as survivors pensions are small for men.[51]

Subtracting the average transfer income from the tax payments leads to the age-specific net tax burden of a representative agent, shown in Fig. 5.5. The reported net tax payments indicate to what extent base year tax and transfer policy affected the annual budget constraint of different age groups. In 1996, agents aged 18 to 60 were net contributors to the public coffers irrespective of gender. Youth cohorts and pensioners in contrast, benefited from the public tax and transfer system.

The age pattern of net tax payments displayed in Fig. 5.5 highlights the relevance of – implicit and explicit – generational contracts, by which consumption possibilities are transferred across cohorts. Fiscal policy in general, and the pay-as-you-go financed social insurance system in particular, impose net tax burdens on working-age cohorts, in order to supplement income of generations who do not dispose of (labor) earnings on their own. However, the periodical and partial perspective on the age-specific net tax burdens does not allow to draw any detailed conclusions regarding the fairness of

---

[51] The irritating swings of average male transfers receipts are caused by variations in the population share of civil servants, who are less frequent in cohorts adolescent during World War II. The irregularities vanish when the civil servant pensions mature in the course of the projection.

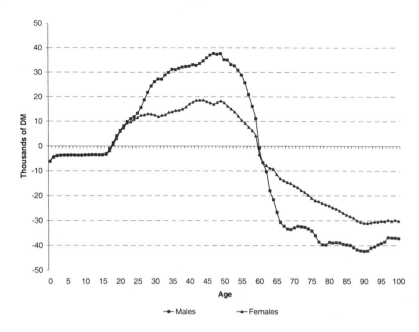

Fig. 5.5. Age-specific net tax payments. Cross section of year 1996

generational contracts. While Fig. 5.5 suggests that net tax payments during working life are unlikely to be compensated by transfers received, one has to remain aware that a fraction of net tax revenue is used to finance non-transfer government spending.

Inspecting Fig. 5.5, there seems to be little evidence for inter-gender redistribution in Germany. The relative net transfer position of women in old-age corresponds well to their relative net tax position during working life. Only for the oldest old, inter-gender redistribution through social insurance schemes, which partly insure wives along with their husbands, seems evident. Again, *prima facie* conclusions drawn from the cross-sectional observations could be misleading. An adequate analysis of inter-gender redistribution requires considering the impacts of mortality and lifetime income differentials, which is only possible adopting the life-cycle perspective of generational accounting.

Public income transfers received in young age before entering into the labor force are rather low, ranging around DM 3,500 annually. However, government spending on youth cohorts is considerably higher, considering the age distribution of net government purchases in the base year, as displayed in Fig. 5.6.[52] In the maximum, public provision of education and youth services amounts to more than DM 13,000 per capita close to age 15 when a major

---

[52] Figure 5.6 does not report separate profiles for males and females, as gender differentials are negligible.

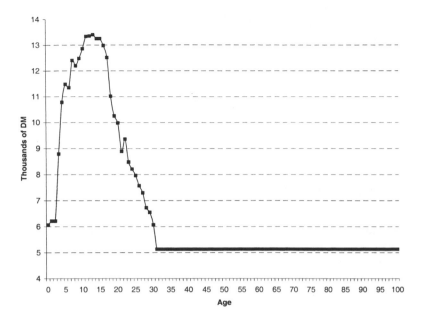

Fig. 5.6. Age-specific net government purchases. Cross section of year 1996

fraction of adolescents is enrolled in secondary education. While education at university level is more costly per student, the population share of those enrolled in education declines, and so does absolute government spending per capita. For age groups older than 30, our calculations do not consider age-related government purchases. Net government spending stays constant at an amount of DM 5,100 irrespective of age.

5.2.4 The Future Economic Environment

Projecting aggregate government net tax revenue and net purchases on the base of the cross sections displayed in Fig. 5.5 and Fig. 5.6 requires a specification of the long-term economic and fiscal policy environment. For our base case calculations, we follow the status quo principle whenever adequate at all. The general rule is to assume that, for all age groups, the base year amount of revenue and spending grows in line with productivity growth, supposed constant. Selecting among plausible growth rates, we have tried to extend the past long-term trend of productivity growth in (West) Germany, as illustrated in Table 5.5.

Comparing the average productivity gain over different periods, it is evident that real productivity growth in per capita terms has continuously slowed down during the past four decades. Predicting the future growth trend, it appears sensible to rely on the more recent productivity development. Therefore, for a benchmark per capita growth is set to a rate of

Table 5.5. Productivity Growth and Interest Rates in West Germany

	Average of Period		
	1960–1997	1970–1997	1980–1997
Real GDP Growth per capita			
– of Population	2.3 %	1.8 %	1.4 %
– of Working Population	2.4 %	1.7 %	1.4 %
Real Interest Rate[a]	3.9 %	3.9 %	4.3 %

[a] Average interest rate on government bonds net of consumer price inflation.
Source: Author's calculations based on SVR (1998), Tabb. 16*, 21* and 42*

1.5 percent per annum, which approximates the average growth rate of the period from 1980 to 1997. For sensitivity tests, it seems reasonable to construct generational accounts using one and two percent growth rates. The former scenario supposes that the downward trend of productivity growth rates would continue, while the latter designs a return to the more favorable growth perspectives of earlier decades.

Besides the corrections of relative profiles concerning the development of pay-as-you-go and civil servant pensions, discussed in section 5.2.2, there are two exceptions to our general rule of uniform growth uprating of absolute tax and spending profiles. The first involves several fiscal policy amendments that had been legally enacted in the base period but not come into their full budgetary effect. Our generally conservative design of the fiscal status quo notwithstanding, enacted policy amendments require consideration, in order to describe current state of government tax and transfer policy properly. Wanting adequate data on the age-specific incidence of the policy measures, we assume that the predicted change in aggregate tax and transfers spreads evenly across all generations, so that the initial absolute payment profiles shift by a uniform proportion. In detail, the base case allows for

- the reduction of the so-called solidarity surcharge (*Solidaritätszuschlag*), a proportional surcharge on the personal labor and corporate tax liability, introduced in 1995 in order to finance the completion of the German unification. The rate of the solidarity surcharge was reduced from 7.5 to 5.5 percent by January 1998. The projections consider that from 1998 on, government revenue from the solidarity surcharge falls in line with the relative change in tax rates, i.e. by 26.7 percent.
- the increment in the normal rate of the turnover tax, from 15 to 16 percent in April 1998. Again, it is assumed that the corresponding change in the average turnover tax rate equals the relative change in aggregate revenue. The additional turnover tax revenue was earmarked to finance an increase in the central government subsidy to Social Security. However, this policy does not affect the overall public sector budget, because the expenditure

increase of the state budget balances the revenue increase of the social insurance budget. Adopting the comprehensive perspective of generational accounting, the value added tax increase merely entails a reduction in the state deficit.[53]

- the abolition of the property tax (*Vermögensteuer*), which had not been introduced in East Germany, in the West German states by January 1997. The aggregate capital tax payment of West German residents is reduced by the base year property tax yield, which was DM 7.5 billion.

- the 1997 changes in contribution rates to social insurance schemes. To be specific, the base year contribution rate to statutory pension insurance, which was 19.6 percent, was increased to 20.3 percent of the payroll. Furthermore, in the East German states, the average contribution rate to statutory health care rose by 0.4 percentage points to 13.9 percent. All affected revenue and expenditure aggregates of the interwoven branches of social insurance are adjusted according to the respective relative change in contribution rates.[54]

- the full establishment of statutory nursery care insurance, introduced with yet limited coverage in 1995. In July 1996, insurance benefits were expanded, while contribution rates were raised from 1.0 to 1.7 percent. We project the long-term revenue and expenditure level of the new social insurance branch starting from its balance in 1997, the year in which the introductory phase had been completed. Nursery care benefits partially replace social assistance payments complementing long-term care expenses. Therefore, we also project social welfare benefits of this type on the base of the 1997 budget, assuming that the sharp decline in aggregate spending observed between 1995 and 1997 was solely due to the introduction of nursery care insurance.

The second exception to uniform growth uprating of absolute fiscal profiles concerns the design of the ongoing economic catching-up process in East Germany. The severe real and monetary shock of German reunification instantly made a significant share of the East German capital stock obsolete, leading into a severe depression.[55] A decade after unification, the East German economy is still struggling for recovery. Despite extensive public direct investment in infrastructure and generous private investment subsidies, productivity and

---

[53] This changes if one constructs separate generational accounts for the pension system, as will be done on Chapter 8.

[54] Since the 1997 public sector budget is available - it actually will be used to test the base year sensitivity of the generational accounts - it would be possible to approximate the contribution rate effects by the actual change in social insurance aggregates between 1996 and 1997. However, the observed variation in aggregates also captures business cycle effects.

[55] A still essential economic analysis of German reunification is provided by Sinn and Sinn (1993).

the standard of living in the East German states only gradually converge to the Western levels.

Some stylized facts may serve to illustrate the persisting economic and social disparities in united Germany. In 1996, gross labor income per capita in the East German States amounted to only 73.6 percent of the Western level. At the same time, labor productivity had reached 59.4 percent of that in West Germany.[56] The wedge between wages and worker productivity fuelled extreme unemployment. According to estimates by Thimann (1996, p. 203), 28.4 percent of the work force were displaced on the East German labor market by the end of year 1995. The labor market disparities in united Germany show through the base year net tax payments of East and West German agents, displayed in Fig. 5.7, which differ substantially for cohorts of working age. In the initial cross section, per capita net tax payments by generations who contribute positively to the public coffers amount to less than one half of the Western level in the East. Furthermore, agents turn into net transfer recipients earlier, due to early retirement programs. In contrast, average net transfer receipts during retirement in the East exceed those in the West German states. With unification, social insurance schemes were immediately extended to East Germany. In the consequence, the average pension payments currently surpass the Western level, because of the high labor force participation rates, in particular of women prevalent in the East German command economy.

The design of the catching up process in the East German states, essential for a realistic projection of prospective government budgets, requires addressing two issues. First, how does regional convergence influence the development of individual age-specific tax and transfer payments? Secondly, what is the expected time of convergence, or put differently, the speed of convergence? Regarding the first issue, one would ideally design the East German recovery process as *cohort-specific*, as younger cohorts are likely to assimilate faster than older generations. However, for lack of adequate data, we adopt the standard cross-sectional perspective of generational accounting. During each year of the convergence process, supposed to start in 1998,[57] the initial East German tax and spending profiles are subjected to constant, *age-specific* growth that is set at a rate assuring equivalence of per capita payments in the East and West German states by the final year of the adjustment period. There is one exception here involving statutory pensions, where we adhere to the cohort perspective, as pension entitlement of current retirees is protected by property rights. Regarding future East German pensioner cohorts, it is assumed that their old-age pension amount at standard

---

[56] The last two figures are reported by Franz and Steiner (2000). Cf. Bonin and Zimmermann (2001) for a detailed analysis of the wage trends during the economic integration of East Germany.

[57] Between 1996 and 1998, East German recovery had basically come to a standstill. Cf. Buscher (1999).

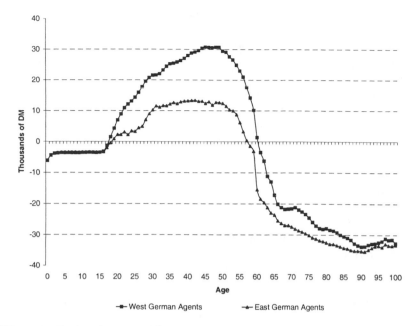

Fig. 5.7. Regional age-specific net tax payments. Cross section of year 1996

retirement age gradually adapts to the Western level, and remains constant upon death.

As for the second issue, projections regarding the speed of the East German adjustment process are extremely uncertain. Estimates regarding the duration of the convergence process range from less than a decade to several generations, although the latter position, based on the two percent convergence rule promoted by Barro and Sala-i-Martin (1991), seems overly pessimistic.[58] In fact, several factors are likely to accelerate the convergence process in united Germany. For example, physical investment in the East German states (including government investment in infrastructure) is rather high, as is human capital mobility [Burda and Funke (1995)]. In face of these alleviating factors, it is assumed in the projections that the East German states will catch-up to the West in the medium term, namely by the year 2010, which is consistent with macro simulations on regional convergence in united Germany conducted by Bröcker and Raffelhüschen (1997). Assessing the status quo generational accounts, one should be aware that this is by no means

---

[58] The two percent rule is based on econometric tests of a central result of endogenous growth theory, stating that productivity growth in undercapitalized areas is faster than in areas that are already rich of capital. Empirical evidence suggests that the speed of convergence does not exceed two percent per annum. Thimann (1996, pp. 34) provides a comprehensive survey of projections concerning the speed of recovery in East Germany.

a pessimistic forecast. After all, the adjustment requires that the labor productivity growth rate in East Germany exceeds that in the West by 3.6 percentage points. Note that, as soon as convergence is reached, the solidarity surcharge, introduced to alleviate the fiscal burdens of the transformation process, is eliminated.

Regional convergence also requires consideration in the projection of future GDP, necessary to construct the macroeconomic generational accounting indicators. As outlined in Chapter 4.6.2, it is convenient to assume that GDP will develop in line with annual productivity growth, corrected for prospective changes in the size of the labor force. As for the labor force, it is projected combining the base year profile of labor force participation by age in united Germany [Statistisches Bundesamt (1997a, Table 6.2)] with the forecasts of the demographic structure underlying the generational accounts. Designing regional convergence, the East German labor force is initially weighed with their reduced labor productivity relative to the West German work force. As the productivity gap vanishes in the course of the catching-up process, the labor force in East Germany gradually gets full weight.

In Germany, the assumption of constant labor force participation rates does not only fit the status quo character of the generational accounting analysis. It could be justified also for empirical reasons. Age-specific participation rates for men have actually declined over the past two decades. The ongoing increase in labor force participation of women, which so far has affected only younger female cohorts, will not necessarily offset this trend [Börsch-Supan (1998, p. 411)].

As generational accounting adopts a present value perspective, projected taxes and public spending (like national and personal income) need to be taken back to the base year using a pre-tax real discount rate. The appropriate discount rate to use is equivocal, because of the varying time structure and the uncertainty of the payments involved.[59] Suppose first that all prospective budget variables were free of risk and certain. Then, the ideal discount factor(s) would be approximated by the term-structure of real return on investment in risk-free assets, like indexed government bonds. However, an empirical realization of this concept would be a difficult task. It first demands that inflation secured government bonds do exist at all (which is not the case in Germany), and that they exist furthermore with a wide range of maturities.[60]

Matters turn out even more intricate considered that future payment flows are actually uncertain. Unexpected demographic or economic events might alter the prospective net tax burden. With uncertainty, the return on risk-free assets does not longer constitute a theoretically meaningful benchmark for

---

[59] The problems of appropriate discount rate choice for generational accounting are fundamental, and have been discussed extensively in the literature. Cf. in particular Havemann (1994), Auerbach et al (1994), CBO (1995) and Diamond (1996).

[60] This argument borrows from Auerbach and Kotlikoff (1999).

discounting. Instead, one has to add a premium for risk to the certain interest rate, which depends on the degree of individual risk aversion.[61] Moreover, as argued by Havemann (1994, p. 104), different risk-adjusted discount rates need to be employed for taxes, transfer payments and government spending, because the risk of these payments is likely to differ. If taxpayers are indeed aware of differences in uncertainty, they assign a rather high discount rate to uncertain future transfers, as they prefer the certain benefit over the uncertain one. By the same line of reasoning, they assign a rather low discount rate to uncertain future tax payments, to buy an insurance against potential fluctuations in taxes. Furthermore, different generations face different degrees of uncertainty regarding particular taxes or transfers.[62]

Unfortunately, very little is known empirically about the various risk adjustments that would be necessary to properly represent the present value of future net taxes. Therefore, generational accountants typically use a pragmatic approach to cope with uncertainty, selecting a uniform discount rate that ranges above the average rate of return on risk-free government bonds to incorporate the premium paid for risk, but below the return on private sector capital, which tends to be more volatile than public payments streams.[63]

Discounting future net taxes at a rate exceeding the interest rate on public borrowing affects the interpretation of the generational accounts. Due to the risk premium included in the discount factor, the future deficits resulting from projected tax revenue and spending levels appear to accumulate debt even faster than they would do in a projection under certainty. As a consequence, the generational accounts of generations whose taxes are raised to redeem intertemporal liabilities of the government, appear higher than under certainty, too. Accelerated discounting translates uncertainty into an implicit tax: Unsustainable time paths of fiscal policy actually do not only change the net tax burden of some cohorts. The resulting potential for tax increases also raises risk, which shows up as an additional burden in the generational accounts [CBO (1995, p. 42].[64]

---

[61] On a more general level, one might question this approach to design the impact of uncertainty. A more appropriate treatment of risk would require computation of shadow prices, i.e. direct adjustment of payment streams, rather than changing the rate of discount. Cf. Arrow and Lind (1970) and Layard and Glaister (1994, pp. 44n).

[62] For example, future pension benefits are considerably safer for current pensioners than for younger generations.

[63] This approach views risk from the perspective of government, which values secure receipts higher than uncertain future resources. As Diamond (1996, pp. 600n) points out, this might not be consistent with the utility-based perspective of the generational accounts. As argued before, agents may discount net tax burdens at a lower than the certain rate.

[64] If government policy improves intergenerational risk sharing, one may argue in favor of a discount rate lower than the risk-free rate. However, incorporation of such second-order effects does not seem really adequate in the context of

Selecting a base case discount rate for the German generational accounts, we follow the standard practice adding a risk premium to the secure real interest rate on government bonds. As was shown in Table 5.5, the long-term average of real interest on government bonds in Germany has been fairly stable, ranging about four percent. For discounting, a risk premium of 100 basis points is added, which leads to a constant social discount rate of five percent. While being arbitrary, the use of this discount rate has the practical advantage that it renders the present base case results comparable to those of other generational accounting studies, which frequently employ a central discount rate around five percent.

The fact that the discount rate is indefinite both theoretically and empirically calls for a sensitivity test. Therefore, we will also present results based on four and six percent discount rates. The six percent scenario assumes that risk aversion is even stronger than in the base case so that uncertainty imposes an even higher implicit tax. In contrast, using a four percent rate of discount which is close to the observed return on secure government bonds, eliminates the aspect of risk from the generational accounts.

This completes the description of the economic parameters and assumptions underlying our construction of the generational accounts for Germany. The following section applies the generational accounts to analyze the intertemporal sustainability of German public finances.

5.3 Generational Redistribution in Germany

5.3.1 Net Tax Burdens of Present Generations

To better understand intertemporal generational redistribution associated with the current state of public finances, it is instructive to investigate the generational accounts for current living generations first. Figure 5.8 displays the generation-specific accounts of representative agents, as well as the gender-specific accounts of male and female cohorts alive in 1996, given the status quo of fiscal policy and assuming constant mortality. Inspecting Fig. 5.8, one has to stay aware that generational accounts are not comparable across age groups, due to their forward looking construction, which neglects all net taxes paid prior to the base year. The accounts do reveal, however, *intra*-generational differences between the net tax burdens of fiscally distinct populations groups (like men and women).

Irrespective of gender, Fig. 5.8 displays a characteristic life cycle pattern of remaining lifetime net tax burdens. For a representative agent who is born in the year 1996, continuation of the initial tax and transfer levels entails a

---

generational accounting, which focuses on first-order redistribution due to fiscal policy (ignoring macroeconomic repercussions). Cf. Auerbach and Kotlikoff (1999, pp. 39n) for an extended treatment of this argument.

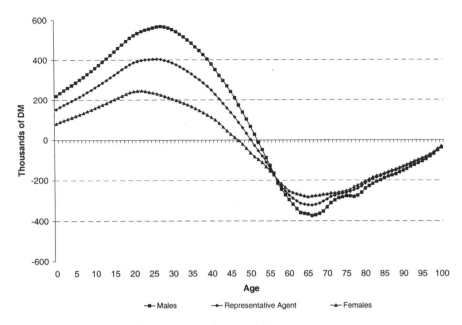

Fig. 5.8. Base case generational accounts for living generations. Base year 1996, status quo mortality. Growth rate 1.5 percent, discount rate 5 percent

positive life cycle tax burden. In present value terms, the lifetime tax payment to the public coffers exceeds transfers received by an amount of DM 151,600. For base year infant cohorts, remaining lifetime net taxes gradually increase. As the generational accounts are based on a narrow transfer concept excluding government purchases concentrated in young age, this is mainly an effect of discounting. Agents gradually attach higher weight to the high tax payments during working age, as the period when the payment will actually be made moves closer.[65] The expected rest-of-life net tax burden peaks for cohorts aged close to 25 in the base year, totalling about DM 400,000 on average. Shortly after being established in the labor force, the present value of agents' net tax payments is particularly high. A long period of high – direct and indirect – tax payments and few transfer receipts in the course of their working life is ahead, while the retirement period with high transfer receipts is still in the distant, heavily discounted future.

After reaching the peak, the generational accounts fall continuously for cohorts who were of working age in the base year. The increase in annual tax payments due to rising average labor income, evident in Fig. 5.3, does not offset the effects of an increasingly shorter working career and less discounted

---

[65] If we assigned education and youth support payments as a transfer, net transfer receipts during youth would be markedly higher. As a result, the generational accounts for young cohorts would increase more sharply with cohort age.

social insurance transfers during retirement. Beyond age 50, a representative agent turns into a recipient of net transfers whose tax payments, over the remaining life cycle, fall short of transfers received. The cohort who had just passed the standard retirement age of 65 receives the maximum rest-of-life net transfer, totaling DM 323,200. For older generations in retirement, the remaining lifetime net benefits progressively decline, mainly as a consequence of shorter life expectancy conditional on age, whereas cohort variations in the pension level, associated with the not yet maturate Social Security system, are of less importance.

As for the tax burdens of men and women, Fig. 5.8 reveals significant gender differences. In absolute terms, net taxes paid by men over the entire life cycle are more than two times as high as those paid by women. Male and female agents born in the base year are expected to pay DM 219,400 and DM 80,100 respectively. Gender differences are even more marked for young cohorts who had already entered into the labor force in the base year. Since women's generational accounts start falling earlier than men's because of the decline in female labor supply during the period of child rearing, the discrepancy of male and female generational accounts reaches DM 350,000 at the maximum around age 30.

As the transfer receipts during the final years of life attain more weight, differences in absolute net tax burdens by gender dwindle for older base year generations. In retirement, the higher annual transfer receipts by men, as displayed in Fig. 5.4, are almost outweighed by the higher life expectancy of female generations. Nevertheless, the remaining lifetime net transfers received by female cohorts in retirement stay, on average, about 15 percent below those received by male cohorts of the same age. Note that the generational accounts of representative base year pensioners gradually approach the female accounts when the cohort share of women increases due to their lower mortality.

Disaggregation of the generational accounts into specific tax and transfer categories, shown in Table 5.6 and Table 5.7 for male and female members of selected living cohorts, provides some basic insight into the sources of gender-specific redistribution in Germany. Regarding indirect taxes and capital income taxation (including seignorage), differences in the absolute tax burdens by sex are not prominent. In general, these taxes impose a slightly higher remaining lifetime tax burden on female than on male cohorts. The longer lifespan of women compensates for their on average smaller annual tax payments. However, women pay less labor income taxes and make lower contributions to statutory social insurance schemes than men, as a consequence of their drastically lower average wage income. The average labor tax burden of base year born women (DM 40,800), for example, is 56.7 percent lower than that of men (DM 94,200). Gender differentials regarding taxes on labor are even more pronounced for older female cohorts in working age who had passed the period of comparatively high female labor force participation.

Table 5.6. The Composition of Generational Accounts: Male Population

Genera-tion's Age	Genera-tional Account	Tax Payments						Transfer Receipts				
		Labor Income	Capital Income	Seigno-rage	VAT	Excise/ Other	Social Insurance Contrib.	Social Security/ Accident	Health/ Long-Term Care	Unem-ployment	General Welfare/ Housing	Youth/ Maternity
0	219.4	94.2	18.5	1.1	57.7	31.4	192.5	50.3	58.4	21.9	17.2	28.2
5	285.6	112.0	22.9	1.4	68.6	37.3	228.7	59.9	57.3	26.1	16.9	24.1
10	358.2	133.0	25.9	1.6	80.7	44.2	271.2	71.2	61.3	31.0	16.7	18.2
15	440.5	157.5	30.5	1.9	93.8	52.0	320.7	84.3	65.6	37.4	17.1	11.5
20	521.7	185.4	35.5	2.2	105.6	58.0	372.3	99.2	69.8	44.8	18.0	5.4
25	560.0	207.4	39.9	2.5	106.6	58.1	405.2	116.8	73.8	49.6	16.9	2.3
30	551.2	215.4	43.7	2.8	105.3	56.1	409.6	138.3	77.9	50.4	14.8	0.2
35	483.7	208.6	45.2	2.9	101.5	52.2	378.7	162.7	81.6	48.5	12.6	0.1
40	379.4	191.3	44.1	2.8	94.8	47.0	333.3	190.9	84.5	47.2	11.1	0.0
45	241.6	163.4	41.4	2.7	86.0	41.1	281.3	230.9	88.5	45.1	9.6	0.0
50	66.4	117.8	37.6	2.4	74.5	34.3	218.2	276.7	91.6	41.7	8.4	0.0
55	-126.1	65.9	32.4	2.1	61.5	27.4	144.9	325.7	93.0	34.2	7.5	0.0
60	-294.7	26.2	27.5	1.8	51.1	21.3	82.5	388.6	93.4	16.2	7.0	0.0
65	-366.2	6.6	22.8	1.5	41.6	16.4	48.2	398.3	97.5	0.5	6.9	0.0
70	-332.2	3.0	17.4	1.1	32.8	12.2	38.5	337.2	92.7	0.0	7.4	0.0
75	-276.5	1.6	12.3	0.8ex	24.7	8.8	30.9	264.4	83.3	0.0	7.8	0.0
80	-239.1	0.1	8.7	0.6	17.8	5.6	24.1	212.0	75.6	0.0	8.3	0.0
85	-188.9	0.0	6.0	0.4	12.8	3.8	18.5	155.6	65.7	0.0	8.9	0.0
90	-151.2	0.0	4.1	0.3	8.7	2.6	13.8	116.9	55.1	0.0	8.8	0.0
95	-104.9	0.0	2.8	0.2	6.2	1.8	8.8	76.5	41.0	0.0	7.1	0.0
100	-36.4	0.0	0.9	0.1	2.0	0.6	2.8	25.4	13.9	0.0	3.5	0.0

Note: Base year 1996, status quo mortality. Growth rate 1,5 percent, discount rate 5 percent. Thousands of DM

Table **5.7.** The Composition of Generational Accounts: Female Population

Generation's Age	Generational Account	Tax Payments						Transfer Receipts				
		Labor Income	Capital Income	Seigno-rage	VAT	Excise/Other	Social Insurance Contrib.	Social Security/Accident	Health/Long-Term Care	Unem-ployment	General Welfare/Housing	General Youth/Maternity
0	80.1	40.8	19.6	1.2	61.2	30.5	98.5	46.3	65.4	10.1	17.6	32.3
5	118.4	48.5	23.3	1.4	72.7	36.2	117.0	55.2	67.1	12.0	17.4	29.0
10	158.5	57.6	27.5	1.7	85.6	42.8	138.4	65.7	73.8	14.3	17.3	24.0
15	201.9	67.8	32.4	2.0	99.8	50.3	162.6	77.8	81.0	17.9	17.9	18.4
20	242.5	79.1	37.6	2.3	112.2	56.3	187.5	91.0	86.7	22.7	18.8	13.3
25	235.3	81.7	42.3	2.7	114.6	56.2	188.9	107.1	90.6	25.5	18.0	9.9
30	204.4	76.2	46.4	2.9	113.4	53.8	177.4	126.5	93.3	24.7	16.6	4.6
35	166.9	71.2	48.3	3.1	109.8	49.4	167.2	147.5	95.7	22.8	14.6	1.4
40	111.9	64.5	47.6	3.1	102.5	43.7	152.7	169.6	98.7	20.5	13.1	0.2
45	28.2	50.6	45.3	2.9	92.1	37.2	127.4	194.6	101.6	19.3	11.9	0.0
50	-64.2	32.3	41.7	2.7	79.8	30.3	96.8	220.0	102.8	14.0	11.0	0.0
55	-153.9	14.4	36.6	2.4	66.7	23.2	62.7	239.2	102.0	8.2	10.4	0.0
60	-251.8	3.3	31.5	2.1	55.8	16.9	44.6	290.6	103.3	1.8	10.3	0.0
65	-281.6	0.5	26.3	1.7	45.7	11.7	38.6	292.4	103.2	0.0	10.6	0.0
70	-268.1	0.2	20.1	1.3	35.9	7.7	33.6	255.8	99.8	0.0	11.4	0.0
75	-251.2	0.1	14.3	0.9	26.4	4.8	28.7	221.6	93.0	0.0	11.9	0.0
80	-204.1	0.0	10.0	0.6	19.2	3.0	20.9	162.2	83.2	0.0	12.3	0.0
85	-164.7	0.0	6.8	0.4	13.2	2.0	15.5	119.0	71.4	0.0	12.3	0.0
90	-129.2	0.0	4.5	0.3	9.3	1.3	11.4	87.3	57.3	0.0	11.5	0.0
95	-89.6	0.0	2.8	0.2	6.2	0.8	7.5	57.9	40.5	0.0	8.7	0.0
100	-30.9	0.0	0.7	0.0	1.7	0.2	2.5	19.6	12.5	0.0	4.1	0.0

Note: Base year 1996, status quo mortality. Growth rate 1,5 percent, discount rate 5 percent. Thousands of DM

Women pay rather high statutory health care contributions in old age out of their pension income. Therefore, the disparity between male and female social insurance contributions, which constitute the single largest fiscal burden irrespective of gender, is altogether smaller. Still, the lifetime contribution to social insurance expected by a base year born men (DM 192,500) exceeds that expected by a representative woman (DM 98,500) by 95.4 percent.

Transfer benefits, on the other hand, are divided rather evenly between males and females. For the base year born generation, government transfers to men, totaling DM 176,000, exceed those to women by an amount of only DM 4,300. Comparison of life cycle social insurance contributions to benefits received reveals that gender redistribution in Germany is effected mainly by the different branches of social insurance. Whereas gender-specific benefits from unemployment insurance reflect the different labor market position of men and women, life cycle transfer receipts from the statutory pension, health and nursery care schemes are basically unaffected by variations in contribution payments by sex. Benefits received by the female generation born in 1996 add up to DM 111,700, compared to DM 108,700 received by male newborns. Since husbands' payroll contributions constitute derivative transfer claims of wives like health care provision and survivors pensions, women are life cycle net beneficiaries of the social insurance system who receive a net transfer of DM 23,300, whereas men are net contributors who face a lifetime contribution amounting to DM 61,900.

As for social assistance payments, male generations generally receive less transfers than female generations. Gender differences remain small in absolute terms though. In young age, they are mainly attributable to maternity benefits, which (empirically, not legally) are limited to women. In old-age, women receive comparatively high general income support payments, serving to complement their rather low average pensions.

These plausible results notwithstanding, one should stay very cautious to draw definite conclusions on the subject of gender redistribution from an analysis of the absolute generational accounts by sex. First, the accounts do not consider aspects of intra-household redistribution, which could imply that tax payments or transfer benefits eventually slide from men to woman, or vice versa. In this respect, the generational account estimates do not improve much upon the relative tax and transfer profiles derived from the micro data, which employ rather cursory assumptions regarding intra-household redistribution. The accounts mainly add the aspect of differential mortality to the analysis, which indeed affects the relative fiscal position of males and females, if only by a comparatively small degree. Secondly, the assessment of absolute generational accounts neglects gender differences in lifetime income. A more clear-cut notion of redistribution would require judging the net tax payments of men and women relative to their respective pre-tax consumption possibilities.

On a more general level, this argument also holds regarding the absolute remaining lifetime tax payments for the representative members of living generations, as displayed in Fig. 5.8. Their factual age-specific fiscal burden can be appraised only by taking into account variations in rest-of-life resources by cohort. In a generational accounting model that abstracts from private intergenerational transfers, lifetime resources of newborn agents only derive from ownership of human capital, which translates into a life cycle stream of annual gross labor income. Capital income, given private agents do not realize a higher rate of return on investment than the discount rate, does not expand the lifetime resources of current newborns. In present value terms, the aggregate return on investment balances the value of the initial investment exactly. However, this perspective is wrong for older living cohorts disposing of assets accumulated prior to the base year. Whereas the return on assets accumulated over the remaining life cycle equals the value of the principal, current holdings of non-human capital, accumulated out of past labor income, generate a revenue stream augmenting lifetime resources neglected if rest-of-life consumption possibilities are approximated by remaining lifetime gross labor income.

To determine the cohort distribution of agents' lifetime pre-tax resources, we follow the usual generational accounting approach of using cross-sectional survey data to assign the corresponding macroeconomic wealth and income aggregates to individual age groups. The CES data allow to distinguish between three sources of personal income – gross wage income including employer's contribution to social insurance, household net financial and real assets, and ownership of enterprises, or stocks.[66] We estimate expected life cycle gross income per capita parallel to the generational accounts, subjecting age-specific absolute gross labor income per agent to mortality by age. The absolute gross income profiles are constructed benchmarking cohorts' gender- and region-specific relative gross labor income position against national gross wage income which in 1996, including imputed earnings of management, amounted to DM 2,228 billion. Future per capita wages are assumed to grow in line with productivity. As with tax and transfer payments, convergence of East German labor income is achieved by gradually shifting the initial age-specific values into the direction of the West German labor income level projected for the final year of the adaptation process.

Similar to government wealth, age-specific private non-human assets can be approximated either by capitalizing the current stream of returns, or by the current (market) value. In practice, since the personal income data reported in the CES are not sufficiently disaggregated to identify capital returns precisely, it is only possible to take the latter approach, dividing the house-

---

[66] Similar estimates are derived by Bonin and Feist (1999) who use slightly different assumptions. The relative age profiles for household wealth, and private stock holdings in particular, are likely to be biased, because CES data are censored due to the exclusion of high-income households.

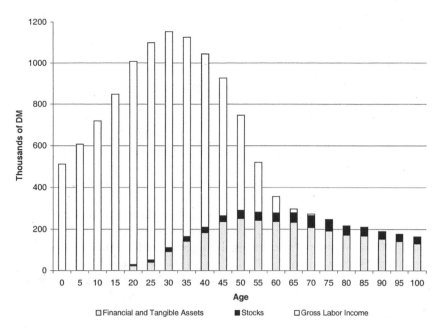

Fig. 5.9. Composition of pre-tax rest-of-life resources for living generations. Base year 1996, status quo mortality. Growth rate 1.5 percent, discount rate 5 percent

hold worth of fiscal and tangible assets net of liabilities evenly among all adult household members.[67] The same approach is employed to assign the market value of household stock holdings. Lacking reliable age-related data regarding ownership of enterprises, we assume that it spreads across generations like ownership of stock assets. To cope with data deficiencies, the estimated relative age profiles for personal wealth and holdings of shares are re-evaluated to the corresponding base year market values, which amounted to DM 10,950 billion and DM 679 billion, respectively [Deutsche Bundesbank (1999a, p. 43)]. As for the value of private enterprises, the 1993 estimate of DM 1,360 billion [Bach (1996, p. 502)], is updated by assuming that it did grow at the same rate as the value of stocks in the period from 1993 to 1996. This adjustment gives us a stock of enterprise wealth of DM 1,952 billion.

Figure 5.9 displays, under status quo mortality, the composition of the remaining lifetime resources available to a representative member of selected living generations before taxation. In present value terms, since private intergenerational transfers or bequests are not taken into account, the consumption possibilities of cohorts who had not entered into the labor force in the base year are limited to gross labor income. According to our estimates, the

---

[67] Surveyed assets evaluate real estate by their uniform value. Therefore, the relative age profile tends to understate the wealth of older cohorts who hold large real estate.

discounted gross life cycle earnings gained by an average agent born in the base year add up to DM 511,300. Supposed no bequests and unchanged labor force participation, future born generations will dispose of a similar amount, enlarged by productivity growth.

For living cohorts up to age 30, the remaining lifetime resources gradually increase, mainly due to discounting effects, as the period of high wage earnings turns less heavily discounted. The present value of lifetime returns on human capital reaches a maximum close to age 25, at little more than one million. Rest-of-life resources also rise, since assets accumulated prior to the base period are increasingly available for future consumption. Capital wealth of the richest generation (of age 30 in the base year) amounts to 9.6 percent of total resources available, which equal DM 1.150 million. Capital asset holdings are particularly high for older cohorts in the labor force. They reach a maximum for the 50-year-old, whose accumulated capital wealth is worth DM 293,800, and remain almost constant for all older cohorts who had not retired in the base year. Nevertheless, the increased capital resources do not compensate cohorts for the reduction in rest-of-life consumption opportunities due to smaller gross labor income. Irrespective of cohort age, stock holdings account for about 20 percent of total capital wealth.

Of course, labor income of pensioner generations is zero, whereas capital resources decline gradually with cohort age. This age pattern would be consistent with a process of capital decumulation in old-age, but might as well be explained by cohort effects. In any case, the age-related decline in consumption opportunities before government intervention appears to be small. Assets disposed of by the oldest-old still amount to DM 163,900. The large amount of asset holdings in the final years of life certainly questions the no-bequest assumption fundamental for the interpretation of lifetime tax burdens as indicated by the generational accounts. Using generations' wealth as displayed in Fig. 5.9 as a reference for cohort-specific fiscal burdens, one has to assume that agents would derive the same benefit from bequests as from their own consumption, which could be seriously misleading. However, a more detailed design of private generational transfers, which would require addressing the empirically unresolved issue to which extent bequests are intended or accidental, is beyond the scope of the present analysis.[68]

Figure 5.10 compares the pre- and after-tax lifetime resources available to base year living generations, which differ by the value of the generational accounts. The comparison shows that generational redistribution induced by the current tax and transfer levels is actually large. Government intervention renders the cohort distribution of remaining lifetime consumption possibilities notably more even. Due to the high tax burdens on the working aged and the generous transfers to retirees, the spread between cohorts' maximum and minimum rest-of-life resources is reduced by about one third. At the

---

[68] Cf. Lüth (2001) for a generational accounting analysis of private intergenerational transfers.

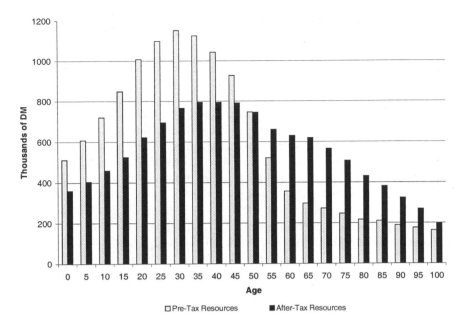

Fig. 5.10. Pre- and after-tax rest-of-life resources for living generations. Base year 1996, status quo mortality. Growth rate 1.5 percent, discount rate 5 percent

same time, maximum resources are shifted to older base year generations. Whereas lifetime resources peak around age 30 before taxation, the highest net resources are left to generations close to age 40 in 1996.

Relative to gross lifetime wealth, the absolute net tax burdens or net transfer receipts are sizeable for most cohorts. The highest lifetime transfer quota is observed for the cohort of standard retirement age 65. The present value of expected government transfers expands consumption opportunities beyond personal assets by an amount of 108 percent. For older cohorts in retirement, the transfer quota steadily declines, but it still exceeds 20 percent of gross wealth in the final year of life. Redistribution toward old cohorts imposes high lifetime tax rates on young generations. The relative fiscal burden reaches a maximum for cohorts at the beginning of their working career (close to age 20 in the base year) who face an average tax rate of 38.3 percent. At 29.7 percent, the life cycle tax rate is markedly smaller for a representative member of the current newborn cohort.

The tax rate perspective also sheds new light onto the question of gender redistribution. Taking into account the specific life cycle income position of men and women, the gender differences in fiscal burdens appear considerably smaller. While the lifetime net tax rate of a male member of the base year born generation equals 31.8 percent, that of a female member is still 24.8 percent. Recall that in absolute terms the fiscal burden of newborn males almost triples the female burden. The observed difference in the life cycle tax rates between genders suggests that the tax and transfer system in Germany is progressive in terms of life cycle resources.

5.3.2 Intertemporal Fiscal Imbalance

Inspecting the generational accounts of living generations, as displayed in Fig. 5.8, little points to the fact that German public finances are in a critical state intertemporally. If current tax and transfer levels stay unchanged, the discounted future net tax payments of two thirds of the current population will be positive and, for the most part, large. In fact, aggregate net payments of living agents to the public coffers upon death, totaling DM 10,398 billion, exceed current government debt (DM 1,993 billion) by far. However, this superficial perspective overlooks the fact that net tax revenue must finance prospective net purchases of the government as well.

Table 5.8 contrasts the generational accounts with the present value of remaining lifetime net government purchases per capita assigned to different cohorts in the projections of government spending. The resulting *cohort deficit*, measuring the cohort-specific per capita amount of government spending not financed by agents' net tax payments, indicates the long-term revenue situation of the public budgets more adequately. Note that, with signs reversed, the cohort deficit can be interpreted as a generational account, too, if one adopts the widest possible definition of personal transfers.

As net government purchases are basically independent of age, the amount of remaining lifetime government spending per capita gradually declines with cohort age. There is only one exception here concerning the youngest living cohorts who are not enrolled in the education system so that government expenditure on schooling is comparatively highly discounted. Still, life cycle government purchases for a base year newborn amount to DM 243,300. Considered that the lifetime net tax payment of a representative agent amounts to DM 151,600 only, a deficit is imposed on public sector budgets, financed either by issuing government debt, which burdens future generations, or by cohort surpluses drawn from other living generations. The latter, as Table 5.8 makes obvious, are much smaller than first suggested by the generational accounts. At the maximum, each member of the 25-year-old generation does not contribute more than DM 266,100 to the public coffers, notwithstanding a net tax payment of DM 403,300.

Aggregation of cohort surpluses and deficits for all present generations reveals that the net tax payments of living agents are actually only sufficient to finance government spending related to them. Public transfers and government purchases exceed the amount of taxes paid by the base year population by just DM 2.3 billion. In the consequence, current tax and transfer levels are unsustainable. If the current life cycle tax rate were maintained for future generations, a large positive contribution of living generations to the intertemporal public budget would be necessary. First, the current living

Table 5.8. Remaining Lifetime Net Government Purchases and Cohort Deficits

Age	Generational Account	Government Purchases	Cohort Deficit[a]	Age	Generational Account	Government Purchases	Cohort Deficit[a]
0	151.6	243.3	92.4	55	-140.0	83.8	226.2
5	204.3	246.7	43.2	60	-272.9	74.2	349.5
10	260.9	221.7	-38.2	65	-321.6	64.2	389.1
15	324.4	188.3	-134.9	70	-293.1	54.4	350.0
20	385.9	156.5	-228.1	75	-259.6	44.3	305.7
25	403.3	135.9	-266.1	80	-214.6	34.7	250.7
30	385.0	121.3	-262.3	85	-171.1	26.7	198.5
35	330.1	114.7	-213.7	90	-134.4	20.2	155.2
40	249.2	108.2	-139.0	95	-92.9	14.6	107.9
45	136.3	100.9	-33.0	100	-32.8	5.1	38.1
50	1.6	92.7	93.8				

[a] Remaining lifetime net government purchases net of generational account.
Note: Base year 1996, status quo mortality. Growth rate 1.5 percent, discount rate 5 percent. Thousands of DM

would have to accumulate funds in order to maintain the generational account of present newborns for future generations. Since net taxes over the entire life cycle currently are smaller than government purchases, each future born agent accumulates additional liabilities worth DM 92,400 in present value terms of the base year, provided that present fiscal policy stays unchanged. Furthermore, the net taxpayers among the initial population would have to redeem the complete outstanding government debt of the base year, because the net tax rate valid for base year newborns (and hence for future generations) is too low to let them share in the debt service.

Under status quo fiscal conditions, since net taxes paid by living cohorts are inadequate to cover interest on government debt, and taxes paid by future cohorts are inadequate to cover net government purchases made for them, the deficits of the public sector would increase progressively in the long term. This process is made obvious by Fig. 5.11, which adopts the conventional perspective of annual deficit budgeting. Using the status quo projections of government revenue and spending underlying the generational accounts, one can calculate, for each year, the corresponding deficit of the government budget, taking into account interest due on government debt which accumulates over time as deficits prevail. As is shown by Fig. 5.11, the non-sustainability of base year tax and spending levels becomes manifest only after a quarter century. In fact, the annual public deficit, expressed as a fraction of the GDP predicted for the same year, first declines, from a quota of 4.6 percent

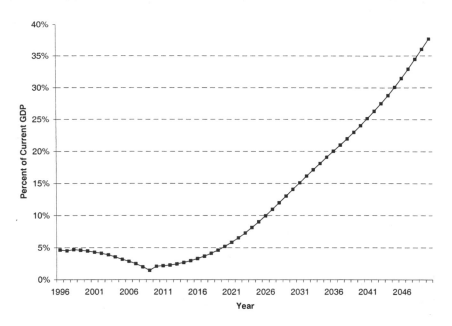

Fig. 5.11. Projected public sector deficit as a percentage of current GDP. Base year 1996, status quo mortality. Growth rate 1.5 percent, discount rate 5 percent

in year 1996 to a minimum of 1.5 percent in 2010.[69] The decline in annual deficits is partly attributable to a favorable demographic environment. In the first years of the projection, comparatively strong cohorts run through the period of high tax payments in the life cycle between age 40 and 50. However, a more important driving force is the recovery of the East German economy.

From the viewpoint of political economy, the long period of moderate and even declining budget deficits ahead seems worrying. It is likely to give decision makers a false security that could prevent early reforms of fiscal policy. Without reforms, deficits start growing faster than GDP as soon as the alleviating budget factors vanish after the year 2010. When tax revenue declines and public spending soars due to population aging, the government, being forced to finance interest payments by issuing new bonds, soon enters into a vicious cycle of ever-growing deficits. Given unchanged tax and transfer levels, the deficit quota will reach the – unrealistic – level of 37.7 percent by the year 2050. Considered the crowding out of private capital associated with rising government borrowing, this is clearly an unsustainable development.

The perspective of yearly budgets is useful, because it highlights the connection between generational accounting analysis and more conventional tools

---

[69] The base year deficit exceeds the official one based on the Maastricht criteria, which was 3.4 percent [Deutsche Bundesbank (1998a)], due to the more comprehensive public budget concept underlying generational accounting.

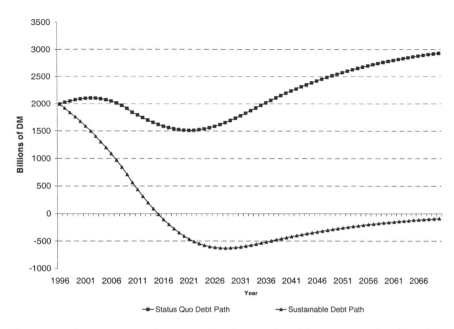

Fig. 5.12. Status quo and sustainable time paths of intertemporal public debt. Present value of base year 1996. Status quo mortality. Growth rate 1.5 percent, discount rate 5 percent

to measure the effects of fiscal policy. Furthermore it renders the long-term consequences of unsustainable public finances more transparent. Returning to the perspective of generational accounting, the deficit path displayed in Fig. 5.11 translates into a time path of intertemporal public debt. Due to the present value character of the calculations, prospective interest payments on accumulated debt vanish from the projection. In present value terms of the base year, the intertemporal liabilities of the public sector are determined by the initial amount of government bonds plus the discounted value of future *primary* government deficits.

Figure 5.12 displays the development of present value public liabilities as projected under status quo conditions. Starting from the initial value of DM 1,993 billion (56.6 percent of 1996 GDP), the present worth of government liabilities, in contrast to the yearly deficit quota, increases in the first years of the projection. Primary deficits of the public sector are positive, which raises intertemporal debt, before government finances run into a period of primary surpluses in 2002, which is projected to last for about two decades. At the maximum around the year 2010, primary surpluses amount to about 2.2 percent of GDP. In line with primary surpluses, the present value of intertemporal public liabilities declines, up to a minimum of about DM 1.500 billion reached in 2020. When demographic aging starts hitting public budgets more seriously, primary deficits rapidly turn large, and exceed six percent of GDP after 2035. Correspondingly, intertemporal liabilities accumulate. This process comes to its end when the demographic transition is complete. As the population reaches a stable state, yearly primary deficits stay constant over time, converging to zero in present value terms.

Supposed that fiscal policy were not restricted by the intertemporal public budget constraint, future deficits, hidden by conventional budgeting, eventually would add up to a present value of DM 1.181 billion, or 59.6 percent of public debt explicit in the base year. Intertemporal liabilities of the government would converge to DM 3.181 billion, which is 90.3 percent of base year GDP. This amount represents the *sustainability gap* of current fiscal policy. Since the government actually must pay off its liabilities, status quo tax levels have to be raised or government spending levels reduced at some point in time. The fiscal policy revision necessary to balance the public sector budget intertemporally is substantial. On a yearly average, the resources available to the government must be enlarged by 3.2 percent of projected GDP. Although any policy change satisfying this condition is feasible, the following analysis refers to the stylized policy scenarios introduced in Section 4.6.2.

Allocating the intertemporal liabilities of the government entirely to cohorts not yet born reveals the severe intertemporal generational distribution conflict possibly associated with unsustainable public finances. The continuation of present tax and transfer levels for the current living imposes a uniform 44.9 percent raise of tax payments on future generations. As a result, representative future-born agents, in growth-adjusted terms, face a lifetime net tax payment of DM 291,900. After the tax raise, the net tax payment of future cohorts exceeds government purchases made for them (DM 243,300 in base year terms, compare Table 5.8). The cohort surplus of DM 48,600 per capita serves to redeem initial government debt. Current generations, in contrast, as seen above, solely pay for their own transfers and government purchases.

Fiscal imbalance between current and future generations resulting from the sustainability gap is large. Compared to the generational account of a current newborn (DM 151,600), the net tax burden of future generations rises by DM 140,300. Accordingly, the life cycle tax rate of a representative agent increases from 29.7 for a member of the base year born cohort, to 57.1 percent for each member of future generations. Relative to life cycle resources, females are hit harder than males by the uniform tax increase. After the policy adjustment, their life cycle tax rate (58.8 percent) exceeds that of men (56.6 percent).

For a representative agent, the relative increment in the life cycle net tax rates of present and future generations – the indicator π used by traditional generational accountants – equals 92.3 percent under status quo conditions. This finding is roughly consistent with the base case results of the more recent generational accounting studies for Germany, surveyed in Table 5.9, although

Table 5.9. Fiscal Imbalance in German Generational Accounting Studies

Source	Base Year	Fiscal Imbalance[a]
Boll (1994)	1989	72.3[b]
Gokhale et al. (1995)	1992	26.2[c]
Boll (1996)	1994	9.4
Raffelhüschen and Walliser(1999)	1995	156.1
Bonin et al. (1999)	1995	107.6[d]
Deutsche Bundesbank (1997)	1996	130.0
Besendorfer et al. (1998)	1996	189.7[e]

[a] Relative increase in generational account for agent born one year after the base year in terms of generational account of base year born agent (π).
[b] West Germany only.
[c] Growth rate 1.25%.
[d] Generational accounts corrected for education and net government purchases.
[e] Public spending on education treated as a personal transfer.
Note: Status quo scenarios. Growth rate 1.5 percent, discount rate 5 percent

intertemporal generational imbalance appears somewhat less severe.[70] Despite using a very different set of relative micro profiles and the inclusion of pension maturation, the present status quo result is particularly close to the findings of Bonin et al. (1999) and Besendorfer et al. (1998) for the base years 1995 and 1996, respectively. This observation suggests that the generational accounting results might be fairly robust with respect to modifications of the underlying micro profiles. The seemingly higher intergenerational imbalance reported by Besendorfer et al. is mainly attributable to a different net tax concept assigning public education spending as a personal transfer. If we did the same, the relative fiscal balance between present and future generations would increase to 205.4 percent in our status quo scenario, while the sustainability gap and therefore the absolute tax increase imposed on future generations stays unchanged.

Assignment of the entire sustainability gap to future born cohorts is an extreme scenario. As the opposite extreme, one might assume that taxation levels are increased in the base year once and for all, which lets current and future generations contribute to cover the sustainability gap. Lump-sum distribution of intertemporal liabilities would burden all generations relative to

---

[70] Inspecting Table 5.9, one should be aware that it is far from providing a consistent time series. As stated in the introduction to this chapter, there is large variation regarding methodic concepts and economic modeling between the studies. The favorable results presented by Gokhale et al. (1995) and Boll (1996) should be regarded with particular caution. Gokhale et al., starting from the base year 1992, perpetuate the unification boom in West Germany indefinitely, whereas Boll excludes public investment from government spending.

their remaining life expectancy. In present value terms of 1996, an annual tax payment (or transfer cut) of DM 1,400 per agent, uprated yearly with productivity growth, is sufficient to redeem intertemporal public liabilities.

Alternatively, current taxation levels need to be raised by a uniform rate of 7.6 percent. The resulting generational account for base year newborns amounts to DM 175,500 or 34.5 percent life cycle resources. It is sustainable for all future generations, although it implies a cohort deficit of DM 67,600. The immediate tax increase substantially enlarges the surplus in the intertemporal budget drawn from living generations of working age. Therefore, the aggregate net tax payments of the living are not only sufficient to redeem base year government debt, but also to fund an intertemporal generational transfer to future generations who, like current newborns, are not asked to fully finance the government purchases made for them.

The funding of future cohort deficits to achieve sustainable public finances is more obvious, if one calculates the sequence of intertemporal government debt given the immediate tax increase, which is contrasted with the unsustainable status quo development of intertemporal public liabilities in Fig. 5.12. In the base year, the uniform tax increase generates additional revenue totaling DM 112.8 billion, which raises the tax quota by 3.2 percentage points, to 45.0 percent of GDP. Hence, the original primary deficit turns into a primary surplus. Government liabilities start declining right from the base year. The favorable demographic and economic environment in the first years of the projection accelerates this development. By the year 2015, the present value of aggregate primary surpluses balances outstanding debt of the base year. As primary surpluses prevail, the government starts accumulating intertemporal assets, which reach a maximum of DM 627.5 billion by the year 2027. In the following years when demographic aging leads to large government spending on transfers and cohort deficits of future generations accumulate, public funds are gradually liquidated, converging to zero in the long term.

The experiment of an unmitigated once-and-for-all tax increase (one may equally opt for an unmitigated cut of transfers or government purchases, or any combination of these policies) is a highly stylized one of course. Nevertheless, it shows how funding strategies could be used to render fiscal policy sustainable in an aging society. This issue will be again discussed in Chapter 7.3.2 when analyzing partial funding strategies for Social Security, which basically work according to the same principle as that at display in Fig. 5.12.

Some counterfactual experiments may help to bring out the main sources of intertemporal generational redistribution in Germany. Table 5.10 displays our main indicators of fiscal imbalance for status tax and transfer levels, supposed that some burdening influences on future public budgets were absent. First, as living generations pass the entire base year liabilities onto future generations under status quo conditions, absence of explicit government liabilities would significantly improve intertemporal fiscal balance. The

Table 5.10. Sources of Intertemporal Fiscal Imbalance

| Scenario | Sustainability Gap[b] | Net Tax Rate[a] | | | |
		Base Year Newborn	Future Newborn	Differ- ence	Lump-sum Tax[c]
Status Quo	3.2	29.7	57.1	27.5	1,410
No Explicit Debt	1.2	29.7	39.7	10.0	530
No East-West Disparity	2.7	29.6	52.8	23.2	1,190
No Population Aging	-0.2	29.7	28.3	-1.4	-80

[a] Generational account as a fraction of present value life cycle income.
[b] Percentage of present value aggregate GDP according to equation (4.24), p. 82.
[c] Annual tax payment per capita of population balancing the sustainability gap.
Note: Base year 1996, status quo mortality. Growth rate 1.5 percent, discount rate 5 percent

sustainability gap falls by more than two thirds, from 3.2 to 1.2 percent of future GDP per annum. In order to maintain net tax levels for the living, future generations face a generational account of DM 202,800.[71] Their lifetime tax rate is reduced by 17.5 percentage points. If the remaining intertemporal burden is assigned lump sum to present and future generations instead, the annual payment achieving fiscal sustainability falls to DM 530, compared to DM 1,400 under the status quo.

A second determinant of intertemporal fiscal imbalance is the persisting fiscal burden from German unification.[72] The deep recession in the East German states following the shock of unification continues to induce sizeable net transfers to the East which, as is indicated by Table 5.11, are only partially balanced by the additional revenue from a number of tax increases enacted to support the unification process. In 1995, the net transfers of the public sector to East Germany reached 5.0 percent of GDP in the West German states.[73] Like in previous years, this transfer was only partly financed by additional tax payments of West German residents. To a major part, it enlarged the government deficit. In fact, unfunded net transfers to the East, ranging between three and four percent of GDP, have sharply enlarged government

---

[71] There remains a cohort deficit for future generations, although the base year living do not accumulate funds to finance it. The cohort deficit is made sustainable by the net tax payments of prospective immigrants.

[72] For a more detailed discussion of the impact of unification on the generational accounts, refer to Gokhale et al. (1995) and, for more recent results, Raffelhüschen and Walliser(1999).

[73] Unfortunately, this seems to be the last year for which official estimates for the size of West-East-transfers are available.

Table 5.11. Transfers to East Germany after Unification (Percent of West German GDP)

	1991	1992	1993	1994	1995
Net Transfers to East Germany[a]	3.8	4.5	4.6	4.2	5.0
Revenue from Tax Amendments	0.6	0.8	0.8	1.3	1.4
Unfunded Net Transfers	3.2	3.7	3.8	2.9	3.6

[a] Public sector spending in East Germany net of East German tax revenue.
Sources: SVR (1995, table 40), Bonin et al. (1999)

deficits since unification. In a period of only five years, from 1991 to 1995, government debt rose from 41.4 to 57.7 percent of the GDP.

The fiscal sustainability impact of past deficits attributable to unification was incorporated implicitly in the base case. The next scenario addresses the fact that the unification related budget pressure is going to continue over the next decade, as net tax payments in the East catch up to the Western level only gradually. To highlight the intertemporal burden entailed by the future need for regional net government transfers, we assume that agents living in the East German states would resemble West German agents right from the base year. Table 5.10 displays that elimination of regional fiscal disparities from the generational accounts reduces the sustainability gap by 0.5 percentage points of present value GDP, which can be translated into a reduction of future generations' life cycle tax rate by 4.3 percentage points. Stated differently, the prospective net transfers to East Germans required to compensate for their low current per capita net tax payments impose a yearly lump-sum burden of DM 210 on each current and future population member.

If both explicit government debt and prospective net transfers to the East did not require financing, current tax and transfer levels would be close to sustainable. The sustainability gap would total only 0.7 percent of present value GDP.[74] Taking a different perspective, the intertemporal fiscal burdens due to past deficits and slow East German economic recovery, totaling 2.5 percent of GDP, would be tolerable if demographic aging did not exert strong pressure on future public budgets. This is shown by a final experiment eliminating the consequences of population aging by assuming that the base year population structure remains constant indefinitely. Technically, this scenario requires endogenous immigration, in order to avoid implausible

---

[74] The sustainability gap and the lump-sum tax indicator are additive with respect to these two experiments, while the net tax rate measure is not, as the disparity experiment affects the lifetime net tax rate of base year newborns.

survival rates for the resident population.[75] With the population structure staying constant, the sustainability gap vanishes, as the favorable base year population share of net taxpayers does not fall over time. The government accumulates even a small intertemporal surplus, amounting to 0.2 percent of annual GDP. The surplus allows to reduce the tax burden of present or future generations. If one supposes, for example, that fiscal policy distributes the intertemporal budget surplus among future generations, lifetime resources available to a representative agent increase by 1.4 percent, compared to those of a current newborn.

A comparison of the three stylized experiments contrasted in Table 5.10 makes evident that demographic ageing is the most serious threat to the intertemporal sustainability of public finances in Germany.

5.3.3 Sensitivity Analysis

The findings presented in the previous sections were based on several economic and demographic assumptions. Like any conditional projection, generational accounting is affected by variations in the underlying parameters. This fundamental ambiguity does not invalidate the method, as long as the measures provided are sufficiently robust, at least qualitatively. Surveying the degree of intertemporal fiscal imbalance indicated by the various generational accounting studies for Germany (cf. Table 5.9) one might get the impression that the method reacts rather sensitively to details of parameterization.

In what follows, the status quo findings are tested for the reaction to demographic variables, base year choice and the design of basic economic parameters. It is demonstrated that the (non-)sustainability outcome is not particularly sensitive to the empirical specification of the generational accounting model. As is good practice of sensitivity analysis, we vary only one parameter at a time, maintaining the status quo setting for all other variables, to work out the relevance of the different empirical uncertainties.

Demographic Variables

Regarding demographics, the status quo analysis sacrifices empirical probability for the sake of *indicator* quality. While the assumption of unchanged future fertility is consistent with past experience, the postulate of unchanged mortality is not, considered ongoing mortality trends. For a gain in *prognostic* quality, the sustainability analysis has to take into account the prospective gain in life expectancy, as designed, for example, by the low mortality scenario.

---

[75] So far, generational accountants have tolerated erratic survival ratios when conducting this experiment, by deducing survival ratios implicitly from aggregate future cohort size. This procedure changes the generational accounts of current newborns, which biases the sustainability indicators.

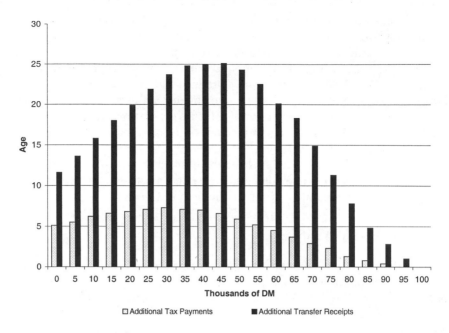

Fig. 5.13. Cohort deficit attributable to increase in life expectancy. Present value of base year 1996. Status quo mortality. Growth rate 1.5 percent, discount rate 5 percent

Decline in age-specific mortality immediately affects the generational accounts, which are defined conditional on expected lifetime. Figure 5.13 displays the change in rest-of-life tax payments and transfer receipts resulting under low mortality conditions for selected base year cohorts.[76] The supposed gain in longevity increases the expected gross tax burdens per capita only by a small amount, because tax payments are concentrated before retirement. Survival rates at working age, already high under status quo conditions, stay largely unaffected by the mortality trend.[77] In contrast, transfer receipts, clustered in retirement, increase markedly due to the longer average lifespan in old-age. Supposed low mortality, life expectancy conditional on age 65 finally exceeds that under status quo conditions by almost four years. Living cohorts aged between 35 and 45 profit most from mortality decline. Their additional transfer receipts are less heavily discounted than those of younger generations who are predicted to benefit from even higher life expectancy.

As is evident from Fig. 5.13, a more realistic specification of future mortality raises cohort deficits. At the maximum, taking into account net

---

[76] Besendorfer et al. (2000) analyze the same in the context of social security.

[77] The increase in life expectancy is designed using a non-linear principle that yields a relatively smaller decline in age-specific mortality for age groups facing relatively smaller mortality. Cf. the Appendix B for details.

government purchases, the additional burden on the public budgets reaches DM 21,700 per member of the 45-year-old generation. For current newborns, the cohort deficit still increases by an amount of DM 8,200. Consequently, acceleration of demographic aging aggravates intertemporal fiscal imbalance. As is shown by Table 5.12, which summarizes the results of the demographic sensitivity tests, the sustainability gap rises sharply in the low mortality scenario, from 3.2 to 4.9 percent of yearly GDP (or 136.2 percent of the base year GDP). Accordingly, the lifetime tax rate difference between present and future generations increases by 13.5 percentage points, to 41.0 percent of lifetime resources. Only a minor fraction (1.6 percentage points) of this increase is due to the tax rate reduction faced by base year born agents, which is attributable to their higher lifetime transfer receipts. In age-neutral per capita terms, the fiscal cost of rising life expectancy equals DM 660 per year.

The low mortality scenario reveals that fiscal policy in Germany, under very plausible conditions, is likely to redistribute between present and future generations even more strongly than is suggested by the already high fiscal imbalance observed for the status quo reference. Whereas the status quo scenario is useful to establish the fact of generational redistribution, the more pessimistic low mortality setting provides the adequate benchmark for assessment of fiscal reforms. Analyzing the intergenerational consequences of policy measures, the prognostic quality of the generational accounts matters, to put their generational impact into the right perspective.[78]

Comparing the low mortality scenario with the high fertility alternative, specified in Section 5.2.1, reveals the differential effect of fertility parameters on the generational account measures. Although the generational accounts, and hence the cohort deficits, basically do not react to changes in fertility, since the calculations abstract from intra-household redistribution,[79] the sustainability gap grows from 4.9 to 5.1 percent of annual GDP. Each newborn agent imposes a burden on the intertemporal public budget, as lifetime net government purchases exceed net tax payments per capita under current fiscal policy. This increase in intertemporal public liabilities is not compensated by the projected higher GDP due to an enlarged labor force. The aggregate GDP effect becomes significant only in the strongly discounted future, while additional public spending obligations occur from the base year.

Also the lump-sum tax measure indicates that rising fertility under current tax and government spending levels impairs fiscal sustainability. Under low mortality conditions, the lifetime present value of sustainability gener-

---

[78] The conflict between indicator and prognostic quality of the generational accounts was a recurring theme in the first part of this study. To this author, the differentiation between (indicative) sustainability and (prognostic) fiscal reform analysis seems to represent a serviceable solution to this conflict.

[79] The increase in average maternity benefits due to the rising number of births per women reduces the lifetime net tax rate faced by newborns by a negligible margin.

Table 5.12. Sensitivity to Demographic Assumptions

| Scenario | Sustainability Gap[b] | Net Tax Rate[a] | | | Lump-sum Tax[c] |
		Base Year Newborn	Future Newborn	Differ- ence	
Status Quo	3.2	29.7	57.1	27.5	1,410
Low Mortality	4.9	28.1	69.2	41.0	2,070
High Fertility	5.1	28.1	65.9	37.8	2,140

[a] Generational account as a fraction of present value life cycle income.
[b] Percentage of present value aggregate GDP according to equation (4.24), p. 82.
[c] Annual tax payment per capita of population balancing the sustainability gap.
Note: Base year 1996. Growth rate 1.5 percent, discount rate 5 percent

ating lump-sum taxes paid by newborn generations (DM 57,900) is smaller than the cohort deficit (DM 100,600). Therefore, a rising number of births creates an imbalance which, as the lump-sum experiment redistributes parts of the cohort deficit of future newborn generations to the living, entails a larger age-neutral burden per capita. Put more generally, policies assigning intertemporal public liabilities to both living and future generations are harmed by rising cohort size, if they maintain a cohort deficit for newborn generations.

In contrast, if the additional cohort deficits occurring in the high fertility scenario are levied on future generations, their lifetime tax rate exhibits the expected normal reaction, falling by 3.2 percentage points. The larger sustainability gap is distributed among a greater number of agents, whose net taxes exceed cohort government purchases, which reduces the per capita burden.[80] Hence, how intertemporal sustainability of public finances is affected by rising future cohort size crucially depends on government policy. Supposed fiscal adjustments are deferred to the future, rising fertility is likely to reduce reported intertemporal generational imbalance.

Notwithstanding this somewhat ambiguous finding, the demographic sensitivity tests clearly indicate that the adverse mortality impact on future budgets is unlikely to be compensated by future changes in fertility behavior. In any case, fiscal imbalance markedly increases compared to the status quo scenario, as the impact of mortality parameters on the intertemporal public budget is much stronger than that of the fertility variables.

---

[80] It is easy to check that the condition for a normal reaction of the difference measure is satisfied. In the low mortality scenario, the sustainable generational account of future generations amounts to DM 356,600 which exceeds net government purchases worth DM 100,600.

Table 5.13. Sensitivity to Base Year Choice

Base Year	Sustainability Gap[b]	Net Tax Rate[a]			
		Base Year Newborn	Future Newborn	Differ- ence	Lump-sum Tax[c]
1995	3.0	33.8	59.3	25.5	1,260
1996	3.2	29.7	57.1	27.5	1,410
1997	3.5	28.5	57.9	29.4	1,540

[a] Generational account as a fraction of present value life cycle income.
[b] Percentage of present value aggregate GDP according to equation (4.24), p. 82.
[c] Annual tax payment per capita of population balancing the sustainability gap.
Note: Status quo mortality. Growth rate 1.5 percent, discount rate 5 percent

Base Year Choice

Since generational accounting starts from crude budget aggregates, the status quo character of the analysis perpetuates the base year state of economic activity indefinitely. Ideally, as is done constructing accrual deficit indicators, one would clear public balances from business cycle effects before extrapolating tax and government spending levels, in order to avoid pro-cyclical behavior of the sustainability measures. The following sensitivity test regarding the development of fiscal sustainability over time is much less ambitious. Using a uniform methodological framework for three consecutive budget pe riods (1995–1997), it illustrates that the volatility of the generational account measures (in a rather stable economic environment) is actually much smaller than is suggested by the 'time series' presented in Table 5.9.

Table 5.13 shows the main sustainability indicators supposed that the economic and demographic status quo of alternative base years is maintained. During the period from 1995 to 1997, according to the generational account measures, public finances in Germany turned significantly more imbalanced intertemporally. In a period of only three years, the sustainability gap increased by 0.5 percentage points. Accordingly, the difference in lifetime tax rates for present and future generations increased from 25.5 to 29.4 percent of lifetime resources. In order to move closer to sustainability, the public sector would have had to raise additional net resources totaling 3.0 percent of GDP in each year from 1995 on. However, fiscal policy of the years 1996 and 1997 failed to hit this target. As is shown by Fig. 5.14, which displays the cohort deficits projected using alternative base years, generations' rest-of-life deficits or surpluses did not change considerably.[81] This finding suggests that politi-

---

[81] To render cohort burdens for different base years comparable, the generational accounts and net government purchases for 1995 and 1997 are expressed in prices of 1996, and corrected for real productivity growth.

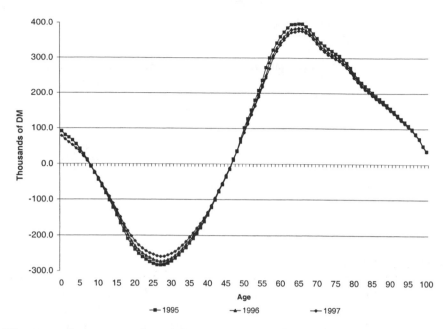

Fig. 5.14. Status quo cohort deficits for base years 1995–1997. Real terms of year 1996. Status quo mortality. Growth rate 1.5 percent, discount rate 5 percent

cal decision makers accommodated net government purchases to fluctuations in net tax revenue during the observed period.

Despite a moderate economic upswing (annual economic growth accelerated from 1.2 percent in 1995 to 2.2 percent in 1997) generational accounts for younger cohorts declined in the period under investigation. For example, the lifetime net tax rate faced by newborn agents decreased from 33.8 to 28.5 percent of lifetime income resources. Since we use an identical set of relative fiscal age profiles throughout, this result mainly reflects shifts in the relative weight of individual taxes and transfers during the period under investigation. From 1995 to 1997, unemployment rates rose sharply, from 9.3 to 11.0 percent of the labor force, which caused a higher share of unemployment benefits in public sector spending combined with marked decline in labor income tax revenue. Either development implies lower projected average net tax payments for cohorts not yet in retirement.

The concurrent decline in net government purchases was not sufficient to fully compensate the intertemporal public revenue loss due to the worsened labor market conditions. Thus, the cohort surplus of generations aged 20 to 35 decreases by up to ten percent, or DM 26,000 per capita, when changing base years from 1995 to 1997. For older agents, whose generational accounts are less affected by the unemployment trend, cohort deficits fall due to per capita decline of net government purchases. However, the net revenue gain for the public coffers remains rather small, since Social Security benefits grew faster between 1995 and 1997 than overall public spending.

The reduction over time of the generational accounts is especially large for the youngest cohorts. In the period under investigation, child allowances, assigned as a transfer to infant household members, were made significantly more generous. Nevertheless, the cohort deficit attributable to the youngest living agents declines if the generational accounting analysis is based on the year 1997, as a sizeable cutback of public education expenditure in this year offsets the higher transfer receipts by the youngest age groups.

Analyzing the development of fiscal sustainability over time illustrates the superiority of an intertemporal budgeting concept over cash-flow deficit analysis. In the year 1997, the primary deficit of the overall public sector budget (DM 6,7 billion) declined sharply compared to the deficit of the previous year (DM 33,0 billion).[82] Nevertheless, fiscal policy did not turn more restrictive. The generational account measures reveal that actually quite the reverse is true. Intertemporally, fiscal policy of the year 1997 was expansive due to the future transfer commitments made with introducing the final stage of statutory nursery care insurance, which are projected to augment generational fiscal imbalance in the long term.

Economic Assumptions

Finally, we test the sensitivity of the status quo indicators regarding the main economic postulates entering our construction of the generational accounts. These concern capitalization of government wealth and investment in the intertemporal public budget constraint, and the rules employed to project and discount future government revenue and spending.

Table 5.14 displays the reaction of intertemporal fiscal imbalance to alternative capitalization assumptions. If the market value of explicit public liabilities is approximated by capitalizing base year public interest payments rather than by the reported nominal value, intertemporal public liabilities increase. In the base year, the average rate of interest due on public liabilities exceeded our central discount rate of five percent. Therefore, the market value of outstanding government bonds is projected to exceed the nominal value, which raises the sustainability gap by 0.6 percent of annual GDP. Accordingly, intertemporal generational imbalance, indicated by the tax rate differential between present and future newborns, rises by 5.1 percentage points, to 32.6 percent of lifetime resources.

Similarly, approximating the market value of government tangible assets by their capitalized base year return rather than by a projection in per capita terms shows base year public finances even less sustainable than under the status quo benchmark. Capitalization of real base year returns on government

---

[82] These figures can be derived from the public sector budgets documented in the Appendix C.

Table 5.14. Sensitivity to Main Economic Assumptions

Base Year	Sustainability Gap[b]	Net Tax Rate[a]		
		Base Year Newborn	Future Newborn	Differ- ence
Status Quo	3.2	29.7	57.1	27.5
Capitalization of				
– Interest on Base Year Debt	3.8	29.7	62.3	32.6
– Return on Tangible Assets	4.0	29.7	63.5	33.9
– Return on Net Investment	1.8	29.7	44.8	15.2
Social Benefits to Civil Servants				
Treated as Government Purchases	2.4	32.0	53.1	21.0
No Maturation of Statutory Pensions	2.9	29.8	54.3	24.5

[a] Generational account as a fraction of present value life cycle income.
[b] Percentage of present value aggregate GDP according to equation (4.24), p. 82.
Note: Base year 1996, status quo mortality. Growth rate 1.5 percent, discount rate 5 percent

assets does not consider that productivity effects could generate additional revenue for the intertemporal public sector budget. Hence, the sustainability gap increases to 4.0 percent of yearly GDP.

The above experiments indicate that the valuation concept regarding government assets influences the sustainability outcome substantially. This is qualitatively important in situations where intertemporal fiscal imbalance is rather small. In the German case study, the selected specification of public sector assets represents the more conservative design, which tends to understate the actual fiscal imbalance. As for public net investment, inclusion as a government purchase which does not yield a return, represents a pessimistic assumption. If one argues instead that public investment generates a return equal to the original investment in present value, the sustainability gap falls markedly, to 1.8 percent of GDP. Thus, the status quo scenario may overstate the existing fiscal imbalance, although evidence for Germany suggests that future direct public revenue from investment is likely to be rather small. However, even in the most optimistic case regarding returns on public investment, the lifetime tax burden of future born agents, according to our data set, needs increase to 44.8 percent, which is 15.2 percentage points above the tax rate faced by base year newborns.

Projecting future government transfer spending, the status quo scenario deviates from conventional growth uprating by incorporation of cohort effects with regard to statutory old-age pensions and social benefits received by civil servants. Table 5.14 indicates that abstracting from cohort effects, one may understate the intertemporal gap in public sector budgets considerably. Supposed no maturation of statutory Social Security payments, the sustainability gap falls by 0.3 percentage points. While the lifetime tax rate of current newborn agents stays almost unchanged as reduced payments in old age are highly discounted, the sustainability gap translates into a 24.5 percentage point higher tax burden for future generations. Maturation effects add 3.0 percentage points to intertemporal generational imbalance.

The impact of rising social services to civil servants on the sustainability of public finances is even more significant. Counting public transfers to civil servants as age-neutral government purchases, as usually done by generational accountants, reduces the sustainability gap to 2.4 percent of yearly GDP, as lifetime net tax payments made by living generations increase considerably. Future generations, in contrast, are unburdened due to the reduced intertemporal liabilities of the public sector. Compared to the status quo, their lifetime tax burden, totaling 53.1 percent of lifetime resources, falls by 4.0 percentage points. One should be aware that this optimistic outcome requires the strong assumption that increased transfer spending to an aging civil servant population is compensated by reduced government spending on active civil servants. The status quo cohort design, despite some uncertainties, definitely represents the more apt scenario.

Table 5.15 displays the main sustainability indicators for a series of experiments conducted in an attempt to bracket what would be the actual long-term productivity growth rate and the appropriate rate of discounting future tax and transfer streams. This test shows that the finding of severe intertemporal fiscal imbalance is very robust. For a range of realistic alternative postulates regarding the long-term development of productivity and interest rates, the sustainability gap does not change by more than 0.2 percentage points of annual GDP. Also the lump-sum tax indicator shows little variation. If the intertemporal liabilities of the public sector are distributed among all living and future agents, the yearly age-neutral tax burden restoring sustainability ranges from DM 1,410 in the minimum (for several growth and interest rate combinations) to DM 1,480 in the maximum (for a two percent growth rate and a four percent interest rate).

Ordering the sustainability gap and the lump-sum tax indicator according to the underlying growth-adjusted discount factor, one detects a u-shaped pattern.[83] Taking into account productivity growth, fiscal imbalance tends to increase, if the discount rate is low, since long-term deficits due to population aging are given high weight, or if the discount rate is high, since future income

---

[83] Ceteris paribus, the sustainability results are determined by the ratio of the growth and interest factor, $\frac{1+g}{1+r}$. Due to the simple projection rules, the assumption of a two percent growth rate in combination with a six percent discount rate is, as one can easily check, closer to the benchmark than a scenario using a one percent growth rate and a five percent rate of discount.

Table 5.15. Sensitivity to Growth and Discount Rate Variations

Growth Rate	Sustainability Gap[b]	Net Tax Rate[a]		Differ- ence	Lump-sum Tax[c]
		Base Year Newborn	Future Newborn		
Discount Rate: 4 %					
1.0 %	3.3	29.7	52.7	23.0	1,420
1.5 %	3.3	29.4	48.4	19.0	1,440
2.0 %	3.4	28.7	44.4	15.7	1,480
Discount Rate: 5 %					
1.0 %	3.2	29.1	62.6	33.5	1,420
1.5 %	3.2	29.7	57.1	27.5	1,410
2.0 %	3.3	29.7	52.4	22.7	1,410
Discount Rate: 6 %					
1.0 %	3.3	27.0	76.6	49.5	1,460
1.5 %	3.3	28.3	68.6	40.3	1,430
2.0 %	3.2	29.2	62.1	32.9	1,410

[a] Generational account as a fraction of present value life cycle income.
[b] Percentage of present value aggregate GDP according to equation (4.24), p. 82.
[c] Annual tax payment per capita of population balancing the sustainability gap.
Note: Base year 1996, status quo mortality

is given low weight. Under status quo conditions, the minimum fiscal imbalance is indicated close to a growth-adjusted discount rate consistent with the combination of a 1.5 percent interest rate and a five percent discount rate, which justifies our benchmark parameterization as a conservative choice.

As is evident from Table 5.15, the hypothetical difference of lifetime tax rates between present on future generations is less robust quantitatively than the sustainability indicators discussed above. Assumed that the sustainability gap is levied exclusively on future generations, generational imbalance varies inversely with the growth-adjusted discount rate. Application of a lower discount factor gives higher weight to agents born in the distant future. Therefore, similar to an increase in fertility, the per capita net tax rates are reduced. The assumption of higher productivity growth makes future born agents richer, which reduces their tax burden relative to lifetime resources. Still, even in the most optimistic scenario, given by a real discount rate of four percent and productivity growth of two percent per annum, the lifetime tax rate of future generations exceeds that of present newborns by more than 50 percent.

The sensitivity analysis reveals that the generational account measures are robust under a wide range of conditions, even quantitatively, and do not depend crucially on uncertain parameterization issues. Although one may combine the various assumptions underlying the generational accounts in a way that leads to the indication of sustainable public finances, this would be, in the light of the present sustainability analysis, an overly optimistic scenario. Long-term oriented fiscal policy can hardly rely on such an extreme setting. Since continuation of current fiscal policy is likely to induce severe fiscal imbalances, fundamental policy changes seem in order in Germany.

In the following chapters, the generational accounting framework is employed to assess policy measures directed at alleviating demographic aging by immigration and reducing the adverse fiscal effects of demographic aging by adaptation of tax and transfer levels.

6. Immigration Policy and Fiscal Sustainability

6.1 Immigration and Generational Accounting

The analysis of the previous chapter has shown that demographic aging imposes the most serious threat to the long term viability of present tax and government spending levels in Germany.[1] Policies directed at augmenting the prospective labor force may help alleviating pressures on public budgets, generated by a rising population share of the elderly. In this context, promotion of female labor force participation, qualification of low skilled workers and a higher standard retirement age are debated policy instruments. Besides, as labor market policy is unlikely sufficient to mitigate the negative fiscal impacts of demographic aging [OECD Secretary (1991)], immigration is proposed frequently as a means to rejuvenate the resident population. Young immigrants, some analysts argue, may replace native working-age contributors to the public coffers, missing due to the permanent fertility decline.[2] For this reason, the long-term demographic and economic impact of immigration is not only being discussed in traditional immigration countries like the United States, Australia or Canada, but also in the countries of western Europe, which generally do not consider themselves as immigration countries.

The impacts of immigration on the long-term demographic structure of aging populations have been assessed for several countries.[3] Sensitivity tests of population projections mostly indicate that the improvement of dependency measures is rather small for reasonable levels of immigration. However, the value of a purely demographic assessment of immigration effects seems limited, since dependency indicators do not accurately design the relation between demographic and fiscal variables, let alone aspects of intertemporal generational redistribution.

The extent to which future migration inflows will mitigate intertemporal fiscal imbalance resulting from an aging population, depends on immigrants' remaining lifetime net payments to the public sector after taking

---

[1] This chapter draws extensively on previous work by Bonin et al. (2000).

[2] This argument is made, for example, by Simon (1991) and Holzmann (1988).

[3] Prominent examples are Ahlburg (1993) for the United States, George et al. (1991) for Canada and Lesthaege et al (1991) for the European Union.

residency. The current position of foreign residents in public tax and welfare systems is generally well-researched.[4] However, cross sectional analysis, focusing on immigrant cohort structure at a certain point in time, fails to address the intertemporal fiscal contribution of immigrants. Evidence regarding lifetime net taxes paid by migrant cohorts in the host country is scarce. Støresletten (2000) assesses the lifetime net fiscal contribution of immigrants to Sweden in the context of a stylized life cycle approach. His findings suggest that the rest-of-life net taxes paid by immigrants after their arrival are positive on average and potentially large, thereby improving fiscal sustainability.

With respect to German public finances, long-term fiscal effects of future immigration have been examined by Börsch-Supan (1994b) and Felderer (1994) who studied the development of public revenue and spending aggregates under alternative migration settings. Unfortunately, the projections are limited to the migration impact on pay-as-you go social insurance schemes. Furthermore, the approach of either study remains fundamentally a demographic one, as specific economic characteristics of immigrants are not identified. Instead, immigrants are supposed to adapt immediately to the behavior of native residents. Bonin (1994) mainly recapitulates the work of Börsch-Supan and Felderer, but widens the scope of the analysis by incorporating taxes paid to and transfers received from the general public budget. Still, the analysis does not treat immigrants as a fiscally distinct subpopulation, nor does it adopt a life cycle cohort perspective.

Sinn (1997), discussing the net contribution of immigrants to pay-as-you go Social Security finances, argues that the present value of immigrant gains for the incumbent population could be large. Supposed each additional immigrant adds a dynastic chain of descendants, whose aggregate payroll contributions, over an indefinite time horizon, balance the aggregate pension claims of the immigrant dynasty in present value terms, the fiscal externality generated by an immigrant equals the present value of her gross life cycle contributions to the system. Based on this theoretical argument, Sinn estimates the immigrant externality to Germans constructing the generational account of immigrant contributions to the pension system, which is large, and considerably larger than the gain from increased fertility.

In this chapter, we employ generational accounts to evaluate the overall intertemporal impacts of immigration to Germany. From the viewpoint of generational accounting, immigration is beneficial for native residents if it moves public finances closer to fiscal sustainability, lowering the per capita tax increment necessary to redeem intertemporal public liabilities. The influence of prospective immigration on the average tax burden of native agents

---

[4] Pioneering studies were undertaken by Simon (1984) and Blau (1984) for the United States. A more recent contribution to the literature was made by Borjas and Trejo (1991). Among others, Riphahn (1998), Simon (1994), Steinmann and Ulrich (1994) and Poschner (1996) have studied the position of foreigners in the German welfare system. The latter also provides a useful survey of the literature.

is evident from the intertemporal budget constraint of the public sector, if one singles out the migrant generational accounts, using equations (4.3) and (4.23):

$$\sum_{y=t}^{\infty} G_{t,y} - W_t =$$

$$\sum_{k=t-D}^{t} P_{t,k} GA_{t,k} + \sum_{k=t+1}^{\infty} P_{k,k} GA_{t,k} + \sum_{y=t}^{\infty} \sum_{k=y-D}^{y} M_{y,k} \frac{GA_{y,k}^{M}}{(1+r)^{y-t}}. \quad (6.1)$$

Future immigrants enter the intertemporal constraint to fiscal policy directly with the base year present value of their rest-of-life net tax payments, made after their arrival in the host country in year y. The double summation on the RHS of equation (6.1a) measures the aggregate net contribution of migrants to the public purse. Besides, immigration affects intertemporal fiscal imbalance through two different channels. First, the presence of migrants potentially changes annual net government purchases, $G_{t,y}$. As with resident generations, the remaining lifetime net tax payments by immigrants in the host country need to be balanced against additional government purchases, in order to measure the full impact of migrants on the sustainability gap. Only if there is a cohort surplus for immigrant generations, the corresponding reduction of intertemporal government liabilities reduces the life cycle tax burden of some – current or future – native cohorts.

Secondly, for a given sustainability gap, immigration increases the number of taxpayers who may share the additional tax payments required to redeem the intertemporal liabilities of the public sector. This demographic effect on the size of the future tax base works both directly and indirectly. The stylized policies used by generational accountants to balance the intertemporal public budget immediately change the immigrant term included in equation (6.1a), raising the generational accounts for those immigrant cohorts who are supposed to share the burden of residents. In addition, the offspring of the immigrant population enlarge the size of future cohorts born in the country, $P_{k,k}$, which, through the second right-hand term of the intertemporal public budget constraint, lowers the per capita net fiscal burden of residents further, if the intertemporal equality (6.1a) is supposed to hold. As a consequence of this favorable long-term tax base effect, immigration might mitigate the intertemporal generational imbalance faced by resident cohorts even if migrant generations accumulate cohort deficits.

Within a generational accounting framework, the intertemporal contribution of immigrants to the public sector has been studied by Ablett (1997). Unfortunately, this study of migration effects on the long-term viability of public finances in Australia ignores differences in average tax and benefit levels between migrants and non-migrants. In the following, we make an attempt to design the fiscal characteristics of future immigrants to Germany explicitly. Disaggregation of the original tax and government spending age profiles allows us to break down the basic generational accounts presented in the previous chapter, into the accounts of German natives and residents of foreign origin. We infer what might be the actual lifetime contribution of future immigrants after taking residency, from current residents' rest-of-life net tax burdens by age and nativity.

A comparable disaggregation of generational accounts was presented recently by Auerbach and Oreopoulos (1999), using data on immigration to the United States, which suggest that the sustainability impact of immigration, although generally positive, could be very small. This finding is in marked contrast to ours. In Germany, which may serve as a case study for other western European countries, the net contribution of prospective immigrants is large supposed that their fiscal behavior resembles that observed in the current cross section of residents of foreign origin. Still, although selective immigration policy might strengthen the positive effect on fiscal sustainability, even high levels of immigration do not eliminate generational fiscal imbalance resulting from demographic aging.

The remainder of this chapter is organized as follows. Section 6.2 introduces our migration scenarios and discusses the estimation of relative net fiscal burdens by nativity from the micro data. Section 6.3 first assesses the generational accounts of current migrant residents, before analyzing the impacts of immigration on fiscal sustainability. The section finally provides some sensitivity tests and shows how active immigration policy might alter our basic findings.

6.2 Migration Scenarios and Parameter Estimates

As was shown in Section 2.6, generational accounts can be broken down for different subpopulations without difficulties, as long as transitions between population groups are excluded. To separate the lifetime net tax burdens of German natives, residents of foreign origin (henceforth also referred to as migrant residents) and future immigrants, it is necessary to carry out all demographic and fiscal projections distinguishing between the three groups within each birth cohort. With regard to future immigrants, we first proceed by assuming that they will resemble current migrant residents, since reliable data regarding immigrant integration and assimilation is scarce.

Our starting point for analyzing the impact of immigration on fiscal sustainability is the status quo of public finances in year 1996, described in Chapter 5. Regarding demographics, we adopt the more realistic *low mortality scenario*, also termed the *status quo migration scenario* in the present context, in order to enhance the prognostic quality of our policy analysis. The main immigration parameters employed to design the status quo migration scenario are displayed in Fig. 6.1 and Fig. 6.2, which plot the projected development of annual net immigration and the age composition of net immigrants respectively.

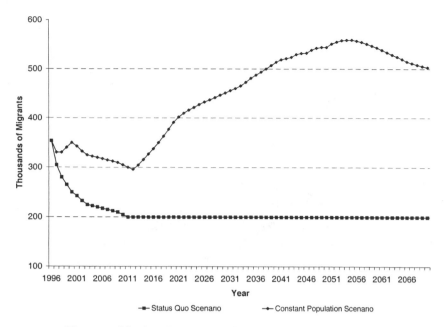

Fig. 6.1. Net immigration in alternative migration scenarios

As discussed briefly in Section 5.2, the status quo migration scenario assumes annual net immigration of 200,000 agents of foreign origin from year 2000 on. This figure is close to the average of annual net immigration to (West) Germany observed for the period 1952-1996, which numbered 191,000 agents. In the first years of the projection, we model a linear decline from the somewhat higher base year figure (220,000) to the supposed long-term value. In addition, in line with official projections, we gradually reduce the annual inflow of immigrants with German ethnicity, mainly from Eastern Europe. From the year 2010 on, net immigration of Germans is supposed to equal zero.

To assign aggregate net immigration by age and gender, we rely on the age and gender composition of net immigration observed in 1996, which is displayed in Fig. 6.2 with regard to age. In the base year, net immigration mainly occurred at an early stage of the life cycle: 43.1 percent of net migrants were of age 15 to 25. More than three quarters of the immigrants were younger than age 30, and 90 percent below age 40. For the status quo migration scenario, we assume that this favorable age structure will stay unchanged in the future. Contrasting the immigrant structure with the age composition of residents in the base period, also displayed in Fig. 6.2, illustrates the possibility to rejuvenate the aging German population through immigration. In 1996, median age of net immigrants was 21 years, while that of the resident population was 38 years. Due to this age advantage, which becomes larger

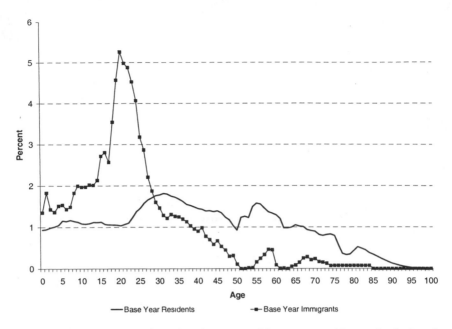

Fig. 6.2. Age structure of net immigrants and base year residents. Autjor's calculations based on Statistisches Bundesamt (1997a, Table 3.11).

over time as the native population ages, immigration reduces both average and medium age of the population in the long term.

Demographic rejuvenation from immigration, under status quo conditions, does not prevent the double aging process. Even if net immigration to Germany continues at historic levels, the median age of the population rises to 50 years by the year 2050, with the population share of agents in pension age doubling from 15.6 percent in 1996, to about 30 percent in the long term. The specific impacts of immigration on the demographic development are revealed comparing the status quo immigration scenario with a population projection excluding migratory flows.[5] As one would expect, this counterfactual experiment, termed the *no migration scenario*, results in more severe demographic aging, as is found inspecting Table 6.1, which displays the development of central demographic indicators for the demographic projections employed in this chapter.[6]

---

[5] This scenario, excluding both immigration and emigration, is different from a projection assuming zero net immigration. With zero net immigration, the population composition changes due to migration, since the age composition of immigrants and emigrants differ [McCarthy and Bonin (1999)].

[6] Similar results regarding the impact of immigration on the long-term demographic structure of the German population have been presented, for example, by the DIW (1995).

Table 6.1. Immigration and Composition of German Population

Year	1996	2000	2010	2020	2030	2040	2050	2060	2070
Total Population(millions)	81.8	81.4	78.6	74.3	68.6	62.0	54.6	47.0	40.3
Population Share (percent)									
< 18	19.4	18.8	15.9	14.2	13.4	12.6	12.0	12.1	12.1
18 – 64	65.0	64.8	63.4	62.7	57.5	53.6	53.4	51.8	51.5
> 64	15.6	16.4	20.7	23.1	29.1	33.8	34.6	36.1	36.4
Migrant Residents	9.0	8.9	8.8	8.6	8.1	7.4	6.2	4.6	2.8
Median Age	38	40	44	49	50	52	54	55	54
Status Quo Migration Scenario									
Total Population (millions)	81.8	82.6	82.6	81.1	78.3	74.6	70.1	65.2	60.7
Population Share (percent)									
< 18	19.4	19.0	16.5	15.3	14.7	14.1	13.8	13.9	14.0
18 – 64	65.0	64.9	63.7	63.4	59.3	56.5	56.4	55.4	55.6
> 64	15.6	16.1	19.8	21.4	26.0	29.4	29.9	30.7	30.5
Migrant Residents	9.0	10.2	12.5	14.5	16.4	18.0	19.5	20.4	20.9
Median Age	38	39	43	46	47	49	50	50	50
Constant Population Scenario									
Total Population (millions)	81.8	82.8	83.9	84.0	84.0	84.0	84.0	84.0	84.0
Population Share (percent)									
< 18	19.4	19.0	16.7	15.7	15.5	15.3	15.4	15.6	15.7
18 – 64	65.0	64.9	63.8	63.6	60.0	58.0	58.5	58.4	58.8
> 64	15.6	16.1	19.5	20.7	24.5	26.7	26.1	26.0	25.5
Migrant Residents	9.0	10.4	13.6	16.7	20.5	24.4	28.2	31.5	33.5
Median Age	38	39	43	45	46	47	46	46	45

Supposed no migration Germany would lose about 20 million people by the year 2070, compared to the status quo scenario. The smaller population is considerably older, too. At the maximum in 2060, median age of the population reaches 55 years, five years more than with constant annual immigration. Accordingly, the aging process sets in earlier. Whereas the population share of pensioners does not exceed 30 percent sooner than 2040 under status quo conditions, this ratio is reached a decade earlier in the no-immigration case. In the long term, the population share of pensioners exceeds 36 percent, which is six percentage points above the status quo benchmark. Without newly arriving immigrants, the fraction of residents who are of foreign origin in the total population converges to zero in the long run of course. Since our demographic model applies the *ius soli* principle to descendants of immigrants, the initial migrant population becomes extinct after a period of hundred years. Although it seems unlikely from today's perspective that Germany could successfully bar immigration, the no-migration benchmark can serve as a lower bound of plausible migration developments. To design an upper bound, termed the *constant population scenario*, we first follow the high migration variant employed by the Federal Statistical Office, considering a constant inflow of 300,000 net immigrants of foreign origin per annum from year 2000 on.[7] Immigration at these levels leads to a continuous increase in population, which approaches a total of 84 million by the year 2011. From 2011 on, when immigration of 300,000 agents per year would not longer prevent population decline, we switch to a different rule to determine annual immigration. Total migration figures are derived endogenously, claiming that immigration guarantees a constant population.

The annual immigration intake preventing population decline in the long term is displayed in Fig. 6.1. Between 2011 and 2020, as the number of deaths in the resident population grows sharply, immigration required to stabilize population size increases to 400,000. In the course of the next decades, necessary immigration continues to rise due to population aging (if at a slower rate) and reaches a maximum of about 560,000 by the year 2055. When the resident population approaches a stable state, the excess of deaths over births converges to a total of 500,000 which needs compensation by immigration.

The constant population scenario requires that annual migration quotas, exceeding 0.6 percent of the resident population in the long term, stay constantly above historic levels in Germany. This does not mean that this scenario would not stand a chance of realization. In fact, administered immigration quotas in traditional immigration countries like Australia or Canada are generally higher than that projected necessary to stabilize the German population.[8] Nonetheless, social costs of integrating a markedly increased number of immigrants are perhaps high.[9] In the constant population scenario, the high intake of immigrants doubles the initial population share of foreign born residents by the year 2030. In 2070, the number of migrant residents exceeds one third of the entire population, compared to 20 percent if status quo immigration levels persist.

Even if endogenous immigration is set to ensure constant total population, its age structure continues to change, since the age composition of im-

---

[7] Parallel to the status quo scenario, we design a linear increase from the base year figure of non-German migrants between the years 1996 and 2000 and account for immigration of ethnic Germans until the year 2010.

[8] Australia, with a total population of about 8 million, sustains an annual intake of 150,000 immigrants, which is an immigrant quota of about two percent. In Canada, current immigration plans provide for 200,000 to 250,000 immigrants. Thus, the immigrant quota is somewhat less than one percent of the current population of 26 million [Appleyard (1993)].

[9] Cf. Steinmann and Jäger (1997) for a theoretical debate of this issue.

migrants differs from that in the resident population. The higher immigrant intake brings additional demographic relief in the long term. The development of both median age and the population share of the pension-aged closely resembles that projected for the high fertility scenario discussed above.[10] In the year 2070, compared to the status quo scenario, median age of the population is lower by five years and the population share of agents in pension age is smaller by five percentage points. However, as particularly high immigration inflows occur only late in the projection, the reduction in old-age dependency evolves very gradually. By the year 2010, the fraction of pension-age cohorts in the population is merely 0.3 percentage points less than under status quo conditions. Even two decades later, the difference does not exceed 1.5 percentage points. In the context of generational accounting, the initial similarity of the status quo and the constant population scenarios is especially relevant, since fiscal impacts of the demographic development during the first decades of the projection attain comparatively high weight due to the present value perspective.

In order to determine the relative fiscal position of German natives and base year residents of foreign origin, we have started from the set of cross sectional tax and transfer profiles introduced in the previous chapter. Unfortunately, the German Consumer Expenditure Survey, from which most fiscal age profiles were retrieved at this stage, does not allow us to disaggregate consumption variables by nativity. Since the CES sample is not representative for residents of foreign origin, we have resorted to additional micro survey data regarding tax payments and transfer receipts by age, provided by the German Socio-Economic Panel (GSOEP). The GSOEP contains a panel of about 6,000 households with approximately 12,000 members, surveyed annually since 1984, which is disaggregated by area of residency, as well as by nationality.

We have used the twelfth, 1995-wave of the GSOEP to estimate the relative fiscal position of migrant residents compared to Germans. In a first step, for most tax and transfer payments incorporated in the generational accounts, separate profiles for Germans natives and residents of foreign nationality, indicating the respective fiscal position by age, were retrieved.[11] As far as possible, the construction of tax and transfer profiles by nativity keeps to the procedures introduced in Section 5.2.2. In principle, we might have used the GSOEP cohort profiles by nativity for our construction of migrant-specific generational accounts directly. However, in face of the comparatively

---

[10] Recall Table 5.3. Old-age dependency is slightly higher in the high fertility scenario, since the supposed increment in birth rates augments the population share of the youth at the expense of the working-aged.

[11] Although the GSOEP allows identification of the nationality of each household member, we have ordered households by the nationality of the household head. Doing so avoids complications assigning household data in households with mixed nationalities (which are few in number).

small sample provided by the GSOEP, in particular regarding migrant residents, we have preferred to benchmark the relative age profiles by nativity taken from the GSOEP against the absolute payment profiles derived from the CES, which (being the much larger sample) seems to provide consistently more dependable age profiles.[12]

To re-evaluate the GSOEP cohort profiles, we observe that the average payment of a representative cohort member taken from the CES, for each tax or transfer of type l, is a weighted average of the average payments per member of the native and migrant subpopulations according to

$$t_{t,k}^l = \frac{P_{t,k}^N}{P_{t,k}} t_{t,k}^{l,N} + \frac{P_{t,k}^M}{P_{t,k}} t_{t,k}^{l,M},$$

(6.2)

for each living generation $t - D \leq k \leq t$. In equation (6.2), the superscripts N and M to a variable denote that it refers to the native or migrant resident subpopulation respectively. To solve equation (6.2) for $t_{t,k}^{l,N}$ and $t_{t,k}^{l,M}$, we claim that the age-specific relative tax and transfer position of German natives and migrant residents, estimated from the GSOEP, is valid for the CES data as well, which allows us to write

$$t_{t,k}^{l,M} = t_{t,k}^{l,N} \frac{\tau_{t,k}^{l,M}}{\tau_{t,k}^{l,N}},$$

(6.3)

where $\tau_{i,k}^{l,N}$ and $\tau_{i,k}^{l,M}$ refer to the age-specific relative fiscal position of natives and migrants respectively.[13] Applying equations (6.2) and (6.3) to benchmark the GSOEP data by nativity against our original tax and transfer profiles, we proceed by assuming that all agents of foreign origin were resident in the West German states in the base year. This assumption, which avoids the distinction between region and nativity effects in East Germany, seems tolerable considered that only 3.4 percent of migrant residents lived in the East German states at the beginning of 1996.[14]

Designing a set of absolute tax and government spending profiles for native and migrant residents, we deviate from the outlined procedure on three

---

[12] This procedure also renders the disaggregated generational accounts generally consistent with those reported in the previous chapter.

[13] In general, due to high variance in the GSOEP data, we had to subject the ratio $\tau_{t,k}^{l,M}/\tau_{t,k}^{l,N}$ to a moving average before using it in equation (6.2).

[14] Cf. Statistisches Bundesamt (1997a, Table3.21.2). Although the base year cross-section of net tax payments made by agents resident in East Germany stays unchanged due to this approach, the disaggregation of net taxes by nativity in the West affects the projected net taxes of East Germans in the long term, since we assume that their payments will converge to the levels observed for Western residents of German nationality. However, the resulting change in generational accounts for East Germans is altogether negligible.

occasions. First, since the GSOEP does not report data on personal consumption, it is impossible to infer the relation of natives' and migrants' indirect tax payments by cohort directly. To overcome this deficiency, we assume that the relative consumption position of the two population groups is determined by differences in life cycle income before taxes.[15] Secondly, we employ uniform profiles to assign statutory health and nursery care benefits by age, since evidence regarding possible differences in morbidity by nativity is inconclusive [Ulrich (1992)]. Finally, civil servants' pension and health support payments are not assigned to migrant residents. Legal regulations prevent agents of non-German nationality from attaining civil servant status.

Figure 6.3 shows the net tax payments assigned to native and migrant residents in the West German states, evaluated for the base year. The fiscal profile of German natives, which dominates the weighted average of equation (6.2), closely resembles the original average net tax profile for the entire West German population. In contrast, the net tax profile assigned to migrant residents exhibits some characteristic features. Until age 20, it is basically equal to the profile applied to German agents, since age-specific net taxes are dominated by health benefits, which are independent of nativity by assumption. For the working-aged, net taxes of migrant residents are consistently smaller than those paid by natives of the same age, notably for older migrants who, on average, appear to profit less from productivity (or seniority) effects to the end of their working career. At age 60, net tax payments of migrant residents for the first time exceed those of native residents. The age pattern of net tax burdens observed close to standard pension age might suggest that migrant residents prefer entering retirement somewhat later than Germans. For cohorts in retirement, average net transfer receipts of migrants are smaller than those of natives. This observation seems consistent with high tax-benefit linkage in statutory pension insurance.

In order to project future tax and transfer payments by nativity, the base year profiles of native and migrant West German residents displayed in Fig. 6.3 are uprated according to the status quo principles set out in Chapter 5. In particular, we apply a constant uniform annual productivity growth rate and assume that policy reforms incorporated in the base case forecasts affect net taxes of native and migrant residents by the same proportion, leaving relative fiscal positions of the two population groups unchanged. For a benchmark, we do not design integration or assimilation effects, which might change the cross sectional migrant net tax profile from a cohort perspective.

As for net government purchases, we differentiate neither by age nor by nativity. There is one exception here, which involves government spending on education, assigned according to education enrolment. Using equations (6.2) and (6.3), we have disaggregated the original West German education pro-

---

[15] The ratio of relative payments by nativity in equation (6.3) becomes a constant in this case, which postulates that all consumption decisions are made at the beginning of the life cycle.

Fig. 6.3. Net tax payments by nativity. Cross section of year 1996

files by nativity, relying on estimates for age-specific education participation of migrant and native residents retrieved from the GSOEP. Note that, as we forecast all net government purchases on a per capita base, each immigrant taking residency in the future is predicted to induce additional public expenditure.

6.3 The Fiscal Contribution of Immigrants

6.3.1 Generational Accounts by Resident Group

Before addressing the potential contribution of prospective migrant cohorts to the intertemporal government budget, it is instructive to analyze the generational accounts for current migrant residents relative to natives. Despite inevitable uncertainties concerning what will be the fiscal position of future immigrants, it seems justified to assume that they are more likely to resemble, in fiscal terms, the current cross section of migrant residents than that of natives. If the remaining lifetime tax payments of immigrants taking residency at a certain age are indeed comparable to the generational accounts of residents of foreign origin who are of the same age, the construction of net tax profiles by nativity leads to a more precise measurement of immigration impacts on fiscal sustainability. In terms of equation (6.1a), the vector

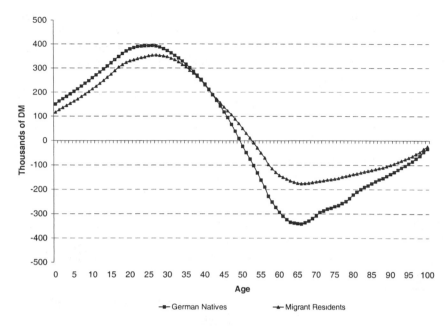

Fig. 6.4. Generational accounts for native and migrant residents. Base year 1996, low mortality scenario. Growth rate 1.5 percent, discount rate 5 percent

of generational accounts for migrant generations resident in the base year, corrected for the annual discount factor, would equal the yearly migrant generational account vectors entering the third RHS term of the intertemporal public budget constraint.[16]

Figure 6.4 displays the generational accounts for base year German natives and residents of foreign origin. In most age cohorts, the population share of migrant residents is initially less than ten percent. As a consequence, the generational accounts reported for German native cohort members closely resemble those of representative cohorts members, such as were analyzed in the previous chapter. As one might expect considering the cross-sectional age distribution of net taxes, the generational accounts of migrant residents exhibit also the typical life cycle pattern. However, compared to native residents, one observes marked differences in age-specific remaining lifetime net tax payments.

Within the base year born cohort, the net fiscal contribution of a migrant member to the intertemporal public budget, totaling DM 116,700, is smaller than that of a German member by an amount of DM 30,000. The difference is even more marked for young working-age cohorts. Migrant residents of age 20 are projected to pay on average DM 49,700 less net taxes upon

---

[16] This argument abstracts from variations in fiscal policy or mortality.

death than German natives of the same age. For cohorts at an early stage of their life cycle, differences in generational accounts by nativity mainly reflect the less propitious income situation of migrant residents relative to natives. According to our estimates, the present value of life cycle labor earnings by residents of foreign origin (DM 424,200) amounts to only 80.7 percent of the lifetime return on human capital of newborn natives (DM 528,600).[17] Taking into account the difference in lifetime income, the net tax burdens faced by the two resident groups are actually very similar. While migrant residents face a lifetime average net tax rate of 27.5 percent, German natives are left with a tax rate of 28.5 percent. This finding suggests that the overall tax and transfer system in Germany is progressive with respect to life cycle income.

Due to lower lifetime earnings and smaller holdings of non-human capital at later stages of the life cycle, base year residents of foreign origin pay significantly less income tax and payroll contributions, but also less indirect taxes.[18] This is evident from a comparison of Table 6.2 and Table 6.3.1, which display how the generational accounts are made up of specific taxes and transfers for native and migrant resident cohorts.

Migrant residents earn less than Germans, since they are endowed with less human capital on average. This is true also for young migrants (probably socialized in the country), who participate significantly less frequently in higher level education than natives.[19] Occupying less qualified jobs in the consequence, non-Germans also face higher unemployment risk. Therefore, benefits received from unemployment insurance are more than 50 percent higher than those of natives for all migrant resident generations. Over the entire life cycle, the unemployment benefits of a representative migrant (DM 25,100) exceed those of a representative native (DM 15,200) by 65.1 percent, which corresponds well with the base year difference in unemployment rates between the two population groups.[20]

For base year cohorts older than age 42, the generational accounts of migrant residents exceed those of natives. The net fiscal position of the two population groups changes quite early in the working career when transfer receipts in old-age start dominating the present value of rest-of-life net taxes due to discounting effects.

---

[17] Schmidt (1997) finds a somewhat smaller difference in labor income by nativity.

[18] The latter result is tautological, since the indirect tax profiles of migrants were constructed assuming that consumption is proportional to life cycle income.

[19] Cf. Schober and Stegmann (1987) and, more recently, Haisken-deNew et al. (1997). In our calculations, this fact is reflected in a lower per capita amount of government education purchases assigned to migrant residents.

[20] In 1996, the unemployment rate of migrant residents was 18.9 percent, while the rate for Germans was 9.2 percent in West Germany. Comparing these two rates, one needs to consider the earnings difference between the two population groups, since unemployment benefits are proportional to previously earned income.

Table 6.2. The Composition of Generational Accounts: Native Population

Genera-tion's Age	Genera-tional Account	Tax Payments							Transfer Receipts			
		Labor Income	Capital Income	Seigno-rage	VAT	Excise/Other	Social Insurance Contrib.	Social Security/Accident	Health/Long-Term Care	Unem-ployment	General Welfare/Housing	Youth/Maternity
0	150.7	70.9	20.1	1.2	62.2	32.3	151.3	58.8	65.3	15.2	17.9	30.2
5	203.3	84.2	23.8	1.5	73.8	38.3	179.5	69.7	66.1	18.0	17.6	26.5
10	259.6	99.8	28.0	1.7	86.7	45.2	212.3	82.3	71.9	21.4	17.5	21.1
15	321.5	117.6	32.9	2.0	100.6	53.0	250.0	97.1	78.4	26.1	17.9	15.1
20	379.6	137.6	38.1	2.4	112.7	59.0	289.2	114.4	84.3	32.3	18.8	9.5
25	393.1	149.9	42.8	2.7	114.3	58.9	306.6	133.2	88.8	36.0	17.7	6.3
30	372.5	151.1	46.7	3.0	113.0	56.6	303.4	154.6	92.5	35.7	15.9	2.5
35	316.0	144.1	48.3	3.1	109.1	52.3	281.4	178.1	95.8	34.0	13.7	0.8
40	234.1	131.8	47.3	3.1	101.8	46.6	251.1	203.9	98.9	32.3	12.2	0.1
45	118.5	109.8	44.7	2.9	91.8	40.1	210.9	237.5	102.5	30.8	10.9	0.0
50	-23.1	75.4	40.7	2.6	79.4	33.0	160.9	273.9	104.7	26.6	9.9	0.0
55	-161.6	40.1	35.5	2.3	66.1	25.8	106.1	303.9	104.2	20.2	9.3	0.0
60	-293.5	14.5	30.4	2.0	55.2	19.5	65.4	358.3	104.5	8.5	9.1	0.0
65	-340.2	3.4	25.3	1.7	45.1	14.2	45.1	359.4	106.0	0.3	9.4	0.0
70	-307.6	1.3	19.6	1.3	35.8	9.7	37.1	300.3	101.7	0.0	10.3	0.0
75	-270.5	0.6	14.0	0.9	26.6	6.3	30.6	245.1	93.4	0.0	11.0	0.0
80	-222.1	0.0	9.8	0.6	19.3	3.8	22.6	183.2	83.6	0.0	11.4	0.0
85	-175.9	0.0	6.7	0.4	13.4	2.5	16.8	132.4	71.7	0.0	11.7	0.0
90	-137.4	0.0	4.5	0.3	9.4	1.7	12.3	96.8	57.8	0.0	10.9	0.0
95	-94.7	0.0	2.9	0.2	6.3	1.1	8.0	63.8	41.0	0.0	8.3	0.0
100	-33.6	0.0	0.8	0.0	1.8	0.3	2.7	22.5	13.0	0.0	3.8	0.0

Note: Base year 1996, low mortality scenario, growth rate 1,5 percent, discount rate 5 percent. Thousands of DM

Table 6.3. The Composition of Generational Accounts: Migrant Resident Population

Generation's Age	Generational Account	Tax Payments						Transfer Receipts				
		Labor Income	Capital Income	Seignorage	VAT	Excise/Other	Social Insurance Contrib.	Social Security/Accident	Health/Long-Term Care	Unemployment	General Welfare/Housing	Youth/Maternity
0	116.7	55.3	16.1	1.0	50.0	25.9	129.1	25.2	61.9	25.1	18.4	30.1
5	162.7	65.9	19.1	1.2	59.3	30.8	153.7	29.8	62.1	29.9	19.1	26.4
10	213.4	78.5	22.7	1.4	70.2	36.4	182.4	35.2	67.2	35.5	20.0	20.3
15	274.6	94.1	26.9	1.6	83.2	43.2	217.0	41.6	72.6	42.3	21.6	13.2
20	329.9	110.6	31.2	1.9	94.1	48.4	250.3	48.9	77.8	49.3	23.4	7.1
25	351.6	124.2	35.2	2.1	95.1	48.5	270.0	57.5	81.5	57.0	24.3	3.2
30	347.1	131.4	38.8	2.4	94.0	46.8	272.6	67.3	84.4	62.0	24.1	1.0
35	305.2	126.1	40.9	2.5	91.6	43.6	249.2	78.3	87.9	58.2	23.9	0.3
40	230.6	111.1	40.7	2.5	86.8	39.2	210.3	90.9	91.8	53.8	23.5	0.0
45	139.1	89.6	38.8	2.3	79.0	33.9	168.2	104.5	95.6	49.9	22.8	0.0
50	50.4	69.1	35.1	2.1	67.9	28.1	134.5	119.3	96.7	48.0	22.6	0.0
55	-50.5	42.5	30.9	1.8	56.7	22.4	91.9	136.9	97.4	40.4	22.0	0.0
60	-142.5	16.3	26.7	1.6	47.6	17.2	47.8	163.1	98.5	18.1	20.0	0.0
65	-175.0	1.3	22.6	1.3	39.3	12.7	22.6	157.7	98.7	0.3	18.2	0.0
70	-168.9	0.0	17.5	1.0	31.1	8.8	17.8	131.6	95.6	0.0	17.9	0.0
75	-157.3	0.0	12.6	0.7	23.4	6.1	14.7	108.5	88.5	0.0	17.9	0.0
80	-138.7	0.0	8.8	0.5	16.9	3.8	11.3	83.6	79.2	0.0	17.4	0.0
85	-121.2	0.0	6.2	0.4	12.0	2.5	8.8	65.0	69.4	0.0	16.7	0.0
90	-100.4	0.0	4.2	0.2	8.4	1.7	6.8	50.2	56.4	0.0	15.0	0.0
95	-70.2	0.0	2.6	0.2	5.6	1.1	4.4	33.0	40.2	0.0	11.0	0.0
100	-24.3	0.0	0.9	0.0	1.9	0.3	1.5	11.2	13.0	0.0	4.7	0.0

Note: Base year 1996, low mortality scenario, growth rate 1,5 percent, discount rate 5 percent. Thousands of DM

Since pensions are closely related to individual earnings histories, Social Security benefits of migrant residents only amount to around 44 percent of natives' pension receipts, as a consequence of lower wage earnings and the typically shorter working career of immigrants.[21] High welfare receipts in pension age compensate migrant residents for their low Social Security income only partially. Therefore, in the maximum at standard retirement age 65, the remaining lifetime net transfer expected for residents of foreign origin, amounting to DM 175,000, exceeds that of native German cohort members by DM 165,200. For older cohorts in retirement, the difference in generational accounts between the two population groups gradually declines, but migrant agents continue to receive significantly less net transfers than natives.

6.3.2 Immigrant Cohort Deficits

As discussed above, calculating what might be the net contribution of future immigrant cohorts to the intertemporal government budget, we employ the cohort pattern of migrant residents' generational accounts, as displayed in Fig. 6.4, for a benchmark.[22] We assign, to each future immigrant of a certain age, the average remaining lifetime net taxes paid by present migrant residents of the same age, considering productivity growth and accounting for fiscal policy impacts. To evaluate the extent to which immigration affects the sustainability gap, net taxes paid by immigrants after taking residency need to be balanced against additional government purchases effected by immigration, which means constructing immigrant cohort deficits.

Table 6.4 summarizes the cohort deficits of base year migrant resident cohorts, which are equal to the cohort deficits we have assigned to immigrants taking residency in the base year. Since the impacts of prospective fiscal policy changes and rising life expectancy are of rather minor importance in our projections, the displayed age pattern of cohort deficits is representative also for immigrants who enter into the host country after the base period.

Similar to young residents, very young immigrants impose a burden on the intertemporal government budget. The present value of their lifetime net payments does not balance the increment in net government purchases due to their presence. For example, each immigrant who enters the country in the year of birth, according to our estimates, enlarges the sustainability gap by an amount of DM 120,000. At age 11, immigrants' remaining net tax payments

---

[21] One may argue that the latter influence on the cross-sectional pension levels does not persist for young migrant generations who stay in the country during their entire working career. Therefore, our estimates are likely to overstate the actual rest-of-life net taxes paid by young migrant cohorts.

[22] As the gender composition of the migrant resident population differs from that of projected immigration, the generational account of a representative immigrant differs from that of a representative migrant resident of the same age. Our computations account for this effect.

Table 6.4. Cohort Deficits of Migrant Resident Generations

Age	Generational Account	Government Purchases	Cohort Deficit[a]	Age	Generational Account	Government Purchases	Cohort Deficit[a]
0	116.7	236.8	120.0	55	-50.5	85.3	135.8
5	162.7	240.0	77.4	60	-142.5	75.4	217.9
10	213.4	216.3	2.9	65	-175.0	65.4	240.4
15	274.6	181.6	-93.0	70	-168.9	55.3	224.2
20	329.9	152.1	-177.9	75	-157.3	44.6	201.8
25	351.6	136.9	-214.7	80	-138.7	34.8	173.5
30	347.1	123.7	-223.4	85	-121.2	26.9	148.1
35	305.2	117.4	-187.8	90	-100.4	20.4	120.7
40	230.6	111.1	-119.5	95	-70.2	14.7	84.9
45	139.1	104.0	-35.0	100	-24.3	5.1	29.4
50	50.4	95.1	44.7				

[a] Remaining lifetime net government purchases net of generational account.
Note: Base year 1996, low mortality scenario. Growth rate 1.5 percent, discount rate 5 percent. Thousands of DM

after taking residency begin to exceed additional government purchases. The maximum cohort surplus is measured for immigrants entering the country close to age 30. Under status quo conditions, each immigrant contributes a net amount of approximately DM 224,000 to reduce the sustainability gap. Cohort surpluses gradually decline for older immigrants, but remain positive for all agents younger than age 48 when taking residency. Older immigrants impose a fiscal burden on the public sector, since they receive large transfers.[23]

If our benchmark is appropriate, i.e. if the net tax payments of prospective immigrants are indeed similar to those of current residents and if immigration raises government consumption, inspection of cohort deficits suggests that attraction of immigrants who are of age 11 to 47 when entering the host country would be particularly beneficial to the resident population. Cohort surpluses drawn from these immigrant generations directly reduce the sustainability gap. At present, most immigration takes place in this favorable age bracket. In 1996, 77.5 percent of all immigrants belonged to cohorts who are lifetime net contributors to the intertemporal public budget, according

---

[23] This seems likely to be true even if one argues that pensions for migrants taking residency at a very late stage of the life cycle are lower than suggested by the current cross section. If this is indeed the case, pensions possibly need to to be complemented with general welfare benefits.

to our estimates. Due to this favorable age composition, the average net contribution of immigrants is likely to be large. Under status quo conditions, we estimate that a representative immigrant pays an amount of DM 103,900, in terms of base year present value, after taking residency. Thus, supposed that the current age distribution of immigrants stays unchanged in the future, immigration will enhance the intertemporal sustainability of public finances.

6.3.3 The Sustainability Impacts of Immigration Policies

Having determined the immigrant cohort deficits, we are now prepared to answer the main question raised at the beginning of this chapter: To which extent may future immigration help alleviating intertemporal fiscal imbalance associated with demographic aging in Germany? This question can be answered inspecting Table 6.5, which displays our main indicators of intertemporal fiscal imbalance for the different migration scenarios specified above. Note that Table 6.5 reports life cycle income tax rates for *native* residents for sake of comparability. Applying the *ius soli* principle to immigrant descendants, we do not observe future newborns in our projection who are identified as of foreign origin.

As we know from our analysis in Chapter 5, continuation of current immigration levels is not sufficient to achieve long-term sustainability of fiscal policy in Germany. Of course, since we employ the same demographic projection, our present status quo results basically reproduce the outcome under low mortality conditions derived in the previous chapter. However, intertemporal government liabilities are somewhat higher due to the more specific treatment of immigrant net tax payments. We now assign migrant-specific generational accounts, which are lower on average, where we employed the net tax levels of representative agents before.

To evaluate the specific sustainability impacts of future immigration to Germany, it is necessary to judge the case of status quo immigration against the polar no migration scenario. Without immigration, public finances are even more seriously imbalanced to the disadvantage of future generations. The sustainability gap of base year fiscal policy increases to 6.1 percent of yearly GDP. If the sustainability gap is levied on future birth cohorts, the average net tax rate imposed on life cycle labor income has to be as high as 95.8 percent, compared to 28.5 percent for base year newborns.[24]

Hence immigration is desirable for future native residents whose lifetime net tax rate is reduced by 23.9 percentage points if current immigration levels are maintained. In absolute terms, a yearly inflow of 200,000 net immigrants extends the life cycle consumption possibilities of each future native

---

[24] This is certainly not a realistic policy option. Recall that the stylized policy experiments used by generational accountants mainly serve to highlight possible generational distribution conflicts.

Table 6.5. Immigration and Intertemporal Fiscal Imbalance

Scenario	Sustainability Gap[b]	Net Tax Rate[a]			Lump-sum Tax[c]
		Base Year Newborn	Future Newborn	Differ- ence	
No Migration	6.1	28.5	95.9	67.4	2,540
Status Quo	5.0	28.5	72.0	43.5	2,140
Constant Population	4.3	28.5	59.3	30.8	1,870

[a] Generational account as a fraction of present value life cycle income.
[b] Percentage of present value aggregate GDP according to equation (4.24), p. 82.
[c] Annual tax payment per capita of population balancing the sustainability gap.
Note: Base year 1996, low mortality scenario. Growth rate 1.5 percent, discount rate 5 percent

by DM 125,700. Alternatively, if the immigration gain is distributed lump-sum across all living and future generations, after-tax resources of native residents increase by DM 400 per annum. The qualitative finding that the positive impact of immigration on the fiscal burdens of natives is large, which stands in marked contrast to generational account estimates reported by Auerbach and Oreopoulos (1999) for the case of immigration to the United States, is robust with respect to growth and discount rate variations. For growth rates between one and two percent and interest rates between four and six percent, the gain from status quo immigration ranges from DM 98,600 to DM 185,200 if it is assigned to future birth cohorts, and from DM 290 to DM 620 per annum if it is distributed according to a lump-sum principle.

Since a representative migrant to Germany generates a cohort surplus under status quo conditions, each additional immigrant improves the intertemporal sustainability of base year tax and transfer levels further. Consequently the sustainability gap in the constant population scenario is smaller than that under status quo immigration. The additional annual revenue required to balance the intertemporal public budget falls by 0.7 percentage points, to 4.3 percent of yearly GDP, which translates into a tax reduction for future native cohorts equaling 12.8 percent of pre-tax resources, or DM 67,400. Compared to the no immigration benchmark, the immigration gain of future natives is as high as DM 193,100. The constant population scenario is more favorable with respect to fiscal sustainability than the high fertility case discussed above.[25] This finding suggests that immigration strategies might be more effective in terms of generational fiscal balance than efforts to raise fertility.

The favorable sustainability impacts of immigration are based on the assumption that the fiscal characteristics of future immigrants will resemble

---

[25] Compare Table 5.12, p. 154.

those of the current foreign worker population who took residency more than a decade ago on average, under rather advantageous labor market conditions. Thus, our base case results fail to account for the integration and assimilation process of immigrants.[26] With net tax levels being closely related to wage earnings, the integration process is likely to imply lower migrant cohort surpluses than those reported in Table 6.4, in particular if high unemployment on regulated German labor markets persists.

In addition, referring to the generational accounts of migrant residents for a benchmark, we assume that the skill structure of immigrants stays unchanged in the future. However, in recent times, the quality of immigrant cohorts has changed considerably due to restrictive immigration policy directed against labor immigration. At present, legal regulations heavily restrict immigration to Germany except for ethnic Germans, citizens of the European Union, family reunions of migrant residents and a limited number of migrants seeking refuge from ethnic or political persecution. As a consequence, the socio-economic characteristics of immigrants who presently attain resident status are likely to differ from those of current migrant residents, a major fraction of which took residency during a period of active labor recruitment in the 1960s and 1970s. While forecasts of prospective immigrant quality seem difficult, changes in the attitude to immigration could quickly alter the presently observed characteristics of immigrants.[27]

In face of these arguments, we have tested the robustness of the immigration impacts on fiscal sustainability, by designing what might be the net taxes paid by immigrants during the period of their integration into the labor market. We expect that after their arrival, immigrants pay less taxes than migrant residents, while being highly dependent on public welfare assistance. We postulate that immigrants, immediately after taking residency, receive the same health and nursery care benefits, maternity assistance, youth support and educational training as migrant residents. As for the remaining transfers and all taxes, we gradually adjust them during the integration period from a zero level in the year of immigration to the per capita payments of migrant residents when integration is complete. Furthermore, compared to the resident foreign worker population, we assign higher general welfare benefits to newly arriving immigrants, until they are fully integrated into the labor market. In the period of taking residency, all immigrants are supposed to gain their living exclusively from this extra welfare benefit, which is fixed at subsistence level. For all tax payments and transfer benefits affected, we assume an exponential adaptation process, which implies that the major share of the adjustment takes place during the final years of the integration process.

---

[26] Cf. Schultz (1998) for a survey of the assimilation literature. For empirical analyses of immigrant assimilation in Germany, consult Seifert (1997) and Dustmann (1996)

[27] Münz et al. (1999) analyze the features of current immigration to Germany in great detail, and outline possible future perspectives.

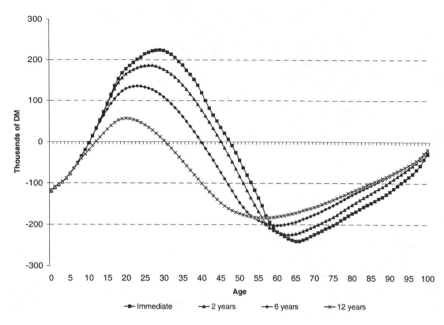

Fig. 6.5. Migrant cohort deficits and duration of integration period. Base year 1996, low mortality scenario. Growth rate 1.5 percent, discount rate 5 percent

The impacts of different integration periods on migrant cohort surpluses, as resulting from our admittedly *ad hoc* design of the assimilation process, are displayed in Fig. 6.5. Accounting for a period of fiscal assimilation reduces cohort surpluses drawn from most working-age cohorts under status quo conditions (implying immediate assimilation). An integration period shortens immigrants' average working career in the host county, which reduces the remaining (labor) tax payments made by older immigrants in particular. As a consequence, with the process of labor market integration slowing down, the maximum migrant cohort surplus gradually shifts toward younger immigrants, whereas older working-age immigrants induce increasingly larger cohort deficits in the intertemporal public budget. These are hardly offset by the reduced cohort deficits caused by immigrants in old-age, which are supposed to gain lower pensions than migrant residents, due to their shorter stay in the country. Note finally that our design of the integration process basically does not change the cohort deficits generated by the youngest immigrant generations. This seems well justified, considered that young immigrants are socialized in the country, and therefore are more likely to resemble migrant residents of the same age.

It is evident from Fig. 6.5 that the average cohort surplus drawn from immigrants, and hence the positive fiscal externality of immigration on the incumbent population, falls with the duration of the integration process. Ta-

Table 6.6. Average Migrant Cohort Surplus and Fiscal Gains of Natives

Scenario	Migrant Cohort Surplus	Immigration Gain[a] Future Natives[b]	Lump-sum[c]
	Integration Scenarios		
Immediate	103,900	125,700	400
2 Years	86,700	122,100	380
6 Years	52,900	108,400	280
12 Years	-8,000	82,300	110
	Immigration Policy Scenarios		
Screening by Skill Level	127,900	156,500	570
Screening by Age	118,900	130,000	440

[a] Per capita reduction in net tax payments compared to no migration scenario.
[b] Immigration gain assigned to native cohorts born after the base year.
[c] Immigration gain assigned to all residents as a constant annual per capita transfer.
Note: Status quo immigration levels. Base year 1996, low mortality scenario. Growth rate 1.5 percent, discount rate 5 percent

ble 6.6 summarizes the consequences on the immigration gain of native residents, assuming status quo immigration levels. If for example, immigrants adapt to fiscal behavior of migrant residents with only a delay of two years, the average net contribution of base year immigrants to the intertemporal public budget falls to DM 86,700, compared to DM 103,900 with immediate integration. Accordingly, the gain of native residents from immigration (compared to the no migration benchmark) is reduced, if rather moderately. To balance the sustainability gap, future German cohorts have to pay an additional amount of DM 3,600, which corresponds to a lump sum burden on all residents of merely DM 20 per annum.

The change in immigration gains turns more significant if immigrant integration takes more time. However, the additional burden on natives is non-linear with respect to the length of the integration period, as the adaptation process of immigrants is designed according to a non-linear principle. If immigrants require six years instead of two to adapt to the net tax levels of migrant residents, the average migrant cohort surplus is reduced to DM 52,900. As a consequence, the immigration gain of future German cohorts decreases by DM 13,700, to an amount of DM 108,400 per capita.

Provided that completion of immigrant integration requires 12 years, the average net contribution of immigrants to the public coffers turns negative. Each additional immigrant enlarges the sustainability gap by an amount of DM 8,000 on average. Nevertheless, the positive fiscal externality on native generations due to immigration remains sizeable. As status quo immigration levels significantly increase population size in the long term, the number of taxpayers who can be made responsible for redemption of intertemporal liabilities increases. Therefore, if the adjustment burden is levied on future born natives (a considerable fraction of which are descendants of immigrants) they still pay DM 82,300 less net taxes than under the no migration scenario. This figure represents the approximate indirect fertility effect of migration on future generational accounts, since aggregate net tax payments of first generation immigrants are close to zero given a 12-year integration period.

Hence, under status quo conditions, the long-term demographic impulse accounts for about two thirds of future generations' gain from immigration. If immigration gains are equally shared by current and future generations, the demographic tax base effect due to immigration remains positive, but is less important. This outcome is due to the fact that the population share of immigrants in the overall population is smaller than that of immigrant descendants in future birth cohorts.

The integration experiments highlight that the speed of fiscal assimilation is a fundamental determinant of the positive fiscal externalities generated by immigration. Fiscal assimilation is supported by smooth labor market integration of foreign workers. Evidence from traditional immigration countries suggests that active screening of potential immigrants may help improving the labor market performance of immigrants [Miller (1999)]. Immigrant skills and age seem to provide particularly successful screens in this regard. To conclude this section, we assess the potential for improving fiscal sustainability by means of selective labor migration policy that discriminates between immigrants.

In a first experiment, we postulate that immigration policy could successfully raise the average skill level of future immigrants above that observed for migrant residents in Germany. As an upper bound of what might be the impacts of successful screening by skills, we claim that migrant cohort surpluses will resemble those of native resident cohorts, rather than those of migrant residents. If this is the case, as is shown in Table 6.6, the cohort surplus drawn from a representative base year immigrant increases markedly, to an amount of DM 115,400. As a result, the lifetime tax rate of future German natives falls to 67.1 percent for status quo immigration levels, compared to 95.9 percent in the no migration case. Accordingly, the immigration gain of future native generations totals DM 156,500 per capita, of which DM 30,800 can be attributed to the impacts of improved immigrant quality. In yearly terms, the per capita gain from qualification-oriented immigration policy amounts to DM 180.

Our second policy experiment designs a screening by age which aims at improving the favorable base year age composition of net immigration further. We assume that the fraction of immigrants in the age bracket between 20 and 35 who exhibit the highest cohort surpluses permanently increases by

20 percent while the absolute immigrant inflow stays unchanged.[28] Our findings, again summarized in Table 6.6, indicate that the positive fiscal externalities from screening immigrants by age are comparatively small. Although the average cohort surplus drawn from immigrants increases considerably, to DM 118,900 per migrant, the net tax burden of future generations, compared to the status quo scenario, falls only by an amount of DM 4,300. This finding suggests that self-selection of immigrants to Germany may guarantee a fiscally satisfactory age composition of immigrants, which would be difficult to improve further by means of active immigration policy. As seems evident from Table 6.6, the more essential task of immigration policy is to support labor market integration of future immigrants.

6.4 Conclusion

This chapter provided valuable insight into the relation between the demographic consequences of immigration and the long-term viability of current tax and transfer levels in Germany. First, from the generational accounting viewpoint, it does not seem likely that intertemporal generational balance can be achieved through immigration, even if future migration quotas would be as high as in traditional immigration countries and prevent population decline. Secondly, measured by the current net tax payments of migrant residents, fiscal externalities of immigration on the incumbent population are potentially large. The positive immigration impact comes from two sources: First, the migrant cohort surplus is positive on average, due to the favorable age composition of immigrants which compensates for their lower per capita net tax payments. Furthermore, immigration enlarges population size, and therefore the number of taxpayers who share in balancing the intertemporal government budget.

Finally, immigration gains strongly depend on how fast immigrants assimilate. Active migration policy, which screens potential immigrants by qualification and promotes the labor market integration of arriving migrants, according our analysis, is advised to improve intertemporal generational balance. Nevertheless, since the adverse intertemporal budget effects of demographic aging are balanced out by immigration only partially, even under very optimistic conditions, there remains a need for substantial fiscal reform, if one believes that generational imbalance to the disadvantage of future generations ought to be reduced. This is the topic of the following chapter, which analyzes the possibilities to improve fiscal sustainability in Germany by reforms of statutory pension insurance.

---

[28] This requires a reduction in the immigration share of all other age cohorts, which is done at a proportional rate in our calculations.

7. Options for Social Security Reform

7.1 Social Security and Fiscal Sustainability in Germany

Analyzing what causes the lack of fiscal sustainability in Germany, we observed in Section 5.3.2 that intertemporal generational imbalance is mainly attributable to three sources – public liabilities of the base period reflecting past fiscal policy, regional economic disparity demanding sizeable government transfers to the East German states which are not completely funded by taxes at present, and most importantly, the fiscal consequences of demographic aging. Although the latter, as shown in the previous chapter, are perhaps to some extent mitigated by immigration, political decision makers cannot hope that demographic rejuvenation will be strong enough to put aging pressure from government budgets. Thus, there is a need for long-term oriented fiscal reform, in order to check intergenerational distribution conflicts resulting from unsustainable tax and transfer levels. In fact, like in many OECD countries, concern that progressive demographic aging could put overwhelming strain on future government budgets has fuelled the debate on fiscal policy reform in Germany. The options to protect public provision of retirement income against demographic aging attract particular attention.[1]

In this context, it is important to note that it is not public provision of pension income *per se*, but the institution of pay-as-you-go pension provision, which comes under pressure during the demographic transition. A pay-as-you-go system does not accumulate funds to serve the entitlement of current contributors to future pensions. Instead, current pension liabilities are financed from current contribution revenue. Assumed that a public pension system of this type does not receive subsidies from other budget authorities, the pay-as-you-go budget constraint as of period i can be written as

$$\sum_{k=i-D}^{D} t_{i,k}^c P_{i,k} + \sum_{k=i-D}^{D} t_{i,k}^p P_{i,k} = 0. \tag{7.1}$$

Equation (7.1) keeps to the notation introduced in Chapter 2. The superscripts c and p of a variable indicate that it refers to contributions to (c)

---

[1] Cf. Thomas (1997) for a general survey with an international focus.

and benefits from (p) the pay-as-you-go system. To see the impact of demographic changes on the pay-as-you-go budget, define $P_{i,k}^c = P_{i,k}$, if $t_{i,k}^c > 0$, and $P_{i,k}^c = 0$, if $t_{i,k}^c = 0$. Furthermore, write $P_{i,k}^p = P_{i,k}$ if $t_{i,k}^p < 0$, and $P_{i,k}^c = 0$ if $t_{i,k}^c = 0$. Thus, $\sum_k P_{i,k}^c$ represents the number of contributors to the system in period i, while $\sum_k P_{i,k}^p$ represents the number of pensioners. Finally, assume that the payroll taxes paid by each contributor and the transfers received by each pensioner are identical, which means that $t_i^c = t_{i,k}^c > 0$ for all agents $P_{i,k}^c$, and $t_i^p = t_{i,k}^p < 0$ for all $P_{i,k}^p$. Then, equation (7.1) can be rearranged to

$$-\frac{t_i^c}{t_i^p} = \frac{\sum_{k=i-D}^{D} P_{i,k}^p}{\sum_{k=i-D}^{D} P_{i,k}^c}. \tag{7.2}$$

Equation (7.2) shows that under a pay-as-you-go system, the level of average payroll contributions relative to pensions is basically determined by the ratio of pensioners to contributors. If old-age dependency increases in the course of the demographic transition, which raises the quotient on the RHS of equation (7.2), either the average transfer level t_i^p has to be reduced, or the average contribution level t_i^c has to be increased, in order to balance the annual pay-as-you-go budget.

Pension claims, acquired through previous contributions to the system, are in general well protected as personal property. With benefits defined, the average contribution level remains the only parameter of choice in equation (7.2). Higher old-age dependency then must go along with higher average contribution levels, which requires an increment in payroll contribution rates unless a rising population share of contributors, for example due to higher labor force participation, replaces contributors missing due to population decline. Rising payroll contributions are problematic, since a fraction of the payroll contribution constitutes a tax on labor earnings in a dynamically efficient economy, which distorts the decision between labor and leisure.[2] With contribution rates increasing, the implicit tax increases too, and therefore the incentives to leave the system.

Generational accounting tests if current payroll contribution levels, given enacted pension replacement rates, can be maintained from an intertemporal perspective. Aggregating the annual pay-as-you-go budgets, as described by equation (7.1), after a period t, and discounting future payments back to the base period, yields the intertemporal budget constraint of a pay-as-you-go system

---

[2] This follows from the well-known Aaron (1966) result that, even with a constant contribution rate, the rate of return in a pay-as-you-go system equals the growth rate of the wage sum, which, in dynamic efficiency, is lower than the interest rate gained on capital markets.

$$\sum_{i=t}^{\infty} \sum_{k=i-D}^{D} t_{i,k}^{c} P_{i,k} (1+r)^{t-i} + \sum_{i=t}^{\infty} \sum_{k=i-D}^{D} t_{i,k}^{p} P_{i,k} (1+r)^{t-i} = 0, \qquad (7.3)$$

which is the basic reference for generational accounting analyses of pay-as-you-go finances [Gokhale et al. (1995), Auerbach et al. (1992b)]. Constructing isolated generational accounts for a pay-as-you-go system, age-specific annual net contributions are defined as $t_{i,k} = t_{i,k}^{c} + t_{i,k}^{p}$. Supposed no migration to limit notation, a rearrangement of equation (7.3) by cohort, after inserting the definition of generational accounts according to equation (2.3), leads to

$$\sum_{k=t-D}^{t} P_{t,k} GA_{t,k} + \sum_{k=t+1}^{\infty} P_{t,k} GA_{t,k} = 0 . \qquad (7.4)$$

Given that pension wealth equals zero (which implies that the provision of public pensions always worked on a pay-as-you-go scheme in the past), equation (7.4), parallel to the intertemporal budget constraint of the overall public sector, illustrates the relation of current and prospective net contribution burdens by generation imposed by a pay-as-you-go-system.[3]

Aggregation of the prospective net contributions under initial tax and benefit levels for all generations provides a direct test whether the pay-as-you-go system is viable in the long term. If aggregate pension liabilities of the system are not balanced by projected contribution payments, contribution rates need to be raised, or benefit levels reduced for some generation, in order to balance the intertemporal pension budget. Using the sustainability approach, by convention, the financing of intertemporally unfunded pension claims is levied on future generations only who are assumed to face a uniform raise in contribution rates, which changes the second LHS term of equation (7.4) to guarantee the equality.[4]

Comparing equations (7.1) and (7.4), it is evident that the intertemporal budget perspective of generational accounting imposes a weaker constraint on the development of contribution and benefit levels than the institutional arrangement of a pay-as-you-go system, which strictly prohibits annual budget imbalances. In a generational accounting framework, by tolerating transitory accumulation of pension liabilities, a given net contribution level can be maintained for some time, if it is counterbalanced by subsequent budgetary surpluses due to demographic recovery or adjustments of the pension system. Provided that base year pension finances work on a pay-as-you-go scheme,

---

[3] In the generational accounting literature, equation (7.4) was used first by Boll et al. (1994) to analyze fiscal sustainability of pay-as-you systems.

[4] In principle, an intertemporal deficit in the pay-as-you-go budget is sustainable provided it is subsidized by the overall government budget. However, unless the general budget runs an intertemporal surplus, this still necessitates an increment in life cycle net taxes for some generation.

the generational accounting test of pension sustainability represents an extreme scenario. It abandons the non-deficit requirement abruptly, suggesting that politics would start trying to shift occurring imbalances in the pension budget into the future through debt.

Adhering, in contrast, to the pay-as-you-go perspective, the revenue and expenditure parameters of the pension system would be adjusted in each year, according to the non-deficit constraint (7.1). In terms of the sustainability gap, continuation of a pay-as-you-go scheme always achieves intertemporal generational balance. A policy rule that meets the pension insurance budget annually must do so intertemporally. From a neoclassical viewpoint, however, continuous pay-as-you-go financing is as extreme a policy as the immediate transition to deficit financing. The government is deprived of its ability to redistribute personal consumption opportunities over time or across generations through accumulation of deficits. The remainder of this section switches between these two polar cases, in order to illustrate the possible generational imbalances induced by the Social Security system in Germany.

Adopting the generational accounting perspective first, it is necessary to extend the basic intertemporal budget constraint given by equation (7.3), to design the peculiarities of the German statutory pension system, which does not only receive contributory revenue. In 1996, 21.5 percent of pension insurance revenue represented a subsidy from the federal budget. Since then, the subsidy quota has increased even further (to 25.1 percent in 1998, according to our estimates), as revenue from an increment in turnover tax rates was earmarked to subsidize pensions. The pension subsidy is usually justified as a compensation for those pension benefits that contravene against the generally close connection between individual earnings (or contributions) and pension income realized by statutory pension insurance in Germany [Hofmann (1996)]. Redistributive elements in the pension system include, for example, credits for child rearing and education, and a lift up of low contributions to a minimum level.

Constructing generational accounts for the pension system, the government grant to the Social Security budget can be approached in different ways. If one accepts that the government subsidy serves to compensate for redistributive elements, which policy makers have added to the pension system, but which could as well be financed from the general budget, one would correct both relative age-specific pension benefits per capita and aggregate pension spending for these benefits. This approach is not taken in the following for two reasons. The first reason is lack of adequate data. While the aggregate costs of redistributive pension measures can be evaluated with some certainty if non-equivalence to contributions serves as the criterion [Schlenger (1998)], it was impossible to estimate their generational incidence from the micro data.

The second reason is that the above justification of the government subsidy seems questionable. In the past, the pension subsidy from the general budget was adjusted repeatedly in discrete steps to avoid an increment in contribution rates, rather than to compensate for additional non-equivalent pension benefits. In fact, the government pension subsidy is linked to both gross wage growth and the development of payroll contribution rates since the 1992 Pension Reform Act. This rule disconnects the pension subsidy from the development of non-contributory pension spending.

The alternative approach taken in the following is to include non-equivalent pension benefits as an expenditure of the Social Security budget, and to account for the government pension subsidy as revenue. This proceeding requires an assumption regarding the incidence of the subsidy, which is uncertain of course. Pension spending on the general government level might be financed by taxes, a crowding out of transfers or net government purchases, a deficit, or a combination of either. Constructing the generational accounts it is henceforth assumed that the government subsidy to Social Security is exclusively financed by non-contributory taxes, postulating that a uniform proportional fraction of each tax payment serves to support the Social Security budget. As for the development of the aggregate subsidy, we assume that it develops in accordance with aggregate pension spending.

Exclusion of deficit financing leads to a lower bound of what might be the actual intertemporal liabilities of statutory pension insurance. If there were a deficit in the general government budget accruing to the Social Security subsidy, the resulting present value of interest payments would have to be incorporated into the intertemporal budget constraint of the pension system (7.4), raising the sustainable pension generational accounts ceteris paribus. The assumption that the non-deficit condition was also valid in the past allows us to treat net pension insurance wealth as zero. In fact, reported pension insurance wealth, which mainly consisted of an operating reserve to smooth fluctuations in contribution revenue, was small in 1996 (DM 29.9 billion). Constructing the intertemporal Social Security budget, we postulate that the operating reserve cannot be used to balance intertemporal pension liabilities. Finally, it is assumed that the institutions running the pension system neither consume nor invest. This assumption is consistent with the design of equation (7.4), which omits net purchases.[5]

Figure 7.1 displays the resulting estimates of pension insurance generational accounts for living generations, and how they differ between genders. The projections of payroll contributions, pension benefits (including the maturation of the system) and tax payment levels (necessary to evaluate the fraction of tax revenue financing the pension subsidy) underlying the accounts are conducted according to the principles set out in Chapter 5.[6] Furthermore, the low mortality scenario is implemented for sake of a realistic reference.

---

[5] To be precise, the (consumptive) administrative spending of the insurance is balanced against the public subsidy.

[6] Migrant-specific net tax profiles are not distinguished in this chapter.

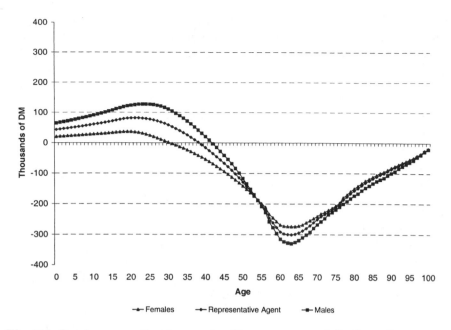

Fig. 7.1. Pension generational accounts with exogenous contributions. Government subsidy to pension insurance financed through taxes. Base year 1996, low mortality scenario. Growth rate 1.5 percent, discount rate 5 percent

The age pattern of pension generational accounts displayed in Fig. 7.1 broadly resembles that of the age-specific rest-of-life net tax payments to the overall government budget, in particular in old-age when pension receipts dominate generations' net tax position. However, for generations not retired in the base year, the present value net contributions to statutory pension insurance are considerably lower than the net tax payments to the overall budget. At the maximum, reached for representative agents at the beginning of their working career, the remaining lifetime contributions to the pension system exceed expected pensions received by more than DM 81,000 in present value terms.

For agents born in the base year, life cycle net contributions to the statutory pension scheme remain positive. Even if current tax and transfer levels are maintained, the implicit life cycle labor tax imposed by the pay-as-you-go system, according to our estimates, totals DM 64,700 and DM 20,500, respectively, for representative male and female cohort members. In terms of life cycle earnings, women are favored by the pension system in Germany. Their lifetime net contribution rate, amounting to 6.3 percent of human capital income, is three percentage points lower than that of newborn men. As is indicated by the small gender difference in pension generational accounts for agents older than age 70, redistribution to the advantage of females is mainly due to the payment of widows pensions and the higher conditional life expectancy of women in retirement.

As evident from Fig. 7.1, agents turn into net beneficiaries of the Social Security system at a rather early stage of their life cycle. Net contributions are negative for representative agents older than age 38, which is also the median age of the population at the beginning of the projections. With 50 percent of the living population being net transfer recipients over their remaining lifetime, and older generations' net transfer receipts being much larger than younger generations' net contribution payments, one should expect that the pay-as-you-go system, despite not being indebted in the base year, accumulates sizeable intertemporal liabilities over time if current contribution and benefit levels are maintained.

The sustainability gap projected for the isolated statutory pension system is indeed large. It amounts to 3.6 percent of yearly GDP, compared to a sustainability gap of 4.9 percent associated with the overall government budget.[7] This result identifies unfunded pay-as-you-go pension claims of present generations as a major source of intertemporal generational imbalance in Germany. In face of demographic aging the current state of Social Security cannot be maintained without accumulation of large debt. If intertemporal liabilities are allocated entirely to generations not yet born, lifetime net contributions to statutory pension insurance faced by a representative member of future generations, totalling DM 203,100, imply an implicit Social Security tax amounting to 39.4 percent of lifetime wages.

The incentive effects possibly induced by this tax burden certainly put the long-term viability of the pension system in doubt. Although one should be aware that the generational distribution conflict is exaggerated by assigning the entire unfunded pension claims to future generations, the mammoth intertemporal generational imbalance revealed by the generational accounts explains why measures aimed at shielding pension income provision against the demographic transition rank very high on the political agenda.

As noted above, fiscal imbalance as indicated by status quo generational accounting is the result of a thought experiment that abandons the non-deficit requirement of the existing pay-as-you-go pension scheme immediately after the base year. To consider the opposite extreme, we maintain the original pay-as-you-go setting indefinitely, adjusting contribution rates periodically. The pay-as-you-go perspective, eliminating intertemporal generational imbalance, translates the sustainability gap of the German statutory pension system into a sequence in time of contribution rates. This approach differs from the generational accounting viewpoint by allocating the burden from demographic aging among all present and future generations. Obviously, any 'real world' development would be found between the two extremes of rigidly

---

[7] In terms of base year GDP, unfunded liabilities of the isolated pension scheme and the overall public budget equal 102.0 percent and 136.2 percent respectively.

maintained pay-as-you-go practice and a policy that switches to the accumulation of debt rolled over to future generations.

Our forecast of payroll contribution rates to Social Security basically exploits the annual budget constraint of a pay-as-you-go system as given by equation (7.1). Projecting age-specific pension benefits and the age composition of the population for each period i, per capita contribution revenue, forecasted under status quo conditions (and hence the current contribution rate), is uniformly adjusted by a factor λ_i set to balance the pay-as-you-go budget in each period. Supposed no policy changes to limit notation, the proportional change in payroll contributions required by a pay-as-you-go scheme is determined by

$$\sum_{k=i-D}^{D} \lambda_i (1+g)^{i-t} t_{t,k}^c P_{i,k} + \sum_{k=i-D}^{D} (1+g)^{i-t} t_{t,k}^p P_{i,k} = 0 \qquad (7.5)$$

or, equivalently,

$$\lambda_i = -\frac{\sum_{k=i-D}^{D} t_{t,k}^p P_{i,k}}{\sum_{k=i-D}^{D} t_{t,k}^c P_{i,k}} \qquad (7.6)$$

for all periods $i \geq t$. Note that $\lambda_i > 0$. In particular, given that the pay-as-you-go scheme worked perfectly in the base period, λ_t equals unity. As the set of age-specific payroll contributions observed in the base period, $t_{t,k}^c$, corresponds to the payroll contribution rate of that year, the contribution rate, for each future period, can be projected by subjecting the initial contribution rate to the proportionality parameter λ_i given by equation (7.6). In the pay-as-you-go model set up by equation (7.5), the development of payroll contribution rates only depends on changes in the demographic composition of the population. In particular, contribution rates are independent from future growth rates, since pension payments are indexed to wages. As a consequence, revenue gains of the pension system due to higher labor productivity are immediately absorbed by higher spending obligations so that contribution rates stay unchanged.[8]

Projecting the future development of payroll contributions to Social Security in Germany, the procedure described so far needs further refinement, in order to cope with the institutional settings of statutory pension insurance. First, parallel to the standard generational accounting approach presented above, the government pension subsidy requires consideration as a revenue in the pay-as-you-go budget constraint. During the first years of the projection, we use the reported government subsidy. From 1998 on, the annual

---

[8] In practice, productivity gains may lower contribution rates in the medium term, if they raise average payroll contributions per capita at a higher rate than g, for example through a reduction in unemployment. However, even in this case productivity gains are unlikely to stabilize contribution rates in the long term, considered tax-benefit-linkage.

amount of the subsidy is extrapolated in line with current legal regulations and tied to gross wage growth. In addition, the subsidy is adjusted, in each period, according to the relative change in the contribution rate to the statutory pension scheme observed in the previous period. Again, it is claimed that a proportional fraction of general tax revenue, in each period, serves to finance the government's subsidy to Social Security.

Secondly, with payroll contributions being treated as endogenous, prospective pension expenditure per capita becomes endogenous, too. In Germany, since the 1992 Pension Reform Act, the yearly increment in pension benefits is linked to the development of *net* wages measured in the previous period, rather than to *gross* wage growth as is stated by the conventional growth uprating rule used to set up equation (7.5). Even when adopting the status quo perspective that political decision makers will not alter tax levels in the future, the change in net wages in a given period still differs from the variation in gross wages by the relative change in payroll contributions to pay-as-you-go social insurance schemes. If, for example, in a given period, the overall contribution rate to social insurance has increased due to demographic changes, net wages grow at a slower rate than gross wages, which reduces the pension increment in the following period and therefore imposes a downward pressure on the Social Security contribution rate.

As a consequence of the net wage indexation of benefits, accurate projection of contribution rates to statutory pension insurance requires the future sequence of payroll contribution rates to the different branches of social insurance. Therefore, we have also projected payroll contributions to statutory health care, nursery care and unemployment insurance, starting from the basic pay-as-you-go principle described by equations (7.5) and (7.6), considering the various payment flows between the different institutions providing social insurance benefits.[9] On this base, net wage growth can be evaluated by forward induction, and the productivity growth adjustment of pension benefits corrected accordingly.[10]

Figure 7.2 displays the projected development of contribution rates to statutory pension insurance under low mortality conditions. Although net wage indexation of pension benefits cushions the increase in Social Security spending, the predicted long-term increase in contribution rates caused by rising old-age dependency is large. At the maximum in year 2055, the contribution rate to Social Security reaches 31.8 percent of the payroll, compared to 19.2 percent in 1996. The change in contribution levels required to guar-

---

[9] For example, a projected change in the payroll contribution rate to statutory health insurance directly affects spending obligations of pension insurance, as retirees are contributors to the public health scheme. It also increases projected spending of unemployment insurance, which pays health care contributions for the unemployed.

[10] The pay-as-you-go model required to project contribution rates when pension benefits are adjusted according to net wages is documented by Bonin (1994).

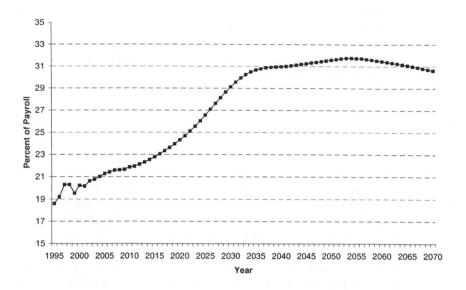

Fig. 7.2. Projected contribution rates to statutory pension insurance. Government subsidy to pension insurance forecasted according to current legal regulations. Low mortality scenario

antee defined pension benefits develops broadly parallel to the demographic aging process. The contribution rates first increase only moderately, and do not exceed 22 percent by the year 2010. When the aging process accelerates during the second and third decades of the next century, however, pension contributions increase sharply, at a rate of about 0.4 percentage points per year. From 2030 on, contribution rates stabilize at a rate exceeding 30 percent of the payroll.

The development of contribution rates, according to our computations, is even more unfavorable than that projected by most analysts who have conducted long-term projections of pension contribution rates recently.[11] This extreme outcome is mainly due to the less cautious assumptions regarding the future development of life expectancy in the low mortality scenario, corresponding to the newest demographic projections by the Federal Statistical Office. If we employ the status quo scenario, which is closer to the assumptions taken by previous forecasts, our model predicts a maximum payroll contribution rate of about 28 percent by the year 2035. Then, the projected time path of contributions is very close to projections conducted for the Advisory Council to the Ministry of Economic Affairs [BMWi (1998)], which

---

[11] Cf. Sinn and Thum (1999) for a survey.

take a moderate position between the 'optimistic' and 'pessimistic' projections currently available.

The pay-as-you-go perspective on a defined benefit plan leads to the same conclusion as the generational accounting analysis above. In the light of the predicted boost in pension contributions, which raises overall contributions to pay-as-you-go insurance to about 60 percent of the payroll in the long term,[12] the viability of the German pension system once again seems in doubt. This is all the more true considered that the projected contribution rates do not capture the full fiscal burden imposed by the provision of pension income. In addition, the pension subsidy provided by the federal government, which, by current regulations, increases in accordance with contribution rates, absorbs a rising fraction of the general tax revenue. For an illustration, one may translate the additional revenue need into fictive equivalents to contribution rates (stated as a fraction of current income) adding to the projected payroll contributions in each year. More accurately, however, the potential fiscal burdens imposed by pay-as-you-go financing of pensions are measured in terms of rest-of-life income, which requires construction of generational accounts.

Supposed endogenous contributions, in order to calculate generations' expected rest-of-life net contributions to Social Security, productivity growth uprating of tax and benefit levels has to be adjusted for the development of contribution rates and the impacts of net wage indexation. The share in general tax revenue financing the increasing amount of government subsidies raises the actual lifetime contribution burden further. Figure 7.3 plots, for selected cohorts, the pension generational accounts corresponding to the predicted time path of endogenous contribution rates. For a comparison, returning to the standard perspective of generational accounting, Fig. 7.3 also reports the accounts under exogenous contributions.

If social insurance budgets are balanced annually by endogenous contribution rates, current regulations imply higher remaining lifetime net tax contributions to Social Security for all living generations. As is evident from Fig. 7.3, pensioner cohorts, although they do not contribute to the pension scheme directly, share in the fiscal burden on the living due to demographic aging. The projected increase in payroll contributions reduces net wage growth and hence projected pension levels. Furthermore, the increase in the government subsidy to the pension system entailed by the increment in contributions is partially assigned to current pensioner cohorts. By assumption, retirees finance the subsidy increase with a proportional share of their tax payments. However, the fiscal burden on current pensioner cohorts, com-

---

[12] Demographic aging also hurts statutory health and nursery care insurance, but less severely, since retirees who are major beneficiaries are also contributors to these schemes. Our model predicts, for the year 2055, contribution rates of 18.2 and 3.7 percent for health and nursery care insurance respectively, compared to 13.5 and 1.7 percent today. A moderate decline in unemployment contributions (from 6.5 percent to 5.7 percent in 2055) is mainly due to economic recovery in the East German states.

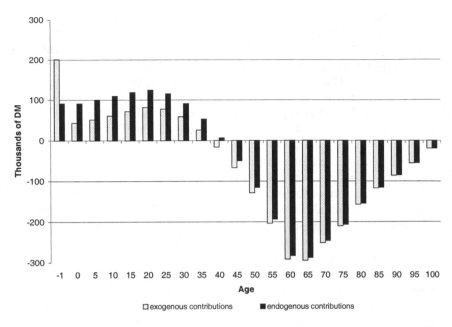

Fig. 7.3. Status quo pension generational accounts for living generations. Government subsidy to pension insurance financed through taxes. Base year 1996, low mortality scenario. Growth rate 1.5 percent, discount rate 5 percent

pared to the exogenous contribution case, is rather small, as the increase in contribution payments unfolds only gradually. For a representative member of the cohort at standard retirement age 65, the additional net contribution to the pension scheme amounts to DM 6,700, or 2.3 percent of the net transfer benefit received under status quo conditions.

The additional fiscal burdens in an endogenous contributions scenario are significantly higher for young cohorts who experience the change in contribution rates while participating in the labor force. The maximum extra burden falls on living cohorts who had not entered the labor force in the base year. For example, a 5-year-old who faces contribution rates exceeding 31 percent of the payroll throughout most of the working career while receiving reduced transfers due to net wage pension indexation, experiences a loss in lifetime consumption opportunities amounting to DM 49,100. As for the base year newborn, the additional net contribution implied by continuation of the current pay-as-you-go pension scheme still totals DM 47,900. In terms of life-cycle returns to human capital, the net contribution to Social Security is more than doubled. It rises from 8.4 to 17.7 percent of present value gross labor income.

Figure 7.3 also displays the pension generational accounts for a member of the cohort born in the period after the base year (of age 'minus one' in

1996). Whereas the status quo perspective of exogenous contributions reveals the potential of severe intertemporal generational imbalance between current and future generations, a rigid pay-as-you-go perspective apparently suggests generational imbalance. As the sustainability gap vanishes if the pension budget is balanced periodically, the generational account measures do not indicate a need for policy revision. Consequently, the change in generational accounts between base year newborns and their immediate successors is small, amounting to about 0.2 percent of the endogenous net contribution over the life-cycle.

However, even if the lifetime difference in the net fiscal burdens of newborn generations is negligible, the above interpretation of Fig. 7.3 is misleading. Although the life-cycle of two consecutive cohorts overlaps except for one period, they experience the sequence of contribution rates and of projected variations in pension levels at different stages of their life-cycle. As a consequence, continuous pay-as-you-go financing could imply sizeable differences in fiscal burdens between cohorts as well. Adopting a life-cycle present value perspective, the actual generational imbalance of the pay-as-you-go scheme is made more transparent through computation of cohorts' internal rates of return on contributions to Social Security.[13]

The internal rate of return to pension contributions for a representative cohort member is defined as the interest rate that leaves the agent undecided between paying a certain amount into the coffers of the pension system and investing the same amount on the capital market. Put differently, it is the discount rate that leads to a zero generational account, i.e. equates the present value of remaining pension contributions paid (including the taxes spent on the government subsidy) and the present value of remaining pension benefits received. As generational accounts are forward looking, it would be misleading to compare internal rates of return for agents at different stages of their life-cycle. Therefore, the method in general only allows to judge generational redistribution between generations who are born in or after the base year and observed over the entire life-cycle. In addition, one can derive consistent internal rates of return for cohorts who have not started making contributions to the pension system, discounting net contribution payments back to the period of their birth. In our model, this is possible for all agents below age 18, since, in accordance with the micro profiles discussed in Section 5.2.2, tax and contribution payments are assigned exclusively to adults.

Computation of internal rates of return to Social Security is a standard practice to evaluate intergenerational distribution within the pension branch of the social insurance system.[14] However, the generational accounting approach to derive internal rates of return in an endogenous contributions sce-

---

[13] The calculation of internal rates of return in a generational accounting framework was first suggested by Raffelhüschen (1998).

[14] Recent contributions to the literature focusing on statutory pension insurance in Germany include Schnabel (1998), Hain et al. (1997) and Eitenmüaller (1996).

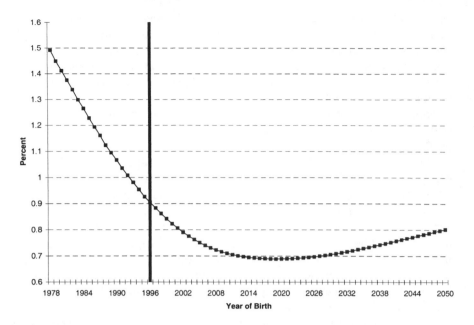

Fig. 7.4. Internal rates of return to pension contributions by birth cohort. Government subsidy to pension insurance financed through taxes. Base year 1996, low mortality scenario

nario differs from conventional analyses in several respects. First, while analysts estimating the private returns to the public pension system are typically concerned with individual heterogeneity within a given birth cohort, generational accounting, taking a macroeconomic perspective, yields the average rate of return for a whole cohort, which is a weighted average of the returns for specific groups of beneficiaries. The generational accounts even allow for the possibility that some cohort members will not participate in the public pension system at all. Secondly, the computations take into consideration that the individual investment in the pay-as-you-go system does not only consist of payroll contributions, but also of tax payments financing the government pension subsidy.

Figure 7.4 displays, for birth cohorts covered with their entire life-cycle contributions in the calculations, the internal rates of return corresponding to the generational accounts in an endogenous contributions scenario. In contrast to Fig. 7.3, the rate of return perspective reveals that continuation of a pay-as-you-go defined benefit plan would lead to generational imbalance. Projected internal rates of return deteriorate for the cohorts born between 1978 and 2020. The impact of population changes is substantial. Rates of return fall by more than one half, from 1.49 percent per annum for a member of the generation who had just entered into the labor force in the base year, to 0.69 percent per annum for a representative agent born in the year 2020.

For a member of the base year birth cohort, we compute a return of contribution and implicit tax payments to Social Security of 0.91 percent per annum. This is markedly higher than the rates based in generational accounting reported by Raffelhüschen (1998), which range between 0.08 percent and 0.58 percent for different long-term scenarios. The more favorable outcome is mainly due to the more significant gain in life expectancy underlying our calculations. In fact, it can be shown that an increment in longevity, prolonging the retirement period, raises returns to Social Security contributions in the model. For example, supposed status quo mortality, the internal rate of return for a base year born agent falls to 0.67 percent. A second factor affecting the internal rate of return positively is the inclusion of maturation effects, which raise average pension benefits.

For cohorts born after the year 2020, the returns to pension contributions gradually improve, but do not again reach the values for current living cohorts not yet in the labor force. As the age composition of the population becomes stable, the rate of return converges to a constant value which lies slightly above 0.8 percent. Due to the macroeconomic perspective of generational accounting, this result is consistent with the fundamental theoretical observation that the rate of return of contributions to a pay-as-you-go pension scheme equals the growth rate of aggregate wages. Once the population arrives at a stable state, in the present status quo world, the sum of wages changes in accordance with the productivity growth rate (1.5 percent), minus the constant rate of population decline (about 0.7 percent).

The fact that the internal rate of return to the pension scheme lies below the secure market rate of return on the capital market reflects the implicit taxation of labor inherent to a pay-as-you-go system. Generational redistribution, in contrast, is due to variations in the sequence of contribution rates faced by consecutive cohorts. Although generational redistribution within pension insurance is a temporary phenomenon associated with the transition to higher old-age dependency, the sharp decline in returns of contributions to the pension system experienced by current young and future cohorts questions the viability of pay-as-you-go financing. There is evidence suggesting that decreasing returns reduce labor supply and the incentives to participate in the pension system [Schnabel (1998)]. As a consequence of such repercussions, contribution rates would increase and rates of return decline even further than is predicted by our status quo scenario. Without policy changes, the pension system therefore could enter into a vicious circle of ever-declining rates of return.

To summarize, whether one adopts the generational accounting or the pay-as-you-go perspective on the long-term development of pension finances in Germany, the results indicate that current revenue and transfer levels are not sustainable during the demographic transition. To avoid intertemporal redistribution to the disadvantage of young and future generations threatening the viability of the pension system, there is a clear and urgent need for an attempt at pension reform, in order to put the system of pension provision in Germany on a sustainable long-term path. However, the rather moderate increase in contribution rates to Social Security over the next decade might seduce short-sighted politicians in postponing the necessary reform effort.

The remainder of this chapter first presents a framework to evaluate the impacts of fiscal policy reform using generational accounts, which is used in Section 7.3 for an assessment of generational redistribution induced by pension reform proposals ranking high on the political agenda in Germany. The principles governing the analyzed reform options – a cut in pension replacement rates, a turn to a broader revenue base of pensions by relying on indirect taxation, and implementation of a partially funded system – are exemplary for the debate on pension reform. Therefore, the following analysis appears of relevance beyond the context of the specific case study.

7.2 The Measurement of Generational Reform Burdens

The static generational accounting framework neglects macroeconomic repercussions and possible efficiency gains. Therefore, fiscal reform is an intergenerational zero-sum-game. Being restricted by the present value intertemporal budget constraint of government, policymakers can increase the consumption opportunities of a generation only at the expense of a higher net tax burden for some other generation. Ruling out positive macroeconomic feedback effects of policy amendments, the task of political decision-makers is to determine how changes in generational accounts should be divided between generations. Put differently, in a generational accounting framework, policy reforms cannot eliminate the fiscal burden from demographic aging, but may help distributing it more evenly across generations, thereby improving long-term viability of public finances.

Assessing the generational impacts of fiscal policy reform, generational accountants conventionally focus on changes in *intertemporal* generational distribution. They ask how a specific policy affects fiscal imbalance between living and future generations. If current fiscal policy is imbalanced to the disadvantage of future generations, policy amendments increasing the net tax payments of living generations are ranked favorably, because they extend the consumption opportunities of future generations. Using the sustainability approach to generational accounting, measures aimed at increasing net taxes paid by living generations reduce the sustainability gap through two different channels. First, the aggregate reform burden imposed on the living reduces intertemporal fiscal liabilities faced by future generations directly. Secondly, if the reform leads to an increment in the lifetime net tax rate of a representative agent born in the base period, net taxes assigned to future generations under unchanged base year policy (now including the reform), increase as well, reducing the sustainability gap even further. As a consequence, reforms that impose identical aggregate reform burdens on living generations might differ in their impacts on the sustainability gap and hence on intertemporal generational imbalance. For an analysis of redistribution between living and future generations through fiscal reform, the aggregate change in net tax burdens for current generations provides the more appropriate reference.

Assessment of fiscal reform impacts under the aspect of intertemporal generational imbalance yields condensed measures for generational redistribution due to policy changes. Living generations are considered only with their aggregate reform burden. However, as was pointed out by Bonin and Feist (1999), to judge attempts at fiscal reform in an effort to improve fiscal sustainability adequately, it is also relevant how the aggregate reform burden spreads among living agents of different age. Reforms leading to an identical outcome in terms of intertemporal generational redistribution might differ significantly with respect to their distributional consequences among the living who have to support them.

In the empirical generational accounting literature, distributional impacts of policy reforms *inter vivos* are typically judged by the corresponding absolute variations in the present value of remaining lifetime net tax payments.[15] Provided that direct income effects dominate the generational welfare impacts of a specific reform, as seems to be the case for several policy options, according to the general equilibrium experiments conducted by Fehr and Kotlikoff (1997), comparison of generational accounts before and after reform is indeed a meaningful approach to indicate reform burdens by age. However, since agents are observed at different stages of their life cycle, it would be misleading to compare the changes in net tax payments due to policy amendments across age cohorts.

For a more purposeful evaluation of the distributional impacts of fiscal amendments among living generations, Bonin and Feist (1999) propose generational account indicators that seek to incorporate three additional aspects into the analysis of inter vivos redistribution by policy reform. First, to render reform burdens faced by members of different age cohorts comparable, it is preferable to cast the change in generational accounts into perspective to pre-reform consumption opportunities, i.e. gross income net of generational accounts, as were displayed in Fig. 5.10.[16] A given absolute reform burden is likely to interfere the less with individual well-being the higher pre-reform wealth of a representative cohort member. The approach to express forgone consumption opportunities due to policy changes in terms of age-specific permanent income is well-known from cohort welfare analysis in computable overlapping generations models [Auerbach and Kotlikoff (1987)].

---

[15] An exception is the study by Franco et al. (1992) who measure the impacts of policy amendments on living generations by the corresponding change in the national savings quota.

[16] A simpler benchmark, used by Borgmann et al. (2001), would be to compare reform burdens by cohort to the remaining life expectancy conditional on age. However, this procedure neglects discounting of future years of life, fundamental to generational accounting.

Secondly, for a comparison between different policy measures, the inter-mingled perspectives of generational redistribution between living and future generations and generational redistribution within the current population require separation. Of course, policies that impose a comparatively high aggregate reform burden on living generations must lead to comparatively high relative changes in cohort consumption opportunities. Focusing on aspects of generational redistribution between living cohorts, it seems preferable to control for level effects of aggregate redistribution between living and future generations, to assure comparability of age-specific relative reform burdens. Finally, per capita measures of cohort reform burdens, as provided by the (absolute or relative) variation of generational accounts by age, do not indicate the number of agents affected by a specific policy. However, the size of the population burdened by a specific reform seems relevant for judging the political feasibility of a reform proposal.

A first concept summarizing the extent of generational redistribution inter vivos by policy reform, which incorporates the different aspects discussed above, is the following measure:

$$\sigma \equiv \sqrt{\sum_{i=0}^{D} \frac{P_{t,t-i}}{\sum_{i=0}^{D} P_{t,t-i}} \left(\frac{RB_i - \overline{RB}}{\overline{RB}} \right)^2}, \tag{7.7}$$

where RB_i denotes the change in the present value remaining lifetime resources due to the policy under investigation, as a percentage of pre-reform consumption opportunities, faced by a representative agent of age i in the base period t. $\overline{RB}$ represents the the reform burden under a hypothetical age-neutral reform that imposes the same aggregate reform burden in the living, so that

$$\sum_{i=0}^{D} \overline{RB} P_{t,t-i} = \sum_{i=0}^{D} RB_i P_{t,t-i}, \tag{7.8}$$

and at the same time satisfies

$$\overline{RB} = cW_{t,i}. \tag{7.9}$$

In equation (7.9), $W_{t,i}$ represents the pre-reform net wealth in period t of a representative member of cohort i.

The measure σ defined by equation (7.7) benchmarks the actual reform burdens faced by specific cohorts, indicated by the relative change in the present value of remaining lifetime consumption opportunities, against an age-neutral reference based on uniform proportional taxation of generations' net wealth before reform. Introduction of this reference makes it possible to judge the extent to which a policy to relieve future generations redistributes among the living. A policy is considered as intergenerationally neutral if $\sigma = 0$, which requires a constant relative reform burden of c on all living agents. For $\sigma > 0$, cohort reform burdens associated with the reform under investigation differ from those of an age-neutral reform, which would impose the same aggregate reform burden on the living, but affect rest-of-life consumption opportunities of agents alive in a uniform proportion. Obviously, the higher the generational variation of relative reform burdens, the more significant is redistribution due to fiscal reform among living generations.

The concept to measure of intergenerational redistribution *inter vivos* given by equation (7.7) punishes large deviations from the age-neutral benchmark. In addition, the measure is sensitive to the fraction of the population burdened more or less, in terms of rest-of-life income, than required to reduce the fiscal burdens of future generations by a certain amount. The measurement concept also neutralizes variations of the aggregate reform burden on living generations. Deviations from the age-neutral benchmark are expressed in terms of the uniform reform burden, which corresponds to the aggregate reform burden imposed on the living. Put differently, σ represents the average deviation of relative reform burdens from the age-neutral reform, which is associated with an aggregate reform burden amounting to one percent of living agents' pre-reform consumption opportunities.[17]

The age-neutral benchmark used by equation (7.7) might be regarded as an implicit value judgment. With constant marginal utility of income, it corresponds to the equity concept of equal relative sacrifice.[18] However, also without referring to normative arguments, the measurement concept seems to provide a meaningful reference. By setting an age-neutral benchmark, it is claimed that analyzed policy amendments are exclusively directed at an improvement of intertemporal fiscal sustainability (by unburdening future generations), and not deliberate means to change the status quo of the income distribution among cohorts.

A second, less ambitious application of the age-neutral benchmark policy suggested by Bonin and Feist (1999) is the construction of political rejection quotas for policy reforms. One might argue that living generations would support fiscal reforms aimed at fiscal relief for future generations, although this leads to a reduction in consumption opportunities for themselves, if they could get an insurance against future fiscal changes with their approval to reform. This argument seems in particular relevant in the context of pay-as-you-go provision of Social Security. Current generations, not having accumu-

---

[17] Note that σ strongly resembles a coefficient of variation. It would in fact be the coefficient of variation of relative reform burdens, if the benchmark relative burden, $\overline{RB}$, equaled the arithmetic mean of actual relative burdens, which it does not.

[18] Arguing that marginal benefits to income are decreasing, one might favor reforms which tax cohort wealth progressively. A hypothetical benchmark reform allowing for progressivity with respect to cohort net wealth is easily constructed, using the following iso-elastic tariff $\overline{RB} = cW_{t,z}^{1+\epsilon}$, where ϵ determines the degree of progressivity and c is used as a scaling factor to satisfy (7.8).

lated personal funds, certainly have an interest in pension reform, if stability
of the pension system improves to their benefit.

Even if one accepts that living generations are generally prepared to bear
reform burdens, it could be reasonable to assume that they would oppose to
policies which they perceive as imbalanced across age groups. To formalize
this argument, one might claim that agents vote against a reform, if it burdens them higher than required by the age-neutral benchmark reform. If this
is the case, the rejection quota in the entire population, denoted by RQ, is
determined by

$$RQ = \frac{\sum_{i=0}^{D} R_i}{\sum_{i=0}^{D} P_{t,t-i}} \quad \text{with} \quad \begin{cases} R_i = P_{t,t-i} & : \ RB_i > \overline{RB} \\ R_i = 0 & : \ RB_i \leq \overline{RB} \end{cases}. \qquad (7.10)$$

The measurement principle described by equation (7.10) condenses generational redistribution among living generations into the share of negative votes
in the population. Alternatively, one may calculate the rejection quota only
for the base year population of voting age. Lacking an explicit model of political economy and neglecting the extent of deviations from the age-neutral
benchmark, the voter concept mainly serves to highlight relative cohort size
of generations particularly burdened by a reform proposal, but the approach
is also neutral against differences in aggregate reform burdens between policy amendments. If aggregate redistribution between living and future generations varies, the age-neutral reform burden, which is serves as the sole
criterion of the voting decision, varies as well.

7.3 The Generational Impacts of Pension Reform

The general accounting framework has been used several times for evaluating reforms of retirement pension financing with regard to their impacts
on generational redistribution. Pioneering studies focusing on Germany were
undertaken by Boll et al. (1994) and Boll (1994, chapter 3) who analyze generational redistribution due to the 1992 Pension Reform Act, which reduced
incentives for early retirement and introduced net wage indexation of pensions (as opposed to gross wage indexation valid before). A more recent contribution to this topic was made by Besendorfer et al. (1998) who investigate
generational redistribution through changes in the pension formula enacted
by the late Kohl administration. Besides, two more radical proposals to reform pension income financing, a tax-financed minimum pension system and
a partially funded system, are assessed in terms of their generational impact. Raffelhüschen (2001a) aims to measure the intertemporal generational
impact of the pension policy amendments by the newly elected Schröder cabinet.

In what follows, the generational accounting framework is employed to
judge different policies to reform pension financing, governing the ongoing

political debate in Germany, by their impacts on both intertemporal and inter
vivos redistribution, in accordance with the concepts developed in the previous section. First, policies are addressed that do not question pay-as-you-go
financing of retirement income in general, but aim at making Social Security
less generous, by cutting replacement rates or broadening the revenue base
of the system. Section 7.3.2 then turns to different strategies accommodating
a cut-down in pay-as-you-go pensions via accumulation of private pension
funds, which are recognized as more effective means to assure sustainability
of Social Security finances despite an unfavorable demographic trend.[19]

7.3.1 Reforming the Pay-as-you-go Pension System

In Germany, the fact that provision of retirement income, at current benefit levels, entails large unfunded liabilities provided that current contribution
levels are maintained, is a long-established result among analysts.[20] Notwithstanding, political decision makers have taken only cautious steps toward
long-term oriented Social Security reform. The most significant effort in this
respect was the transition to net wage indexation in 1992, moderating pension expenditure growth when contribution rates increase due to demographic
aging. However, for the most part, politics reacted to (short-term) revenue
needs of the pension system by discrete adjustments of the government subsidy. This strategy, from the generational accounting perspective, does not
improve fiscal sustainability at all, if it is not counterbalanced by changes in
net taxes. What is originally a deficit of the pay-as-you-go-system, eventually
turns up as a deficit of the government sector. Accordingly, indexation of the
public pension subsidy to changes in payroll contributions, as established by
the 1992 Pension Reform Act, does not improve fiscal sustainability, as indicated by the generational accounts, although it does reduce predicted payroll
contribution rates.

The public debate on long-term pension financing in Germany gained new
impetus when, in 1998, the Kohl government introduced the so-called *demographic factor* into the pension formula, which would have linked pension net
replacement levels, i.e. the ratio of average pensions to average net income, to
the development of longevity in old-age. This reform, scheduled to take effect
from 1999 on, was immediately suspended, after the 1998 general election, by
the newly appointed Schröder administration. The current plan, henceforth
also referred to as the *Riester plan* (termed after the Minister of Labor and
Social Affairs) for convenience, is to reduce pension net replacement rates by
means of temporary consumer price inflation (CPI) indexation of pensions. In
addition, the yield of an increment in energy taxation has been ear-marked
to raise the public subsidy to pension insurance.

---

[19] The following analysis strongly borrows from Bonin and Feist (1999).

[20] Cf. Grohmann (1981) for an early analysis of the aging pressure on Social Security in Germany.

As a first policy experiment, we analyze the generational impacts of the now deleted demographic factor reform. The demographic factor, proposed by Rürup (1998), was designed in reaction to the prolonged average stay of pensioners in retirement due to declining mortality.[21] As enacted by the Kohl administration, the demographic factor was determined to translate, with a lag of eight years, a relative increment in life expectancy conditional on standard retirement age 65 into a half proportional cut in the pension net replacement rate. In technical terms, this means that pension net replacement rates would develop according to:

$$NR_i = NR_{i-1} \left[1 - 0.5 \frac{\hat{e}_{i-8}^{65} - \hat{e}_{i-9}^{65}}{\hat{e}_{i-8}^{65}} \right] \tag{7.11}$$

where NR_i denotes the net replacement rate and $\hat{e}_i^{65}$ represents life expectancy conditional on age 65 in period i. As is evident from equation (7.11), the demographic factor improves the ratio of contributive revenue and pension spending obligations as life expectancy increases. However, for reasons of what has been considered as generationally fair by politics, only 50 percent of the pension burden due to mortality decline is levied on retirees.

Obviously, the effectiveness of the demographic factor reform depends on the prospective development of longevity in old-age. If we used the demographic status quo scenario, which keeps to base year mortality rates, the reform basically would not reduce projected pension expenditure at all. In the low mortality scenario, life expectancy conditional on age 65 is predicted to increase significantly. Until the year 2050, it rises from 14.9 to 18.3 years and from 18.7 to 22.5 years for men and women, respectively. The changes in the net replacement rates corresponding to the supposed longevity trend, computed on the base of equation (7.11), are displayed in Fig. 7.5, which supposes that the demographic factor is introduced in the year 2000. Decline in replacement rates is almost linear.[22] Starting from the base year net replacement rate of about 70 percent, the projected pension level approaches 63 percent by the year 2059 and stays constant thereafter. Thus, in the low mortality scenario, the demographic factor achieves an even more significant reduction in pensions than proclaimed by government institutions, if only at a later period. According to the BMA (1997b), the demographic factor reform would lead to a replacement rate of 64 percent by the year 2030.

---

[21] For a general critique of the demographic factor approach, which fails to address the financial problems of pay-as-you-go financing due to fertility changes, cf. Schmähl (1998) and Krupp (1999). Under certain conditions, introduction of a demographic factor is equivalent to an increment in standard retirement age if entry to retirement is flexible [Breyer and Kifmann (1999)].

[22] Between 2000 and 2004, replacement rates decline gradually faster than in later periods. Due to the time lag built into the demographic factor, we resort to changes in life expectancy observed prior to the base year. In the low mortality scenario, mortality falls at a somewhat lower rate than that experienced over the recent past.

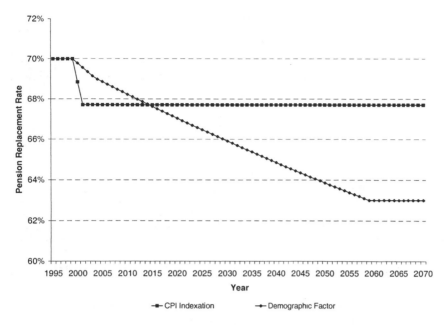

Fig. 7.5. Net replacement rates of pensions with demographic factor and CPI indexation. Low mortality scenario

Nonetheless, the impacts of the demographic factor reform on intertemporal generational imbalance remain small, which is evident from an inspection of Table 7.1 surveying the impacts on intertemporal generational imbalance of the different pay-as-you-go reform scenarios analyzed in this section. Since the pension cut through the demographic factor takes place very gradually, the reductions in primary deficits due to the reform are rather highly discounted. Consequently, despite the substantial long-term pension cut, the sustainability gap falls merely by 0.6 percentage points of yearly GDP. Compared to the status quo, the reduction in pension levels experienced by living generations extends the consumption opportunities of future generations (who face a lifetime net tax rate of 65.1 percent) by 4.1 percent, but generational imbalance between representative members of current and future generations still amounts to 36.2 percent of lifetime income. The sustainability gap, and hence generational imbalance, remains substantially higher than under status quo demographic conditions.[23] This finding suggests that introduction of a demographic factor, as designed by equation (7.11), does not even compensate for the spending impacts of mortality decline.

After abolition of the demographic factor, the current strategy to stabilize pension financing, scheduled by the Schröder administration, includes

---

[23] Compare Table 5.10, p. 149.

Table 7.1. Pay-as-you-go Reform and Intertemporal Generational Imbalance

| | | Net Tax Rate[a] | | |
Scenario	Sustainability Gap[b]	Base Year Newborn	Future Newborn	Differ-ence
Status Quo	4.9	28.1	69.2	41.0
Demographic Factor	4.3	28.8	65.1	36.2
Riester Plan	4.2	28.9	64.2	35.3
– CPI Indexation	4.5	28.4	66.3	37.9
– Green Tax Reform	4.6	28.7	67.1	38.4

[a] Generational account as a fraction of present value life cycle income.
[b] Percentage of present value aggregate GDP according to equation (4.24), p. 82.
Note: Base year 1996, low mortality scenario. Growth rate 1.5 percent, discount rate 5 percent

two separate measures. The first reform element is a so-called *green tax reform* that raises taxation of energy consumption and transfers the additional tax yield as a subsidy to the Social Security budget, in order to reduce payroll contributions. Supposed inelastic demand for energy, which would guarantee a positive tax yield even in the long term, the green tax reform, in the static generational accounting framework, may lead to a better pooling of demographic risk, because it shifts the revenue base of the pay-as-you-go system from direct to indirect taxation. If the latter is spread more evenly over the life cycle, revenue of the pension system reacts less sensitively to changes in the age composition of the population.[24]

Designing what might be the impacts of the green tax reform, we have started from estimates of its budget effects provided by government authorities [BMF (1999)]. Table 7.2 displays, for the period from 1999 to 2003 when the proposed increment in energy tax rates gradually takes full effect, the annual changes in aggregate energy taxes and the government pension subsidy to Social Security (supposed equal to the cut in contribution revenue) considered in the projections of personal tax and benefit levels. The green tax reform is introduced in two stages. At the first stage, implemented in

---

[24] The static design of generational accounting implies that the enacted energy taxation is inefficient as a Pigou tax, in contrast to the intentions of the Schröder cabinet. This seems possible considered that the tax increment remains rather moderate, and that the electricity tax hits the German energy market in a process of liberalization. In the context of a dynamic second-best world, the impacts of green tax reform, directed at removing two negative externalities (on the environment and on labor supply) at a time, are uncertain. Whether green taxes actually yield a 'double dividend' is a debated topic in the literature. Cf., for example, Schneider (1997) and Ruocco and Wiegard (1997).

Table 7.2. Estimated Budget Impact of Green Tax Reform

	1999	2000	2001	2002	2003
Gasoline Tax[a]	7.1	4.5	4.2	4.2	4.2
Electricity Tax	4.2	1.6	1.2	1.2	1.2
Pension Subsidy[b]	15.0	3.6	3.6	5.4	5.4

[a] Includes taxes on gas and mineral oil.
[b] Equal to reduction in payroll contributions.
Note: Changes as against previous year. Billions of DM
Source: Author's calculations based on BMF (1999)

1999, taxes on gasoline, gas and mineral oil were increased and a new tax on electrical power consumption was introduced. Keeping to our standard practice, we proceed by assuming that the electricity tax is eventually borne by consumers. The aggregate electricity tax revenue is assigned according to agents' relative spending on power consumption by age, as identified from the CES.[25] In 1999, the raise in the pension subsidy enacted was higher than the predicted revenue gains from energy taxation. To compensate for the initial deficit, it is supposed that the additional green tax revenue is not entirely transferred to the pension insurance budget in the years 2000 and 2001.

The second stage of the green tax reform foresees a regular, more moderate increment in tax rates on gasoline and electricity consumption, in each year between 2000 and 2003. Projected revenue of DM 5.4 billion is used to subsidize pension contributions.[26] From 2003 on, it is assumed in the projections that the link between energy tax revenue and pension subsidies established by the green tax reform will be maintained. In each period, the government pension subsidy is adjusted by the observed change in absolute green tax revenue. As a consequence of this procedure, the quota of government subsidies relative to contribution revenue starts falling below the initial level in the long term, since the energy tax base is projected to decline, in the course of the demographic aging process, at a faster rate than the tax base of payroll contributions.

Strictly speaking, the above outlined approach to design the long-term evolution of the green tax reform violates the valid non-affectation principle (*Nonaffektationsprinzip*). In Germany, it is generally illegal to restrict

---

[25] The alternative assumption that energy taxes are borne by capital holders changes the generational effects of the reform quite substantially. If, instead, the energy taxes were borne by labor, the green tax policy would hardly have any effect on generational distribution among living cohorts.

[26] For the year 2000, we predict a somewhat higher revenue effect of the green taxes, which reflects that energy taxation was not in effect during the entire year 1999.

parliamentary budgeting rights by earmarking tax revenue for specific tasks. However, in practice, it is possible to circumvent this regulation, as it is done during the introductory phase of the green tax reform. On a more general level, one may criticize the green tax reform concept for breaking with the insurance principle realized by the German Social Security system. As the risks insured by the pension scheme are mainly earnings-related, the appropriate way of financing them would be through an earnings-related tax. In Germany, tax-transfer elements cannot serve to justify pension financing through general tax revenue, as current government subsidies to Social Security already exceed spending on non-individual-equity components included in pension benefits.[27]

The second element of the Riester reform plan is temporary suspension of net wage indexation of pensions, in 2000 and 2001. Due to the contribution rate effects of the green tax measures and an income tax reform to the advantage of families, recently enacted, net wages are expected to grow considerably faster than gross wages during this period. As a consequence, if net wage indexation of pensions were maintained, pension expenditure would grow at a faster rate than contributions (developing in line with gross wages). In face of the resulting upward pressure on payroll taxes to Social Security, the Schröder administration has proposed temporary CPI indexation of pensions for two years. This temporary measure will reduce the pension net replacement rate permanently, depending on net wage growth and price inflation realized.

In order to estimate the impact of temporary CPI indexation on pension levels relative to net wages, we use official projections of the inflation rate and nominal gross wage growth [BMF (1999)]. The corresponding changes in net wages are computed by correcting gross wage growth for changes in the pension contribution rate due to green tax reform, as predicted by our pay-as-you-go model. Under the specified conditions, we calculate that CPI indexation lowers the net replacement rate of pensions to 67.7 percent by the year 2001.[28] Supposed a permanent return to net wage indexation, the replacement rate stays constant at this level from 2002 on. Thus, as is shown in Fig. 7.5, which allows to compare the impacts of the demographic factor and CPI indexation strategies to lower pension levels, the latter leads to a more

---

[27] Cf. Thompson (1983) for a definition of the insurance and tax-transfer perspective on Social Security, and for a discussion of the respective financing implications.

[28] The impacts of CPI indexation on the net replacement rate depend on the actual development of net wages. According to government estimates, the inflation rate equals 0.7 and 1.6 percent in 2000 and 2001 respectively, while nominal net income grows at 3.7 percent and 3.5 percent. Thus, in real terms, pensions relative to net wages are projected to fall by 3.0 in 2000, and by 1.9 percent in 2001. In our model, however, the replacement rate stays somewhat higher than has been officially proclaimed, as the positive net wage effects of the income tax reform in 2000 are not included in the generational accounts.

moderate decline in statutory pension income, relative to net wage income. However, in the short run, the relative pension cut is much more significant. It takes until the year 2015 for the demographic factor reform to unfold as a more effective means to curb pension expenditure growth.

As is shown in Table 7.1, the combined impacts of the two different reform strategies making up the Riester plan reduce the sustainability gap to 4.2 percent of annual GDP, compared to 4.9 percent in a scenario without reform. Accordingly, the difference in lifetime tax rates of current and future newborn generations falls to 35.3 percentage points, which is 5.7 percentage points less than under status quo conditions, but only 0.9 percentage points less than that indicated for the abolished demographic factor concept. This finding suggests that the alternative policy bundle favored by the new government achieves little in improving the long-term viability of pension finances.

Separating the two reform concepts, one can see that temporary CPI indexation has a stronger impact on intertemporal fiscal imbalance than the green tax reform. However, amelioration of fiscal sustainability is less significant than that achieved by a demographic factor. Given low mortality, the more radical initial reduction in relative pension levels due to CPI indexation, despite being less heavily discounted, does not compensate the effects of the more significant cut in pension spending associated with the demographic factor in the long term. Although it raises the lifetime tax rate faced by current newborns to almost the same level as the demographic factor (28.7 percent), the policy to subsidize pension contributions by green tax revenue, among the analyzed reforms, turns out as the least powerful strategy to reduce the sustainability gap. In comparison to the status quo, intertemporal generational imbalance is reduced by only 2.6 percent of future generations' gross lifetime resources.

We now proceed to the analysis of redistribution among living generations associated with the different reform scenarios. In our specific context, aspects of redistribution inter vivos seem of particular relevance, considered that the policy measures are very similar in their effect on intertemporal generational imbalance. Selecting between the introduction of a demographic factor and the Riester plan, decision makers might prefer the policy interfering less markedly with the current distribution of remaining lifetime resources among cohorts.

Figure 7.6 displays, for each living cohort, the changes in discounted rest-of-life net tax payments, i.e. the generational accounts, due to the demographic factor reform, expressed in terms of pre-reform consumption opportunities upon death to assure comparability. For a benchmark, Fig. 7.6 also plots the age-neutral reform burden associated with a hypothetical reform which, as defined in Section 7.2, would impose the same aggregate reform burden on the living, but reduce pre-reform wealth of each cohort in the same proportion. In the aggregate, implementation of the demographic factor reduces consumption opportunities of the living before reform by an amount of

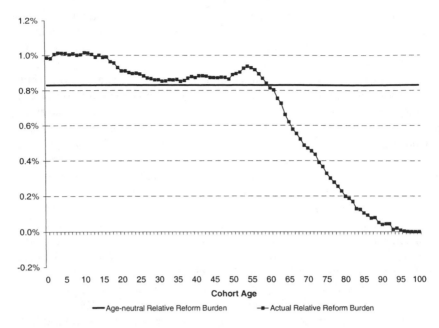

Fig. 7.6. Actual and equal relative burden of demographic factor reform. Percentage of pre-reform rest-of-life consumption opportunities. Base year 1996, low mortality scenario, growth rate 1.5 percent, discount rate 5 percent

0.83 percent. The reform hits all generations, although the burden on current retirees remains rather moderate, as the demographic factor reduces pension benefits only gradually. The reform burdens are higher for non-pensioner cohorts whose pre-reform wealth is taxed at a rate of 0.8 to 1.0 percent by the demographic factor. The maximum burden, close to 1.0 percent of pre-reform resources, falls on the youngest base year cohorts who face the full reduction in the pension replacement rate due to the demographic factor when retired.

The demographic factor reform raises the generational accounts of all base year cohorts below age 60 in the base year, by a higher proportion than the age-neutral benchmark reform would require. Therefore, if agents burdened more than necessary reject reforms to the advantage of future generations, as postulated by equation (7.10), the demographic factor fails by a safe majority. Table 7.3 shows that 79.0 percent of the population, or 67.9 percent of the voting population, would oppose it. Nevertheless, the age pattern of relative reform burdens displayed in Fig. 7.6 suggests that the burdens imposed by the demographic factor are spread rather evenly among living generations. In fact, relative reform burdens, on a weighted average, deviate from the age-neutral relative burden only by 0.26 percentage points, supposed the latter is normalized to one percent of pre-reform income.

Table 7.3. Pay-as-you-go Reform and Generational Imbalance *inter vivos*

Pension Policy	Equal Relative Burden[a]	Rejection Quota		Variation of Burden[b]
		Voters	Population	
Demographic Factor	0.83	67.9	79.0	0.26
Riester Reform	0.79	42.5	46.0	0.55
– CPI Indexation	0.60	45.9	37.0	0.44
– Green Tax Reform	0.19	39.1	49.9	1.30

[a] Percent of living generations' pre-reform rest-of-life consumption opportunities.
[b] Weighted average deviation of generations' actual reform burdens from equal relative burden.
Note: Base year 1996, low mortality scenario. Growth rate 1.5 percent, discount rate 5 percent

Figure 7.7 displays the relative reform burden on living generations imposed by temporary CPI indexation of pensions. This policy transfers 0.60 percent of living generations' aggregate wealth before reform to future generations. The age distribution of relative reform burdens is markedly different from that observed under the demographic factor reform. Since the maximum pension cut comes into effect almost immediately, the reduction in lifetime consumption opportunities faced by current pensioner cohorts is more substantial. The highest reform burden falls on cohorts entering retirement when the policy of CPI indexation unfolds its full effect on replacement rates. At the maximum, pre-reform lifetime resources of a representative 58-year-old are reduced by about 1.1 percent. The reform burdens of younger base year cohorts gradually decline, as they get more heavily discounted so that agents younger than 44 are burdened less than required by the age-neutral reform.

Approval to temporary CPI adjustment of pensions could be higher than to a demographic factor. As the policy change concentrates reform burdens that might be regarded excessive on older and therefore smaller cohorts, only 37.0 percent of the population are burdened more than required by an age-neural policy. However, overall redistribution among living generations due to CPI indexation, as indicated by the average generational variation of relative cohort reform burdens, increases. Normalizing the reform impacts so that they correspond to a one percent cut in aggregate lifetime consumption opportunities of the living, actual burdens deviate from the uniform age-neutral benchmark by 0.44 percentage points, which is 0.18 percentage points higher than with the demographic factor reform.[29]

---

[29] The impacts of the demographic factor reform and of temporary CPI indexation become more similar, if mortality decline is less significant.

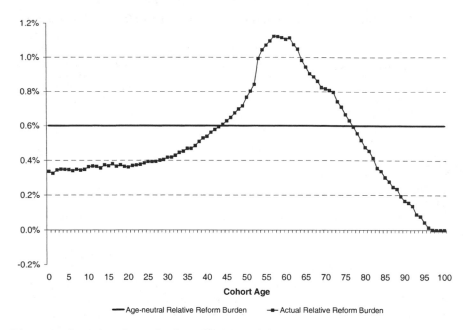

Fig. 7.7. Actual and equal relative burden of CPI indexation. Percentage of pre-reform rest-of-life consumption opportunities. Base year 1996, low mortality scenario. Growth rate 1.5 percent, discount rate 5 percent

The green tax element of the Riester plan shows a rather special age pattern of reform burdens relative to pre-reform consumption opportunities. As displayed in Fig. 7.8, two peculiarities are noticeable. First, two local maxima are observed. Base year cohorts of age 50 to 65 are left with comparatively high burdens, ranging above 0.4 percent of lifetime wealth before reform. Agents in these age groups do not benefit from the reduction in payroll contributions made possible by the reform, but their energy consumption over the remaining life cycle, subject to green taxes, is still high. However, if our design of the green tax measures is correct, very young base year cohorts face an even higher reform burden, close to 0.8 percent of lifetime income for a representative base year newborn. As noted above, the very favorable tax base in the introduction period of the green taxes shrinks over time when the population ages. This process forces the government, in order to avoid a deficit, to cut the transfer to Social Security down. This process eventually drives the public subsidy quota below the initial level. Therefore younger cohorts, while bearing the full burden of raising energy taxation, gain comparatively less from the subsidization of payroll contributions than older base year generations.

A second peculiarity of the green tax reform is that it does not impose a burden on all living generations. Agents of age 21 to 37 in the base year

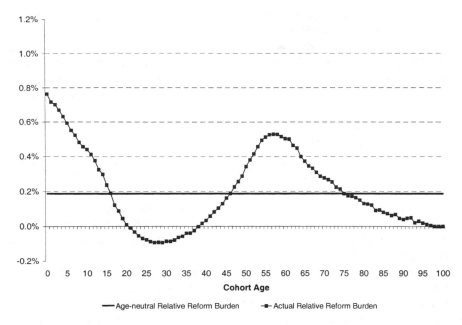

Fig. 7.8. Actual and equal relative burden of green tax reform. Percentage of pre-reform rest-of-life consumption opportunities. Base year 1996, low mortality scenario. Growth rate 1.5 percent, discount rate 5 percent

actually benefit from the reform. For them, fiscal relief from the immediate reduction in payroll contribution more than outweighs the green tax payments over the remaining life-cycle in present value terms. As the green tax concept does not transfer the entire revenue from the tax increase to future generations, the aggregate burden on living generations due to the reform is less substantial than that of the strategies cutting pension benefits discussed above. On the average of all living generations, the green tax policy reduces rest-of-life consumption opportunities before reform by merely 0.19 percent, compared to 0.83 percent for the demographic factor and 0.60 percent for CPI indexation.

The fact that the reform burden on living generations is actually very small is obscured focusing on the sustainability gap (compare Table 7.1). As the green tax policy raises the lifetime tax rate of current newborns, setting the reference for future generations' net tax payments when using the sustainability approach to generational accounting, the reduction in the sustainability gap is almost as high as that associated with CPI indexation (which imposes a two times higher burden on the living). In contrast, focusing on the reform burdens of the living, the green tax reform turns out as a measure mainly redistributing consumption opportunities between different age cohorts, rather than reducing fiscal burdens in the future. Supposed that one percent of living generations' pre-reform income were to be transferred to future generations by means of a green tax policy, cohort reform burdens would on average deviate by considerably more than one percent from a uniform taxation of pre-reform wealth. Still, the fiscal relief for some living generations could gain support for the reform. Only 39.1 percent of the voting population reject the green tax policy, if they support reforms burdening less than the age-neutral benchmark policy.

Table 7.3 summarizes the impacts on living generations of the different reforms of pay-as-you-go pension financing discussed in this section. It shows that the Riester plan, which combines temporary CPI indexation with green tax subsidies to Social Security, in the aggregate, imposes almost the same burden on living generations as the abandoned demographic factor reform. With burdens due to the two separate reform elements adding up, the transfer of consumption opportunities between living and future generations amounts to 0.79 percent of pre-reform resources, compared to 0.83 percent under the demographic factor policy.

However, in terms of generational redistribution among living generations, the policy scheduled by the Schröder administration appears considerably less balanced than the demographic factor concept. Either of its two reform elements interferes more significantly with the pre-reform cohort distribution of consumption opportunities. As a consequence, the average generational variation of cohort reform burdens imposed by the Riester plan (0.55) doubles that of the withdrawn modification of the pension formula (0.26).[30] The latter, however, taxes a vast majority of the population at a higher rate than a uniform sacrifice to unburden future generations, relative to permanent income before reform, requires. Put differently, according to our estimates, the Riester plan seeks to enhance political support for pension reform, at the expense of a more uneven distribution of reform burdens.

7.3.2 Proposals for Partially Funded Pension Systems

The previous section focused on reform options directed at restoring intergenerational balance within the existing pay-as-you-go scheme, none of which were sufficient to assure long-term sustainability of public finances. As a more effective means to reduce demographic pressure on pension systems, analysts frequently propose a (partially) funded system of Social Security. In a funded system, the increasing demand for old-age pensions in an aging population is met through the accumulation of a personalized capital stock in good time. Transition to a funded system puts a double fiscal burden on cohorts living

---

[30] The generational impacts among living generations of the Riester plan are a weighted average of the two reform components, the weights being defined by the respective aggregate reform burdens. Thus, generational redistribution due to CPI indexation dominates the more significant distributional impacts of the green tax measures.

during the transition period who In order to accumulate an asset for their own retirement, have to forego part of their current income, but at must finance the spending obligations of the expiring pay-as-you-go system the same time. Nonetheless, the introduction of a partly funded system can be pareto-superior if the economic distortions originating from pay-as-you-go financing are eliminated. In other words, the dynamic efficiency gains could be sufficient to compensate the generations living through the transition.[31]

The possibility of Pareto improving transitions has been challenged recently, notably by Fenge (1996) and Geanakopolos et al. (1998).[32] Nevertheless, there seems to be consensus among analysts that transition to a funded system is in order, if not necessarily for theoretical reasons, then for pragmatic reasons, to cope with the imminent crisis of pay-as-you-go Social Security due to population aging, which requires replacing missing human capital with physical capital [Sinn (2000)]. The main question open to debate then is how to assign the adjustment burdens during the transition among different cohorts.

Generational accountants have analyzed rather stylized transitions to a capital reserve system several times. In fact, the generational accounting framework provides a useful benchmark for intertemporally balanced partial funding strategies. Using generational accounts, such strategies can be derived by calculating the unmitigated once-and-for-all increment in contribution and/or reduction in benefit levels eliminating the intertemporal liabilities of the pension system, thereby assuring intertemporal fiscal balance among generations. The mechanics of such a stylized partial funding strategy have been discussed above, in the context of hypothetical policies assuring sustainability of overall public finances.[33] Since the adjustment of contribution rates or pension benefit levels takes place immediately, the pension insurance scheme runs surpluses in the first decades, when the ratio of contributors to pensioners is still favorable. As soon as the demographic situation worsens, the accumulated assets are employed to partially finance the pension claims of an increased number of retirees.

Funded systems that take intertemporal generational balance as the only reference do not assign yearly surpluses of the pension scheme as savings to private individuals. As additional restrictions regarding correspondence between cohort savings over time and funded pension claims are not considered,

---

[31] The efficient pension transition literature is extensive. Major papers include Homburg (1990), Raffelhüschen (1993), Breyer and Straub (1993), Feldstein (1998) and Kotlikoff et al. (1998).

[32] Pareto improvement by pension funding depends on the extent to which contributions to Social Security imply a tax on labor. In practice, this is an empirical question, depending on the specific institutional design of pay-as-you-go insurance. Cf. Börsch-Supan (1998a) for a summary of the debate on the efficient transition hypothesis.

[33] Recall the interpretation of Fig. 5.12, on pp. 145n.

these schemes could be run only by government authorities evening out the distribution of funds across future pensioners. In the following, the generational distribution impacts of more realistic proposals for transition to partial funding are evaluated. The strategies investigated opt for personalized pension accounts, in order to put pension wealth out of the reach of greedy politicians. The analysis focuses on two reform concepts prominent in Germany – the partial funding proposal put forward by the Advisory Council to the Ministry of Economic Affairs (AC) [BMF (1998b), Sinn (1999)] and the so-called balancing reform (*Ausgleichsreform*), as suggested by Raffelhüschen (1997).[34]

The Advisory Council's proposal for partial funding combines a defined total benefit plan with constant total contributions and time-variable savings contributions. For each pensioner cohort, pensions financed by contributions complement pension income from annuitized personal savings up to the defined benefit level. Accordingly, payroll contributions to the pay-as-you-go part of the system vary over time, depending on the returns from capital accruing to pensioner cohorts. Since the sum of pension contributions and savings contributions is fixed, private savings rates vary over time as well, and so does the share in cohorts' capital pensions in total pension income, which reflect different cohort histories of savings to the funded part of the system.

The overall contribution rate necessary to stabilize the partially funded system proposed by the Advisory Council and therefore the development of pension contributions, depends on the guaranteed pension income replacement level. Supposed that the current pension level of 70 percent were to be maintained and capital accumulation starts in 2000,[35] we calculate that combined pension and savings contributions to the pension scheme have to be fixed at 27.0 percent of the payroll under low mortality conditions. In our model, the constant overall contribution turns out to be markedly higher than the one originally recommended by the Advisory Council (24.5 percent). This is mainly the result of the underlying more significant gain in longevity, which depreciates annuities. Moreover, our calculations, for a benchmark, do not design a cut in replacement rates.

Figure 7.9 displays how the partially funded pension system proposed by the Advisory Council unfolds over time. The upper diagram shows the pension contributions, and the residual private savings rates, required to lift up the capital pensions accruing to pensioners to the defined benefit level in *each future year*. The lower diagram shows how pension income is divided between capital and pay-as-you go pensions for *each future pensioner cohort*, distinguished by year of entry into retirement, supposed to occur at standard retirement age 65. Obviously, the pension income of current retirees, who did

---

[34] Other proposals for transition to partially funded pensions come from Buslei and Kraus (1996), Börsch-Supan (1998b) and Neumann (1998).

[35] In addition, it is assumed that the government will continue to subsidize the system, at a constant rate of pension expenditure.

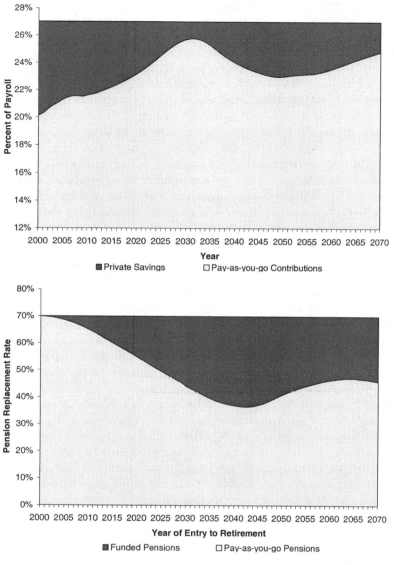

Fig. 7.9. Contributions and pension levels under AC partial funding proposal. (**a**) Contribution rates. (**b**) Pension replacement rates. Low mortality scenario. Growth rate 1.5 percent, interest rate 5 percent

not accumulate pension assets in the past, is financed entirely from pension contributions.

Pay-as-you-go contributions start from the current value of about 20 percent and then rise steadily as the population ages, reaching a maximum of 25.8 percent close to the year 2030, shortly before demographic pressure reaches a first peak. The increase in pay-as-you-go contributions is much lower than predicted for an unfunded system (compare Fig. 7.2), since pensions from private funds become increasingly available.

In the first years after the reform is introduced when private savings contributions exceed five percent of the payroll, personalized funds accumulate rapidly. Therefore, cohorts reaching retirement in the decades of demographic crisis between 2030 and 2050, receive more than 40 percent of their guaranteed pension income as a return to personal pension savings. Consequently, the pay-as-you-go contribution rates decline after 2030, although demographic aging continues. From 2050 on, the observed variation in the endogenous parameters of the system is mainly due to echo effects. Cohorts active during a period of comparatively high pension contributions accumulate relatively small funds, which again leads to comparatively high pension contributions for the cohorts being in the labor force when they retire. Once the echo effects will have subsided, savings contributions to the funded system stabilize close to three percent of the payroll, and agents derive about 35 percent of their pension income from capital funds.

As the status quo perspective of generational accounting neglects macroeconomic repercussions, personal savings enforced by the transition to partially funded systems are not considered in the calculations.[36] In the generational accounts, partial funding strategies show only with the changes in contribution and public pension benefit levels due to the gradual cut-back of the pay-as-you-go pension scheme. As displayed in Table 7.4, which summarizes the effects on intertemporal generational redistribution of the different partial funding strategies analyzed in this section, transition to a funded system, as suggested by the Advisory Council, significantly enhances fiscal sustainability. Even if the current generous replacement rate is maintained, the sustainability gap falls to 2.8 percent of annual GDP, which is 2.1 percentage points less than under status quo conditions.[37] As tax payments of living generations increase due to reduced pay-as-you benefits and increased pension contribution payments, the reform extends the consumption opportunities of future generations by 14.1 percent of life cycle income. Fiscal imbalance between present and future newborns falls from 41.0 to 23.1 percent of lifetime resources.

In terms of intertemporal generational balance, the Advisory Council's proposal is certainly superior to the reforms within the pay-as-you-go system

---

[36] In a static model with perfect capital markets, the present value of returns on savings equals the amount saved. Taking into account dynamic changes in gross factor income, it is shown by Raffelhüschen and Risa (1996) that the generational accounts could misrepresent the generational welfare impacts of transition to a funded system.

[37] One should not expect that reform of statutory pension financing is sufficient to fully eliminate intergenerational imbalance which, as was shown in Chapter 5, is caused by several structural problems affecting the overall government budget.

Table 7.4. Funding Strategies and Intertemporal Generational Imbalance

Scenario	Sustainability Gap[b]	Net Tax Rate[a]		
		Base Year Newborn	Future Newborn	Differ- ence
Status Quo	4.9	28.1	69.2	41.0
AC Proposal				
– Base Year Pension Level	2.8	32.0	55.1	23.1
– Riester Plan	2.4	32.2	51.9	19.7
Balancing Reform	2.5	30.9	51.6	20.7

[a] Generational account as a fraction of present value life cycle income.
[b] Percentage of present value aggregate GDP according to equation (4.24), p. 82.
Note: Base year 1996, low mortality scenario. Growth rate 1.5 percent, discount rate 5 percent

discussed in the previous section. Figure 7.10 allows to judge the distributional impacts of the Advisory Councils' funding strategy among the living. It is evident that the aggregate reform burden due to the reform, which totals 2.91 percent of current generations' pre-reform wealth, is distributed rather unevenly between cohorts. Supposed that the reform does not make an effort to reduce targeted pension benefits below the current level, all agents who retire before the reform comes into effect are not burdened at all. Defined pensions accruing to current pensioner generations are fully guaranteed by pay-as-you-go contributions.

For working-age cohorts, the reform burdens as a fraction of pre-reform income are almost proportional to the remaining years in the labor force. In the maximum, for agents close to age 15 in the base year, entering the labor market when the partial funding strategy is implemented, the reform reduces consumption opportunities by about 6.2 percent. These generations bear the double transition burden: they have to guarantee full pay-as-you-go pensions for present pensioner generations, which requires an increment in pension contributions, while receiving reduced public pension benefits when they retire. The double burden falls only in the long term. As is evident from Fig. 7.10, the youngest base year cohorts, retiring after 2050, will receive higher pay-as-you-go pension benefits than their parents. At the same time, they will be contributors to the pay-as-you-go scheme during a period of comparatively low contribution rates, between 2030 and 2050. Consequently, the relative reform burden decreases among the very young, although it remains as high as 5.4 percent of lifetime resources for a base year newborn.

The static generational accounting analysis suggests that the pension reform designed by the Advisory Council would concentrate the aggregate

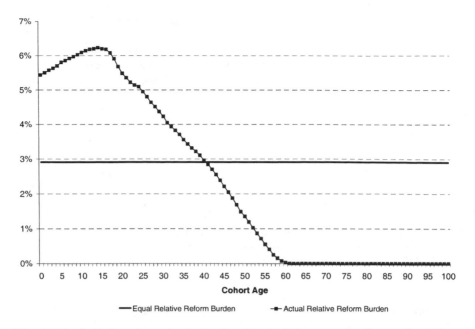

Fig. 7.10. Actual and equal relative burden of AC-proposal – Status Quo. Percentage of pre-reform rest-of-life consumption opportunities. Base year 1996, low mortality scenario. Growth rate 1.5 percent, discount rate 5 percent

adjustment burden to the advantage of future generations on young base year cohorts. Only 42.6 percent of the voting population, but 53.7 percent of the entire population are burdened more than a generationally balanced reform requires. Moreover, since base year cohorts older than age 40 bear comparatively moderate burdens (if at all), the generational variance in reform burdens is considerable. On average, the reform burdens deviate from the age-neutral benchmark by 0.79 percentage points. Macroeconomic efficiency gains due to enforced savings which, if they occur, would extend the pre-tax reform income of younger generations in particular, could moderate the imbalanced distribution of reform burdens indicated by Fig. 7.10. Nevertheless, if one believes that the burdens of transition to a partially funded pension scheme should be distributed evenly, it might be advised to complement the reform plan of the Advisory Council with additional measures aimed at a reduction of the adverse distributional impact inter vivos.

One measure to achieve a generationally more balanced outcome, it turns out, is to combine the Advisory Council's funding strategy with the Riester plan for a pay-as-you-go reform. As shown in Section 7.3.1, both temporary CPI indexation and the introduction of green taxes let current pensioners contribute to the task of unburdening future generations. Moreover, the green tax subsidy to pay-as-you-go contributions could bring fiscal relief to

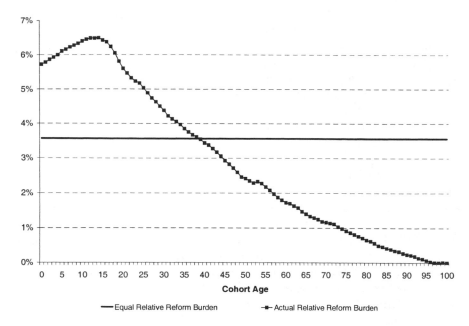

Fig. 7.11. Actual and equal relative burden of AC-proposal – Riester plan. Percentage of pre-reform rest-of-life consumption opportunities. Base year 1996, low mortality scenario. Growth rate 1.5 percent, discount rate 5 percent

young working-age cohorts, which face high reform burdens under the partial funding policy. If the measures of the Riester reform are combined with the Advisory Council's partial funding plan, a constant pension and savings contribution rate totaling 24.6 percent of the payroll stabilizes the pension scheme. This significant reduction in combined contribution rates, compared to the status quo scenario, is not only due to the cut in defined benefits. The green tax subsidy to the pay-as-you-go part of the pension system reduces payroll contributions and accelerates private savings in the introductory period, which in turn reduces the pay-as-you-go contributions required during the years of demographic crisis.

As shown in Table 7.4, combination of the funding proposal by the Advisory Council with the Riester reform improves intergenerational fiscal balance further. As the sustainability gap falls to 2.4 percent of annual GDP, the difference in tax rates between present and future newborns, compared to the status quo, is reduced by more than one half, to 19.7 percent of lifetime resources. Figure 7.11 displays the corresponding variation in living generations' remaining lifetime consumption opportunities. Although the age pattern of the reform burden broadly resembles that observed for the isolated partial funding strategy, which of course dominates the reform effects, the distribution of burdens relative to the age-neutral reference turns out more even. The cut in defined benefits and the green tax payments burden pensioner cohorts, exempted before, and in particular agents who are in the final years of their working life in the base year. This brings the relative reform contribution of the latter closer to the age-neutral sacrifice of 3.56 percent.

In contrast, the relative reform burden for younger working-age cohorts does not increase sizably due to the Riester reform. Their profit from the green tax subsidy, which lowers contributions to the reduced pay-as-you-go system, compensates the green tax burden and the loss in defined benefits. One should also note that in the context of the Advisory Council's partial funding strategy, the green tax policy does not burden the very young excessively, as it would do in a non-funded system. Young cohorts benefit, in proportion to the aggregate reform burden on living generations, from accelerated capital funding made possible by the green tax subsidy, which reduces their pay-as-you-go contributions over the life-cycle. As the distributional impacts of the Riester reform counterbalance inter vivos redistribution induced by the Advisory Council plan to some extent, the generational variation of reform burdens compared to the age-neutral benchmark falls to 0.52. From the perspective of generational balance, the pension reform scheduled by the Schröder administration seems to open a favorable opportunity for transition to a partially funded system.

Even if combination with supplementary reform measures may partly offset generational redistribution among living generations due to the Advisory Councils's partial funding strategy, one could argue that the distribution of the reform impacts is rather unequal, because the burden of transition is levied mainly on young cohorts. An alternative strategy aiming at unburdening future generations through a partial funding policy while achieving a balanced distribution of reform burdens among living generations, is the balancing reform advocated by Raffelhüschen (1997, 1998, 1999d). Like the funding plan of the Advisory Council, the balancing reform starts from a constant overall pension and savings contribution rate, set at 23 percent of the payroll. After an introductory period, which combines defined pay-as-you-go benefits with a significant cut in replacement rates, to 61 percent of net wages, the reform changes to a defined pension contribution plan adjusting pay-as-you-go pensions in each period so that to balance contributive revenue. Declining pay-as-you-pension pension levels are complemented by returns on savings contributions to pension funds.

Figure 7.12 displays how the balancing reform unfolds over time. The upper diagram shows the development of pay-as-you-go contributions and the residual savings contributions. Due to the considerable initial reduction in pension levels, phased in between 2000 and 2005, the contribution rates necessary to balance defined pay-as-you-go pensions decline during the introduction phase of the reform, which opens space for a rapid accumulation of funds despite the rather moderate overall contribution rate. From 2017 on, when contribution rates required to finance the defined pay-as-you-go bene-

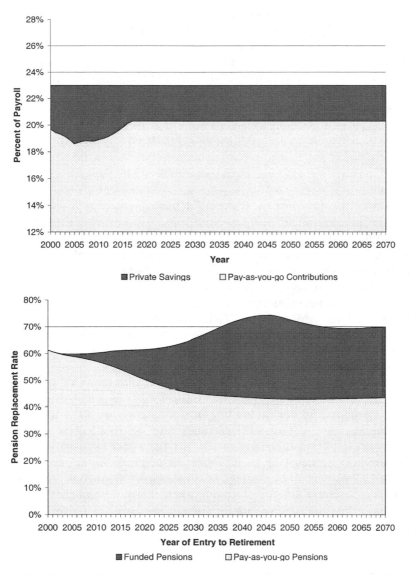

Fig. 7.12. Contributions and pension levels under balancing reform. (a) Contribution rates. (b) Pension replacement rates. Low mortality scenario, growth rate 1.5 percent, interest rate 5 percent

fits would exceed the initial value of 20.3 percent due to demographic aging, the balancing reform turns to a defined contributions plan. Pension contributions are fixed at 20.3 percent of the payroll, and correspondingly savings contributions at a rate of 2.7 percent. Maintaining pay-as-you go practice, pension contributions are fully transferred to retirees in each year. As the ratio of contributors to pensioners deteriorates over time, publicly provided pensions per capita decline. In the long term, the pay-as-you go scheme replaces only about 43 percent of net wages.

The lower diagram of Fig. 7.12 shows the development of pension levels, by year of entry to retirement, implied the balancing reform. Due to the introductory cut in pay-as-you-go benefits implemented with the reform, cohorts retiring closely after the year 2000 when the reform comes into effect (as well as current pensioners) face considerable decline in pension income.[38] As these generations do not have the opportunity to accumulate substantial personal pension assets, the replacement rate falls below 60 percent of net wages for cohorts retiring close to the year 2005. While pay-as-you-go pension levels continue to decline for subsequent pensioner cohorts, whose retirement reaches more and more into the regime of defined pay-as-you-go contributions, returns on pension wealth increase and prevent more substantial decline in pension replacement levels. For agents retiring until 2020, combined pay-as-you-go and funded pension income replaces about 61 percent of net wages.

Afterwards, the rapid accumulation of pension funds in the introductory period of the system starts to pay off. Generations entering retirement in the years of demographic crisis can replace up to 31.2 percent of their net wages with income from pension assets. Thus, overall pension income even exceeds the base year replacement rate for some cohorts. In the long term, pension income returns almost to the initial replacement level of 70 percent, of which about one third is financed by personal funds.[39]

Inspection of Table 7.4 reveals that in terms of intertemporal generational redistribution, the balancing reform is basically as effective as the Advisory Council's proposal for partial funding in combination with the Riester plan. The balancing reform reduces the sustainability gap to 2.5 percent of annual GDP, which implies a difference in net tax payments between present and future newborns amounting to 20.7 percent of gross lifetime wealth, compared to 19.7 percent if the strategy of the Advisory Council is implemented. The balancing reform achieves the reduction in intertemporal fiscal imbalance with a lower lifetime net tax rate for current newborns. Therefore, although the balancing reform appears slightly more imbalanced across generations in relative terms, it extends the net lifetime consumption opportunities of future generations by more than the Advisory Council plan (combined with the Riester reform) in absolute terms. Introducing the balancing reform, the lifetime

---

[38] To estimate the change in rest-of-life replacement rates, the development of pension generational accounts conditional on age 65, given the balancing reform, is compared to that under status quo conditions, representing a constant 70 percent replacement rate.

[39] Our calculations are rather optimistic with respect to the long-term rate of real interest on pension assets, set at the discount rate level of five percent. Supposed smaller returns, for example at a rate of three percent, overall replacement rates would never exceed the – generous – initial level of 70 percent.

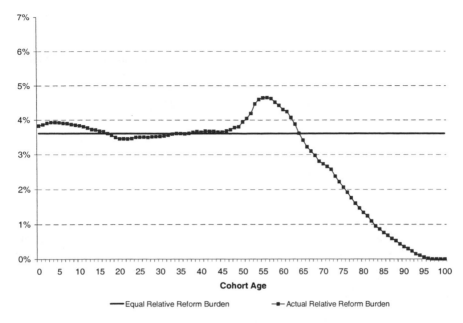

Fig. 7.13. Actual and equal relative burden of balancing reform. Percentage of pre-reform rest-of-life consumption opportunities. Base year 1996, low mortality scenario. Growth rate 1.5 percent, discount rate 5 percent

net tax rate of future generations falls to 51.6 percent, which is 0.3 percentage points less than under the partial funding strategy of the Advisory Council.

Even if the two partial funding strategies impact similarly on fiscal sustainability and impose almost the same aggregate burden on living generations, they differ markedly in terms of generational redistribution inter vivos. This is evident from Fig. 7.13, which displays how the burden of transition is distributed among living generations by the balancing reform. First, the sizeable immediate reduction in cohorts' pay-as-you-go replacement rates assigns a higher share of the aggregate reform burden on the living to current pensioner cohorts. For example, the balancing reform reduces the pre-reform consumption opportunities of a representative 75-year-old by 2.1 percent, whereas the Advisory Council plan, combined with the Riester reform, imposes a burden of only 1.2 percent.

Secondly, similar to the effects of the CPI strategy discussed in the previous section, the cut in replacement rates leads to a particularly high burden on cohorts between age 50 and 60 who, compared to the status quo, will face a sizeable pension cut when old, but do not benefit much from the reduction in pay-as-you-go contributions made possible by less generous pension payments. Besendorfer et al. (1998, p. 231) have argued that a high burden on these cohorts would be justified for normative reasons, since the change in

Table 7.5. Funding Strategies and Generational Imbalance *inter vivos*

Pension Policy	Equal Relative Burden[a]	Rejection Quota Voters	Rejection Quota Population	Variation of Burden[b]
AC Proposal				
– Base Year Pension Level	2.91	42.6	53.7	0.79
– Combined with Riester Plan	3.56	38.9	50.8	0.52
Balancing Reform	3.61	47.7	56.8	0.21

[a] Percent of living generations' pre-reform rest-of-life consumption opportunities.
[b] Weighted average deviation of generations' actual reform burdens from equal relativ burden.
Note: Base year 1996, low mortality scenario. Growth rate 1.5 percent, discount rate 5 percent

fertility behavior of these cohorts is one of the main reasons for the forthcoming demographic crisis.

Most striking, however, is the distribution of reform burdens among agents younger than age 50 who face an almost uniform loss in consumption opportunities that, in proportion to their pre-reform income, is almost equal to the reform burden required by the age-neutral benchmark reform. In contrast to the partial funding plan of the Advisory Council, the balancing reform does not shift excessive reform burdens to the young, since it allows to maintain lower pay-as-you-go pension contributions, while the gradual decline in contribution financed pensions (shown in Fig. 7.12) corresponds well to the cohort distribution of pre-reform resources.

It is evident from Fig. 7.13 that the balancing reform indeed achieves a rather even distribution of the transition burden due to partial funding, as it is claimed by the advocates of the proposal. The burdens imposed interfere with the distribution of rest-of-life income before reform mainly for older and therefore smaller cohorts. Accordingly, as shown in Table 7.5, which summarizes the measures of generational distribution inter vivos for the funding proposals analyzed in this section, the generational variation of relative reform burdens is very small. Supposed the reform were to transfer one percent of living generations' pre-reform wealth to future generations, the average deviation from an equal relative sacrifice would not exceed 0.21 percentage points. This is the lowest variance of reform burdens measured for any of the reforms analyzed in this chapter. In particular, redistribution among living generations induced by the balancing reform is considerably less severe than that tolerated by the alternative Advisory Council strategies. Note that the rejection quota concept is not particularly useful in the context of the balancing reform. For most age groups, the rejection is based on very small burdens in excess of the age-neutral benchmark.

7.4 Conclusion

This chapter demonstrated that generational accounting provides powerful tools for addressing issues of generational redistribution through Social Security. The method unveils unfunded liabilities accumulated by public pension schemes. Some general insights are gained from the German case study. First, pay-as-you-go financing of pension income is not sustainable in face of demographic aging and might entail sizeable generational redistribution. If existing pension claims were guaranteed by issuing public bonds (also indirectly through government subsidies), intertemporal redistribution of consumption opportunities between present and future generations possibly would be overwhelming. In contrast, if pension claims were guaranteed by raising payroll contributions (tolerating high tax rates), the system would redistribute among both current and upcoming generations, since internal rates of return deteriorate.

Secondly, as the demographic crisis due to double aging is severe in most industrialized countries, reforms within the institutional frame of pay-as-you-go financing are unlikely sufficient to achieve long-term viability of Social Security. Considering inter vivos generational redistribution through pay-as-you-go reforms, strategies opting for a gradual long-term cut of defined benefit levels (like the introduction of a demographic factor) might be preferable to an immediate pension cut. Broadening the tax base for pension financing by relying on indirect taxation could interfere considerably with the current income distribution among living generations, but is unlikely an effective means to stabilize Social Security in the long term.

Finally, from the static generational accounting perspective, unmitigated transition to a partially funded pension system is the recommended strategy to improve intertemporal generational balance of fiscal policy. Accumulation of personalized pension wealth allows to cut unfunded pay-as-you-go benefits down in the years of demographic crisis. However, while being most suitable to reduce fiscal pressure on future generations, partial funding strategies could markedly change the present cohort distribution of consumption opportunities among the living, depending on the specific institutional provisions of the funded scheme. The design of the transition to partially funding of pension income should take care of redistributive effects inter vivos. If the variance of reform burdens among living generations is sizeable, it seems advisable, for political feasibility, to implement additional measures counterbalancing unwanted generational redistribution.

8. Whither Generational Accounting?

Within less than a decade, generational accounting has become a well-established concept among analysts to address issues of generational redistribution through public sector budgets. The considerable success of the method is owed to the fact that it responds to growing concerns of policy debates about the long-term sustainability of public finances in a changing demographic and economic environment. As the present study has shown, generational accounting translates these concerns into practicable and accessible measures of generational redistribution, which move beyond the short-sighted traditional perspective of cash-flow budgeting.

Nevertheless, one should be aware that the answers to the intricate questions of generational redistribution and fiscal sustainability given by generational accounting stay far from perfect, even if one does not challenge the validity of the underlying neoclassical life cycle paradigm. Although the sustainability approach improves upon the methodological shortcomings of the initial residual concept, conversion of the theoretical notion that fiscal policy is constrained by the intertemporal public budget into a concrete set of personal, cohort-specific net tax burdens raises serious theoretical and empirical problems.

In particular, the static interpretation of the intertemporal public budget employed by generational accountants, appealing for its simplicity, may confuse the generational distribution of net tax payments with generational redistribution, i.e. reallocation of consumption opportunities among cohorts due to fiscal policy. Ignoring behavioral reactions to individual net tax burdens and their possible impacts on macroeconomic variables, including pre-tax factor income, the generational accounts are limited to the measurement of first-order redistribution, which may represent cohorts' actual fiscal burdens quite inadequately. This aspect is especially relevant when using generational accounts as an instrument to evaluate the generational impacts of alternative fiscal reforms (as done in Chapter 7). Adhering to a static perspective, policy changes stay an intertemporal zero-sum game. They cannot raise or reduce aggregate pre-tax consumption opportunities for present and future generations.

In order to move beyond a pure if intertemporal bookkeeping exercise, generational accounting has to show greater awareness for macroeconomic repercussions of fiscal parameters on generational redistribution. The tools to analyze generational redistribution in a dynamic context are at hand with macroeconomic simulation models designing multi overlapping generations, and have been used for stylized generational accounting analyses of fiscal policy that seek to separate the cohort distribution of net tax burdens from the measurement of generational welfare. Still, it remains an important task for future research to reconcile the theoretical results of dynamic macro simulation concepts with the essentially empirical perspective of conventional generational accounting.

The distinction between generational welfare effects and generational accounts points at a central methodological issue that remains to be resolved by generational accountants. Breaking down the intertemporal budget of the government in order to derive a set of cohort-specific life cycle fiscal burdens mingles two different analytical perspectives. On the one hand, the focus on the public budget highlights the intertemporal financing requirements faced by the government, which addresses the long-run sustainability of a specific fiscal parameter setting. Testing fiscal sustainability requires to measure payment flows. On the other hand, the focus on generational accounts illustrates the possible welfare impacts of fiscal policy on individuals, which addresses generational redistribution due to fiscal policy. Assessing generational redistribution requires to measure fiscal incidence. Unfortunately, even in a static framework, these two perspectives are not necessarily congruent and add ambiguities to the interpretation of the generational account indicators.

The conflict between the government and the personal sector perspectives is evident having to assign government spending and revenue to individual age cohorts. The standard approach, taken in the empirical part of this volume, to allocate tax and transfer flows to the reported taxpayer of transfer recipient when they occur, fits the financing perspective of the government. The fact that tax and transfer incidence is likely to slide within the personal sector has little influence on the sequence in time of government revenue and spending condensed to the sustainability gap. However, the corresponding generational accounts, ignoring aspects of private intergenerational redistribution, could measure the cohort distribution of fiscal burdens inadequately.

Generational accountants have made occasional attempts at the design of sliding tax or transfer incidence, most prominently with regard to the generational distribution of tax burdens on capital subject to differential investment incentives. Future research would have to make an effort to rectify the generational account measures of generational redistribution more systematically. Incorporation of the reaction of income transfers within the private sector to fiscal policy draws a wedge between the aggregate present value of generational accounts and aggregate net tax revenue entering the intertemporal government budget. To clarify the different perspectives, one could use the cohort deficit concept suggested in this study to address the cash flows effected by each individual, while using generational accounts to indicate the generational redistribution of individual fiscal burdens through the public sector budget. The distinction between generational accounts and cohort deficits also offers the opportunity to cope with the theoretically and empirically indefinite conception of the personal net tax burden, for government spending not assigned as a personal transfer benefit adds invariably to the cohort deficit.

Separating the issues of fiscal sustainability and generational redistribution more accurately would also help to integrate private intergenerational bequests into the generational accounting method, ignored until recently. Adopting the perspective of the intertemporal financing constraint faced by the government, private bequests are indeed irrelevant, since they do not raise revenue for the government (ignoring inheritance taxation). To balance the intertemporal public budget, the government has to adjust envisaged net taxes for some generation irrespective of bequests, which gives rise to efficiency effects supposed a distortionary tax and transfer system. In contrast, the impacts of fiscal policy on bequests obviously matter considering generational redistribution. To indicate public interference with private consumption opportunities satisfactorily, one may have to correct the generational accounts for crowding out or crowding in of private inheritance.

A distinction between cohort deficits and generational accounts finally could help solving the fundamental problems of discount rate choice, not definitely resolved to date by generational accountants, who prefer to rely on sensitivity tests for a range of discount rates. Proper risk adjustment of discount rates, used as a substitute for accurate shadow pricing of flows, has to take into account the differing risk perspective of the government and private agents. Thus, it might be appropriate to employ separate discount rates for the construction of the intertemporal public budget, accounting for the government risk of running unsustainable finances, and for the computation of generational accounts, accounting for individual risk of facing generational redistribution.

Notwithstanding unresolved conceptual problems, which are partially due to the novelty of the method, it seems hardly in doubt that the generational accounting approach is superior to conventional cash-flow budgeting as an instrument to assess the long-term sustainability of public finances and the related issue of generational redistribution. This observation does not answer the question whether generational accounting should replace deficit accounting as the central indicator of fiscal activity, as claimed by some advocates of the method. Considered that the analytical programs of the two concepts are rather complementary, this question actually seems somewhat pointless. The insights gained from conventional deficit accounting rest in the realm of budget planning and execution, whereas generational accounting takes a theory-based, conceptual perspective on the intertemporal and generational impacts of government finances.

To raise awareness for the future effects of fiscal decision making, it seems advised to complement the short-sighted perspective of conventional budget statistics with a non-arbitrary, long-term oriented concept like generational accounting. Acceptance of the new concept could be improved by highlighting the aspects it has in common with familiar budget measures, rather than stressing its opposite features. The sustainability approach to indicate fiscal imbalance, resting on aggregation of conventional primary deficits, partially reconciles the periodical budget perspective with the intertemporal concept of generational accounting. To stress the method's connection with the conventional budget perspective further, it could be helpful in future applications to translate the individual generational account measures into familiar macroeconomic budget aggregates. For example, one could characterize a set of sustainable fiscal policies designed for a counterfactual benchmark, by the corresponding sequence of government revenue and spending variables.

Provision of generational accounts by official entities is likely to improve the empirical accuracy of generational accounting, as it would open the opportunity to collect a data base really adequate for the method. Then, some of the empirical issues, which have limited the analytical scope of generational accounting so far, might be resolved more satisfactorily. In particular, it may become possible to evaluate the government stock of assets and the return accruing to it more realistically and to use cohort profiles instead of cross-sectional profiles to assign government revenue and spending. Furthermore, an improved data base may allow better identification of generational accounts for different population groups, to broaden the analysis of intergenerational redistribution by considering aspects of intra-generational redistribution. Parallel to recent extensions of computable dynamic generation models, separation of the generational accounts by income classes would be a welcome future extension of the representative agent concept.

Regular calculation of generational accounts, preferably according to a uniform international standard, is also prerequisite to draw more measured comparisons of intertemporal fiscal sustainability across countries. Reported fiscal imbalance, reacting to business cycle effects or short-termed loosening or tightening of fiscal policy, can be unstable over time (although it is not in the German case study). Therefore, comprehensive conclusions about international differences in fiscal imbalance and generational redistribution require a time series of observations. Possible instability of the generational account measures also complicates the interpretation of national generational accounting results derived for an isolated point in time. As a straightforward solution, future applications of the method could start from more sophisticated budget constructs that correct for periodical influences government revenue and spending aggregates.

Thus, there seems to be ample scope to improve the generational account measures. The urgent need to develop generational accounting into a standard (and standardized) statistical tool of long-term fiscal policy analysis and government planning is established by the structural demographic and economic changes challenging societies around the globe in the first half of the next century. Generational accounting forces us to direct our attention to the future, shortly before the impending aging process sets in, and to think over the long-term viability of current government policies. For many countries, like for Germany, the generational accounting view into the future is disquieting. Directing fiscal policy on a sustainable path will require considerable prudence and fiscal restraint. Politicians need to answer the question how to reduce unfunded government commitments soon. If they hesitate, they could unleash distributive conflicts between generations that could reach beyond the scope of our imagination.

A. Appendix: Proofs

A.1 Separability of Generational Accounts

This appendix serves to proof the proposition that, for each age cohort, the generational account for a representative agent, defined by equations (2.1) and (2.4), represents the weighted average of the accounts for any set of population subgroups $P_{t,k}^1, ..., P_{t,k}^m, ..., P_{t,k}^n$ aggregating to the base year population $P_{t,k}$ so that $\sum_m P_{t,k}^m = P_{t,k}$, the appropriate weights being defined by the initial share of a population subgroup in the total population born in the same year k:

$$GA_{t,k} = \sum_m \frac{P_{t,k}^m}{P_{t,k}} GA_{t,k}^m. \tag{24}$$

In equation (24), the generational account for each population group, $GA_{t,k}^m$, is defined parallel to the standard definition (2.1). Therefore, it holds that

$$GA_{t,k}^m = \sum_{i=t}^{k+D} t_{i,k}^m S_{i,t,k}^m. \tag{A.1}$$

for all generations $t - D \leq k \leq t$. To proof proposition (24), first note that the age-specific average net tax payments of cohort k, $t_{t,k}$, are a weighted average of the net tax payments of all subgroups. The respective weights are given by the shares of each subpopulation in future years. Respecting that $S_{i,t,k}^m P_{t,k}^m$ measures the number of m-type individuals resident in the base period t who survive until period $i \geq t$, one may express $t_{i,k}$ as

$$t_{i,k} = \sum_m t_{i,k}^m \frac{S_{i,t,k}^m P_{t,k}^m}{\sum_m S_{i,t,k}^m P_{t,k}^m}. \tag{A.2}$$

Similarly, the survival ratio $S_{i,t,k}$ of a whole base year resident generation k upon year $i \geq t$ can be written as the weighted average of subgroup survival probabilities. In this case, the respective weights are given by the age-specific base year population shares of the subpopulations. This leads to

$$S_{i,t,k} = \frac{\sum_m S_{i,t,k}^m P_{t,k}^m}{P_{t,k}}. \tag{A1.3}$$

Substitution of equations (A.2) and (A1.3) into equation (2.1) yields

$$GA_{t,k} = \sum_{i=t}^{k+D} \frac{\sum_m S_{i,t,k}^m P_{t,k}^m}{P_{t,k}} \sum_m t_{i,k}^m \frac{S_{i,t,k}^m P_{t,k}^m}{\sum_m S_{i,t,k}^m P_{t,k}^m}. \tag{A.3}$$

Finally, a rearrangement and simplification of (A.3) proofs the proposition (2.12), considering (A.1):

$$GA_{t,k} = \sum_m \frac{P_{t,k}^m}{P_{t,k}} \sum_{i=t}^{k+D} t_{i,k}^m S_{i,t,k}^m. \tag{A.4}$$

A.2 Invariance of the Relative Fiscal Imbalance

This appendix serves to proof that the disaggregation of the generational account representative for future born generations, $GA_{t+1,t+1}$, into a set of generational accounts $(GA_{t+1,t+1}^1, ..., GA_{t+1,t+1}^m, ..., GA_{t+1,t+1}^n)$ representative for members of subpopulations $P_{t+1,t+1}^m$, where $\sum_m P_{t+1,t+1}^m = P_{t+1,t+1}$, does not affect the relative change in life cycle tax burdens indicated for agents born in periods t and $t+1$, if the population share of the distinct population classes is time invariant. For this proof, it is sufficient to show that

$$\frac{GA_{t+1,t+1}}{GA_{t,t}} = \frac{GA_{t+1,t+1}^m}{GA_{t,t}^m} \tag{A.5}$$

is true for the generational accounts measured for any population group m. First note that equation (4.13) can be rearranged to

$$\frac{GA_{t+1,t+1}^m}{GA_{t,t}^m} = \frac{GA_{t+1,t+1}^n}{GA_{t,t}^n}. \tag{A.6}$$

Next, substitution of equation (4.14) into equation (A.6) and shortening the resulting fraction on the RHS by $GA_{t,t}^n$ yields

$$\frac{GA_{t+1,t+1}^m}{GA_{t,t}^m} = \frac{GA_{t+1,t+1}}{\sum_m \frac{P_{t+1,t+1}^m}{P_{t+1,t+1}} GA_{t,t}^m}. \tag{A.7}$$

Noting that the generational accounts for the base year living can be broken down according to equation (2.12), it is easy to see that the denominator in equation (A.7) condenses to $GA_{t,t}$. Hence (A.7) is equal to the proposition (A.5) if it is true that $P_{t+1,t+1}^m / P_{t,t}^m = P_{t,t}^m / P_{t,t}$ for all subpopulations m, i.e. if the cohort share of the population classes does not change between periods t and $t+1$.

A.3 Normal Reaction of Future Generational Accounts

The purpose of this appendix is twofold. First, the conditions for a normal reaction of the generational account, representative for cohorts born after the base period t, to variations in aggregate size of future birth cohorts are derived. Secondly, it is shown how this generational account reacts to policies that change the life cycle net taxes of cohorts living in the base period t, supposed future demographic conditions vary.

In order to compute these two partial derivatives, it is useful to write the conventional definition of the generational account representative for cohorts born after the base period t, $GA_{t+1,t+1}$, given by equation (4.9), as

$$GA_{t+1,t+1}(P_{k,k}, GA_{t,t-i}) = \frac{\varphi(P_{k,k}, GA_{t,t-i})}{f(P_{k,k})}, \qquad (A.8)$$

where $k > t$, $0 \leq i \leq D$, and $f(P_{k,k}) > 0$. In equation (A.8), $\varphi(\cdot)$ represents the residual of the public sector intertemporal budget constraint as defined by equation (4.1). $f(\cdot)$ stands for the set of future newborn generations which are weighed with their fiscal potential in present value terms. The signs of the partial derivatives are given by $\frac{\partial f}{\partial P_{k,k}} > 0$, $\frac{\partial \varphi}{\partial GA_{t,t-i}} < 0$, and $\frac{\partial \varphi}{\partial P_{k,k}} = GA_{t,k}^G > 0$.

Each additional agent born in period $k > t$ increases the residual in the intertemporal budget constraint by the base year present value of net government purchases upon death, $GA_{t,k}^G$, allocated to her according to equation (4.5). This amount is labeled like a generational account here, to indicate that it is constructed parallel to the present value of private net tax payments. For $GA_{t,k}^G > 0$, it is sufficient that projected per capita net government expenditure is positive for all age cohorts.

Differentiating equation (A.8) with respect to future cohort size yields

$$\frac{\partial GA_{t+1,t+1}}{\partial P_{k,k}} = \frac{GA_{t,k}^G f(P_{k,k}) - \varphi(P_{k,k}, GA_{t,t-i})}{[f(P_{k,k})]^2}. \qquad (A.9)$$

As the denominator of equation (A.9) is positive, a necessary and sufficient condition for an inverse relation between the number of agents born after the base period t and the generational account representative for future born generations is that $GA_{t,k}^g f(\cdot) - \varphi(\cdot) < 0$. Thus, a normal reaction of $GA_{t+1,t+1}$ requires that

$$GA_{t,k}^G < \frac{\varphi(P_{k,k}, GA_{t,t-i})}{f(P_{k,k})} = GA_{t+t,t+1}. \qquad (A.10)$$

This proofs the first proposition that an increase in future cohort size reduces the net tax burden representative for future generations, if the marginal revenue gain of the government from net taxes exceeds the marginal increase in net government purchases associated with a new population member.

To derive the second proposition regarding the fiscal policy response of future generational accounts, start from the partial derivative of equation (A.8) with respect to $GA_{t,t-i}$ which reads as:

$$\frac{\partial GA_{t+t,t+1}}{\partial GA_{t,t-i}} = \frac{\partial\varphi/\partial GA_{t,t-i}}{f(P_{k,k})} < 0. \tag{A.11}$$

Equation (A.11) confirms an inverse relation between the life cycle tax burdens of living and future generations. Now differentiate equation (A.11) with respect to $P_{k,k}$ to yield

$$\frac{\partial\left(\frac{\partial GA_{t+t,t+1}}{\partial GA_{t,t-i}}\right)}{\partial P_{k,k}} = -\frac{\partial\varphi/\partial GA_{t,t-i}}{[f(P_{k,k})]^2} > 0. \tag{A.12}$$

Equation (A.12) shows that rising future cohort size reduces the sensitivity of the generational account representative for cohorts born after the base year, $GA_{t+1,t+1}$, to changes in the generational accounts of the living in absolute terms. This means that the negative slope of the function $GA_{t+1,t+1}(P_{k,k}, GA_{t,t-i})$ turns flatter as future cohort size increases.

B. Appendix: The Demographic Model

This appendix gives an introduction to the computable demographic model used to generate the demographic projections underlying the generational accounts. The model is based on the discrete and deterministic algebraic formulation of the component method proposed by Leslie (1945). The standard procedure has been extended to distinguish between genders and to incorporate immigration.[1]

Let $\bar{P}_i = (P_{i,i}^f, ..., P_{i,i-j}^f, ..., P_{i,i-D}^f, P_{i,i}^m, ..., P_{i,i-j}^m, ..., P_{i,i-D}^m)$ denote a row vector containing the age structure of the resident population at the beginning of period i, disaggregated by gender. In the vector $\bar{P}_i$, $P_{i,i-j}$ represents the number of agents resident in period i who were born in period $i - j$, whereas the superscripts are added to distinguish between the female (f) and male (m) members of a birth cohort. Then, supposed no migration, the composition of the population resident at the beginning of period $i + 1$ is determined by

$$\bar{P}_{i+1} = \bar{P}_i \, LM_i. \tag{B.1}$$

In equation (B.1), LM_i represents the so-called *Leslie matrix* as valid in period i. The Leslie matrix is defined as

$$LM_i = \begin{bmatrix}
f_{i,i}^f & \zeta_{i,i}^f & 0 & \cdots & 0 & f_{i,i}^m & 0 & 0 & \cdots & 0 \\
f_{i,i-1}^f & 0 & \zeta_{i,i-1}^f & \cdots & 0 & f_{i,i-1}^m & 0 & 0 & \cdots & 0 \\
\vdots & \vdots & \vdots & & \vdots & \vdots & \vdots & \vdots & & \vdots \\
f_{i,i-D+1}^f & 0 & 0 & \cdots & \zeta_{i,i-D+1}^f & f_{i,i-D+1}^m & 0 & 0 & \cdots & 0 \\
f_{i,i-D}^f & 0 & 0 & \cdots & 0 & f_{i,i-D}^m & 0 & 0 & \cdots & 0 \\
0 & 0 & 0 & \cdots & 0 & 0 & \zeta_{i,i}^m & 0 & \cdots & 0 \\
0 & 0 & 0 & \cdots & 0 & 0 & 0 & \zeta_{i,i-1}^m & \cdots & 0 \\
\vdots & \vdots & \vdots & & \vdots & \vdots & \vdots & \vdots & & \vdots \\
0 & 0 & 0 & \cdots & 0 & 0 & 0 & 0 & \cdots & \zeta_{i,i-D+1}^m \\
0 & 0 & 0 & \cdots & 0 & 0 & 0 & 0 & \cdots & 0
\end{bmatrix}$$

---

[1] Useful introductions to the component method on a textbook level are given by Pflaumer (1988) and Bretz (1986).

The single columns of the Leslie matrix contain age- and gender-specific fertility and survival ratios, which determine the development of the population structure. To be specific, $\zeta_{i,i-j}^{f}$, where $0 \leq j \leq D$, denotes the probability that a woman born in the course of period $i - j$ (hence of age j at the beginning of period i) survives until the beginning of period $i + 1$, reaching age $j + 1$. $\zeta_{i,i-j}^{m}$ represents the analogous likelihood for a man of age j. Recurring to a life table, the required vector of survival rates $(\zeta_{i,i}, ..., \zeta_{i,i-j}, ..., \zeta_{i,i-D+1})$ can be derived as

$$\zeta_{i,i-j} = \frac{L_{j+1}}{L_j} \tag{B.2}$$

for all $0 \leq j < D$, where L_j stands for the life table function of the total number of years lived through by the survivors of a fictive start cohort of 100,000 between exact age j and $j + 1$.[2]

Furthermore, the Leslie matrix contains age-specific fertility probabilities, which design the reproductive behavior of the population. In detail, $f_{i,i-j}^{f}$, with $0 \leq j \leq D$, stands for the average number of girls given birth to in period i by a representative woman born in period $i - j$ (thus of age j at the beginning of period i), who survive through the beginning of period $i + 1$. Correspondingly, $f_{i,i-j}^{m}$ denotes the number of surviving boys given birth to by a representative j-year-old woman during period i. Of course, biology renders $f_{i,j} = 0$ for most ages j.[3] Equation (B.1) weighs the number of surviving girls and boys per woman with the cohort size of the potential mothers. The resulting total constitutes the female and male generation of age zero at the beginning of period $i + 1$, $P_{i+1,i+1}$.

Assuming that the likelihood of giving birth is distributed evenly across the entire year span, the average number of male and female newborns per mother of age $i - j$ is given by

$$f_{i,i-j}^{m} = \frac{L_0^m}{100000} \frac{\rho}{1+\rho} \frac{F_{i,i-j} + \zeta_{j,i-j}^{w} F_{i,i-j-1}}{2} , \tag{B.3a}$$

$$f_{i,i-j}^{f} = \frac{L_0^f}{100000} \frac{1}{1+\rho} \frac{F_{i,i-j} + \zeta_{j,i-j}^{w} F_{i,i-j-1}}{2} . \tag{B.3b}$$

In equations (B.3a) and (B.3b), the third term on the RHS serves to calculate the total number of births expected per woman aged j at the beginning of period i. $F_{i,i-j}$ stands for the age-specific fertility rate as of period i for women of exact age j. Aggregation of age-specific fertility rates yields to the

---

[2] It is not exact to set into the relation the number of survivors at age $j+1$ and j, because the representative individual aged j at the beginning of period i is aged j years and a half on average.

[3] Here and in the remainder of this appendix, the superscripts f and m are omitted to limit notation, where a statement holds equally for both male and female cohorts.

total fertility rate as of period i. With probabilities of giving birth evenly distributed over time, the exact age of the average j-year-old mother at the beginning of period i is j years and a half. Therefore, fertility rates at age j and $j + 1$ require consideration. In principle, each fertility rate has a 50 percent chance of realization. However, as not all potential mothers survive to age $j + 1$, fertility at age $j + 1$ needs to be corrected for the probability of death at age j.

The second term on the RHS of equations (B.3a) and (B.3b) divides the total number of newborns per woman into boys and girls by application of the gender ratio ρ, which is defined as the number of newborn boys per 100 newborn girls. The gender ratio is treated as a time invariant natural constant. Throughout the projections a value of $\rho = 1.05527$ is used, which corresponds to the gender ratio in Germany over the period 1986–1995. Finally, the gender-specific survival ratio of a newborn agent in the first year of life, which can be computed from the life table according to the first term on the RHS of equations (B.3a) and (B.3b), is used to translate the total figure of girls and boys born in the course of period i into the corresponding number of zero-year-old which are still alive at the beginning of period $i + 1$.

Allowing for immigration, the change in population composition between periods i and $i + 1$ does not only depend on age-specific fertility and mortality. The basic projection according to equation (B.1) needs to be extended by the age vector of net immigrants taking residence in the course of period i and surviving until the start of period $i + 1$. Let $\bar{M}_i = (M_{i,i}^f, ..., M_{i,i-j}^f, ..., M_{i,i-D}^f, M_{i,i}^m, ..., M_{i,i-j}^m, ..., M_{i,i-D}^m)$ denote a row vector comprising the number of net immigrants born in period $i - j$ who enter the country during period i, separated by gender. Then, the age composition of the surviving immigrants, who augment the resident cohorts at the beginning of period $i + 1$ can be computed by applying a migrant-specific Leslie matrix, denoted as LM_i^M, to the migrant vector $\bar{M}_i$:

$$\bar{M}_{i+1} = \bar{M}_i \, LM_i^M. \tag{B.4}$$

If all immigrants were to take residence at the beginning of period i, the Leslie matrix for the resident population would be equally valid for immigrant cohorts (provided demographic characteristics do not differ). However, assuming that migration takes place continuously in the course of period i, the Leslie matrix for immigrants needs to be adjusted, since, at the beginning of period $i + 1$, immigrants stay in the host country for only half a year on average. The adjusted survival and fertility rates entering the immigrant Leslie matrix, indicated with superscript M, are derived from residents' rates in period i according to

$$\zeta_{i,i-j}^M = \sqrt{\zeta_{i,i-j}}, \tag{B.5a}$$

$$f_{i,i-j}^M = \frac{f_{i,i-j}}{2} \tag{B.5b}$$

for $0 \leq j \leq D$. Equation (B.5a) implies that likelihoods to survive identically and independently distributed over time. Under this condition, the likelihood to survive one year is the product of the probabilities to survive two times half a year. Therefore, immigrant survival probabilities are higher compared to residents. Equation (B.5b) claims that the number of births observed for the average immigrant woman is reduced by one half in comparison to a resident woman of identical age, as a consequence of her shorter stay in the host country.

In the presence of immigration, the two Leslie equations (B.1) and (B.4) need to be combined, in order to generate the structure of the population resident at the beginning of period $i + 1$. We get

$$\bar{P}_{i+1} = \bar{P}_i L M_i + \bar{M}_i L M_i^M. \tag{B.6}$$

The updated population vector generated by equation (B.6) constitutes the starting point for the subsequent projection of the population development between the periods $i + 1$ and $i + 2$, etc.

Due to the ergodic properties of the component method, the population structure always converges to a stable state in the long term, if the components of the Leslie matrices stay constant over time [Keyfitz (1977)]. In the stable demographic state, all cohorts grow at the same constant annual rate, as does the population. The demographic projections employed in this study indeed converge to a stable long-term state. However, in general certain adjustments of survival and fertility rates were incorporated in the sequence of Leslie matrices.

In order to correct the initial set of survival rates by age for expected gains in life expectancy at birth, our model opts for the exponential adjustment procedure suggested by Pflaumer (1988, pp. 38n).[4] Assume average life expectancy at birth starts changing in period i. Assume further that the final state of life expectancy at birth is reached after a period of N years. Then, our projection manipulates the initial set of age-specific survival rates according to

$$\zeta_{i+n,i+n-j} = (\zeta_{i,i-j})^{\omega_n} \quad \text{with} \quad \begin{cases} \omega_n = \Omega^{\frac{n}{N}} & : \quad 1 \leq n \leq N \\ \omega_n = \Omega & : \quad N < n \end{cases} \tag{B.7}$$

for all $0 \leq j < D$. In equation (B.7), $\Omega \geq 0$ represents a level parameter which is determined by the final state of life expectancy. Letting $\hat{e}_{i+N}$ represent life expectancy at birth reached from year $i + N$ on, the level parameter is obtained solving

$$\hat{e}_{i+N} = \sum_{i=0}^{D} \left(\frac{L_i}{100000} \right)^{\Omega} \tag{B.8}$$

---

[4] This method also finds support by Butz (1983).

for Ω.[5] If Ω equals unity, equation (B.8) represents the life table definition of life expectancy at birth. For $0 \leq \Omega < 1$, the adjustment of age-specific survival rates according to equation (B.7) raises survival probabilities derived from the initial life table. Life expectancy at birth increases correspondingly.[6]

The nonlinear variation of survival ratios according to equation (B.8) has the advantage of generating comparatively higher gains in life expectancy for age cohorts facing a relatively high mortality risk, which corresponds well with the empirical evidence. The exponential change in survival rates leads to a more pronounced aging process than a proportional adjustment of survival rates would do. In addition, as the adjustment factor ω_n, according to equation (B.7), also moves nonlinearly during the transition period, the method places the major share of the mortality reduction in the first years of the adjustment process. To a certain degree, this proceeding helps in coping with uncertainties regarding long-term mortality trends.

As generational accounts generally react less sensitive to variations in reproductive behavior than to changes in mortality, our demographic model opts for a simpler formulation of fertility trends. It is assumed that variations in the total fertility rate are evenly distributed among all age cohorts, neglecting the possibility of corresponding changes in average proliferation age. Furthermore, the transition to the final total fertility rate is designed as linear. Let $TFR_i = \sum_{j=0}^{D} F_{i,i-j}$ denote the total fertility rate valid in period i. Given that total fertility begins to change in period i and that transition to the final state requires N years, the initial number of newborns per mother is adjusted according to

$$f_{i+n,i+n-j} = (1+\psi_n)f_{i,i-j} \quad \text{with} \quad \begin{cases} \psi_n = \frac{n}{N}\left(\frac{TFR_{i+N}}{TFR_i} - 1\right) & : \ 1 \leq n \leq N \\ \psi_n = \frac{TFR_{i+N}}{TFR_i} - 1 & : \ \ N < n \end{cases}$$

$$(B.9)$$

for all $0 \leq j \leq D$. Provided that survival rates stay constant, equation (B.9) leads to a proportional adjustment of all age-specific fertility rates by a uniform factor ψ_n. Thus, proliferation age is supposed constant.

---

[5] Equation (B.8) has no closed form solution for Ω. However, the level parameter can be easily obtained using basic search algorithms. Like life expectancy, the level parameters are gender-specific.

[6] In the extreme where $\Omega = 0$, life expectancy at birth reaches D. All agents would live through to the maximum age. $\Omega < 0$ is not permitted, since it implies survival ratios greater than unity. The empirically irrelevant case of falling life expectancy would require choosing a value of Ω greater than unity.

C. Appendix: German Public Sector Budgets

Table C.1. Composition of the German Public Sector Budget 1995. Billions of DM

Revenue	West	East	Total	Expenditure	West	East	Total
Taxes				Social Insurance			
Labor Income	318.5	28.1	346.6	Social Security[a]	352.6	75.3	427.9
Capital Income	94.0	3.9	97.9	Statutory Health[a]	198.9	40.8	240.1
Seignorage	5.7	1.3	7.0	Nursery Care	7.5	1.6	9.2
Turnover[b]	225.2	16.5	241.7	Unemployment	51.8	42.6	94.4
Excise	30.8	2.4	33.3	Accident	13.9	3.5	17.4
Gasoline	55.4	9.5	64.9	Maternity Assistance	6.5	0.7	7.2
Insurance	13.1	1.0	14.1	Child Allowances	16.2	4.4	20.6
Vehicle	11.8	2.0	13.8	Social Welfare	45.9	6.3	52.2
Other	1.8	0.2	2.0	Housing Support	3.2	2.5	5.8
Contributions				Education Support	2.7	0.6	3.3
Social Security	232.5	51.1	283.6	Youth Services	19.9	5.8	25.7
Statutory Health	180.1	44.7	224.8	Education[c]	102.0	22.5	124.5
Nursery Care	12.9	3.1	15.9	Government Purchases[d]	369.3	86.7	456.0
Unemployment	84.3	4.1	88.4				
Accident	16.1	3.5	19.6				
Deficit[e]			159.9	Interest Payments			129.6

[a] Includes transfers to civil servants.
[b] Includes duty.
[c] Net of investment.
[d] Non age-specific spending.
[e] Includes provision for pension of civil servants.
Source: Author's calculations based on BMA (1996c) BMF (1996), Statistisches Bundesamt (1996a,b), BLK (1997)

Table C.2. Composition of the German public sector budget 1996. Billions of DM

Revenue	West	East	Total	Expenditure	West	East	Total
Taxes				Social Insurance			
Labor Income	291.0	24.7	315.7	Social Security[a]	357.4	88.6	446.0
Capital Income	104.2	4.4	108.6	Statutory Health[a]	207.2	39.8	247.0
Seignorage	5.7	1.3	7.0	Nursery Care	16.9	3.5	20.4
Turnover[b]	226.3	17.5	243.8	Unemployment	67.5	37.9	105.4
Excise	31.1	2.6	33.6	Accident	13.8	4.1	17.9
Gasoline	58.2	10.0	68.3	Maternity Assistance	6.2	0.7	7.0
Insurance	13.3	1.0	14.3	Child Allowances	29.3	8.0	37.3
Vehicle	11.7	2.0	13.7	Social Welfare	44.2	5.8	50.0
Other	1.8	0.2	2.0	Housing Support	3.7	2.9	6.6
Contributions				Education Support	2.6	0.4	3.1
Social Security	245.4	53.9	299.3	Youth Services	20.0	5.8	25.8
Statutory Health	189.4	45.2	234.6	Education[c]	97.8	21.1	118.9
Nursery Care	18.2	4.3	22.6	Government Purchases[d]	340.5	79.2	419.8
Unemployment	84.7	4.0	88.7				
Accident	16.5	3.3	19.8				
Deficit[e]			163.5	Interest Payments			130.5

[a] Includes transfers to civil servants.
[b] Includes duty.
[c] Net of investment.
[d] Non age-specific spending.
[e] Includes provision for pension of civil servants.
Source: Author's calculations based on BMA (1997a) BMF (1997), Statistisches Bundesamt (1997a,b), BLK (1997)

Table C.3. Composition of the German public sector budget 1997. Billions of DM

Revenue	West	East	Total	Expenditure	West	East	Total
Taxes				Social Insurance			
Labor Income	289.7	24.1	313.8	Social Security[a]	367.2	91.5	458.7
Capital Income	99.2	5.3	104.5	Statutory Health[a]	204.8	39.3	244.1
Seignorage	5.8	1.2	7.0	Nursery Care	23.3	4.8	28.1
Turnover[b]	229.5	18.3	247.8	Unemployment	66.1	39.4	105.5
Excise	31.1	2.7	33.8	Accident	13.5	4.0	17.5
Gasoline	56.3	9.7	66.0	Maternity Assistance	6.3	0.7	7.0
Insurance	13.1	1.0	14.1	Child Allowances	31.8	8.7	40.5
Vehicle	11.7	2.0	13.7	Social Welfare	39.2	5.3	44.5
Other	1.7	0.2	2.0	Housing Support	3.8	2.9	6.7
Contributions				Education Support	1.7	0.3	2.0
Social Security	254.9	56.7	311.6	Youth Services	22.7	6.6	29.3
Statutory Health	191.2	46.7	237.8	Education[c]	76.8	13.9	90.7
Nursery Care	24.7	6.0	30.7	Government Purchases[d]	352.0	73.3	425.3
Unemployment	75.9	12.8	88.6				
Accident	16.6	3.4	20.1				
Deficit[e]			142.5	Interest Payments			135.9

[a] Includes transfers to civil servants.
[b] Includes duty.
[c] Net of investment.
[d] Non age-specific spending.
[e] Includes provision for pension of civil servants.
Source: Author's calculations based on BMA (1998) BMF (1998a), Statistisches Bundesamt (1998a,b), BLK (1997)

References

Aaron, H. (1966), "The Social Insurance Paradox," *Canadian Journal of Economics and Political Science*, 32, pp. 371–374

Ablett, J. (1996), "Generational Accounting - An Australian Perspective," *Review of Income and Wealth*, 42, pp. 91–105

Ablett, J. (1997), "A Set of Generational Accounts for Australia: Baseyear 1994/95," *The Economic and Labor Relations Review*, 8, pp. 90–109

Ablett, J. (1999), "Generational Accounting in Australia," in A. Auerbach, L. Kotlikoff, and W. Leibfritz, eds., *Generational Accounting around the World*, Chicago: University of Chicago Press, pp. 141–160

Ablett, J. and Z. Tseggai-Bocureziou (2000), "Lifetime Net Average Tax Rates in Australia since Federation: A Generational Accounting Study," *The Economic Record*, 76, pp. 139–151

Ahlburg, D. (1993), "The Census Bureau's New Projections of the US Population," *Population and Development Review*, 19, pp. 159–174

Altamiranda, M. (1999), "Argentina's Generational Accounts: Is the Convertibility Plan's Fiscal Policy Sustainable?," in A. Auerbach, L. Kotlikoff, and W. Leibfritz, eds., *Generational Accounting around the World*, Chicago: University of Chicago Press, pp. 141–160

Altonji, J., F. Hayashi, and L. Kotlikoff (1992), "Is the Extended Family Altruistically Linked? Direct Tests Using Micro Data," *American Economic Review*, 82, pp. 1177–1198

Altonji, J., F. Hayashi, and L. Kotlikoff (1997), "Parental Altruism and Inter Vivos Transfers: Theory and Evidence," *Journal of Political Economy*, 105, pp. 1121–1166

Andel, N. (1998), *Finanzwissenschaft*, 4th ed., Tübingen: Mohr

Appleyard, R. (1993), "Trends in International Migration in the 1990s," in G. Luciani, ed., *Migration Policies in Europe and the United States*, Amsterdam: Kluwer Academic Publishers, pp. 33–52

Arrow, K. and R. Lind (1970), "Uncertainty and the Evaluation of Public Investment Decisions," *American Economic Review*, 60, pp. 364–378

Atkinson, A. and J. Stiglitz (1980), *Lectures on Public Economics*, London: McGraw-Hill

Auerbach, A. (1997), "Quantifying the Current U.S. Fiscal Imbalance," *National Tax Journal*, 50, pp. 387–398

Auerbach, A. and L. Kotlikoff (1987), *Dynamic Fiscal Policy*, Cambridge: Cambridge University Press

Auerbach, A. and L. Kotlikoff (1999), "The Methodology of Generational Accounting," in A. Auerbach, L. Kotlikoff, and W. Leibfritz, eds., *Generational Accounting around the World*, Chicago: University of Chicago Press, pp. 31–41

Auerbach, A. and P. Oreopoulos (1999), "Analyzing the Fiscal Impact of U.S. Immigration," *American Economic Review, Papers and Proceedings*, 89, pp. 176–180

Auerbach, A. and P. Oreopoulos (2000), "The Fiscal Effects of U.S. Immigration: A Generational Accounting Perpective," in J. Poterba, ed., *Tax Policy and the Economy*, Vol. 14, Cambridge: MIT Press, pp. 123–156

Auerbach, A., B. Baker, L. Kotlikoff, and J. Walliser (1997), "Generational Accounting in New Zealand: Is there Generational Balance?," *International Tax and Public Finance*, 4, pp. 201–228

Auerbach, A., J. Braga de Macedo, José Braz, L. Kotlikoff, and J. Walliser (1999), "Generational Accounting in Portugal," in A. Auerbach, L. Kotlikoff, and W. Leibfritz, eds., *Generational Accounting around the World*, Chicago: University of Chicago Press, pp. 471–488

Auerbach, A., J. Gokhale, and L. Kotlikoff (1991), "Generational Accounting: A Meaningful Alternative to Deficit Accounting," in D. Bradford, ed., *Tax Policy and the Economy*, Vol. 5, Cambridge: MIT Press, pp. 55–110

Auerbach, A., J. Gokhale, and L. Kotlikoff (1992a), "Generational Accounting: A New Approach to Understanding the Effects of Fiscal Policy on Saving," *Scandinavian Journal of Economics*, 94, pp. 303–318

Auerbach, A., J. Gokhale, and L. Kotlikoff (1992b), "Social Security and Medicare Policy from the Perspective of Generational Accounting," in J. Poterba, ed., *Tax Policy and the Economy*, Vol. 6, Cambridge: MIT Press, pp. 129–145

Auerbach, A., J. Gokhale, and L. Kotlikoff (1994), "Generational Accounting: A Meaningful Way to Evaluate Fiscal Policy," *Journal of Economic Perspectives*, 8, pp. 73–94

Auerbach, A., J. Gokhale, and L. Kotlikoff (1995), "Restoring Generational Balance in US Fiscal Policy: What will it Take?," *Economic Review*, 31, pp. 2–12

Auerbach, A., J. Gokhale, L. Kotlikoff, and E. Steigum (1993), "Generational Accounting in Norway: Is Norway Overconsuming its Petroleum Wealth," Working Paper no. 9305, Federal Reserve Bank of Cleveland

Auerbach, A., L. Kotlikoff, and W. Leibfritz (1999), *Generational Accounting Around the World*, Chicago: University of Chicago Press

Bach, S. (1996), "Zur Neuregelung der Vermögen- und Erbschaftsteuer," *DIW-Wochenbericht*, 1996, pp. 497–506

Baker, B., "Generational Accounting in New Zealand (1999)," in A. Auerbach, L. Kotlikoff, and W. Leibfritz, eds., *Generational Accounting around the World*, Chicago: University of Chicago Press, pp. 347–367

Ball, L., D. Elmendorf, and G. Mankiw (1998), "The Deficit Gamble," *Journal of Money, Credit and Banking*, 30, pp. 699–720

Banks, J., R. Disney, and Z. Smith (2000), "What Can we Learn about Pension Reform from Generational Accounts for the UK?," *The Economic Journal*, 110, pp. F575–F597

Barro, R. (1974), "Are Government Bonds Net Wealth," *Journal of Political Economy*, 82, pp. 1095–1117

Barro, R. (1990), "Government Spending in a Simple Model of Endogenous Growth," *Journal of Political Economy*, 98, pp. 108–126

Barro, R. and X. Sala-i-Martin (1992), "Convergence Across States and Regions," in A. Cukierman, Z. Hercowitz and L. Leiderman, eds., *Political Economy, Growth and Business Cycles*, Cambridge: MIT Press, pp. 141–195

Barro, R. and X. Sala-i-Martin (1995), *Economic Growth*, New York: McGraw-Hill

Bartenwerfer, J. (1990), *Mikroökonomische Querschnittsanalysen des individuellen Erwerbsverhaltens*, Vol. 1109 of Europäische Hochschulschriften, Reihe 5: Volks- und Betriebswirtschaft, Frankfurt a.M.: Peter Lang

BBF – Bundesministerium für Bildung und Forschung (1998), "Grund- und Strukturdaten 1998/99," Bonn

Berenguer, E., H. Bonin, and B. Raffelhüschen (1998), "Generational Accounting in Spain: Has Public Sector Grown too Much?," Documents de Traball de la Divisió de Ciències Juridiques, Econòmiques i Socials No E98/30, University of Barcelona

Berenguer, E., H. Bonin, and B. Raffelhüschen (1999), "Spain: The Need for a Broader Tax Base," European Economy, Reports and Studies, 1999(6), 71–85

Besendorfer, D., H. Bonin, and B. Raffelhüschen (2000), "Reformbedarf der sozialen Alterssicherung bei alternativen demographischen Prognosen," Hamburger Jahrbuch für Wirtschafts- und Gesellschaftspolitik, 45, pp. 105-122

Besendorfer, D., C. Borgmann, and B. Raffelhüschen (1998), "Ein Plädoyer für intergenerative Ausgewogenheit: Rentenreformvorschläge auf dem Prüfstand," ifo Studien, 44, pp. 209–231

Birg, H. (1998), "Demographisches Wissen und politische Verantwortung," Zeitschrift für Bevölkerungswissenschaft, 23, pp. 221–251

Birg, H. (2000), "Migration, Geburtendefizit und Alterung in Deutschland," in M. David, T. Borde and H. Kentenich, eds., Migration, Frauen, Gesundheit, Frankfurt a.M.: Mabuse, pp. 187–196

Birg, H., E.-J. Flöthmann, T. Frein, and K. Ströker (1998), "Simulationsrechnungen zur Bevölkerungsentwicklung in den alten und neuen Bundesländern im 21. Jahrhundert," Vol. 45 of Materialien des Bundesinstituts für Bevölkerungsforschung und Sozialpolitik, Bielefeld

Blanchard, O. (1993), "Suggestions for a New Set of Fiscal Indicators," in H. Verbon and F. van Winden, eds., The political economy of government debt, Amsterdam: North-Holland, pp. 307–25.

Blanchard, O. and S. Fischer (1989), Lectures on Macroeconomics, Cambridge: MIT Press

Blanchard, O. and P. Weil (1992), "Dynamic Efficiency, the Riskless Rate and Debt Ponzi Games under Uncertainty," NBER Working Paper no. 3992, Cambridge

Blau, F. (1984), "The Use of Transfer Payments by Immigrants," Industrial and Labor Relations Review, 37, pp. 222–239

Blejer, M and A. Cheasty (1991), "The Measurement of Fiscal Deficits: Analytical and Methodological Issues," Journal of Economic Literature, 24, pp. 1644–1678

BLK – Bund-Länder-Kommission für Bildungsplanung und Forschungsförderung (1997), "Ausgaben der Gebietskörperschaften für Bildung und Wissenschaft in den Jahren 1994 (Ist), 1995 und 1996 (Soll)," Bonn

BMA – Bundesministerium für Arbeit und Sozialordnung (1991), Sicherung bei Pflegebedürftigkeit – Fakten und Argumente, Bonn

BMA – Bundesministerium für Arbeit und Sozialordnung (1996a), "20. Bekanntmachung zum Risikustrukturausgleich, Verältniswerte für den monatlichen Ausgleich 1996," Bundesarbeitsblatt, pp. 71–73

BMA – Bundesministerium für Arbeit und Sozialordnung (1996b), "Soziale Pflegeversicherung – Leistungsempfänger nach Altersgruppen und Geschlecht, 31. Dezember 1995," Bundesarbeitsblatt, p. 158

BMA – Bundesministerium für Arbeit und Sozialordnung (1996c), "Arbeits- und Sozialstatistik, Hauptergebnisse," Bonn

BMA – Bundesministerium für Arbeit und Sozialordnung (1997a), "Arbeits- und Sozialstatistik, Hauptergebnisse," Bonn

BMA – Bundesministerium für Arbeit und Sozialordnung (1997b), "Vorschläge der Kommission 'Fortentwicklung der Rentenversicherung'," Bonn

BMA – Bundesministerium für Arbeit und Sozialordnung (1998), "Arbeits- und Sozialstatistik, Hauptergebnisse," Bonn

BMF – Bundesministerium für Finanzen (1996), "Finanzbericht 1997," Bonn
BMF – Bundesministerium für Finanzen (1997), "Finanzbericht 1998," Bonn
BMF – Bundesministerium für Finanzen (1998a), "Finanzbericht 1999," Bonn
BMF – Bundesministerium für Finanzen (1998b), "Grundsätzliche Reform der gesetzlichen Rentenversicherung, Gutachten des wissenschaftlichen Beirats beim Bundesministerium der Finanzen," Bonn
BMF – Bundesministerium für Finanzen (1999), "Deutschland erneuern - Zukunftsprogramm zur Sicherung von Arbeit, Wachstum und sozialer Stabilität," Bonn
BMI – Bundesministerium des Inneren (1996), "Modellrechnungen zur Bevölkerungsentwicklung bis zum Jahre 2040," Bonn
BMWi – Bundesministerium für Wirtschaft (1998), "Grundlegende Reform der gesetzlichen Rentenversicherung," Bonn
Boll, S. (1994), *Intergenerationale Umverteilungswirkungen der Fiskalpolitik in der Bundesrepublik Deutschland, Ein Ansatz mit Hilfe des Generational Accounting*, Vol. 66 of Finanzwissenschaftliche Schriften, Frankfurt a.M.: Peter Lang
Boll, S. (1996), "Intergenerative Verteilungseffekte öffentlicher Haushalte - Theoretische Aspekte und empirischer Befund für die Bundesrepublik Deutschland," Economic Research Group of the German Bundesbank, Discussion Paper no. 6/96, Frankfurt a.M.
Boll, S., B. Raffelhüschen, and J. Walliser (1994), "Social Security and Intergenerational Redistribution: A Generational Accounting Perspective," *Public Choice*, 81, pp. 79–100
Bomsdorf, E. (1993), *Kohortensterbetafeln für die Geburtjahrgänge 1923 – 1993, Modellrechnungen für die Bundesrepublik Deutschland*, Vol. 13 of Reihe Versicherungswirtschaft, Bergisch Gladbach: Josef Eul
Bonin, H. (1994), "Auswirkungen von Immigration auf den öffentlichen Sektor in Deutschland," MA-Thesis, University of Kiel
Bonin, H. and K. Feist (1999), "Pension Reform in Germany and Redistribution between Living Generations," University of Freiburg, Discussion Papers of the Institute for Public Finance, no. 78
Bonin, H. and B. Raffelhüschen (1999), "Public Finances in the European Union - Is Convergence Sustainable?," University of Freiburg, Discussion Papers of the Institute for Public Finance, no. 77
Bonin, H. and K. Zimmermann (2001), "The Post-Unification German Labor Market," in R. Riphahn, D. Snower and K. Zimmermann, eds., *Employment Policy in Transition, The Lessons of German Integration for the Labor Market*, Heidelberg: Springer, pp. 8–30
Bonin, H., J. Gil, and C. Patxot (2001), "Beyond the Toledo Agreement - The Intergenerational Impact of Spanish Pension Reform," *Spanish Economic Review*, 2001, forth
Bonin, H., B. Raffelhüschen, and J. Walliser (1999), "Germany: Unification and Ageing," *European Economy, Reports and Studies*, 1996(6), pp. 57–70
Bonin, H., B. Raffelhüschen, and J. Walliser (2000), "Can Immigration Alleviate the Demographic Burden?," *Finanzarchiv*, 57, pp. 1–21
Borgmann, C., P. Krimmer, and B. Raffelhüschen (2001), "Rentenreformen 1998–2001: Eine vorläufige Bestandsaufnahme," *Perspektiven der Wirtschaftspolitik*, 2001, forth
Borjas, G. and S. Trejo (1991), "Immigrant Participation in the Welfare System," *Industrial and Labor Relations Review*, 44, pp. 195–211
Boskin, M. and L. Kotlikoff (1985), "Public Debt and U.S. Saving: A New Test of the Neutrality Hypothesis," *Carnegie-Rochester Conference Series on Public Policy*, 23, pp. 55–86

Bovenberg, L. and H. ter Rele (1999a), "Generational Accounting in the Netherlands," in A. Auerbach, L. Kotlikoff, and W. Leibfritz, eds., *Generational Accounting around the World*, Chicago: University of Chicago Press, pp. 325–345

Bovenberg, L. and H. ter Rele (1999b), "Netherlands: Finances and Ageing," *European Economy, Reports and Studies*, pp. 133–148

Bröcker, H. and B. Raffelhüschen, "Fiscal Aspects of German Unification: Who is
Stuck with the Bill? (1997)," *Applied Economics Quarterly*, 45, pp. 139–162

Bretz, M. (1986), "Bevölkerungsvorausberechnungen: Statistische Grundlagen und
Probleme," *Wirtschaft und Statistik*, 4, pp. 233–260

Breyer, F. and M. Kifmann (1999), "Erhöhung der Regelaltersgrenze oder Kürzung
des Rentenniveaus?," *Wirtschaftsdienst*, 79, pp. 288–292

Breyer, F. and M. Straub (1993), "Welfare Effects of Unfunded Pension Systems
when Labor Supply is Endogenous," *Journal of Public Economics*, 50, 77–91

Börsch-Supan, A. (1991), "Aging Populations: Problems and Policy Options in the
U.S. and Germany," *Economic Policy*, 12, pp. 104–139

Börsch-Supan, A. (1994a), "Savings in Germany – Part 1: Incentives," in J. Poterba,
ed., *Public Policy and Household Saving*, Chicago: University of Chicago Press,
pp. 81–104

Börsch-Supan, A. (1994b), "Migration, Social Security Systems, and Public Finance," in H. Siebert, ed., *Migration: A Challenge for Europe*, Tübingen: Mohr,
pp. 119–142

Börsch-Supan, A. (1998a), "Zur deutschen Diskussion eines Übergangs vom
Umlage- zum Kapitaldeckungsverfahren in der gesetzlichen Rentenversicherung,"
Finanzarchiv, 55, pp. 400–428

Börsch-Supan, A. (1998b), "Germany: A Social Security System on the Verge of Col-
lapse," in H. Siebert, ed., *Redesigning Social Security*, Tübingen: Mohr, pp. 129–
159

Buchanan, J. (1958), *Public Principles of Public Debt*, Homewood: Richard Irwin

Buiter, W. (1997), "Generational Accounts, Aggregate Saving and Intergenerational
Distribution," *Economica*, 64, pp. 605–626

Burda, M. and M. Funke (1995), "Eastern Germany: Can't we be more Optimistic?," *ifo Studien*, 41, pp. 327–354

Buscher, H. (1999), "Kommt der Aufschwung im Jahr 2000?," *ZEW Konjunktur-
report*, 2, May, pp. 1–2

Buslei, H. and F. Kraus (1996), "Wohlfahrtseffekte eines graduellen Übergangs auf
ein nierigeres Rentenniveau," in V. Steiner and K. Zimmermann, eds., *Soziale
Sicherung und Arbeitsmarkt*, Baden-Baden: Nomos, pp. 57–92

Butz, W. (1983), "Methoden zur Fortschreibung der Sterblichkeit in Bevölkerungs-
projektionen," *Zeitschrift für Bevölkerungswissenschaft*, 9, pp. 229–240

Cardarelli, R. and J. Sefton (1999), "UK: Rolling Back the UK Welfare State?,"
European Economy, Reports and Studies, 1999(6), pp. 193–206

Cardarelli, R., J. Sefton, and P. Agulnik (2000), "The Pensions Green Paper: A
Generational Accounting Perspective," *The Economic Journal*, 110, pp. 598–610

Cardarelli, R., J. Sefton, and L. Kotlikoff (2000), "Generational Accounting in the
UK," *The Economic Journal*, 110, pp. F547–F574

CBO – Congressional Budget Office (1995), "Who Pays and When? An Assessment
of Generational Accounting," Washington D.C.

Chamley, C. (1981), "The Welfare Costs of Capital Income Taxation in a Growing
Economy," *Journal of Political Economy*, 89, pp. 468–496

Chouraqui, J., R. Hagemann, and N. Sartor (1990), "Indicators of Fiscal Policy: A
Re-Examination," OECD Working Paper no. 78, Paris

Cornes, R. and T. Sandler (1996), *The Theory of Externalities, Public Goods and
Club Goods*, 2nd ed., Cambridge: Cambridge University Press

Crettez, B., K. Feist, and B. Raffelhüschen (1999), "France: Generational Imbalance and Social Insurance Reform," *European Economiy*, 1999(6), pp. 87–99

Cutler, D. (1988), "Tax Reform and the Stock Market – An Asset Price Approach," *American Economic Review*, 1988, 78, pp. 1107–1117

Deutsche Bundesbank (1995), "Fortschritte im Anpassungsprozeß in Ostdeutschland und der Beitrag der Wirtschaftsförderung," *Monthly Report*, July, pp. 35–52

Deutsche Bundesbank (1996), "Die Wirtschaftslage um die Jahreswende 1995/96, Öffentliche Finanzen," *Monthly Report*, February, pp. 39–50

Deutsche Bundesbank (1997), "Die fiskalische Belastung zukünftiger Generationen – eine Analyse mit Hilfe des Generational Accounting," *Monthly Report*, November, pp. 17–30

Deutsche Bundesbank (1998a), "Stellungnahme des Zentralbankrates zur Konvergenzlage in der Europäischen Union im Hinblick auf die dritte Stufe der Wirtschafts- und Währungsunion," *Monthly Report*, April, pp. 17–40

Deutsche Bundesbank (1998b), "Gegenwärtige und künftige Belastungen der Gebietskörperschaften durch den Personalaufwand," *Monthly Report*, August, pp. 61–82

Deutsche Bundesbank (1999a), "Zur Entwicklung der privaten Vermögenssituation seit Beginn der neunziger Jahre," *Monthly Report*, January, pp. 61–82

Deutsche Bundesbank (1999b), *Monthly Report*, July

Diamond, P. (1965), "National Debt in a Neoclassical Growth Model," *American Economic Review*, 55, pp. 1126–1150

Diamond, P. (1996), "Generational Accounts and Generational Balance: An Assessment," *National Tax Journal*, 49, pp. 597–607

Dinkel, R., C. Höhn, and R. Scholz (1996), *Sterblichkeitsentwicklung – unter besonderer Berücksichtigung der Kohortenansatzes*, Vol. 23 of Schriftenreihe des Bundesinstituts für Bevölkerungsforschung, Munich: Boldt

Disney, R. (1996), *Can we Afford to Grow Older – A Perspective on the Economics of Aging*, Cambridge: MIT Press

DIW – Deutsches Institut für Wirtschaftsforschung (1995), "Alternde Gesellschaft, Zur Bedeutung von Zuwanderungen für die Altersstruktur der Bevölkerung in Deutschland," *DIW-Wochenbericht*, pp. 579–589

Dustmann, C. (1996), "The Social Assimilation of Immigrants," *Journal of Population Economics*, pp. 37–54

Eitenmüller, S. (1996), "Die Rentabilität der gesetzlichen Rentenversicherung, Kapitalmarktanaloge Renditeberechnung für die nahe und die ferne Zukunft," *Deutsche Rentenversicherung*, pp. 784–798

European Commission (1999), ed., *Generational Accounting in Europe*, Vol. 1999(6) of European Economy, Brussels

Fehr, H. (1999), *Welfare Effects of Dynamic Tax Reforms*, Vol. 5 of *Beiträge zur Finanzwissenschaft*, Tübingen: Mohr

Fehr, H. and L. Kotlikoff (1996), "Generational Accounting in General Equilibrium," *Finanzarchiv*, 53, pp. 1–27

Feichtinger, G. (1979), *Demographische Analyse und populationsdynamische Modelle, Grundzüge der Bevölkerungsmathematik*, Wien: Springer

Feist, K., B. Raffelhüschen, R. Sullström, and R. Vanne (1999), "Finland: Macroeconomic Turnabout and Intergenerational Redistribution," *European Economy*, 1999(6), pp. 163–178

Felderer, B. (1983), *Wirtschaftliche Entwicklung bei schrumpfender Bevölkerung*, Heidelberg: Springer

Felderer, B. (1994), "Can Immigration Policy Help to Stabilize Social Security Systems," in H. Giersch, ed., *Economic Aspects of International Migration*, Berlin: Duncker und Humblot, pp. 197–226

Feldstein, M. (1974), "Social Security, Induced Retirement, and Aggregate Capital Accumulation," *Journal of Political Economy*, 82, pp. 905–926

Feldstein, M. (1998), "Privatizing Social Security: Introduction," in M. Feldstein, ed., *Privatizing Social Security*, Chicago: University of Chicago Press, pp. 1–29

Fenge, R. (1996), "Pareto-Efficiency of the Pay-as-you-go System with Intergenerational Fairness," *Finanzarchiv*, 52, pp. 357–363

Franco, D. (1995), "Pension Liabilities - Their Use and Misuse in the Assessment of Fiscal Policies," European Commission Economic Papers no. 110, Brussels

Franco, D. and N. Sartor (1999), "Italy: High Public Debt and Population Ageing," *European Economy, Reports and Studies*, 1999(6), pp. 117–132

Franco, D., J. Gokhale, L. Guiso, L. Kotlikoff, and N. Sartor (1994), "Generational Accounting: The Case of Italy," in A. Ando, L. Guiso, and I. Visco, eds., *Savings and the Accumulation of Wealth: Essays on Italian Household and Government Saving Behavior*, Cambridge: Cambridge University Press, pp. 128–160

Franz, W. and V. Steiner (2000), "Wages in the East German Transition Process: Facts and Explanations," *German Economic Review*, 1, pp. 241–269

Färber, G. (1988), *Probleme der Finanzpolitik bei schrumpfender Bevölkerung*, Frankfurt a.M.: Campus

Färber. G. (1997), "Zur Entwicklung der Personal- und Versorgungsausgaben im öffentlichen Dienst," *WSI-Mitteilungen*, 50, pp. 426–438

Fullerton, D. and D. Rogers (1993), *Who Bears the Income Tax Burden?*, Washington: Brookings

Gandenberger, O. (1981), "Theorie der öffentlichen Verschuldung," in F. Neumark, ed., *Handwörterbuch der Finanzwissenschaft*, 3rd ed., Vol. 3, Tübingen: Mohr, pp. 6–49

Geanakopolos, J., O. Mitchell, and S. Zeldes (1998), "Would a Privatized Social Security System Really Pay a Higher Rate of Return?," NBER Working Paper no. 6713, Cambridge

George, M., F. Nault, and A. Romaniuc (1991), "Effects of Fertility and International Migration on Changing Age Composition in Canada," *Statistical Journal of the United Nations*, 8, pp. 13–24

Gokhale, J. and B. Raffelhüschen (1999), "Population Aging and Fiscal Policy in Europe and the United States," *Economic Review*, 35, pp. 10–20

Gokhale, J., B. Page, and J. Sturrock (1999), "Generational Accounting in the United States: An Update," in A. Auerbach, L. Kotlikoff, and W. Leibfritz, eds., *Generational Accounting around the World*, Chicago: University of Chicago Press, pp. 489–517

Gokhale, J., B. Raffelhüschen, and J. Walliser (1994), "Fiskalpolitik im vereinten Deutschland - Droht zukünftigen Generationen der Leviathan?," University of Kiel, Discussion Papers of the Institute for Public Finance no. 48

Gokhale, J., B. Raffelhüschen, and J. Walliser (1995), "The Burden of German Unification: A Generational Accounting Approach," *Finanzarchiv*, 52, pp. 141–165

Gramlich, E. (1990), "Fiscal Indicators," OECD Working Paper no. 80, Paris

Greiner, A. and W. Semmler (1999), "An Inquiry to the Sustainability of German Fiscal Policy: Some Time-Series Tests," *Public Finance Review*, 27, pp. 220–236

Grohmann, H. (1980), *Rentenversicherung und Bevölkerungsprognosen*, Schriftenreihe Sonderforschungsbereich 3 der Universitäten Frankfurt und Mannheim, Mikroanalytische Grundlagen der Gesellschaftspolitik, Vol. 2, Frankfurt a.M.: Campus

Grohmann, H. (1981), "Die gesetzliche Rentenversicherung im demographischen Wandel," in Bundesministerium für Arbeit und Sozialordnung, ed., *Langfristige Probleme der Alterssicherung in der Bundersrepublik Deutschland*, Bonn, pp. 1–94

Hagemann, R. and C. John (1997), "Fiscal Reform in Sweden: What Generational Accounting Tells Us," *Contemporary Economic Policy*, 15, pp. 1–12

Hagemann, R. and C. John (1999), "Generational Accounts in Sweden," in A. Auerbach, L. Kotlikoff, and W. Leibfritz, eds., *Generational Accounting around the World*, Chicago: University of Chicago Press, pp. 397–412

Hagemann, R. and G. Nicoletti (1989), "Ageing Populations: Economic Effects and Implications for Public Finance," OECD Department of Economics and Statistics Working Paper, no. 61, Paris: Organization for Economic Cooperation and Development

Hain, W., S. Eitenmüller, and S. Barth (1997), "Von Renditen, Gerechtigkeit und Reformvorschlägen," *Sozialer Fortschritt*, 46, pp. 213–226

Haisken-deNew, J., F. Buechel, and G. Wagner (1997), "Assimilation and other Determinants of School Attainment in Germany: Do Immigrant Children Perform as well as Germans?," *Vierteljahreshefte zur Wirtschaftsforschung*, 66, pp. 169–179

Haveman, R. (1994), "Should Generational Accounts Replace Public Budgets and Deficits," *Journal of Economic Perspectives*, 1994, 8, pp. 95–111

Höhn, C., U. Mammey, and H. Wendt (1990), "Bericht 1990 zur demographischen Lage: Trends in den beiden Teilen Deutschlands und Ausländer in der Bundesrepublik Deutschland," *Zeitschrift für Bevölkerungswissenschaft*, 16, pp. 135–205

Hofmann, J. (1996), "Versicherungsfremde Leistungen und Bundeszuschuß in der gesetzlichen Rentenversicherung," *Sozialer Fortschritt*, 45, pp. 126–128

Holtz-Eakin, D. (1994), "Public Sector Capital and the Productivity Puzzle," *Review of Economics and Statistics*, 76, pp. 12–21

Holzmann, R. (1988), "Ageing and Social Security Costs," *European Journal of Population*, 3, pp. 411–437

Homburg, S. (1990), "The Efficiency of Unfunded Pension Schemes," *Journal of Institutional and Theoretical Economics*, 146, pp. 640–647

Jagob, J. and O. Scholz (1998), "Reforming the German Pension System: Who Wins and Looses? – A Generational Accounting Perspective," Institute for Germany Studies Working Paper no 12/98, Birmingham

Jensen, S. and B. Raffelhüschen (1995), "Intertemporal Aspects of Fiscal Policy in Denmark," EPRU Working Paper 1995-22, Copenhagen

Jensen, S. and B. Raffelhüschen (1997), "Generational and Gender-Specific Aspects of the Tax and Transfer System in Denmark," *Empirical Economics*, 22, pp. 615–635

Jensen, S. and B. Raffelhüschen (1999a), "Denmark: Challenges Ahead and Needs for Social Security Reforms," *European Economy, Reports and Studies*, 1999(6), pp. 43–56

Jensen, S. and B. Raffelhüschen (1999b), "Public Debt, Welfare Reforms, and Intergenerational Distribution of Tax Burdens in Denmark," in A. Auerbach, L. Kotlikoff, and W. Leibfritz, eds., *Generational Accounting around the World*, Chicago: University of Chicago Press, pp. 219–238

Jensen, S., B. Raffelhüschen, P. Jacobsen, and M. Junge (1996), "Generationsregnskab for danmark," *Nationaløkonomisk Tidsskrift*, 134, pp. 39–60

Kakwani, N. and M. Krongaew (1999), "Thailand's Generational Accounts," in A. Auerbach, L. Kotlikoff, and W. Leibfritz, eds., *Generational Accounting around the World*, Chicago: University of Chicago Press, pp. 413–446

Kane, T. (1986), "The Fertility and Assimimilation of Guestworker Populations in the Federal Republic of Germany: 1961 – 1981," *Zeitschrift für Bevölkerungswissenschaft*, 12, pp. 99–131

Kellermann, K. and C.-H. Schlag (1998), "Produktivitäts- und Finanzierungseffekte öffentlicher Infrastrukturinvestitionen," *Kredit und Kapital*, 31, pp. 315–342

Kempen, E. van (1996), "Betaalt de baby de boom," *Economisch Statistiche Berichten*, 81, pp. 724–728

Keuschnigg, C., M. Keuschnigg, R. Komann, E. Lüth, and B. Raffelhüschen (1999), "Austria: Restoring Generational Balance," *European Economy*, 1999(6), pp. 149–162

Keuschnigg, C., M. Keuschnigg, R. Komann, E. Lüth, and B. Raffelhüschen (2000), "Public Debt and Generational Balance in Austria," *Empirica*, 27, pp. 225–252

Keyfitz, N. (1977), *Applied Mathematical Demographics*, New York: Wiley

Kitterer, W. (1986), "Die Einkommens- und Verbrauchsstichprobe des Statistischen Bundesamtes (EVS)," in H. Lindner, ed., *Aussagefähigkeit von Einkommensverteilungsrechnungen für die Bundesrepublik Deutschland*, Tübingen: Mohr, pp. 25–101

Kitterer, W. (1994), "Tax- versus Debt-Financing of Public Investment: A Dynamic Simulation Analysis," *Kredit und Kapital*, 27, pp. 163–187

Kitterer, W. (1996), "Intergenerative Belastungsrechnungen ('Generational Accounting') - Ein Maßstab für die Belastung künftiger Generationen?," in A. Oberhauser, ed., *Finanzierungsprobleme der deutschen Einheit IV, Spezielle Finanzierungsprobleme im Zeitablauf*, Berlin: Duncker und Humblot, pp. 215–257

Kotlikoff, L. (1979), "Social Security and Equilibrium Capital Intensity," *Quarterly Journal of Economics*, 93, pp. 233–53

Kotlikoff, L. (1986), "Deficit Delusion," *Public Interest*, 84, pp. 53–65

Kotlikoff, L. (1988a), "The Deficit is not a Well-Defined Measure of Fiscal Policy," *Science*, 241, pp. 791–795

Kotlikoff, L. (1988b), "Intergenerational Transfers and Savings," *Journal of Economic Perspectives*, 2, pp. 41–58

Kotlikoff, L. (1992), *Generational Accounting, Knowing Who Pays and When for What we Spend*, New York: Free Press

Kotlikoff, L. (1993), "From Deficit Delusion to the Fiscal Balance Rule – Looking for a Sensible Way to Measure Fiscal Policy," *Journal of Economics*, 7(suppl.), pp. 17–41

Kotlikoff, L. and W. Leibfritz (1999), "An International Comparison of Generational Accounts," in A. Auerbach, L. Kotlikoff, and W. Leibfritz, eds., *Generational Accounting around the World*, Chicago: University of Chicago Press, pp. 73–102

Kotlikoff, L. and J. Walliser (1995), "Applying Generational Accounting to Developing Countries," IED Discussion Paper Series No. 67, Boston

Kotlikoff, L. and B. Raffelhüschen (1999), "Generational Accounting Around the Globe," *American Economic Review, Papers and Proceedings*, 89, pp. 161–166

Kotlikoff, L., K. Smetters, and J. Walliser (1998), "Opting out of Social Security and Adverse Selection," NBER Working Paper no. 6430, Cambridge

Krupp, H.-J., "Grenzen von Rentenanpassungsformeln (1999)," *Wirtschaftsdienst*, 79, pp. 474–479

Laitner, J. and T. Juster (1996), "New Evidence on Altruism: A Study of TIAA-CREF Retirees," *American Economic Review*, 86, pp. 893–908

Lampman, R. and T. Smeeding (1983), "Interfamily Transfers as Alternatives to Government Transfers to Persons," *Review on Income and Wealth*, 29, pp. 45–66

Layard, R. and S. Glaister (1994), "Introduction," in R. Layard and S. Glaister, eds., *Cost-Benefit Analysis*, 2nd ed., Cambridge: Cambridge University Press, pp. 1–56

Lechner, M. (1998), "Eine empirische Analyse des Geburtenrückgangs in den neuen Bundesländern aus Sicht der neoklassischen Bevölkerungsökonomie," *Zeitschrift für Wirtschafts- und Sozialwissenschaften*, 118, pp. 463–488

Lee, R.. and J. Skinner (1999), "Will Aging Baby Boomers Bust the Federal Budget," *Journal of Economic Perspectives*, 13, pp. 117–140

Leibfritz, W. (1993), "Germany," in D. Jorgenson and R. Landau, eds., *Tax Reform and the Cost of Capital: An International Comparison*, Washington: Brookings, pp. 166–190

Leibfritz, W., W. Büttner, and U. van Essen (1998), "Germany," in K. Messere, ed., *The Tax System in Industrialized Countries*, Oxford: Oxford University Press, pp. 128–158

Leslie, P. (1945), "On the Use of Matrices in Certain Population Mathematics," *Biometrica*, 33, pp. 183–212

Lesthaege, R., H. Page, and J. Surkyn (1991), "Sind Einwanderer ein Ersatz für Geburten?," *Zeitschrift für Bevölkerungswissenschaft*, 17, pp. 281–314

Levy, J. and O. Doré (1999), "Generational Accounting for France," in A. Auerbach, L. Kotlikoff, and W. Leibfritz, eds., *Generational Accounting around the World*, Chicago: University of Chicago Press, pp. 239–276

Lindbeck, A. and J. Weibull (1986), "Intergenerational Aspects of Public Transfers, Borrowing and Debt," *Scandinavian Journal of Economics*, 88, pp. 239–267

Lüth, E. (2001), *Private Intergenerational Transfers and Demographic Aging. The German Case*, Heidelberg: Physica

Lüth, E. and A. Dellis (1999), "Belgium: Can Fiscal Policy Cope with Debt and Ageing?," *European Economy, Reports and Studies*, 1999(6), pp. 29–42

Lundvik, P., E. Lüth, and B. Raffelhüschen (1999), "Sweden: The Swedish Welfare State on Trial," *European Economy, Reports and Studies*, 1999(6), pp. 179–192

Mammey, U. (1990), "35 Jahre Ausländer in der Bundesrepublik Deutschland – Die demographische Entwicklung," in C. Höhn and D. Rein, eds., *Ausländer in der Bundesrepublik Deutschland*, Vol. 20 of Schriftenreihe des Bundesinstituts für Bevölkerungsforschung, Bielefeld, pp. 55–82

McCarthy, T. (1995), "Ageing Populations and the Pension System: Time Bomb or False Alarm?," Economics Department Working Paper, no. 60/10/95, Maynooth College, Kildare

McCarthy, T. and H. Bonin (1999), "Ireland: EU Transfers and Demographic Dividends," *European Economy, Reports and Studies*, 1999(6), pp. 101–116

Mehra, R. and E. Prescott (1985), "The Equity Premium: A Puzzle," *Journal of Monetary Economics*, 15, pp. 145–162

Miller, P. (1999), "Immigration Policy and Immigrant Quality: The Austalian Points System," *American Economic Review*, 89, pp. 192–197

Münz, R., W. Seifert, and R. Ulrich (1999), *Zuwanderung nach Deutschland: Strukturen, Wirkungen, Perspektiven*, 2nd ed., Frankfurt a.M.: Campus

Modigliani, F. (1961), "Long-Run Implications of Alternative Fiscal Policies and the Burden of the National Debt," *Economic Journal*, 71, pp. 730–755

Neumann, M. (1998), "Replacing Germany's Public Old Age Pension System with a Fully Funded System: Options for Transition," in K. Morath, ed., *Verläßliche soziale Sicherung*, Bad Homburg, pp. 53–63

OECD Secretary (1991), "Demographic Challenges and Migration Policies," in OECD, ed., *Migration, The Demographic Aspects*, Paris, pp. 7–14

OMB - Office of Management and Budget (1994), "Analytical Perspectives," Budget of the United States Government, Fiscal Year 1995, Washington D.C.

Oreopoulos, P. (1999), "Canada: On the Road to Fiscal Balance," in A. Auerbach, L. Kotlikoff, and W. Leibfritz, eds., *Generational Accounting around the World*, Chicago: University of Chicago Press, pp. 199–217

Pflaumer, P. (1988), *Methoden der Bevölkerungsvorausschätzung unter besonderer Berücksichtigung der Unsicherheit*, Vol. 377 of Volkswirtschaftliche Schriften, Berlin: Duncker und Humblot

Poschner, H. (1996), *Die Effekte der Migration auf die soziale Sicherung*, Vol. 30 of Reihe Wirtschafts- und Sozialwissenschaften, Weiden: eurotrans

Prognos (1998), *Auswirkungen veränderter ökonomischer und rechtlicher Rahmenbedingungen auf die gesetzliche Rentenversicherung in Deutschland*, Vol. 9 of DRV Schriften, Berlin

Raffelhüschen, B. (1993), "Funding Social Security through Pareto-Optimal Conversion Policies," *Journal of Economics*, 7 (suppl.), pp. 105–131

Raffelhüschen, B. (1996), "A Note on Measuring Intertemporal Redistribution in Generational Accounting," University of Freiburg, Discussion Papers of the Institute for Public Finance, no. 53

Raffelhüschen, B. (1997), "Sanfte Umstellung," *Finanzen*, 12, pp. 21–22

Raffelhüschen, B. (1998), "Interne Renditen gemäß der Generationenbilanz," in Deutsches Institut für Altersvorsorge, ed., *Renditen der gesetzlichen Rentenversicherung im Vergleich zu alternativen Anlageformen*, Frankfurt a.M., pp. 36–49

Raffelhüschen, B. (1999a), "Generational Accounting: Method, Data and Limitations," *European Economy, Reports and Studies*, 1999(6), pp. 17–28

Raffelhüschen, B. (1999b), "Generational Accounting in Europe," *American Economic Review, Papers and Proceedings*, 88, pp. 167–170

Raffelhüschen, B. (2000), "Aging and Intergenerational Equity: From Paygo to Funded Pension Schemes," in H.-G. Petersen and P. Gallagher, eds., *Tax and Transfer Reform in Germany and Australia*, Vol. 3 of Australia Center Series, Berlin: Berliner Debatte Wissenschaftsverlag, pp. 263-284

Raffelhüschen, B. (2001a), "Eine Generationenbilanz der deutschen Wirtschafts- und Sozialpolitik," in O. Graf von Lambsdorff, ed., *Freiheit und Soziale Verantwortung*, Frankfurt a.M.: Frankfurter Allgemeine Verlagsanstalt, pp. 241–260

Raffelhüschen, B. (2001b), "Aging, Fiscal Policy and Social Insurances: A European Perspective," in A. Auerbach and R. Lee, eds., *Demographic Change and Fiscal Policy*, Chicago: University of Chicago Press, forth

Raffelhüschen, B. and A. Risa (1996), "Reforming Social Security in a Small Open Economy," *European Journal of Political Economy*, 11, pp. 469–486

Raffelhüschen, B. and A. Risa (1997), "Generational Accounting and Intergenerational Welfare," *Public Choice*, 93, pp. 149–163

Raffelhüschen, B. and J. Walliser (1996), "Generational Accounting, Eine Alternative zur Messung intergenerativer Umverteilungspolitik," *Wirtschaftswissenschaftliches Studium*, 25, pp. 181–188

Raffelhüschen, B. and J. Walliser (1997), "Was hinterlassen wir zukünftigen Generationen? Ergebnisse der Generationenbilanzierung," in E. Knappe and A. Winkler, eds., *Sozialstaat im Umbruch*, Frankfurt a.M.: Campus, pp. 65–89

Raffelhüschen, B. and J. Walliser (1999), "Unification and Aging: Who Pays and When?," in A. Auerbach, L. Kotlikoff, and W. Leibfritz, eds., *Generational Accounting around the World*, Chicago: University of Chicago Press, pp. 277–298

Razin, A. and E. Sadka (1995), *Population Economics*, Cambridge: MIT Press

Rele, H. ter (1997), "Generational Accounts for the Dutch Public Sector," CPB Netherlands Bureau for Economic Policy Analysis, Research Memorandum no. 135, The Hague

Riphahn, R. (1998), "Immigrant Participation in the German Welfare Program," *Finanzarchiv*, 55, pp. 163–185

Ronning, G. (1991), *Mikroökonometrie*, Heidelberg: Springer

Rürup, B. (1998), "Zur Berücksichtigung der Lebenserwartung in der gesetzlichen Rentenversicherung," *Deutsche Rentenversicherung*, 1998, pp. 281–291

Ruocco, A. and W. Wiegard (1997), "Green Tax Reforms: Understanding the Double Dividend Hypothesis," *Zeitschrift für Umweltpolitik und Umweltrecht*, 20, pp. 171–198

Samuelson, P. (1958), "An Exact Consumption-Loan Model of Interest with or without the Social Contrivance of Money," *Journal of Political Economy*, 66, pp. 467–482

Sartor, N. (1999), "Generational Accounts for Italy," in A. Auerbach, L. Kotlikoff, and W. Leibfritz, eds., *Generational Accounting around the World*, Chicago: University of Chicago Press, pp. 299–323

Schlenger, M. (1998), *Versicherungsfremde Leistungen in der Gesetzlichen Rentenversicherung*, Vol. 86 of Schriften des Karl-Bräuer-Instituts des Bundes der Steuerzahler, Wiesbaden

Schmähl, W. (1992), "Changing the Retirement Age in Germany," *Geneva Papers on Risk and Insurance*, 17, pp. 81–104

Schmähl, W. (1998), "Perspektiven der Alterssicherung – Anmerkungen zu Konzeptionen und Konzepten," in B. Seel, ed., *Sicherungssysteme in einer alternden Gesellschaft*, Frankfurt a.M.: Campus, pp. 154–177

Schmidt, C. (1997), "Immigrant Performance in Germany, Labor Earnings of Ethnic German Migrants and Foreign Guest-Workers," *Quarterly Review of Economics and Finance*, 37, 379-397

Schmidt, C. and K. Zimmermann (1992), "Migration Pressure in Germany: Past and Future," in K. Zimmermann, ed., *Migration and Economic Development*, Berlin: Springer, pp. 201–230

Schnabel, R. (1998), "Rates of Return of the German Pay-As-You-Go Pension System," *Finanzarchiv*, 55, pp. 374–399

Schneider, K. (1997), "Involuntary Unemployment and Environmental Policy: The Double Dividend Hypothesis," *Scandinavian Journal of Economics*, 99, pp. 45–59

Schober, K. and H. Stegmann (1987), "Ausländische Jugendliche – Demographische Entwicklung sowie Ausbildungs- und Beschäftigungssituation," in E. Hönekopp, ed., *Aspekte der Ausländerbeschäftigung in der Bundesrepublik Deutschland*, Beiträge zur Arbeitsmarkt- und Berufsforschung 114, Nuremberg: Bundesanstalt für Arbeit, pp. 195–242

Schultz, T. (1998), "Immigrant Quality and Assimilation: A Review of the US Literature," *Journal of Population Economics*, 11, pp. 239–252

Seifert, W. (1997), "Integration of "new" and "old" immigrant groups in Germany," *Vierteljahreshefte zur Wirtschaftsforschung*, 66, pp. 159–169

Simon, J. (1984), "Immigrants, Taxes and Welfare in the United States," *Population and Development Review*, 10, pp. 55–69

Simon, J. (1991), "The Case for Greatly Increased Immigration," *The Public Interest*, 102, pp. 89–103

Simon, J. (1994), "On the Economic Consequences of Immigration: Lessons for Immigration Policies," in H. Giersch, ed., *Economic Aspects of International Migration*, Berlin: Duncker und Humblot, pp. 227–248

Sinn, H.-W. (1987), *Capital Income Taxation and Resource Allocation*, Amsterdam: North-Holland

Sinn, H.-W. (1997), "The Value of Children and Immigrants in a Pay-as-you-go Pensino System: A Proposal for a Partial Transition to a Funded System," CES Working Paper no. 141, University of Munich

Sinn, H.-W. (1999), "Die Krise der Gesetzlichen Rentenversicherung und Wege zu ihrer Lösung," in Bavarian Academy of Sciences, ed., *Yearbook 1998*, Munich: Beck, pp. 95–119

Sinn, H.-W. (2000), "Pension Reform and Demographic Crisis: Why a Funded System is Ueful and why it is not Useful," *International Tax and Public Finance*, 7, pp. 389–410

Sinn, G. and H.-W. Sinn (1993), *Jumpstart: The Economic Unification of Germany*, Cambridge: Cambridge University Press

Sinn, H.-W. and M. Thum (1999), "Gesetzliche Rentenversicherung: Prognosen im Vergleich," *Finanzarchiv*, 56, pp. 104–135

Sommer, B. (1994), "Entwicklung der Bevölkerung bis 2040, Ergebnis des achten koordinierten Bevölkerungsvorausschätzung," *Wirtschaft und Statistik*, 1994, pp. 497–503

Statistisches Bundesamt (1991), *Allgemeine Sterbetafel für die Bundesrepublik Deutschland, (Gebietsstand vor dem 3.10.1990), 1986/88* Fachserie 1, Bevölkerung und Erwerbstätigkeit, Reihe 1.S.2., Stuttgart: Metzler Poeschel

Statistisches Bundesamt (1996a), *Statistical Yearbook for the Ferderal Republic of Germany 1996*, Stuttgart: Metzler Poeschel

Statistisches Bundesamt (1996b), *Volkswirtschaftliche Gesamtrechnungen, Fachserie 18, Reihe 1.3, Hauptbericht*, Stuttgart: Metzler Poeschel

Statistisches Bundesamt (1997a), *Statistical Yearbook for the Ferderal Republic of Germany 1997*, Stuttgart: Metzler Poeschel

Statistisches Bundesamt (1997b), *Volkswirtschaftliche Gesamtrechnungen, Fachserie 18, Reihe 1.3, Hauptbericht*, Stuttgart: Metzler Poeschel

Statistisches Bundesamt (1998a), *Statistical Yearbook for the Ferderal Republic of Germany 1998*, Stuttgart: Metzler Poeschel

Statistisches Bundesamt (1998b), *Volkswirtschaftliche Gesamtrechnungen, Fachserie 18, Reihe 1.3, Hauptbericht*, Stuttgart: Metzler Poeschel

Steigum, E. and C. Gjersem (1999), "Generational Accounting and Depletable Natural Resources: The Case of Norway," in A. Auerbach, L. Kotlikoff, and W. Leibfritz, eds., *Generational Accounting around the World*, Chicago: University of Chicago Press, pp. 369–396

Steinmann, G. and M. Jäger (1997), "How many Immigrants can a Society Integrate," Institut für Volkswirtschaftslehre und Bevölkerungsökonomie, Volkswirtschaftliche Diskussionsbeiträge no. 11, University of Halle

Steinmann, G. and R. Ulrich (1994), *The Economic Consequences of Immigration to Germany*, Heidelberg: Springer

Stijns, J.-P. (1999), "Generational Accounting for Belgium," in A. Auerbach, L. Kotlikoff, and W. Leibfritz, eds., *Generational Accounting around the World*, Chicago: University of Chicago Press, pp. 161–176

Støresletten, K. (2000), "Sustaining Fiscal Policy Through Immigration," *Journal of Political Economy*, 108, pp. 300-323

Summers, L. (1981), "Capital Taxation and Capital Accumulation in a Life Cycle Growth Model," *American Economic Review*, 71, pp. 533–544

SVR – Sachverständigenrat zur Begutachtung der gesamtwirtschaftlichen Entwicklung (1995), *Im Standortwettbewerb, Jahresgutachten*, Stuttgart: Metzler-Poeschel

SVR – Sachverständigenrat zur Begutachtung der gesamtwirtschaftlichen Entwicklung (1998), *Vor weitreichenden Entscheidungen, Jahresgutachten*, Stuttgart: Metzler-Poeschel

Takayama, N., Y. Kitamura, and H. Yoshida (1999), "Generational Accounting in Japan," in A. Auerbach, L. Kotlikoff, and W. Leibfritz, eds., *Generational Accounting around the World*, Chicago: University of Chicago Press, pp. 447–469

Thimann, C. (1996), *Aufbau von Kapitalstock und Vermögen in Ostdeutschland*, Vol. 74 of Schriften zur angewandten Wirtschaftsforschung, Tübingen: Mohr

Thomas, G. (1997), "Retirement Income Financing Reform – A General Issues Paper," *European Economy, Reports and Studies*, 1997(4), pp. 167–190

Thompson, L. (1983), "The Social Security Reform Debate," *Journal of Economic Literature*, 21, pp. 1425–1467

Turner, D., P. Richardson, and S. Rauffet (1993), "The Role of Real and Nominal Rigidities in Macroeconomic Adjustment: A Comparative Study of the G7 Economies," *OECD Economic Studies*, 21, pp. 89–137

Ulrich, R. (1992), "Der Einfluß der Zuwanderung auf die staatlichen Einnahmen und Ausgaben in Deutschland," in H.-J. Hoffmann-Nowotny, G. Buttler and G. Schmitt-Rink, eds., *Acta Demographica 1992*, Heidelberg: Physica, pp. 189–208

United Nations (1988), "Economic and Social Implications of Population Aging: Proceedings of the International Symposium on Population Structure and Development," New York

Van den Noord, P. and R. Herd (1993), "Pension Liabilities in the Seven Major Economies," OECD Economics Department Working Papers no. 142, Paris

Vaughn, K. and R. Wagner (1992), "Public Debt Controversies: An Essay in Reconciliation," *Kyklos*, 45, pp. 37–49

VDR, – Verband Deutscher Rentenversicherungsträger (1996), "Rentenbestand am 31. Dezember 1995," VDR Statistik, Vol. 116, Würzburg

Villela Malvar, R. (1999), "Generational Accounting in Brazil," in A. Auerbach, L. Kotlikoff, and W. Leibfritz, eds., *Generational Accounting around the World*, Chicago: University of Chicago Press, pp. 177–198

Wagner, H. (1992), "Seigniorage und Inflationsdynamik: Einige grundlegende Zusammenhänge," *Kredit und Kapital*, 25, pp. 335–358

Wilhelm, M. (1996), "Bequest Behavior and the Effect of Heirs' Earnings: Testing the Altruistic Motive of Bequests," *American Economic Review*, 86, pp. 874–892

Druck: Strauss Offsetdruck, Mörlenbach
Verarbeitung: Schäffer, Grünstadt